A Concise History of British
Presence in India

A Concise History of British Presence in India

Establishing and Withdrawing an Empire

by

Barid Baran Mukherjee

2024

Copyright © 2024, Barid Baran Mukherjee
All rights reserved.

No part of this publication may be reproduced or transmitted in any form or by any means, electronic or mechanical, including photocopy, recording or any information storage and retrieval system now known or to be invented, without permission in writing from the publisher, except by a reviewer who wishes to quote brief passages in connection with a review written for inclusion in a magazine, newspaper or broadcast.

Published in India by Prowess Publishing,
YRK Towers, Thadikara Swamy Koil St, Alandur,
Chennai, Tamil Nadu 600016

ISBN: 978-1-5457-6015-4

Library of Congress Cataloging in Publication

To

My Father

Contents

Dedication v

Author's Preface. xv

Acknowledgements xvii

Abbreviations xix

List of Illustrations xxi

Introduction 1

Chapter 1. The British East India Company, 1611 – 1772 11

    1.1   Mughal Empire at the time of the arrival of the EIC 11

    1.2   The East India Company as Traders 13

        1.2.1   Beginnings. 14

        1.2.2   EIC and other European Traders. 15

        1.2.3   Job Charnock – Bengal. 19

        1.2.4   Chaos in the Mughal Empire 23

        1.2.5   Decline of Mughals and Consequences 24

        1.2.6   Bengal – Robert Clive and Battle of Plassey. 29

        1.2.7   The EIC gaining supremacy outside Bengal 31

        1.2.8   Post-Plassey developments. 34

    1.3   Observation 38

Chapter 2. East India Company rulers from Bengal 1772 – 1858 41

- 2.1 Beginning of Company Rule 41
- 2.2 The Administration of the EIC and Territorial Expansion 42
  - 2.2.1 Company Employees, Trafficking and Indian Drain ... 42
  - 2.2.2 Administrative Reforms 43
  - 2.2.3 Governor-Generals and administration 45
  - 2.2.4 Territorial Expansions 53
- 2.3 Rammohan Roy 61
  - 2.3.1 Causes of Social Degradation 62
  - 2.3.2 Rammohan and Reformation 64
- 2.4 Institutions and Western Education 71
  - 2.4.1 Girls' Education 79
  - 2.4.2 Effects of Western Education 80
- 2.5 The Sepoy Mutiny 81
- 2.6 Trade, Economics, Industry and Infrastructure Building 85
  - 2.6.1 Trade and Economics 85
  - 2.6.2 Industry 90
  - 2.6.3 Survey Work 94
- 2.7 Observations 95

Chapter 3. British Raj 1858 – 1919 101

- 3.1 Post-mutiny Administration 101
- 3.2 Crown rule – Viceroys / Governor-Generals 103

3.3 Genesis of Indian politics and Foundation of Indian
    National Congress 107
    3.3.1 Preparation for Indian National Congress 114
    3.3.2 Congress in its early days and the
          Administration 116

3.4 Lord Curzon – Bengal Partition and Consequences 119

3.5 Swadeshi Movement 124

3.6 Trends of Congress Politics (1906 – 1914) 127

3.7 Anarchist Movements 128
    3.7.1 Major Activities in Bengal 129
    3.7.2 International Activities 131

3.8 Muslim League 134

3.9 Minto – Morley Reform Act of 1909 136

3.10 During World War I 137

3.11 Observations 139

Chapter 4. British Raj 1919 – 1926 145

4.1 Government of India Act 1919 145

4.2 Hindu Mahasabha 147

4.3 Gandhi and the Indian National Congress 148

4.4 The Rowlatt Act and Amritsar Massacre 150

4.5 Congress becoming a mass organization 152

4.6 The Chauri Chaura incident 156

4.7 The Swaraj Party 157

4.8 Anarchist Movement – Second Phase 160
  4.8.1 Gopi Nath Saha 160
  4.8.2 Benoy, Badal and Dinesh 161
  4.8.3 Bhagat Singh. 162
  4.8.4 Chandrashekhar Azad 163
 4.9 Observations. 164

Chapter 5. British India 1926 – 1938. 167
 5.1 The Simon Commission and after Effects 167
 5.2 Fate of the Simon Report. 170
 5.3 Salt Satyagraha (Dandi March) and Outcome. 171
 5.4 The Gandhi – Irwin Pact 176
 5.5 Economic Instability 180
 5.6 Final RTC and Government of India Act, 1935 183
 5.7 Period of Political Stalemate 185
  5.7.1 Subhas Chandra and J. L. Nehru in Europe. 186
  5.7.2 Nehru as Congress President 187
 5.8 Elections of 1937 and Post–Election Incidents 187
 5.9 Subhas Chandra as Congress President. 190
 5.10 Observations. 194

Chapter 6. British India 1939 – 41. World War II, Phase 1 . . .201
 6.1 Beginnings 201
  6.1.1 Escape of Subhas Chandra Bose 207

		6.1.2	Atlantic Charter and aftermath 209
	6.2	Observations. 211	

Chapter 7. British India 1942 – 45. World War II, Phase 2 . . .213

	7.1	The Cripps' Mission and Responses 213	
	7.2	Quit India Movement. 216	
	7.3	The Penultimate Viceroy 219	
	7.4	Subhas Chandra Bose, Azad Hind and Indian National Army 220	
	7.5	Final days of Subhas Chandra Bose .223	
	7.6	After Subhas. 225	
	7.7	Calcutta Famine. 226	
	7.8	The Simla Conference, 1945 227	
	7.9	After the Second World War 229	
		7.9.1	New Elections 1945 – 46 and Other Issues. 229
		7.9.2	INA Trial. 229
		7.9.3	Consequences of the Trial 230
		7.9.4	Parliamentary Delegation and interim Government . . .232
		7.9.5	Elections and after effects 232
	7.10	Observations. 233	

Chapter 8. British India 1945 – early 1947 237

	8.1	Cabinet Mission Plan and Outcome .237
	8.2	Interim Government 241

- 8.3 Muslim League's Direct Action Day 244
  - 8.3.1 The Great Calcutta Killings. 244
  - 8.3.2 Noakhali Riots 250
- 8.4 Fate of Interim Government 252
- 8.5 Observations. 253

Chapter 9. British India March – August 1947 259

- 9.1 Lord Mountbatten's Appointment 259
- 9.2 Mountbatten – Last Viceroy of India 262
  - 9.2.1 London office 262
  - 9.2.2 Delhi office 263
  - 9.2.3 The Balkan Plan 264
  - 9.2.4 Implementation. 266
  - 9.2.5 Commonwealth Membership and Dominion Status. 267
  - 9.2.6 The Simla Episode 268
  - 9.2.7 Menon's Draft Plan. 271
- 9.3 Post–Simla Agreements 272
  - 9.3.1 The statement of His Majesty's Government (HMG) 272
  - 9.3.2 Implementation of Nehru Mountbatten Plan ... 273
  - 9.3.3 The Status of Bengal 274
  - 9.3.4 Third June Plan – Radio Broadcast and June 4 Press Conference 274

	9.3.5	India's Independence Act 276
	9.3.6	Consequences of Third June Plan 276
	9.3.7	Independence Bill 276
	9.3.8	Settlement of Bengal and Punjab 277
	9.3.9	Re-appointment of the Governor-General 277
9.4	Boundary Commission – Partition and Boundary Line 279
9.5	Announcement of Independence Day 282
9.6	Gandhi in Calcutta with Suhrawardy 282
9.7	Pledges and India's Obligations 284
9.8	Princely States – Accession to India 286
9.9	Observations 289

Conclusion 293

Glossary 311

Appendix 1. The Bengal Renaissance 319

Appendix 2. Princely States 351

Appendix 3. Scholastic Europeans in India 361

Appendix 4. List of Governor-Generals and Viceroys 365

Bibliography 367

Index 379

Author's Preface

During my childhood I saw my grandmother and father wear khadi clothes, and regularly spun threads on wooden wheels at home which were woven to make their attire. I listened to them curiously when they told and retold the stories of their experience of the last decade before freedom. Many of my schoolmates belonged to families who lived in refugee colonies set up in our neighborhood. They came from East Bengal after the Partition. I heard horrible stories of the final days of their stay in their homeland and forced migration. Those incidents of my growing days influenced me to write this work.

When I grew up, the joyful spirit of the first independence day was kept alive in the minds of the people of Serampore, a small suburban town north of Calcutta. Serampore became the birthplace of several patriotic anarchists like Hrishikesh Kanjilal, Gopinath Shah, Jitendranath Lahiri, and was a hub of Congress politics from before the 1930s. The British missionaries who ran the Serampore College did not oppose the growing nationalism among the students who made Serampore a political hub. I could talk to several freedom fighters of my neighbourhood who sacrificed their material life. They inspired me with stories of their selfless struggle and involvement in different freedom movements during the 1940s. These incidents instigated nostalgic feelings which I cherish even now. Due to the generation gap, the majority of people are now ignorant of this glorious history. However, the history of the British period in India has attracted many scholars. In my reading, I found that among many historical works, several writings conveyed faulty perspectives on certain incidents.

Some important facts of history, like why the British agreed to transfer power to Indian hands and why partition of India became inevitable, or what were problems with the Kashmir accession to India, etc. are some of the topics many people are confused about. Also unclarity exist about the inter-relationships among Gandhi, Nehru, and Subhas Chandra, or even on the last days of Subhas Chandra Bose. These issues are often debated even today. I proceeded with this work with the intention to clarify for myself some of these confusing issues.

Assuming that a majority of readers favor reading simple and linear stories, I planned to write this book by simply stating the facts of the events as they occurred in succession. I attempted to inform the readers how the British imperial rule posed to extract Indian resources, and how Indian people were affected as the Indian economy gradually declined because of recurrent war expenditures, and why the British ultimately decided to withdraw. I highlighted how the Indian people suffering from ignorance, were enlightened through western education initiated by the British, and added a glimpse of the Bengal Renaissance as an appendix to inspire Indian youths to realize how a downtrodden society was transformed through education and personal initiatives. It is my hope that this one volume will help clarify many questions which today still cause confusion.

Acknowledgements

The inspiration of writing this volume came from my predecessors and family members who sacrificed their material life for the cause of Indian independence. A desire to write this story, which I have cherished since my school days, has been materialized after more than four years of uninterrupted work. It further developed with advice of Mr. Peter de Vries of New Zealand, who presently resides at Serampore. He shares responsibilities in editorial work of the *Carey Day Souvenir* published annually by Serampore College, and devotes himself to digitizing the accession of old manuscripts and books and the entire collection at Carey Library and Research Centre of Serampore College, India, on a voluntary basis.

Mr. De Vries grasped the concept of this Indian story and helped making line edits. He looked after the flow of thoughts and made the expressions of the text more explicit. He thoroughly checked the text, and even shared the credit of creating new maps to avoid problems of copyright. Spending his valuable time and energy on this work, his help was indispensable to bring the standard of this book to this printable form. My heartfelt thanks to him for his generous help.

I am indebted to the intellectual contributions of Sivanath Sastri, Subhas Chandra Bose, V. P. Menon, and Alan Campbell-Johnson, in particular, because their works provided genuine information which guided me to write this story. What these writers wrote were reflections of their personal experiences. Interpretations on economical aspects presented here were based on works by B. R. Tomlinson.

Sri Kalyan Das resized and enhanced the pictures.

My thanks are due to the team Prowess Publishing and Software Solutions, Guindy, Tamil Nadu 600016, specially to Mr. Abdul Rasheed and Mr. Murali Mohambari and the team, for their patience, cooperation and excellent work.

I acknowledge all who encouraged me to work on this project.

Last but not least I must reveal that my daughter Soma and son-in-law Arjun Rathore, and their two daughters Lily and Tata, cooperated with me and provided me with leisure and an undisturbed work environment and all facilities at their home in Dallas, Texas, to compile this work.

Abbreviations

CWC   Congress Working Committee

EIC   East India Company

EIR   East India Railway Company

NWFP   North Western Frontier Province

RTC   Round Table Conference

League Muslim League

HMG   His / Her Majesty's Government

SEAC   South East Asia Command

List of Illustrations

Fig. 1   Fort St. George, Madras. By Thomas Daniell, London
         1797 (British Library Archive)..............................16

Fig. 2   Old Tank and Old Mission Church, Calcutta, 1787.
         Thomas Daniell (British Library Archive)...................21

Fig. 3   Old Fort Ghat, Calcutta. Thomas Daniell 1787
         (British Library Archive)..................................22

Fig. 4   Robert Clive (of Plassey). By Francesco Bartolozzi
         (National Galleries of Scotland)...........................30

Fig. 5   Map of India at height of Mughal Reign, 1707 38

Fig. 6   Map India 1760...40

Fig. 7   Old Court House and Writers Building, 1786.
         By T. Daniell (British Library Archive)....................44

Fig. 8   New Court House Calcutta, 1786. By T. Daniell
         (British Library Archive)..................................44

Fig. 9   Old Government House. By Thomas Daniell, 1788
         (British Library Archive)..................................46

Fig. 10 Warren Hastings. Engraved from Painting of Zoffany,
         in his *Memoir*, London: J. Murray, 1787...................46

List of Illustrations

Fig. 11   St. John's Church, Calcutta 1786–88. By T. Daniell (British Library Archive). 50

Fig. 12   Marquis Wellesley. By J. Young (National Galleries, UK). 52

Fig. 13   White Town. "A Street in Calcutta," *Illustrated London News*, 1855. 56

Fig. 14   Chitpore Road, 1867. Blacktown. By William Simpson (Wikimedia). 56

Fig. 15   Tagore Castle, North Kolkata (Public Domain). 57

Fig. 16   Government's House at Ganeshkhind (after 1949 Pune University). 57

Fig. 17   Viceroy's House upon completion 1931. Later called Rashtrapati Bhavan. 58

Fig. 18   Map India 1805 61

Fig. 19   Rammohan Roy. By Rembrandt Peale, 1833 (Wikipedia). . . .62

Fig. 20   Dwarkanath Tagore. Portrait Bengal Club, Calcutta, 1827 (Wikimedia). 70

Fig. 21   Pontoon Bridge. By Johnston & Hoffman (Public Domain). . .93

Fig. 22   Map India 1857 100

Fig. 23   Salt March 12 March - 5 April 1930 (Rue des Archives. citeco.fr) 175

Fig. 24   Salt March 12 March - 5 April 1930 (Wikipedia). 175

Fig. 25   Gandhi's Quit India Speech, 8 August 1942. (navyuvaz.blogspot.com) 176

Fig. 26   Second Round Table Conference, London Sept 1931 (British Library Archive). 177

Fig. 27	Jawaharlal Nehru and Subhas Chandra Bose (Public Domain)	191
Fig. 28	Gandhi and Subhas Bose (Public Domain)	206
Fig. 29	Civil Disobedience Bombay, 1942 (G. G. Parekh, orato.world/2023/05/09)	218
Fig. 30	Map India Partition August 1947	278
Fig. 31	Gandhi and Suhrawardy in Beliaghata, Calcutta, September 1–4, 1947 (Public Domain)	283
Fig. 32	News of Independence Friday August 15, 1947 (The Statesman)	285
Fig. 33	Gandhi and Mountbatten, one week before Independence (Public Domain)	286
Fig. 34	Map Princely States 1904	288
Fig. 35	Growth of Calcutta with its suburbs (NATMO, Salt lake, Calcutta)	322
Fig. 36	Henry Louis Vivian Derozio (Public Domain)	325
Fig. 37	Statue of David Hare, Calcutta (Wikipedia)	326
Fig. 38	Madhusudhan Dutta. By Atul Bose (Victoria Memorial Collection)	336
Fig. 39	Bankim Chandra Chattopadhyay (Public Domain)	336
Fig. 40	Sivanath Sastri (Public Domain)	337

Introduction

This work traces the history of British presence in India covering about 330 years – a period that was rich with social and political interactions of people of two different identities with conflicting longings. It is a story of Indian polity from the beginning of the East India Company's journey as traders in the early 17th century to withdrawal of the British Raj with the partition of India in 1947. The subject is the territory which was directly under British rule (excluding the Princely States, Burma, and other areas in South East Asia conquered by the British up to 1837).

The British East India Company (EIC) came to India solely with commercial interests during Mughal rule. With the break-up of their empire, the Company began occupying the territories and took gradual possession of the resources they had acquired. At the time, India was the richest country in the world,[1] but fell into a state of prostration.[2] In the middle of the 19th century, after the Sepoy Mutiny, Parliament established Imperial (or British) Raj, replacing the EIC with Crown rule, which was withdrawn within 90 years following.

Histories written on the East India Company and the British Raj taken together or separately, are many and among the best of its type. Eurocentric works focus generally on the activities of colonists, their administrators, their political aspirations and achievements, and social life in the colonial environment. They sometimes highlight Gandhi's role in Indian politics and Ram Mohan Roy's role in social reforms. These works are rich with rare information, but some are written in story form. Being more imaginative, they leave some relevant facts unmentioned. In recent years, some commanding works on the economy of the EIC and British Raj were published.

Indian historians published a detailed history of the British in India that included political discourses, and the colonial economy. At one time they preferred to narrate Indian patriotism and write biographies of nationalists. More recent Indian historians tend to delve into assembling fragments of history taking into account subaltern perspectives. They interpret Indian history through inclusion of many characters of social and cultural relevance. These are obviously analytical studies referring to Postcolonial interpretations to serve academic interests. Today, historians are still working on India and continue to do so in the future.

William Dalrymple, an award winning historian, while describing his personal experience of a visit to the Red Stone Mughal Fort at Allahabad wrote,* "I visited it ... neither the guards at the gate nor their officers knew any of the events that had taken place there, none of the sentries had even heard of the Company whose cannons still dot the parade ground where Clive's tent was erected..."[3] Dalrymple was naturally surprised because even the Fort's employees did not know the history of their workplace. The majority of Indians are ordinary people of multiple mentalities. Attempts have been made to make this story plain sailing to attract the attention of all types of readers.

William Faulkner once said, "The past is never dead." To keep the past living, past events need to be saved from the danger of being lost. This is a rewriting of history but crafted to cater to the needs of this story, as well as to explain some shaded and forgotten areas. The Bengal Renaissance, for example, is mostly forgotten; and causes of the partition of India or persons responsible for it are still debated. The Kashmir issue too leaves the international onlooker dazed.

---

* Note: This fort, originally built by Emperor Akbar in 1583, was garrisoned by British troops to protect Shah Alam II as a part of the Allahabad Treaty signed by Robert Clive and Mughal partners after the Battle of Buxar in 1765. Following conflicts of claims and counterclaims this fort became the military store of the EIC after 1801.

The purpose of this work is to highlight major political and military developments of the EIC by which it empowered itself to rule India; and focusing on those persons and events of special attraction which caused the British to withdraw from India. We explore how it was done. This study emphasizes the making of modern India in relation to what India was before English education was available. It shows how political concepts grew leading to the founding of the Indian National Congress (Congress) and how Congress matured politically and was gradually enriched to strive for a completely free India. This is a concise history presented as a linear story in one volume. Major events are discussed in sequence to enable general readers and scholars to track how the political progress of Congress coupled with economic situation of the Raj, shifted the British trajectory, despite the contradictory agenda of Muslim League. Whenever possible, empirical and authentic perspectives have been given priority over unverifiable theories while narrating the text.

The contents are presented in nine chapters. The history of the EIC in Chapter 1 & 2 highlights how Company men secured trading rights, built forts and factories, and took over the entire territory. It explains how India was modernized during the Bengal Renaissance.

This work tells how the European rivals and local power factors like Marathas, Sikhs, Jats, and rulers of Mysore and Hyderabad who sprung up after the decline of Mughals, were eliminated by the Company after it was established by securing the Bengal base. What were the primary administrative and military developments during the period of Robert Clive, Warren Hastings, Cornwallis, Wellesley and Dalhousie, that drove the EIC to rule India? It was felt necessary to highlight the reformer Rammohan Roy, who laid the base of modern India when the EIC began occupying the territories. He and others sparked the growth of western style education, triggering the Bengal Renaissance, which became the vanguard of political movements throughout India.

The chronology in the text of Chapter 1 is interrupted because regional fragmentation of the Mughal empire and British engagements took place simultaneously in different places. To avoid more interruptions, some relevant incidents of this history like the Bengal Renaissance has been presented as appendixes. Since the foundation of British Indian rule was laid in Bengal, and a cultural renaissance began in Bengal, it is unsurprising that Bengal became the hub of Indian politics, trade and commerce until the end of World War I. So the elements of British history of Calcutta, nay Bengal, are rich in comparison to those of the rest of India.

The EIC did not face any united opposition from the Indian rulers, but the British Raj, after Congress was organized, faced an integrated pan Indian opposition. The EIC changed institutional policies to expand the British market in India, and the British Raj changed policies to sustain itself under domestic pressures triggered by the Sepoy Mutiny. The Raj was responsible for retaining control of Indian capital under imperial guidance. Its policies were dictated by the party in power in London. The Raj's obligation was to earn from India and pay back loans, interest (on capital expenditure such as the Indian railways), home charges, maintain a military to protect the empire, create a market for British goods, as well as maintaining itself. But the Raj was failing to manage the economy to comply with imperial aspirations.

The history of the British Raj laid out in Chapters 3 to 9 reviews a period of about 90 years. It considers the administration and imperial aspirations of the Raj, as well as the formation of major political parties. Thirty years after the Raj was formed, the Indian National Congress was founded. It had a clear nationalist agenda. Two decades later the Muslim League was organized to look after the Indian Muslim minorities. The story narrates the conflicts between imperialism and nationalism and Muslim League's insistence for a separate Muslim domain.

Chapter 3 narrates the legal and administrative systems that gave the Raj an imperial character, the genesis of nationalist politics, tenures of some of the Viceroys who indirectly helped build up the domestic political base, the beginning of constitutional relaxation, and the situation during the World War I. The final thirty years described in chapters 4 to 8 tell how this period was crucial for the Raj as the political conflicts with Congress intensified in stages once Gandhi rose to become the national leader, the complex political situation during the World War II, and Muslim League becoming a significant factor in Indian politics. These chapters also narrate the activities of younger Congress leaders, the effects of World War II on the Indian economy and the British decision to withdraw.

The economic instability during the War and subsequent global depression at a time of increased domestic pressure compelled the Raj to pass the Government of India Act 1935, which formed the foundation of the Indian constitution until 1950. These chapters highlight the 1940s – the Raj's most fraught period when Britain's conservative government grappled with rapidly changing political conditions in India, the Quit India movement, when the post war economy of Britain languished, administration weakened, and the Labour Party came into power.

In this changed situation the newly elected liberal government decided to withdraw from India keeping India united, and to prioritize rebuilding war ravaged Britain. The story narrates how problems arose in the procedure of selecting a single recipient to take charge of British India when the Muslim League demanded a separate territory for the Muslims (called Pakistan). It relates why the transfer of power was constrained, and how the penultimate (second before last) Viceroy was replaced by Lord Mountbatten.

During this time, the administration passed many Acts and Bills and set up several Commissions. Chapters 6 to 8 track how Congress leaders negotiated and organized a movement underpinning those government laws and how the present administration became untenable failing to deal with subsidiary issues. Chapter 9 narrates how Lord Mountbatten was appointed as the last Viceroy, how he endeavoured to make plans for the transfer of power, and why he failed keeping India united.

Prior to the founding of Congress, Rammohan Roy sought justice for Indians. Emerging Congress appealed to the British Raj for social and economic justice, and over time Congress claimed self-rule under the Raj. When Gandhi was elevated to leadership, he demanded complete freedom of a united India, contradicting Muslim League's demand for a separate electorate for the Muslims with administrative support. This story, addressed chronologically, depicts how the survival of the Raj was stymied due to backlash of Indian politicians coupled with the financial burden of two great wars. This situation caused a swing of the British trajectory towards withdrawal.

The Indian middle classes were the architects and participants of social and political activities. This story of the British Raj has been written with a limited perspective and is confined to the activities of elite middle class Indians only. It has little scope to include the so-called underprivileged classes, though they usually are important actors in social histories.

The withdrawal of Britain was a significant event in world history. Its course changed in a phase-like manner through the decisions of a few influential persons. The text includes notes on the political biography of some of these persons, a cast of characters at the centre of the drama such as Rammohan Roy, Aurobinda Ghosh, Mahatma Gandhi, Jawaharlal Nehru, Subhas Chandra Bose, etc. History demands intellectual biographies. People still gossip over the cause of death of Subhas Chandra, his relation with Nehru and Gandhi, and debate the causes of the partition of India. Biographical notes may clarify several of these confusing notions. Accused of being tolerant to Muslims and causing many Hindus to be uprooted during partition, Gandhi was assassinated five months after independence. Gandhi's death fascinated Mountbatten, who said, "Mahatma had achieved in death what he had been striving to achieve in life, an end to India's communal violence. … One which he would consider a fitting final chapter of his life."[4]

The context of the past is relevant for this work as it determined the course of Indian history. The ancient history of India adheres to Hindu way of life; a liberal society, which developed a unique culture and philosophy inscribed in its scriptures. The Europeans appreciated the ancient Indian cultural roots and rediscovered it. The glory of ancient India had been lost as people became inert being deprived of education under Muslim rule. They could not assert resistance for the first one hundred years under British rule even after being economically exploited.

Furthermore, the texture of Indian society is unique. Terms like Hindu and Muslim are associated with India. Many Indian Muslims are converts and prefer to maintain a separate identity. As Hindus were in majority within the Mughal dynasty, the British inherited both Hindu and Muslim subjects. During the early nineteenth century the Indian Muslim population grew to 30%, but unlike the Hindus, the majority of them avoided modern education.

Indian epics were written and rewritten from time to time from Takshashila (Punjab) to Rajagriha (Bihar). India was a self-contained geographical unit surrounded by oceans and the largest mountain range of the world, leaving a marginal provision for the movement of people in the northwest sector, which witnessed many historical invasions. From ancient times, India has been a physically and culturally distinct entity. For 5,000 years Indians followed a uniform culture. Throughout the subcontinent, ancient sacred establishments were built where the same Sanskritized scripture is being read.

Sanskrit was the foundational and sacred language of the Hindus spoken throughout India, which came into disuse after Muslim rulers introduced Persian as the official language. Sanskrit was modified into different local languages and dialects. Even now Indians speak 23 different languages and more than 300 dialects. The cultural uniformity existing with social divisions, has a long history which evolved through inclusiveness of people born in this land. National identity is a perception of its people in an international context. Even so, Indian uniformity was lost due to linguistic barriers, and Europeans hesitated to accept India as a nation. National aspirations remained dormant but was revived when English became the lingua franca of British India. Indian nationalism grew in this fertile context, and Congress was founded as a platform for all Indians irrespective of caste, creed and religion.

For decades, Indians longed for independence. The strong emotional feelings expressed on August 15, 1947, have faded away among the present generation. Young Britishers are also indifferent about the British colony where many of their forebears lived and worked. This work may incite interest among a younger generation of Indians and British, and especially the students of colonial history.

The *Observations* at the end of each chapter analyzes the political and or economic conditions of sub-periods. The story ends with a summary of the text. The *Conclusion* that completes this book highlight the main theme and additional information to enhance the story.

Appendices:

1. The Bengal Renaissance - deals with certain 19th century individuals who contributed to the making of a modern Indian state, and helped form the embryo of Indian nationalism.
2. Accession of the Princely States - territories under British command which have not been treated in the text. Their accession was achieved by the last viceroy to include them under the provisions of the Indian Independence Act.
3. Selected British scholars - who cooperated with the British administration, but avoided being in direct politics, and worked for welfare of the Indian subjects.
4. A List of Governor-Generals and Viceroys.

The major structure of this work relies on Dutt,[5] Sastri,[6] Menon,[7] Bose,[8] and Alan Campbell-Johnson,[9] in particular, who all wrote their work based on their personal experiences. V. P. Menon was serving under the Raj administration from 1935 to 1947 and his book is the source of the majority of dates of events presented in this work. Campbell-Johnson was press attaché of Mountbatten and his book is a helpful diary of the time. Information on the economic situation was borrowed mainly from Tomlinson.[10]

References:

1. Angus Maddison, *Contours of World Economic History: Essays of Macro Economic History* (Oxford: Oxford University Press, 2007), 329.
2. Paul Bairoch, *Economics and World History, Myths and Paradoxes* (Chicago: University of Chicago Press, 1995), 95.

3. William Dalrymple, "The East India Company: The Original Corporate Raiders," *The Guardian*, 4 March 2015, page 16 (2019).
4. Dominique Lapierre and Larry Collins, *Freedom at Midnight* (New Delhi: Vikas Publishing House, 1997), xx.
5. Romesh Chunder Dutt, *Literature of Bengal: Attempts to Trace the Progress of National Mind and Various Aspects of Literature* (Calcutta: I.C. Bose & Co., Stanhope Press, Bow Bazar St., 1877).
6. Sivanath Sastri, *Ramtanu Lahiri O Tatkalin Banga Samaj*. 3rd edn. (Kolkata: Rubi Publishers, 2019). (translation: Ramtanu Lahiri and Contemporary Bengali Society).
7. V. P. Menon, *The Transfer of Power in India* (Princeton, NJ: Princeton University Press, 1957).
8. Subhas Chandra Bose, *The Indian Struggle 1920–1942* (New Delhi: Oxford University Press, 1997).
9. Alan Campbell-Johnson, *Mission with Mountbatten* (New Delhi, Calcutta: AICO Publishing House, 1951).
10. B. R. Tomlinson, "India and British Empire, 1880–1935," *Sage Journal*, Vol. 2, Issue 4 (1975), University of Cambridge, Published online 26 July 2016; Ibid, "The Political Economy of the Raj: decline of Colonialism," *Journal of Economic History*, Vol. 42, no. 1 (March 1982), 133–137.

CHAPTER 1

The British East India Company, 1611 – 1772

This chapter describes how the East India Company obtained Mughal permission to settle in the coastal enclave of Surat. It then used its resources for nearly 150 years to expand its trading network from north to south and east to west of India before obtaining the power to rule from Bengal. From 1765, the Bengal Presidency became the main base of future expansions.* This chapter begins with a brief account of the people and administration of the Mughal regime at the time when the Company reached India.

1.1 Mughal Empire at the time of the arrival of the EIC

The Mughal regime created by Akbar (1556–1605), became the most powerful empire being extended up to Gandhar (after Babur's invasion in Kandahar). At first, several territories in the South remained outside their direct rule. Their territory was populated with 100 million people – much

---

* Note: The EIC operated simultaneously from three trading posts that gradually evolved into provincial centres. The Madras Presidency was founded in 1640 (along the Coromandel Coast), the Bombay Presidency in 1661 (West coast), and the largest, the Bengal Presidency, in 1700.

more populated than the contemporaneous Ottoman Empire. The British traders witnessed the pomp of this empire as well as its decline with the death of Aurangzeb (1658–1707). After its decline, the empire survived only in name, as regional power factors emerged. Until 1707 the European traders were insignificant, being confined to coastal enclaves with their legalized trading posts.

The Mughal administration worked along with Hindu elites who owned trade and industry. This coexistence gave rise to a common language – Urdu – a hybrid of Hindi grammar and modified Persian alphabet. Persian and Urdu were the lingua franca of educated persons. When underprivileged Hindus converted to Islam to enjoy royal favor, the Muslim population grew in number. The Mughals maintained a separate social order from the Hindus. Indian Muslims were fewer compared to other Muslim ruled countries and social institutions of converts retained Hindu influences.

Hindus under the Muslim dynasty were protective of their culture which was not much affected even as the political systems changed. Because Persian was the official language, their Sanskrit based educational institutions were suppressed. Islamization grew from the time of Sultanates, providing the converts political backing. When the predecessors of the Mughals gradually increased societal pressure to convert, Hindus responded by reinforcing their culture with social barriers to create an orthodox society. Since then the Hindu community formed some irrational customs to escape Islamic influence imposed on them.

The Mughals adopted traditional Hindu laws, and ruled with help of a decentralized administration. Mainly led by Hindu princes, these heads of states acted as local authorities and managed the land and the people. They collected revenues on behalf of the central administration in Delhi, themselves receiving proportionate shares in cash and kind on contract basis. Land was the main source of state revenue. One sixth of the total revenue collected by the Mughals were dues paid to local princes. In central India the administration rested on allegiances with local authorities.

The rural economy was vibrant but suffered as the proportion of central share gradually increased. In 1580 Emperor Akbar introduced a centrally regulated system for collection of land revenue through decentralized units under the ultimate control of the Mughal rulers in Delhi. The territory was segregated as political mosaics bound to the monarch. If local authorities attempted to revolt, they were replaced by the emperor's own officials empowered to collect taxes and control the administration.

The civil and criminal legal systems followed Hindu laws. Emperor Akbar did not discriminate against Hindus. But subsequent generations beginning from Shah Jahan (1592–1666) prohibited construction of Hindu temples. Aurangzeb (1659–1707) tried to introduce Muslim culture and Sharia law through forced conversions, and demolished Hindu temples. This oppression prompted discontent among the Hindus. Aurangzeb was the last powerful Mughal emperor. Under his reign the Mughal empire reached its greatest extent. After him the empire declined.

The immediate rulers of a large area in the west and north were the Marathas, Rajputs, Jats and Sikhs. Such local units were sometimes provinces or semi-independent petty states. In the Deccan alone there were over thousands of fortified segments under control of Hindu *zamindars*. Most of them were allowed to enforce their command for revenue collection, which, at the end of the seventeenth century, totalled more than 230 million rupees annually. Aurangzeb's religious intolerance caused many Hindu kings to rise to power in defiance to the emperor. This resistance played a major role in European attempts to trade with the Mughals as under subsequent rulers the Mughal territory fragmented to the advantage of the European traders.

1.2 The East India Company as Traders

Right from its start, the British East India Company (EIC) interacted with European rivals and local kings and princes under the Mughal Empire. The EIC struggled for one and a half centuries in an alien political environment before they settled in Bengal, making it their base for gradual expansion.

1.2.1 Beginnings

The East India Company (named as *Association of Merchants Adventure*) formed in 1599 by some London merchants, was entrusted to start trading with the East Indies. Queen Elizabeth I issued a charter on New Year's eve of 1600 under the name of *London East India Company* enabling the Company to share in the East Indian spice trade. This lucrative trade had been the monopoly of the Portuguese and Dutch nations. The venture had started but in 1623 the Company was temporarily halted after the Amboina Massacre in the Dutch Indies. Then the EIC focused on the overseas textile trade from their base on the Indian west coast created in the early seventeenth century.

Sir Thomas Roe, ambassador of King James I, sailed from London in March of 1615 and began negotiations with the court of Mughal emperor Jahangir. He secured Company's rights to land its first factory (warehouse) and residential facilities in 1616 at Surat, Gujarat, strategically located in the western fringes.* But they had to encounter Portuguese merchants. Only a few years earlier, in 1608, William Hawkins, showed interest in Surat and he, as commander of a Company vessel, was the first Englishman to land in Surat remaining under the Portuguese. A partial control of the Bombin (Bombay) port was acquired in 1612. It was a major entry point to India. Bombay was subsequently secured by the EIC from the Portuguese through the Crown.

India was a rich source of silk, cotton, gems, ivory, peacock feathers, and especially good quality saltpetre, an important ingredient of gunpowder. It attracted European nations to trade these items in the overseas market. Also, there were demands for woven textiles like calico,

---

* Note: In response to a letter, sent by James I through Thomas Roe, Jahangir wrote back that the governors were instructed to allow the traders to sell, to buy, and transport to their country with pleasure. According to some other authors formal permission was granted in 1613. Emperor Farrukhsiyar, grandson of Bahadur Shah I, who conspired to throw over Aurangzeb, was the emperor between 1713–1719. In 1717, Farrukhsiyar gave official permission to the EIC to continue trading free of duty, a century after Jahangir's *firman*.

muslin, chintz bedspread, and Chinese tea (exchanged against Indian opium). Calico trading became a lucrative business in course of time from the Madras base.

The Mughals used technical help from the British for the operation of their ships in return for allowing the EIC to trade. When their mutual understanding improved, the EIC was allowed to set up a small trading post at the Malabar Coast alongside other European traders like the Portuguese, Dutch and French. The Danes also had a sole base in Tanjore. There were local traders and middlemen too. Over time, the Malabar coast became a destination for native non-Muslim traders when they required Marathas' protection against Aurangzeb.

Growth of European commercial interests was perceptible with the rise of their naval power. They established trading posts in Asian countries from Persia in the West to Japan in the Far-east. In India the British EIC ultimately became the dominant factor after taking over their rivals.

1.2.2 EIC and other European Traders

The EIC interacted with their European rivals who established Indian trade before the British came. The Portuguese reached India before any other European nations as they reached Calicut just six years after Vasco da Gama discovered the sea route to India via the Cape in 1498. They began from Cochin in 1505 and conquered Goa from the Bijapur Sultanate and made it their capital. Bombay was their harbour from 1535 and Portuguese India was extended up to Daman & Diu in the West, and Bandel and Chittagong in the East. The church they founded in Bandel in 1599 still exists as the oldest church in Bengal. But the Portuguese were driven out by the Mughals.

The EIC built their fort in 1639 in the South with permission from the King of Chandragiri. The place was at the proximity to the production center of the weavers. Known as Fort St. George, named after England's patron Saint, this was their first fortified factory (Fig. 1). It was established by Francis Day in 1640. Mr. Day was a factor up the coast at Masulipatnam, sent down south in 1639 to decide on a place to erect a new factory. St. George was selected as the main trading center in South India when demand for calico grew as a fashionable textile in Europe. The city that grew around it became known as Madras. The southern region surrounding it became an export hub for southeastern nations too, and this British base became profitable from its inception. Company employees were allowed to trade individually.

Fig. 1 Fort St. George, Madras. By Thomas Daniell, London 1797 (British Library Archive).

Local power units reached Madras around this time. But the EIC's main rivals were the French who settled up the coast at Masulipatnam in 1669 and in Pondicherry in 1673. During the First Carnatic war beginning in 1740 Fort St. George was briefly occupied by the French company (1747–48) but victory after a second Carnatic War (1749–54) ensured British dominance over the French. The EIC came to an understanding with the King of Arcot from 1750 and used his help to acquire some territories in the Carnatic region. The 4th Nizam granted the Guntur district (Kondavid) to the French Company in 1753 (Aurangabad treaty), being obliged by their help to rise to the throne. Soon the rest of the Circars area was also granted to the French. In 1759 through the conquest of Masulipatnam the Circars extending up to the Chilka Lake in the north were transferred to the British from the French. The French threat increased again between 1770–1780 when the Company suffered a loss from the region.

The economy in the southern region improved with European investments. The Portuguese were predominant pepper traders. The Dutch challenged them first, and only later the EIC took command over this trade. From 1661 when the Portuguese were losing control of Bombay, Charles II obtained Bombay as a dowry due to his marriage with the Portugal princes Catherine Braganza. They got married in Bombay and later in 1669 this island went to the EIC.

The Portuguese lost dominance in the South after the Dutch conquered Cochin in 1663. As the British power grew, Dutch investments were gradually restricted, and at the end of the eighteenth century they gave up their Malabar base. But the French remained strong, and to combat a growing rivalry in this area, the EIC bought Fort St. David at Cuddalore, originally a property of the Nayak of Gingee, from the Marathas in 1690 as an alternate fortified trading area. The French occupied Mahi in 1725, challenging the British ambition. Subsequently Haidar Ali of Mysore rose to power in the early 1760s with the conquest of north Malabar, and made alliance with the French to counter the British occupation. Thus, political complications grew in the southern parts due to the presence of competing European powers and local units. The French increased their presence significantly after winning the first Carnatic war.

Bengal in the Northeast was known as a profitable trading zone since antiquity. In 1638 the Company received permission from Emperor Sahajan to trade in Bengal. Subsequently the EIC set up trading posts in Balasore (1651), Hooghly (1651), Malda (1657), Cossimbazar (1659), Patna (1659), and Dacca (1668).[1] A subsidiary company known as *The English Company Trading in The East* formed in 1661 under the EIC established factories in these places; and the Charter of 1700 issued permission to trade in the East to be extended until repayment of the advances made to them.

Agents were appointed in the bases usually each with three assistants except in Cossimbazar where Job Charnock was the fourth assistant.

As stated before, the Portuguese were first the European settlers in Bengal. Dutch traders also had set up trade posts in Chinsurah and Patna, as well as other places in Bengal from 1635 onwards. During the French occupation of the Low countries, these posts were taken over by the British in 1795. Upon Napoleon's defeat, they were given back to the Dutch, but becoming unprofitable, ceded to the British in 1824 by a treaty. The settlement in Chandanagar was established in 1673 as the main French base in Northern India. This settlement was twice occupied by the British. The Danes secured Serampore in 1755 from their southern base at Tranquebar, and hosted William Carey and his fellow missionaries from the early 19th century when missionary activities were prohibited in British occupied territory. The British occupied Danish Serampore twice, and finally purchased all Indian Danish settlements in 1845.

The main attraction of European settlers in Bengal were the textile manufacturing centers in the entire area along the west bank of the Hooghly extending up to Bandel north of Calcutta. Additional advantage was the Saptagram port situated near Bandel. This was the oldest port on the bank of Hooghly, then a mighty river.

During the last half of the 1660s, the Marathas increased their strength in the west. The EIC, then prominent in the western coast, made Bombay their headquarters and fortified their area from 1669. Bombay and its surrounding area was also a lucrative source of earning. From 1674, Shivaji was an independent Maratha king. But he was in trouble with Aurangzeb from the late 1660s. Shivaji favored the EIC's presence along the west coast, aspiring to use British power with advanced naval force to combat the Mughals. Thus the British trading network grew in the South, east and west of India within 50 years of their arrival.

Robert Clive joined Fort St. George as a clerk in 1744 when he was only nineteen. In Britain, the EIC was able to loan one million Pounds to the government to oblige the Parliamentarians. The nation was at war with France. In South India, Fort St. David withstood the French attack after the fall of Fort St. George, but it also went to French hands. Clive learnt the art of war and proved his efficiency on the battlefield as a commander by defeating the French at their base in Pondicherry. His skill established the EIC in Bengal when Calcutta was taken over in 1756. Fort St. David remained French until 1785, when it was taken back by the British. The British lost interest in maintaining this fort after the French threat was over.

From the second half of the 17th century it became clear that India was a lucrative business center for European traders. With the growth of a consumer economy in Britain after 1660, the Companies' import of Indian fine textiles as luxury goods to Europe exceeded £300,000 in 1670, reaching nearly £2 million in 1740, after getting access to the East. The pay bill for spice exports alone through Dutch and British traders was 17,000 cavalrymen. Trading activities brought wealth to Indian businessmen and weavers as well. By 1678 some 80,000 weaving jobs were created in Bengal alone.[2]

1.2.3 Job Charnock – Bengal

For the British history of India, the fertile riverine basin of Bengal is significant. The EIC laid the foundation of British rule in 1757, about hundred years after Job Charnock was first appointed as their representative in Cossimbazar (1658). The operation in Cossimbazar was initially looked after by Streynsham Master, president of Madras, but in 1681 Bengal was made an independent agency under William Hedges. He was sent by the Court of Directors in London, to secure a trade licence from the Bengal Governor Shaista Khan at Murshidabad, from the base at Hooghly. While negotiations were continuing, Charnock was appointed as chief at Patna in 1664 and remained there till 1680, when he took charge of Cossimbazar. Climbing up the ranks, he was appointed as chief Bengal agent in 1685, but he could not resume his office immediately as the Cossimbazar post was seized by the Nawab of Bengal.

In 1686, Job Charnock took charge of Hooghly. Located close to the Bay of Bengal, Hooghly (Hughly) became the Company's eastern headquarters. The Directors instructed the Company to fortify their area plagued by conflicts over the level of duties between the British traders and the Mughal government. This led to the first Anglo-Indian War (1685–90). In 1689, Charnock became commander of a naval fleet to capture Chittagong of the Mughals. The British campaign which was fought on many fronts failed against an overwhelming Mughal army. The conflict was so intense that the British traders were forced to sail back with its squadron to the safety of Madras.

Meanwhile in the West, after the death of Shivaji, Aurangzeb introduced poll tax for non-Muslim traders. As the local British authorities refused to cooperate, their relation with the Mughals became so embittered that the commander of their garrison had to abandon allied areas. But Elihu Yale (1687–99), the Company's president of Fort St. George, secured an undisturbed base by applying anti-piracy law. Eventually the British offered apologies and restitution at Aurangzeb's Court in 1690, and new terms for trade were negotiated.

Nawab Shaista Khan in 1687 and his successor Ibrahim Khan (1689–1701), the last *Subedar* of Bengal, allowed the EIC to resume trading from the Hooghly. He gave the Company a duty-free trading facility against payment of Rs 3,000 Charnock returned, but planned to shift the settlement to a safer zone further south of their Hooghly establishment.

From the middle of the seventeenth century, the Saptagram port, one of the main attractions of foreign traders, lost its importance due to siltation. Betor (near present Shibpur), down on the Hooghly's west bank, rose to greater importance. To avail new facilities, two indigenous business families – the Setts and the Basaks – acquired property in Betore. Subsequently, a clan of the Setts moved across the river, and bought property near the present position of Calcutta General Post Office (GPO).

Charnock shifted the Company's Hooghly base near the Seths' establishment around 1690 (the exact year of his settlement is unknown). By that time the Setts had already developed the area by digging Laldighi (Fig. 2) and establishing a market, the Lalbazar. Calcutta (Kolkata) was inhabited since that time, though not as a city. Charnock made Calcutta the EIC's headquarters. It is said that Charnock lost his job with the Company, but stayed in Calcutta and died in January 1693. The developments in

Calcutta encouraged the London Directors in 1694 to found the British establishment from here. Parliament planned to restrict the monopoly of EIC by allowing other companies to operate. The EIC continued to dominate the Indian trade by absorbing rival companies. And so its journey began from Calcutta. In April of 1700, the Company's permission to trade was extended with the condition that Government advances were paid back.

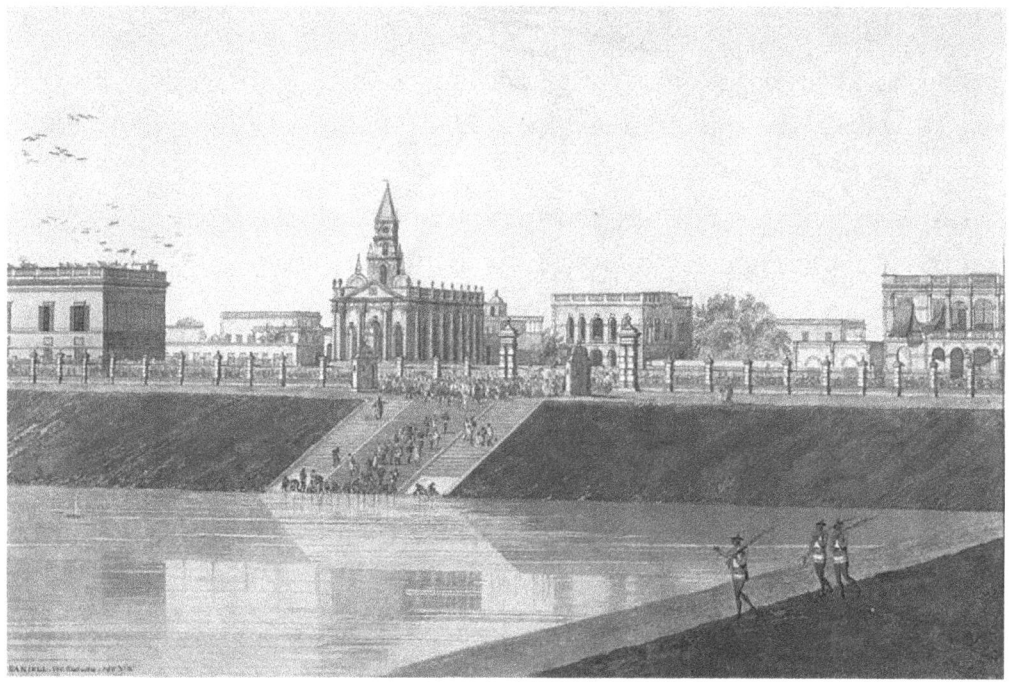

Fig. 2 Old Tank and Old Mission Church, Calcutta, 1787.
Thomas Daniell (British Library Archive).

In due course Calcutta became a place of commerce, the seat of administration, and the stronghold of Britain's colonial operation. The Calcutta Fort, which became operational from 1773, became the transit point of army operations to protect Indian territories as well as facilities outside India. For 350 years, a colonial metropolitan economy developed Calcutta from a small tradepost to the "Star of the East," the symbol of English power and authority. It developed as the largest city of the British Empire after London. All these events happened after 1757, but Calcutta began from Job Charnock's time.

The Company started with the lease of three villages – Kolkata, Sutanuti and Govindpur – from zamindar Sabarna Chowdhary. Judiciary power over its inhabitants was obtained in 1698 from Prince Azim-ush Khan, one of the grandsons of Aurangzeb, against an incentive of 16,000 Rupees in 1698. In 1699 the EIC purchased Seth's property to erect the (old) Fort William which was completed in 1702 by Charles Eyre (Fig. 3). In 1700, Calcutta became a separate presidency (administrative unit) of the EIC with its limited area in Bengal, but accountable to London. The Company already had secured trading rights in Bombay and Madras and each of these enclaves had obtained the status of presidencies.

As the trade improved and the number of bases increased, the Company needed a fully equipped military power to protect their assets. The presence of the French East India Company was then a significant factor. But French authority restricted resources for Indian establishments to hold it out indefinitely, and limited their traders' freedom. It became an advantage for the EIC to proceed with taking over the fragmented units when the Mughal empire was prone to decline.

Fig. 3 Old Fort Ghat, Calcutta. Thomas Daniell 1787 (British Library Archive).

1.2.4 Chaos in the Mughal Empire

After Aurangzeb's death (1707), his sons' struggle for succession resulted in the loss of power of the Mughal Empire. Taking advantage of this power vacuum, local territorial rulers gained regional power, even as they were in conflict with each other (Fig. 5 Map 1707). The empire effectively broke up. This chaotic situation was favorable for European traders, especially the British and the French, to expand their bases from the early 18th century. The Marathas, one of the main challengers of the Mughals, ravaged large parts of central India, causing the fragmentation of the empire.

During this time, the Nawabs of Bengal became financially independent on the support of Jagat Set, a Bengal banker. The Nawabs, however, maintained good relations with central Mughal authorities by accepting their sovereignty. When Murshid Quli Khan was the Nawab of Bengal (1717–27), European traders were permitted to operate from Bengal. Nawab Alivadri Khan (1740–56) accepted the EIC's presence in Calcutta under certain conditions; and Farrukh Siyar (1713–19), the Mughal Emperor himself, granted EIC the freedom of trade and duty free export against yearly payments from 1717 onwards. He also permitted the EIC to take access to 38 villages around Calcutta. Those were ultimately purchased by the Company at the cost of Rs 8,120. The EIC was also permitted to trade using Madras issued coins in Calcutta.[3]

The grant of 1717 was a remarkable British triumph as they could outright purchase three adjacent villages. The British were encouraged to settle in Calcutta and focus on Bengal. Alivardi Khan, who was Nawab from 1740, supported the EIC's presence as it improved the economy of Bengal. Then all European traders were required to pay money to the Nawab's officers to resist recurring attacks of Maratha plunderers.

Siraj-ud-Daula reigning from 1756 was the successor of Alivardi. Siraj, unlike his predecessors, was anti-Hindu and repressive. He lost the favor from the Hindu community and the local kings. It is said that to get rid of Siraj, some Hindu Rajas of the Bengal Subah – like Mohendra, Ramnarayan, Rajballav, Krishnadas, and Krishnachandra – decided to take help of the British establishment in a meeting held in the house of Jagat Set in presence of Mir Zafar. This was the period when decline of the Mughal Empire was perceptible.

1.2.5 Decline of Mughals and Consequences

The Mughal Empire started to disintegrate from the early eighteenth century, which coincided with the simultaneous expansion of the EIC. The following paragraphs depict how the fragmented Empire brought advantage to European traders.

In the late 17th century Aurangzeb's career proved to be unsuccessful in south central India when his war venture prolonged with predicaments for decades. He was obliged to accommodate aristocratic Deccani groups from defeated territories of Bijapur and Golconda after the war. It caused the locally established Irani and Hindustani groups, who were also nobles and once supported Mughals, to lose faith in him and stopped cooperating with the empire. It limited the empire's tax collection from the areas which supplied a major share of revenue. It resulted in fund shortage in the central coffer.

A time came when the empire forcibly increased taxes to maintain a stable military establishment. It annoyed the zamindars and peasants and they refused to cooperate. Also Aurangzeb came into conflict with Hindu Marathas for his religious intolerance. About twenty-seven years of engagement to secure Deccan and Hyderabad consumed so much of the resources that by 1707 his treasury was almost exhausted. Then eighteen months of succession war followed Aurangzeb's death, accelerating the Mughals' decline.

A lax empire becoming less powerful began to collapse. The local hierarchies – the zamindars, princes, provincial governors, etc. – began to assert independence, weakening the central authority. Nader Shah of Iran saw an opportunity and invaded India in 1739, defeating the Mughals in the battle of Karnal. He captured the capital and looted the Mughals' wealth valued at the time as £87 million, in gold, silver, and precious stones including the Koh-I-Noor. All major sources that financed the empire were exhausted. The looted Koh-I-Noor ultimately reached a museum in London. The Afghans repeatedly invaded northwestern India between 1748 and 1762.

The Marathas' increasing strength from 1707 made their presence in northern central India spectacular. Their rise caused Mughal's revenue to decrease further. Financial weakness of the central authority encouraged local powers to assert themselves. This forced change, and a modified system of rent collection was introduced to increase revenue earnings. In Bengal, for example, a *diwan* – an imperial revenue officer – was posted after 1713 as a subordinate to Nawab Murshid Quli Khan who was authorized to collect revenues from Hindu Bengal zamindars. In Oudh also a similar system was put in practice. But the new tax collection system proved to be unsuccessful.

Bengal was ruled from Murshidabad and extended influence over Bengal, Orissa and Bihar. The Bengal Nawabs did not defy Mughals' supremacy, but were semi-independent with their own troops. After becoming financially independent through Jagat Set's help, the Nawab entered into direct trade with British, French, Dutch, and Danish East Indian Companies, and used earnings mainly to compensate losses incurred due to roving Marathas. They had paid a large sum of money to appease Marathas who plundered Bengal five times between 1741 to 1751. They said that they obliged the Hindu zamindars of Bengal who called them. The zamindars, however, were scared of the plunderers as they often demolished temples overwhelming every opposition. European traders operated legally from the coastal belts, and their protection was guaranteed by the Mughal Emperor. But local units often disregarded their privileges. To ensure their security, those traders began fortifying their territory, often extending their original holdings. When they were objected to by the local kings, Europeans became offensive. Thus the scaffolding of law broke gradually down. The British traders took a major advantage of this unstable situation, unlike the French who responded initially reluctantly.

Because Aurangzeb through his favoritism of Muslim people disrupted the social fabric of the Hindu majority, the non-Muslim regional powers took measures to protect their own authority and status. They encouraged the elites and growth of a body of Hindu literature. But these kings did not support the Hindu peasantry, nor did they make any attempt to establish a united Hindu dominated rule.[4] The Marathas, Jats and Sikhs were powerful, but they did not feel the need to develop the concept of a state. Their lack of integration favored the British merchants with superior military power to gradually take over separate territories as their fight was confined to limited areas within a declining central authority.

The Jats around Delhi, Hindu Marathas of Deccan, Sikhs of Punjab, and Rajputs of Rajasthan, all enjoyed partial autonomy under the Mughals and became powerful under a weak administration. The farmers and the overall cultivation was at their control and their wealth increased during the late 17th century. Like the zamindars, they looked after the interest of the subjects and received their support in return. They even encouraged local diffusion of knowledge and culture. These units became so powerful that they gradually challenged imperial authority across central and northern India.

Jats. Jat zamindars were prominent in Agra – Mathura region. They had revolted before in 1669–70 being alarmed at Aurangzeb's oppression of Hindu culture. The zamindars openly plundered consignments of goods in transport caravans which compelled Aurangzeb's army to step in to subdue the Jats.[5] This Jat revolt went beyond imperial control. The agitators received support of the Rajputs' houses who were in isolation. When by the 1750s at Bharatpur a new Jat kingdom was formed that promoted Hindu culture, the central authority yielded and came to an understanding and assured them security. The Jat revolt was the beginning of their dissociation from the Mughal family.[6] Jats however, were careful to maintain a non-committal relationship with the British.

Marathas. Marathas were in conflict with the Mughals since Shivaji rebelled against them during his brief service in their establishment. Later Shivaji made connections with the Sultanates who commanded tributary states from Deccan to Gujarat in the west under the Mughals. He received Poona base as grant from the Sultanate, which developed into the nucleus of Shivaji's Maratha state. Its main source of income was cotton produced by small industries. The Deshmukhs, who were rural chiefs who controlled the politics of the Deccan, helped Shivaji to rise.

Shivaji ultimately rose to the helm of power by increasing revenue earnings in an extended Maratha territory that overlapped with Mughal hierarchies. This expansion drift caused ongoing conflicts between Marathas and Mughals. After the death of Shivaji and his son Shambhuji's murder, Shahu, a grandson of Shambhuji was raised to court in 1708. A Brahmin community, the Peshwas, served the Maratha territory as administrative advisors and finance managers from Shivaji's time. Shahu from 1713 onwards, also utilized Peshwas for the same purpose.

The Peshwas prompted the Marathas to advance northward and assault the Mughals. They attacked Gujarat and Malwa, and extended up to Peshawar. Bhopal was defeated in 1717. Shahu admitted Baji Rao Peshwa as his commander. Then Peshwa enlisted the help of his favorite men Holkars and the Shind families to increase Maratha military power against the Mughals. The Marathas pampered the Rajputs too who were Aurangzeb's enemies.

The Peshwas controlled the entire Maratha-drive, but they betrayed Sahu and captured power from him. Baji Rao Peshwa (1720–40), also based in Poona, became de facto ruler of the Maratha state. Peshawas' office (1720–1761) was hereditary and received patronage of literate elites. These elites gradually excelled in administration, banking and economic operations, and even in warfare, which further extended the Peshwas' territory.

Baji Rao was a master of guerrilla warfare and took over the Nizam of Hyderabad who enjoyed Mughal backing. Once Nizam's supplies were cut off, he was forced to come to an agreement and paid a one of "contribution" in 1728. This was the usual Maratha technique to win over opponents. In the same year, the Marathas reached Rajasthan, raided Delhi in 1737, caused the Mughal emperor to cede Malwa in 1739, and extended their territory towards Agra. During this northward march, the Marathas assisted the Rajputs in their fight against the Mughals. After Baji Rao died in 1740, their frontier extended to Delhi, Rajasthan and Punjab. Thus Marathas became a major force in India.

They occupied Bihar under the Bengal province and forced the Nawab to cede Orissa. At the southern Deccan, the Nizam was also forced to yield and share Karnataka with the Marathas. Thus large regions where the Mughals used to collect revenue, turned to become revenue payers to the Marathas. They admitted Brahmins into administration and commerce of the extended area. The Peshawa administration supported the overall development of Marathi literature and culture which was initiated by Shivaji, and helped to open avenues for education, developing a Maratha aristocracy.

The third Peshwa suffered a major financial loss during the southern expedition. To make it up he preferred to boost the agricultural bases employing soldiers to work as peasants, but neglected their military training. Their renewed expedition in the northwest brought a large area under the Peshwas. But in 1761, due to the poor condition of their artillery, the Marathas were badly defeated in the Third Panipat War by the Afghan troops of Ahmed Shah Abdali (Durani), who was invited by a group of Indian Muslims. This terminated the Maratha supremacy within 40 years of their rise. The Maratha reversal helped the military commander Hyder Ali (c1720–82) to attack Mysore between 1764 and 1771; and the weakened Maratha power was finally concluded by Lord Wellesley, to which we will return later.

Hyder Ali enabled the English power to emerge and expand in the South with their Bengal base intact. The Company already had bases in Bombay and Madras, and had established Mayor Courts by Royal assent of George I in 1726 for management of their presidencies. But by 1740 the British-French rivalry increased as both tried to extract gains by weakening the position of opponents. Their conflict spilled over in the south. During this period of rivalry, Robert Clive proved himself as a successful administrative and military leader after his successful defeat of the French, earlier alluded to. Clive was afterwards sent to Bengal where he established the Company as ruler.

1.2.6 Bengal – Robert Clive and Battle of Plassey

After Southwest India was restored to the British, Robert Clive (Fig. 4) was dispatched to Calcutta in December 1756, after the new Nawab Siraj-Ud-Dula occupied Calcutta. Clive decided to consolidate his military in Bengal for a stronger step against local rulers instead of appeasing them. He knew that British artillery was superior to that used by Mughals. Clive challenged Siraj-Ud-Daula and defeated him with help of Mir Zafar and other local Hindu kings, in the battle of Plassey. It is said that Clive presented five canons to Raja Krishnachandra, a Hindu king of Krishnanagar, after his victory. These canons are still preserved at the Krishnanagar Rajbati.

The Company's attempt to collect tax from Calcutta villagers annoyed Siraj-Ud-Daula and he objected to the EIC's lawful rights. He also denied the fortification of their settlements. The Nawab became displeased at Company-men's impolite behavior with his ambassador whom he had sent to negotiate. He then plundered the EIC at Cossimbazar, and the next day marched towards Calcutta, where he captured the Company's Fort on June 20, 1756. The EIC was clearly not ready for this sudden encounter. Completely overwhelmed by the sudden attack, the British men had no choice but to abandon the Fort and withdraw to their ships. Siraj's attack caused destruction of the European quarter and casualties of British soldiers and civilians who were locked in a small room without adequate ventilation. This event became infamously known in Britain as the Black Hole event. In addition, apart from humiliation, the Company suffered a huge loss of investors' money.

Robert Clive upon his arrival assessed the situation and used local politics in his favor. He enlisted the help of local kings and persuaded Mir Jafar to turn against his leader, defeating Siraj and his French allies in the Battle of Palashi (Plassey) in June 1757. Thus cunning and treachery won the day. Calcutta was restored, and Mir Jafar's aspiration to capture Siraj's throne was fulfilled. Now Clive had secured Bengal for the Company, restitutions were paid, land tenures were handed over, and taxation on Indian goods was abolished. Winning this battle was just the first phase of the conquest of Bengal (see the following).

Clive wished to modify the Company's legal code to better control private traders, against the advice of London. Clive was also ambitious to obtain a monopoly over the French trade in Bengal. The British – French rivalry ameliorated in Europe after the Treaty of 1740, but Joseph François Dupleix (1697–1763), a shrewd French merchant who arrived in 1742 used the Indian Princes to encircle British bases. He was recalled in 1754 after his intrigues were ruined by Robert Clive. Clive's advantage was that the French East India Company worked with limited liberty as it had to follow remote instructions from home. The French ambition in the east was concluded after Clive attacked French Chandannagar in January 1757 and kept it under British military control until the Treaty of Paris, 1763.

Fig. 4 Robert Clive (of Plassey). By Francesco Bartolozzi (National Galleries of Scotland).

1.2.7 The EIC gaining supremacy outside Bengal

The following paragraphs describe the circumstances in which different territories came under British rule. British supremacy was established between 1757 and 1765, ending the chaos that began from the 1740s. The British–French conflicts occurred from 1744 to 1763 with military conflicts and diplomacy mostly in southern India. There were succession disputes in the Carnatic and Hyderabad, and European interventions began by supporting rival native claimants. After winning in 1760, British control was established in the Carnatic region by taking over the French troops. The Allahabad Treaty of 1765 – discussed with the 'Post Plassey Developments' – consolidated the EIC's power in Bengal, and carried on with the annexation of successive territories. During this process, between 1755 to 1765, the British engaged simultaneously in wars in the South and in the Northeast.

i) Punjab. In the same year Clive won in Plassey, Ahmed Shah – an Afghan ruler – invaded adjacent areas of Lahore in Punjab, and secured a part of the eastern side of the Indus in 1757 for forcible revenue collection. Marathas, Persians, Sikhs, and remnants of Mughals continued to occupy Punjab, making the place volatile culturally and politically. Troops of Ahmed Shah returned to take over Hindu Marathas who concluded in 1761, as alluded to. Ahmed Shah took help from Safder Jang, the Nawab of Oudh, but major support came from Najib-ud-Daula – an Afghan and former imperial commander. He supplied his Ruhela troops in the Panipat War of January, 1761. The Afghans put Shah Alam II as a puppet emperor, but retained Lahore under their own successors. The Princely rulers surviving at the periphery of the residual area accepted the Mughals, but retained their own authority.

Ranjit Singh was chief of Sukerchakia, a small territory in western Punjab. He approached Lahore in 1799 and was obliged to become administrator of Lahore by the grandson of Ahmed Shah Abdali. Ranjit Singh declared himself as the Maharaja of Punjab in 1801 after extracting the remaining territories of the Mughals along with its adjacent regions of Multan, Kashmir, and Peshawar. During his eastward advancement, Singh encountered for the first time British resistance. Finally, around the 1850s, Punjab became occupied by the British, as described later.

ii) Rajputs. Rajputs are a large multicomponent cluster of classes sharing common social status but of geographically distinct origin. These Hindu warriors were never united. Muslim regimes and Mughals ruled over them, but to appease them gave them administrative responsibility as governors. Aurangzeb landed in conflict with them, and some Rajputs sheltered Marathas who were in opposition to the Mughals. The Rajputs resisted the Mughals and even deceived Aurangzeb, ensnaring his son Prince Akbar to keep authority over Marwar. They, however, fell victims of the chief of the Marathas until they accepted British suzerainty in 1818 at the end of the Maratha war.

iii) Hyderabad. The surviving provincial Governors who worked as administrators in remote areas not directly connected with the Mughals' territory became autonomous. One of them, Asaf Jah, assumed the title "Nizam-ul Mulk" at the courtesy of the Sayyid brothers. Asaf withdrew to Hyderabad in 1724 and fought against Mughal troops for autonomy. Then from 1740, he was made the Viceroy of the southern portion of the Mughal territory allowing him to function as Mughal administrator. He founded the Nizam dynasty of the Hyderabad state.

After the death of Asaf Jah in 1748, his sons began to contend for the throne aided by domestic neighbors and foreign forces. They could not retain their domain because of internal administrative problems. Ultimately Asaf Jah IV signed a treaty for a subsidiary allowance with the British Governor of Madras in 1799 and stayed on as head of the Princely State. Thus the British completed the capture of the Deccan plateau. The Jah dynasty continued their rule as Nizam of Hyderabad until incorporated under independent India in 1948.

iv) Mysore. In Mysore, Hyder Ali, a son of a Mughal Faujder (military service) of Sira in Karnataka, became a caretaker after the death of Aurangzeb. Hyder Ali maintained his allegiance with the Mughals, and cleverly seized the throne of Mysore from a Hindu dynasty in the second half of the 18th century. Unlike the Mughals, he concentrated his resources by collecting direct taxes through the zamindars, and built up a powerful modern army which checked the British approach to Malabar Coast in 1766. From 1757 to 1763 in the battle of Wandiwash the British decisively defeated the French forces.

After the EIC was established in Calcutta, the British military supported the Maratha kings and the Nizam against Hyder Ali. In the first Mysore War of 1767–69, Hyder Ali outflanked the British in his unexpected march to the outskirts of Madras. The British were forced to sign the Treaty of Madras with him in 1769. But in 1771 when Marathas attacked Hyder Ali, the British refused to help them. Hyder maintained good relations with the French, and he had access to the French Mahe port on the western coast. The British captured Fort Mahe by defeating the French. When the British refused to vacate Mahe, Hyder Ali declared the Second Mysore War (1780–84). During the third Anglo – Mysore Wars (1790–92), the kingdom of Mysore was defeated and ended with the signing of the treaty of Seringapatam.

Precedently the EIC had set up their administration in Calcutta, but Lord Cornwallis refrained from engaging in war. However, when Tipu Sultan – Hyder's son – violated the treaty, Tipu was killed in the Fourth Anglo – Mysore war in May of 1799, and the Mysore capital was captured by Lord Wellesley who had begun a major territorial expansion. The EIC took over direct control of Mysore, restoring Wodeyar to the throne at the care of a British Commission.

v) Awadh (Oudh). The Mughal Subah of Awadh in the northwest gained de facto independence after the first decade of the 18th century. The state had its own Nawab-successors who even diverted revenues due to be sent to Delhi, withdrew from attending the court, and maintained their own military power but kept allegiance to Delhi. Shuja-Ud-Daula (1732–75) was the governor of Awadh. He maintained a friendship with Shah Alam II. The rest of the history of Awadh is linked with Clive's Bengal after Plassey.

1.2.8 Post-Plassey developments

Let us return to Bengal after the Battle of Plassey. Robert Clive put Mir Jafar on the throne at Murshidabad. In exchange, the Company was promised payment of Rupees 2.25 crores. Additional payments made to English officers exceeded Rupees 20 lakhs, and Clive himself secured a zamindary from which he earned lakhs of Rupees. The EIC had secured their Calcutta settlement free from disturbance after 1757.

The loyalists of Siraj and Hindu zamindars of Patna and Midnapur did not accept Mir Jafar as a puppet Nawab. Mir Jafar himself, not being a decisive administrator, came into conflict with his disloyals. The Company's base remained in Calcutta. Clive's legal authority was initially not ascertained by the Calcutta Council. However, soon after he was appointed as the Governor of Calcutta Presidency.

But external threats arose. In 1759 Shah Alam II, a son of the Mughal Emperor of Delhi, travelled to the Bihar border, but had to return as he was not properly received by the Bengal authorities. After his father was murdered in Delhi, Shah Alam II returned to Bengal again and proclaimed himself as emperor. When he proceeded to capture Murshidabad, Mir Jafar pushed him back to western Bihar with help of the British army. By this time, the Marathas proceeded towards Midnapur after they had occupied Orissa.

After paying a part of the committed sum to the Company, the Murshidabad treasury was exhausted. Since the soldiers' wages were overdue, they revolted. The Company also claimed a full payment of the dues. Mir Jafar, being incapable of paying, handed over Chittagong to the EIC. The Nawab took an advance from Mir Qasim, his son-in-law who claimed his succession from the Nawab, and became a de facto ruler of Bengal. He made a secret treaty with the Company's governor and leased Burdwan and Midnapur. By October of 1760, Mir Jafar was forced to surrender to the British and was replaced by Mir Qasim. Mir Zafar retired to Calcutta with a military escort.

The Company officers brought back Shah Alam II to Bengal. Mir Qasim, being suspicious of the Company's intentions, shifted his capital to Bihar to keep himself beyond the British influence. Shah Alam had been proclaimed to be the successor of the Mughals, but he was not confident to march to Delhi without British help. In the meantime, Mir Qasim refused Shah Alam's entry into Murshidabad. This caused the company officers to become annoyed. Then Mir Qasim executed a zamindar of Bihar for being disloyal. He also increased the rate of trade duties for the British. When he was challenged by the traders, Mir Qasim allowed concessions to the Company, but not to the private traders, who disagreed to pay taxes violating all norms. The Murshidabad court alleged this as a misconduct. The English traders then desperately forced tax paying native businessmen to withdraw their business, disrupting the overall tax collection in Bengal.

With the decline of treasury income, Mir Qasim gradually became powerless. The British officials and traders exploited the Nawab's weakness by extorting money from the public. They openly demanded bribes, and failing payments the unprotected villagers were forced to yield. In this chaotic condition the Company commissioners became self-made tax collectors in the resource-rich cities of Dacca, Patna, and Cossimbazar.

Even in Calcutta tax free trading became normal by ignoring the Nawab's officials. In an extreme situation, British private traders of oil, paddy, betel nuts, cotton and silk textiles demanded permits to be issued by the Company totally bypassing the Murshidabad office. They even started construction of factories without permission. The native producers were forced to sell commodities below market rates and the local traders were driven away at the indulgence of the administration. Natives had no protection. They were tortured to disclose their treasures; the prosperous weavers and artisans were cursed like slaves. In this terrible situation when the Company officers were de facto rulers, plunder reached its climax in various forms from Bengal. Large sums of money were dispatched to Britain privately which remained unaccounted for. This was the beginning of forcible looting from India in absence of any formidable law.

Several English men, including Warren Hastings, were government agents for delivering orders to the Nawab on behalf of Clive staying in Murshidabad. Hastings investigated trading abuses, and complained before the Board of Council in Calcutta that the Nawab's authority was completely disavowed. However, his urge to stem this abuse was given little attention. In disgust Warren Hastings resigned from Company service. From 1762–63, the English merchants started forcing the Council not to interfere in tax free trading and influenced officials to make a treaty proposal with Nawab to abolish the customs duty. Mir Qasim declined to accept it because the revenue was already halved. When the situation went out of the hands of Mir Qasim, he came to the conclusion that it was inevitable for him to start an armed conflict with the English. The Nawab's men initially detained some Company's ships and murdered some British soldiers.

This incident instigated the Calcutta Council to prepare for a war on Mir Qasim by reinstating Mir Jafar. Mir Qasim sent his trained forces to combat the advancing British force towards Mursidabad. The Nawab took over the Cossimbazar base, and British men who were captured during the conflict were taken to Munger in Bihar. Unfortunately, Mir Qasim was surrounded by treacherous men. They joined the British force with the Bengal army causing the Nawab to lose. Mir Qasim's next encounter was also marred by treachery by one of his trusted men, and the Munger Fort was lost. The Nawab's great mistake was losing the support of his own subjects after he murdered his respectable prisoners including Jagat Seth.

Mir Qasim prepared for revenge and requested the governor of Awadh, Suja-Ud-Daulah, for help in the operation against the English. Suja was very close to Shah Alam II, then the Emperor of Delhi. Suja along with Shah Alam agreed to side with Mir Qasim, and the trio pitched camps in Buxar. Finally, Suja asked for a large contribution from Mir Qasim. Another sad treachery happened when Reihardt Somber* betrayed Mir Qasim to join Suja with his soldiers, arms and ammunition. He looted his former master's camp, captured Mir Qasim and brought

---

* Note: Mr. Somber, an Austrian, belonged to the French army in India. In 1760 he was recruited by Mir Qasim. Somber was instrumental when Patna was re-occupied by killing many English men. Mir Qasim brought him to Buxar to lead one group of his troops but he betrayed him.

him to Suja. Shah Alam II remained indifferent. Next, Suja-Ud-Daulah prepared himself for war against the British troops. Under Hector Munro, newly employed British troops advanced towards Buxar and easily defeated their opponents in an encounter near Arah, and advanced further to take on Suja in Buxar.

Suja Ud Dulah was decisively defeated in the battle of Buxar in October 1764, in presence of Shah Alam II. This victory of Britain was something more than that they could achieve in Plassey. Shah Alam II joined the victors. Mir Qasim after being released lived like a commoner in a hut in Delhi and died there bringing to an end the Nawabi rule in Bengal. The Buxar incident was a repetition of dishonesty and treachery on the Indian battlefield.

This win in Buxar secured the EIC a consolidated extended trading center because in August 1765, King Shah Alam II formally granted the Company the Diwani of Bengal, Bihar, and Orissa with the power of tax collection (Fig. 6 Map 1760). This grant increased the Company's secured income. It is said that Shah Alam's order that dismissed his own revenue officers, replacing them with British traders, was dictated by Clive himself from his Buxar tent.

Though the British East India Company suffered a setback in Madras after the success of Dupleix in 1746, its supremacy was restored between 1749 and 1764 after Dupleix was withdrawn in 1749. Also, the Nawab of Bengal failed to defeat the British in their own territories due to treachery. The EIC already had secured sources of income from the farm lands and manufacturing units in 24 Parganas, Burdwan, Midnapur, and Chittagong. The present offer brought additional opportunities for the Company to increase their revenue earning. They earned millions of Pounds which was dispatched to Britain between the Battle of Plassey and Waterloo. The success of Buxar was the ultimate success, and it compelled EIC to accept administrative responsibility for a larger territory for which they were unprepared. Clearly this unexpected development needed a larger western styled administrative structure that required more manpower.

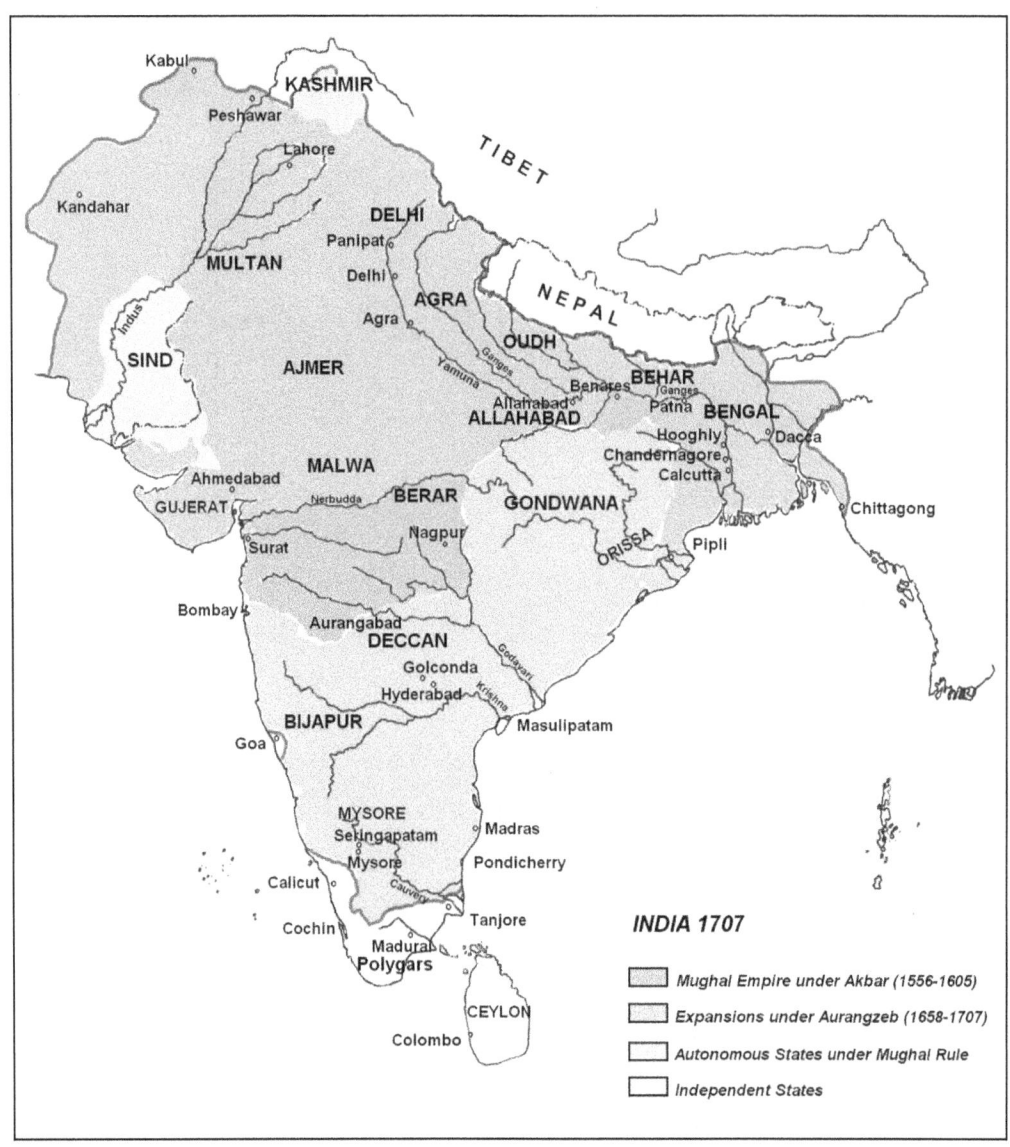

Fig. 5 Map of India at height of Mughal Reign, 1707.

1.3 Observation

The Company wrestled Bengal from the Mughals' command after a long struggle for about one hundred and fifty years, and used it as the base for future expansion. This was possible due to farsightedness of Job Charnock, and the military skill of Robert Clive who used native sepoys to defeat the larger army of Siraj-ud-Daula enriched with French troops.[7] The fragmented regional powers that continued after the collapse of the Mughal Empire with its degraded political stability were gradually occupied over one hundred years. This British Company also had to encounter other European rivals, especially the French in the southern region. Southern territories were conquered after they were weakened by the Marathas.

The illegal drainage of Indian resources began shortly after Siraj was defeated, and it was done mostly by force with administrative support at a lower level. Warren Hastings, recruited as the first Governor-General of Bengal, was in Company service but failed to protect the natives. Rather than listening to Hastings, the Calcutta council yielded to the pressure of traders and its own employees. Robert Clive's achievement to get financial access to Bengal increased the earnings of the traders. The Company enriched the British economy. This situation forced Britain to set up a proper administration to rule over a wider territory with the intention of further expansion.

References:

1. The dates of establishment of factories in Bengal are given in *Hedges' Dairy*, Vol. III, pages 194–95. Refer, Dirom Gray Crawford, *A Brief History of the Hughly District* (Calcutta: Bengal Secretariat Press, 1903), 14. William Hedge was the first British agent in Bengal from 1686 and his diary was published in 1687.
2. Barbara D. Metcalf and Thomas R. Metcalf, *A Concise History of India* (Cambridge: Cambridge University Press, 2005), 45–46.
3. Michael Edwardes, *British India 1772–1947* (New Delhi: Rupa, 10th Edn. 2019), 7.
4. Ibid, 5.
5. Burton Stein, *A History of India*, revised and edited by David Arnold (Sussex, UK: Wiley-Blackwell, 2010), 182.
6. Ishita Banerjee-Dube, *A History of Modern India* (Cambridge: Cambridge University Press, 2015), 5.
7. Penelope Carson, *East India Company and Religion 1698–1858*. Vol. 7 of the World of the East India Company (Woodbridge, UK: Boydell Press, 2012), 226.

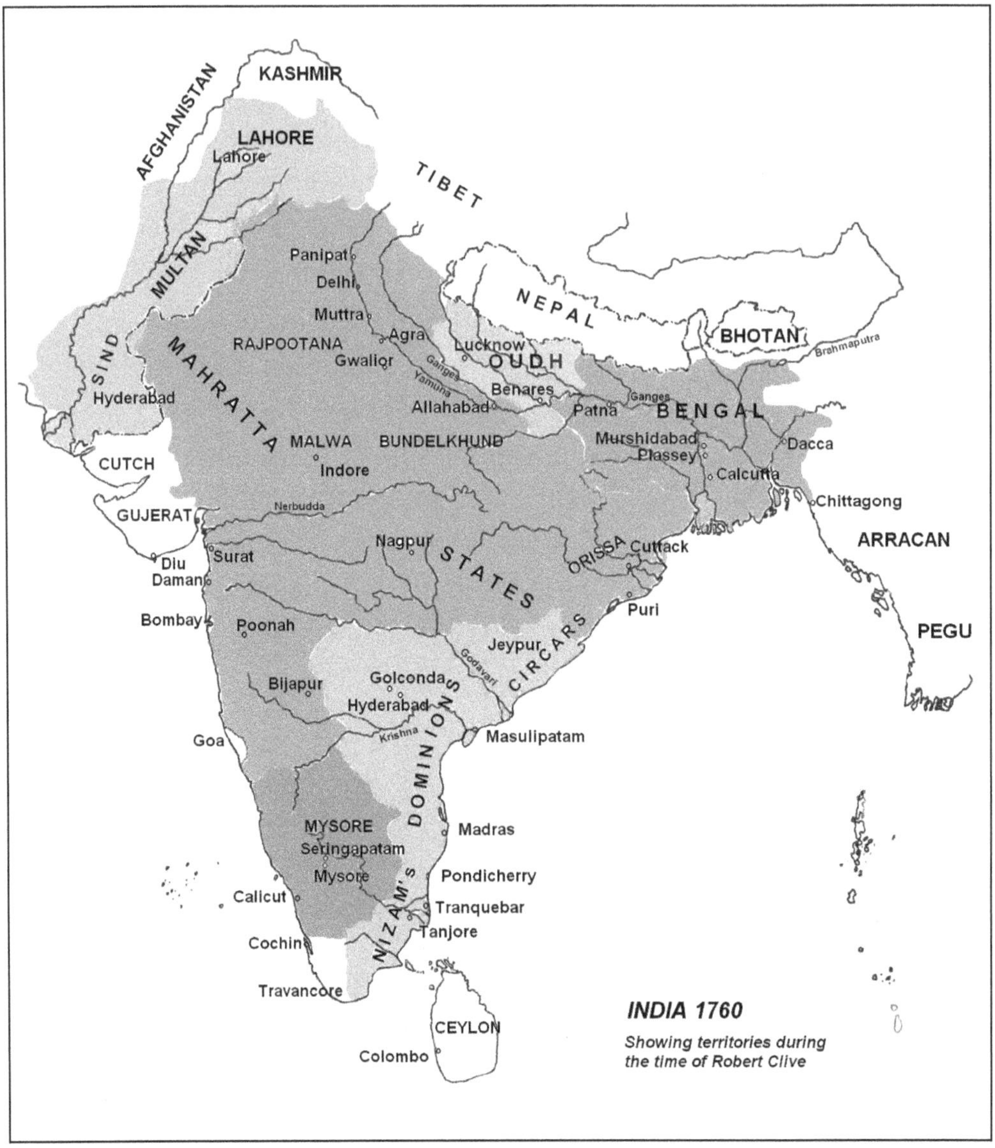

Fig. 6 Map India 1760.

CHAPTER 2

East India Company rulers from Bengal 1772 – 1858

This chapter deals with a history of about 85 years of the EIC when much of its power was shifted to London before British Parliament took over its total control terminating it. It describes how the administration gradually changed and how the socio-political conditions in Bengal improved with the introduction of western education. During this period the EIC expanded its territory, while encouraging trade and commerce all over India. The events culminated in the so-called Sepoy Mutiny; its causes and consequences will be discussed.

2.1 Beginning of Company Rule

Robert Clive left India for two years after his 1765 Buxar victory. He returned Awadh to Suja-Ud-Daula, making this state a buffer between Bengal and the North West Frontier which was disturbed. By controlling the Company servants' payments, he attempted to tame Bengal's plunder. He appeased them by allowing provisions for extra income through a trading company in which the servants became shareholders. He also saved on military expenditure by reducing the army men's extra income, even surviving a white mutiny. Clive allowed a deputy nawab in Murshidabad to keep control over police and magistrates, but nominated a Company man to act for him. This dual system ensured firm Company's control over Bengal and Bihar. He also engaged his force to check Dutch ambitions that grew with an understanding with the Nawab. However, Clive was criticized for suppressing the Calcutta Council, and for failing to check ongoing Company's losses.

2.2 The Administration of the EIC and Territorial Expansion

2.2.1 Company Employees, Trafficking and Indian Drain

With renewed growth of revenue earnings, the Company's remittances to Britain increased, creating a high demand for Company's bonds. This growth also attracted a considerable number of keen young British applicants signing up to travel to Calcutta. Some of them joined as officers, others as clerks. Upon their arrival, an army of native employees were ready to teach ignorant newcomers survival skills in an alien environment.

With the increase of manpower and in absence of formidable legislation, corruption in the administration became rampant. Some young company servants earned as much as £40,000 yearly from trafficking and illegal trade; funds which remained outside the official EIC transfers to Britain.[1] Corruption grew so much that it drastically reduced the EIC's earnings. Also the import of silver, from Britain to Bengal which was used for exchange, declined from 1757. There was a shortage of food grains in Bengal too. As a result, the local people's earnings tended to decline from the 1760s, and many of them had only limited purchasing power. The Company's administration was not equipped to manage food distribution during this period of shortage, and so a famine broke out in 1769–70. It caused the reduction of one third of the population in Bengal due to death and migration.

Since Clive allowed company servants – including civil servants, soldiers, surgeons and even chaplains – to be legal traders, their earnings were high until the end of the 18th century. Some British residents in Bengal acquired a monopoly in saltpetre and opium trade until the Company imposed restrictions in 1770. Employees increased their personal income by taking a percentage of tax-farming or revenue collection. In addition, they received gifts from Nawab's men. For fifteen years from Plassey (1757), these EIC employees were power brokers in Bengal. The 1760s were the most corrupt decade.[2] Even the Army officers were managing to draw double allowances for campaigns up to 1810. Thus an unaccounted amount of Indian money was privately dispatched to Britain. This plunder began in some form or another in Mir Qasim's time.

The British Parliament appointed a committee to survey the company's financial condition between 1757 and 1766 and found it unsatisfactory. The share price of the EIC had doubled overnight in 1772 (seven years after the Diwani was granted), but the bubble burst over the months following as revenue collection fell unexpectedly. The EIC was now burdened with debts of £1.5 million in addition to an unpaid tax bill of £1 million owed to the Crown. Thirty European banks failed once this news was disclosed. The Company was uncertain of obtaining a Bank loan in England. In that situation the Company Directors appealed for sanction of £1 million from London. To bail out the Company from this situation, the Parliament decided to initiate immediate reforms.

2.2.2 Administrative Reforms

Parliament voted for reforming the Company's administration through the Regulatory Act 1773 by forming a central authority to bring partial control over the EIC, and appointing a Governor-General for Bengal with authority over Bombay and Madras provinces. The Governor-General had the right to introduce new laws based on exigencies of the moment. The Company had long felt the need to establish a Supreme Court with judges with legal powers over the occupied area. From 1662, Charles II authorized the execution of judicial power to the Company through Mayor's Courts established in Calcutta (Fig. 7), Bombay and Madras provinces. But these Court's did not introduce any legal binding for running the administration.

Fig. 7 Old Court House and Writers Building, 1786. By T. Daniell (British Library Archive).

Fig. 8 New Court House Calcutta, 1786. By T. Daniell (British Library Archive).

The first Supreme Court (Fig. 8) started in Calcutta from 1774, replacing the Mayor's Court. The EIC was also authorized to function as a state with military power. From the 1790s, the Company became a managing agency of Indian trade for the British Government, which had now increased its control to prevent abuses. It became a world leader in the export of calico, indigo dye, cotton, silk, spices, and Chinese tea.

As the next step of reform, the Bengal Judiciary Act of 1781 was introduced extending the jurisdiction of the Supreme Court over persons residing in Bengal, Bihar and Orissa, including the European residents so that Company's revenue collection remained undisturbed. Warren Hastings, the first Governor–General, further extended Indian legal systems – both civil and criminal – to district levels. High Courts were established a century later in 1882, under the Indian High Courts Act, 1861.

Calcutta became the Company's capital. The Governor-General was chief of government. This Act also enabled the officers of commercial settlements to become Governors of the provinces. He was the principal negotiator. His salary was Rs 10,000 per month – highest of all Company officers. The Governor-General remained accountable to the Secretary of State for India in London, and through him to Parliament. His posting was in the capital, and he worked with the support of an executive council. The presidencies of Bombay and Madras had Governors who worked in consultation with an advisory council. Later Lord Canning assigned different departments for the council members but the basic structure of governance remained unchanged.

The Company began recruiting Indian sepoys for defence of their acquired territory and for coercing other areas including neighboring Princely States. The total expenditure for maintenance of the troops was met by collecting taxes from local people which was gradually raised as territorial expansion continued. India's indigenous economy was vibrant and sustainable. But the Company forcibly introduced British goods to ensure the British market in India. Thus commercial exploitation started with administrative support. In 1784 a double government system was introduced through the Pitt's India Act. Many company servants, especially those engaged in tax collection, got the opportunity to become administrators.

2.2.3 Governor-Generals and administration

The basic responsibility of the Governor-General was to increase British earnings with royal sceptre. He retained power for expansion of the territory. Some of the Governor-Generals generously tried to diffuse western culture and education among Indians, and recover ancient Indian knowledge. The Governor-General's residence was Buckingham House (Fig. 9), a rented house southwest of Calcutta's commercial centre. After 1799, Wellesley constructed a grand Government House in the same locality.

Fig. 9 Old Government House. By Thomas Daniell, 1788 (British Library Archive).

Fig. 10 Warren Hastings. Engraved from Painting of Zoffany, in his *Memoir*, London: J. Murray, 1787.

When all the presidencies were brought under direct control of Bengal, Warren Hastings (Fig. 10) was appointed as the first Governor-General of Bengal, having previous experience in Murshidabad court. He had helped Robert Clive to lay the EIC's foundation, but resigned. However, after a short stint in Madras he was called back to Bengal as governor of Fort William in 1772. When Hastings took charge, Bengal was a poor state due to economic depression and a famine.

Warren Hastings set up the legal system terminating despotism but kept an oriental touch. He allowed both Hindu and Muslim subjects to enjoy separate religious custom-based laws. Hindus, an amalgam of Hindu, Sikhs, Buddhists, and Jains, lacked comprehensive legal texts, and for them a separate arrangement was made. Muslims were segregated because they followed laws set out in the Quran and Hadith. This new system accepted all individuals as basic units of a society and intended to provide uniform legal rights and obligations. But legal pluralism was not avoided.

Religious affiliation in marriage, contracts, and successions between different Hindu sects were not uniform. To codify Hindu Laws written in Sanskrit, Hindu pandits were employed. Their versions were translated into English for use in the legal system. Nathaniel Brassey Halhed made the first translation of *Gentoo Code* in 1773 from Persian into English. It was then rewritten by the Sanskrit scholar William Jones. Hindu laws are said to have been compiled with help of pundits from ancient treaties and medieval texts in the *Dharmas*; the legal maxims being found in *Smrities*.

As we have seen, when Warren Hastings took charge the Bengal province was devastated by wars and famine. He dismissed the old dewani system of tax collection, and replaced it with a centrally controlled colonial system of land tenures. District collectors were recruited who had no permanent interest in the lands, and would not squeeze the peasants. Revenue administration was left mainly with the old natives as the trained European officials were few in number.

This system was like a commercial corporation. Neither the Europeans or Indians collectors were honest. They used to apply force for tax collection. The British collectors were ill paid and greedy and dependent on natives due to their unfamiliarity with the land. The direct tax collection had fallen behind due to the devastation caused by the famine. According to Sivanath Sastri,[3] from January to August of 1770 one crore people died in Bengal, but only 76,000 died in Calcutta.

An official report written by Edmund Burke stated, "The EIC's financial problem could drag the government down to an unfathomable abyss …" In 1773 the Company was saved by history's first "mega bail-out."[4] But financial reports of EIC between 1768 to 1772 did not show any fall in revenue tariff even though one third of the taxpayers died or were displaced by famine.

Warren Hastings' letters to London depicted that the quantum of loss of revenue was compensated by excess collections with immediate effect from the remaining two thirds of the population. This meant that the subjects living in misery were made to compensate for the loss by paying excess taxes and interests. The Governor-General had to act under pressure from a regulatory board, and was explainable to the Parliament even though there were public resentments. This escalation of misery after the famine caused a revolt in North Bengal. In his historical novel *Devi Chaudhurani* (published in 1887), Bankim Chandra Chatterjee painted Bhabani Pathak's character with reflections of old memories of the expedition led by Lt. Brenan against the Sanyasi and Fakir Rebellions in 1787.

The Company was against immediate expansion, but Warren Hastings got involved at several war fronts to mitigate post-Mughal political situations. In a war with the Marathas he made a long term treaty even having well trained troops. However, he occupied Ahmedabad. His tenure required augmenting military forces with more Indian sepoys, many of them with Portuguese blood, in the way Clive himself did after the Plassey. Hastings recruited more Rajputs and higher class Hindus, permitting them to celebrate festivals in the cantonments.[5] But Warren Hastings was instrumental in conspiring against Maharaja Nanda Kumar. It is said that the Governor-General had manipulated a case of forgery against the Maharaja and condemned him to death following an old act of 1729. The Maharaja was an Indian tax collector.

The EIC's military strength increased to 1,55,000 men with cavalry during the Napoleonic wars. In the South, the Madras presidency became engaged with Hydar Ali, who had French support. When Madras drifted into war, Hasting's help was required. This war venture was expensive and badly affected the Company's finances. However, Warren Hastings himself earned fortune, but not as much as Clive earned. Hastings was fond of collecting diamonds.

Hastings could not work freely until 1776, as the Council members did not cooperate with him. In 1781 he was able to appoint Britishers of his choice and combined the posts of the judges of the Civil Courts with the Post of Magistrate. In addition, he reintroduced the posts of revenue collectors, but eliminated the Provincial Council. In this manner the Civil Court, remaining under the Nawab of Murshidabad, was in effect brought under the Governor-General. Hastings' successor Lord Cornwallis finally eliminated the power of the Nawab over the affairs of criminal justice. Several powers of the Nawab were restricted around 1780. A double governor system was introduced through the Pitt's Act passed by the Parliament in 1784 at the end of Hasting's tenure.

Back home, Warren Hastings was impeached in 1788 for mismanagement and corruption. Edmund Burke rallied against the way the returned officers of EIC were buying Parliamentary influences. They bribed MPs to oblige the Parliamentary Office by using their Indian plunder.[6] After a long public process, Hastings was finally acquitted in 1795 with an understanding that he did more good for Britain than bad.

From the tenure of the first Governor-General of Bengal, India witnessed the beginning of social and cultural changes. Hastings thought about establishing Fort William College. He encouraged Mr. Halhed to create Bengali fonts for writing and printing Bengali grammar which was completed by 1777. He took interest to get the *Gita*, the famous Hindu scripture, translated from Sanskrit into English. Hastings founded the Calcutta Madrasa in 1781 to encourage Muslims to study and practice law. He supported the foundation of the Banaras Sanskrit College in 1782 and he endorsed Sir William Jones's achievements by patronizing the Asiatic Society of Bengal in 1784. James Augustus Hicky published the *Bengal Gazette*, the first English newspaper in 1780, but in 1782 his press was seized for circulating controversial views. Some other newspapers like the *Calcutta Gazette*, *Bengal Journal*, *Oriental Magazine* or *Calcutta Amusement* and the *Calcutta*

Chronicle came into publication between 1782 and 1786. Hastings also laid the foundation stone of the Compagnie's St. John's Church in 1784 (Fig. 11).

Sir William Jones was a judge of the Supreme Court, and as a researcher he interpreted the *Trimurti*, an ancient symbol of Hindu culture, and dug out the *Manu Samhita (Smriti)*, a Sankrit text to set laws for Hindu marriage and hierarchy. Jones also endeavored to elaborate the Indian history with archaeological discoveries of *lipis* (written on stones, etc.) through the Asiatic Society. He was a pioneer to uncover ancient Indian history and wisdom that almost was lost. All these attempts to recover the ancient Indian glory received support of the first Governor-General. Though his personal life was not free from controversy, Warren Hastings was one of the most competent administrators who laid the foundation of modern India.

Fig. 11 St. John's Church, Calcutta 1786-88. By T. Daniell (British Library Archive).

Lord Charles Cornwallis (1786–93) succeeded Warren Hastings after a 20 month interregnum under John Macpherson (1785–86). Cornwallis divided the civil service into executive and judicial branches as a measure to suppress corruption. He reformed the tax collection procedures and allowed the zamindars to collect taxes on behalf of the government to augment revenue collections. To modify the administration, he rejected native collectors' supremacy and excluded Indians from all senior positions in administration and army as he thought Indians dishonest. The new system increased British earnings from land revenue but widened racial divides fostering white superiority. The natives were subordinates in work places.

Cornwallis curtailed extra income of employees, but their service conditions improved with respectable salary and better post retirement facilities. This system attracted young Englishmen to flock to India until World War I. The majority of new recruits came to make money, and did little for their subjects. None of the land revenue earned by the government was used for rural improvement.

Cornwallis' reformed the EIC's view on proprietorial rights of lands, which were incorporated as written documents under the Permanent Settlement Regulation II of 1793. This law conferred legislative authority to landlords with property rights on a permanent basis – it was inheritable and transferable. This procedure limited government jurisdiction, but ensured a stable earning, and it abolished tax collection through government agents, checking dishonestly but squeezing the taxpayers. The Permanent Settlement served government purposes, but was harmful to the peasants as they became landless laborers. The land ownership was given to the zamindars but the rents belonged to the sovereign.

Under this system the post-assessment tax was payable to the landlords, and the rent payable to the state by the landlords. These were due to be foreclosed if remained unpaid. It caused a widespread failure of timely tax payments by the peasants. Landlords enjoyed power to force default farmers to sell properties. In this manner, thousands of farmers of Bengal became landless and were evicted from their own land. Rich native merchants of Calcutta with no interest in the soil, purchased land to become landlords. The rent was a constant source of earning. This system constrained productivity, and the rural economy was destroyed. The impoverished farmers lived without any protection.

When landlords became affluent with the flow of easy money, they engaged *Jotedars* – the intermediary tenure holders to control the agriculture.

But the holding's characters were not consolidated. In South India the *Ryotwari Settlement* was introduced, awarding rights to the peasant-cultivators. Government retained the right to revise assessments every twenty years outside Bengal. The system started from Mysore after 1800 when economic recovery was encouraged after successive wars.

Throughout India, Forest dwellers, such as Santals of the Chotanagpur Plateau, were free hunter-gatherers from antiquity. When the Company began to manage forestry, their rights on the natural resources were withdrawn. When they turned to become invaders of agricultural settlements, they were subjected to armed incursions in the 1820s. During this time, the Santals revolted and created their own laws.

Wastelands, long used as grazing fields, were contracted by creating private property rights to ensure political stability and revenue earnings. This was done through the Permanent Settlement Law when one third of Bengal was still waste land. The owners of animal herds used these fields for grazing as their livelihood. They enjoyed natural rights for generations, and when evicted, they became plunderers and robbers. A special law was framed to control them, and the system continued until 1839. The mercantile phase that started from 1757 continued until it was replaced by a free trade system in 1813.

Fig. 12 Marquis Wellesley. By J. Young (National Galleries, UK).

2.2.4 Territorial Expansions

Warren Hastings reluctantly began to expand EIC territory. Cornwallis too was unwilling to engage in wars. However, under Lord Wellesley (1798–1805) (Fig. 12) and his successors, the EIC's territorial claims encompassed all of India from Afghanistan to Burma, taking 50 years to turn a trading area into full British hegemony. Wellesley was ambitious to make India an empire more like "a sacred trust with a permanent possession" as he said.

Before Wellesley, Charles Cornwallis restrained Tipu Sultan through a treaty in 1792 which ended the third Anglo–Mysore War. Though a military man himself, Cornwallis was careful to avoid an outright war. "Barbarian Tipu has forced us into war," he once said. Tipu –the tiger of Mysore– was over-ambitious. Wellesley, however, was less cautious. With help of the Nizam of Hyderabad, he attacked the Sultan causing his death on 4 May 1799 at Seringapatam, even as Tipu Sultan used French trained troops. Wellesley did not stop the plunder of Mysore after winning the fourth Anglo–Mysore War (1798–99). It is said that Napoleon advanced up to Egypt to oblige Tipu. They both lost. The Princely state of Tanjore also fell to Wellesley in 1799. Finally, the entire coast of Carnatic Malabar was annexed.

Tipu's sons instigated the Vellore Mutiny in 1806 from prison when sepoys were ordered to change traditional headgear and their savings style, and not to use ornaments and the caste marks. These were traditional military customs in Mysore with a religious touch. The Muslim sepoys murdered several British officers while they slept because they felt their religion was endangered when sepoys were ordered to wear new headgears resembling British hats. The natives said, "you took our country and now would take our religion."

Wellesley expanded quickly by taking over the Marathas in north and central India by engaging a strong garrison with Indian sepoys. He secured control over the region between the Ganges and Yamuna near Allahabad. Within just six years, the Company's territory extended from southern India to Poona, Rajputana, and Sindh. Punjab remained outside Wellesley's net. He persuaded Shah Alam II to obtain control of Delhi though he was against re-establishing the Mughals.

Remnants of the Maratha confederacy lost coherence, except the Sindhias of Gwalior and the Holkars who thrived through military rivalry. The Holkars became powerful. In 1802, Wellesley neutralized the Peshwas of Poona, putting him on the throne following the Bassein treaty. He conquered Delhi in 1803 (Fig. 18 Map 1805). The Maratha native rulers were eclipsed after the defeat of Holkar in 1804. Finally, Lord Hastings (1813–23) eliminated the constant threat of the Maratha plunderers, the *Pindaris* in 1817, and in the following years Gujarat was incorporated in Company's domain.

Wellesley opened the College of Fort William in 1800 in Calcutta to train civil servants in Indian languages, customs, manners, and culture before their posting. Also, the London Company directors established a College at Haileybury in England in 1804 for training of new recruits in civil service to prepare them for the Indian foreign conditions. Fort William College became a center of cultural interaction between eastern and western intellectuals.

When the Company's earnings increased from their expanded territory, Lord Wellesley desired to make the British presence in India more glamorous and planned to rebuild the old government house into a palace, and even before informing the court of directors he began its construction (presently Raj Bhawan, Kolkata). The building was completed in January of 1803 after four years from the time of laying the foundation when Wellesley engaged Tipu in Mysore. A total of £178,000 were spent for the land and the building, which looks like a well-furnished palace.

This grand building contains a central hall on the ground floor, the marble room and throne room on the first floor. The ballroom was on the second floor along with guest rooms. The Governor-General used the Council Chamber on the first floor to preside over the meetings with the Executive and the Legislative councils. The throne room was used during the prize distribution ceremony of Fort William College. Lord Curzon made the building even more pompous. Wellesley built a second governmental residence at Barrackpore overlooking the river.

Lord Minto (1807–13) favored a civilized system. He restricted military activities and resolved conflicts through diplomacy. But the British became apprehensive of the Russian presence causing security threats along the borders of the northwestern frontier (Afghanistan). Then Ranjit Singh was ruling Punjab with formidable power of religious militancy at the partial command of European officers. Minto made a treaty with Singh and avoided wars. He in 1809 brought Tripura (in the East) under the British which continued as a Princely State.

Lord Moira revived the older policy of expansion to maintain peace. He inducted Gorkhas into the British army, arrested the plundering by Marathas, and finally secured central India under control. Subsequent Governor-Generals supported social reforms as well as concluded territorial expansions with the conquest of remaining areas. From this latter part of the EIC's regime, Indian city life began to bring transformation through increasing western influence. From the early nineteenth century Bombay and Madras became large cities after Calcutta. Learning English helped Indians to interact with Europeans. Wealthy Indians developed friendly relations with high ranking British officers. European elites aided diffusion of western culture among Indian youths. The children of elite families got opportunities to associate with European talents privately. Besides the British, there were Italians, Germans, and French nationals who took residence in white Calcutta and other cities. From the tenure of the Earl of Moira, Marquis Hastings (1813–23), western culture became prevalent in the metropoles.

The social and cultural reformation of India began in Calcutta through the Bengal Renaissance (Appendix 1). This movement transformed India from orthodoxy into a modern society. It was similar to the upheaval during the European Renaissance which freed Europeans from religious dependence. City life in India tended to progress, but rural life remained neglected. Meanwhile, territorial expansions continued though at a slower pace after Wellesley (Fig. 18 Map 1805). Europeans and wealthy Indians used to lead luxurious lifestyles within a typical city culture. In Calcutta, Europeans settled in the central part of Calcutta known as "White Calcutta." It was planned with wide roads and splendid, spacious buildings (Fig. 13), raised on land reclaimed from tiger infested forests. In contrast, the native houses in the northern part of Calcutta were unplanned. This was "Black Calcutta" (Fig. 14). Some wealthy natives erected palatial buildings surrounded by thatched hovels, creating a unique city heritage (Fig. 15 Tagore's Castle).

Fig. 13 White Town. "A Street in Calcutta," *Illustrated London News*, 1855.

Fig. 14 Chitpore Road, 1867. Blacktown. By William Simpson (Wikimedia).

East India Company rulers from Bengal 1772 – 1858 57

Fig. 15 Tagore Castle, North Kolkata (Public Domain).

Fig. 16 Government's House at Ganeshkhind
(after 1949 Pune University).

Fig. 17 Viceroy's House upon completion 1931. Later called Rashtrapati Bhavan.

Government Houses in the major cities were magnificent. Pune Government's Mansion completed in 1871 is a picturesque architectural blend of Roman-Hindu style (Fig. 16). Victoria Memorial Hall in Calcutta built by Curzon was a copy of the Agra's Taj Mahal. New Delhi's Viceroy's house with 340 rooms and halls (Durbar hall and Asoka hall) exhibits the symbols of Roman might with Indian architectural elements blended in (Fig. 17). Bombay and Madras were no exception. Exhibiting power and wealth, these mansion's expenditures were borne from Indian resources.

Lord Amherst (1823–28) initiated the first war against Burma. Khasi Hills in the east were brought under control in 1823 through a subsidiary arrangement. Lord Combermere, Commander-in-Chief, stormed the Indian forces of Bharatpur. By the middle of 1825, Dutch properties in Bengal were handed over to the British in exchange for their possessions in Sumatra. Native infantry mutinied at Barrackpore and qualified Indians claimed their rights to sit in court trials for the first time. The Jury Bill of 1826 allowed Indians to act as juries in criminal cases before the Supreme Court, but were restrained to sit as Grand Juries while dealing with the cases of Christian convicts. (In Madras an association was founded in 1860 to protest against the special favors for Christians).

During the Renewal of the Charter in 1833 when William Bentinck (1828–35) was the Governor-General, the Parliament ordered the EIC to administer the territory on behalf of the Crown. The sole power of legislation rested on the EIC and restrictions on missionary activities were revoked. Lord Bentinck abolished Sati in Bengal in 1829, restored press freedom, and formally approved English education in 1835 at Macaulay's recommendation. Bentinck reduced official corruption, drinking, and gambling habits of the European residents. He instructed Sindh to come into commercial relations with the British after the Russians reached up to central Asia, and obliged Ranjit Singh of Punjab with gifts. Charles Metcalfe, a civil servant, took charge for a short period before Lord Auckland (1836–42) took over.

Lord Auckland involved himself in the first Afghan War wrongly apprehending that Russians were nearing the British post. This war was a disaster as many British and Indian soldiers were killed. Ranjit Singh died in 1839, and Auckland returned home in 1842. Lord Ellenborough (1842–44) was appointed next, but his appointment was revoked two years later though he occupied Gwalior. After Ranjit Singh, the territory was left under the Sikh army as his son was a boy. Sikhs refused the British army to allow passage through their territory during the first Afghan War. Since then relations between the British and Sikhs had been strained. The first Sikh War was bloody and hard fought by the Sikhs, but they were defeated in 1845 by Hardinge, and the British annexed the land east of Sutlej extending to the Beas river which contained the mountain range.

During the tenure of Hardinge (1844–48), the mountain region surrounding the Kashmir valley was sold to the Hindu king of Jammu, Raja Gulab Singh, under the Treaty of Amritsar, 1846. Kashmir–Jammu, including Ladakh, Gilgit and Baltistan, was recognized as an independent Princely State under Gulab Singh from 1848. About five years of civil wars in Punjab was followed by the second Anglo–Sikh War of 1848–49.

The Sikh empire fell under Lord Dalhousie who joined as the Governor-General in 1848. These battles were expensive. Lord Dalhousie (1848–56) made decisive history by including Punjab into British territory in 1848, which covered the entire mountain region between the Indus and Ravi under the Sikhs. This inclusion added four million subjects to British India. Parliament renewed the Company Charter in 1853 by giving more power to the Crown over the EIC and decentralizing its administration. Awadh (Allahabad) was included in EIC's territory in 1854. Territorial expansion of Indian territories was complete by 1857 (Fig. 22 Map 1857).

Though Punjab, Agra, and Allahabad officially became part of the Bengal Presidency, all were allowed to remain under the administration of a lieutenant governor with greater independence. Punjab was left under a few autonomous administrators and free from legal codes, deviating from the Permanent Settlement Act. Punjab prospered through improvements in agriculture, using natural facilities of its vast river-system.

After the capture of Punjab, Dalhousie seized Burma. He also annexed the Princely States without any direct heirs. The cities of Jaipur, Udaipur, Nagpur, and Jhansi, and all their estates which lacked proper male heirs, were confiscated. Thus the British secured an expanded both source area and markets.

Lord Dalhousie, the penultimate Governor-General, delineated the acquired territories with a defined geographical boundary, thus making India a legal entity (Fig. 22 Map 1857). He created an infrastructure for easing communication provided with railways, telegraph lines, roadways, and ocean transport systems. He also completed about 500 miles of canals for irrigation and local transportation. He strengthened the British hegemony in the Indian colony.

The period between the tenure of Warren Hastings and Marquess Dalhousie brought unification of political territories. In this period a moribund fragmented society was transformed to a modern Indian society in a new atmosphere created by institutional education. Lord Canning (1856–58) witnessed the Sepoy Mutiny as the last Governor-General of the EIC.

Fig. 18 Map India 1805.

2.3 Rammohan Roy

Rammohan Roy (Fig. 19) was the prime architect of modern India. He arrived at a crucial period of history when the native population was crippled with unreason and bigotry remaining under a prolonged Muslim rule. Rammohan Roy started a process of reformation when the EIC's expansion was in progress. The following paragraphs highlight how a vibrant society degraded and how Rammohan initiated societal reformation.

Fig. 19 Rammohan Roy. By Rembrandt Peale, 1833 (Wikipedia).

2.3.1 Causes of Social Degradation

The People of ancient Indian society learnt literature, mathematics, and logic in Takshashila and Nalanda universities and were culturally rich. Hindus retreated when Buddhism was spreading. A new order was introduced for their descendants and traditional society sunk in ignorance from the early 12th century with the advent of Muslim rule, when an alien political power imposed slavery on the Hindu natives.

Societal degradation began with growing psychological pressures on native women who were forced to marry Muslims. Forced religious conversions increased child marriage, female infanticide, and Sati. Sati

Rajput widows sacrificed themselves with their dead warrior husbands out of fear of exploitation. When women needed masculine protection, society became male dominated. To avoid forced conversions, society accepted Hindu orthodox practices to integrate the natives into classes. The caste system became a tool to serve the personal interests of priests, as people grew accustomed to live under their dictation. Kings, gurus and seniors of a family also waged influence on people. Thus limiting free-thinking and learning, the individual and social strength degraded. Physical survival became a priority and education and intellectualism became a thing of the past. Social taboos which had no link with scriptures became a priority.

Muslims being ignorant of the local commercial system received guidance from native business communities who were privileged money lenders. They exploited the poor of their own community who were segregated into lower castes. The ruling class took advantage of the social divisions. Nawabi despotism forced wealthy natives to survive by commending and self-concealment. Truth became secondary to pretence. Ordinary people followed them and in their attempts to gain favors, they were not ashamed of falsehood. The goodness and honesty that survived was eliminated during British rule with the introduction of new revenue collection policies and court procedures. It did not attempt to uncover the truth, but rather claimed evidence to prove the truth using witnesses which indulged in falsehood. The entire system bred greediness, bribing and cheating. Morality was so low that Macaulay had to make critical comments about the character of Indians.

The Muslim regime replaced Sanskrit with Persian as the official language. Once Sanskrit lost official status it was suppressed, and Hindu scriptures became limited and were not preserved. The priestly community distorted the meaning of scripture knowingly or unknowingly to serve personal interest. Indigenous languages failed to flourish. Written languages became obscure.

Spoken language changed from the middle ages from basic Sanskrit to Prakrit or Pali, depending on the rulers or dominant religion. Regional languages like Magodhi, Gandhari, Dharmapada, Maharashtri came into existence. However, in the southern states, the ancient Dravidian language was resilient and developed its literature. Buddhist scriptures were preserved in Pali. Prakrit flourished in the 15th century as a written language through literary work. But education could not flourish as writing became obsolete.

The Bengali language evolved late from Apabhramsha. Literary work in Bengali was confined to poetry, especially among the Vaishnavas from the 16th century. There is no record of prose writing in Bengali, but spoken Bengali was not primitive. Bengali devotional songs of Ramprasad practiced from the early 18th century are similar to modern Bengali.

2.3.2 Rammohan and Reformation

Kalachand Vidyalankar (1713–1846), a Vaisnavi descendant, tried to reform education and prohibit untouchability, but he was only influential in a limited area of East Bengal (now Bangladesh). Rammohan was the first Indian to stand up against the negative legacy of medievalism. He was the first Bengali to use Bengali prose writing as a vehicle to disseminate his message.

In 1816, Sir Edward Hyde's (Chief Justice, Supreme Court Calcutta) wrote to his friend Mr. Harrison, a judge in England, introducing Rammohan Roy as a Calcutta Brahmin whom he knew, and who was well known for his intelligence and active interference among the principal native inhabitants, and also intimate with many English gentlemen of distinction.[7] Rammohan had already made his mark.

Rammohan Roy (1772–1833) grew up in an orthodox Brahmin family in rural Bengal with no scope for western exposure. When he was a boy, his wise parents sent him to Patna to learn Persian. According to Sastri, Rammohan stayed there until he was fifteen, and acquired knowledge in Persian and Arabic.[8] He was influenced by Arabian philosophers to be a free thinker and a believer of monotheism. When he was sixteen years old he wrote a book in Arabic in which he defied Hindu idolatry.

Young Rammohan witnessed the terrifying death of his sister-in-law as a Sati, and ever since rallied against debased social customs such as sati, polygamy, purdah, child-marriage and dowry. When he failed to adjust to living with his orthodox family, he left home and wandered in the heat of Punjab and the biting cold of Tibet. He disliked the idolatry practiced by Buddhist priests in Tibet and returned to Bengal. Rammohan learned Sanskrit in Banaras and read the *Vedas* and the *Upanishads* and ancient Hindu scriptures and learnt from *Mimamsa* philosophy how to discriminate by applying logic. He realized that orthodoxy and the caste system caused the society to decay. He wrote *Gift to Deists* in Persian in 1803.

In his twenties, Rammohan returned home from Banaras. His father inspired him to learn English. He took a service with the EIC and learnt English in association with Englishmen. His final posting was as dewan of a William Digby, a Company collector at Rangpur. From there he started his societal reformation work. People used to assemble at his residence to discuss their problems with him, and he attempted to help to resolve controversial issues. In 1814 he left his job, and began a private legal consultancy with his expertise in Dewani laws, earning a fortune, but spending most on charity.

From Rangpur, Rammohan went to Calcutta with a mission to start social reformation. His tall and handsome look, his speaking talent, forceful personality and lofty ideas attracted liberal minded persons of Calcutta who would share in his mission. An association, the *Atmiya Sabha* was established in 1815 to enable a superstitious society to imbibe the logic and wisdom of Vedas and Upanishads, and free it from blasphemy and bigotry. He was convinced that superstitions ate the truth. To ventilate new ideas to common people, Rammohan sharpened the Bengali language first and translated the ancient Vedic knowledge from Sanskrit into Bengali. He published in *Sambad Kumudini*, a Bengali newspaper. He also supported *The Bengal Gazette* published by Ganga Kishore Bhattacharya for improving Bengali prose writing.*

---

* Note: Ganga Kishore was a compositor in Serampore Mission Press. He also edited the *Bengal Gazette* from Serampore- a weekly newspaper. Any copy of the *Bengal Gazette* was not available, though its imminent publication was advertised in the Government Gazette in May, 1818. Ganga Prasad began Bengali prose writing. Ramram Basu along with William Carey started writing Bengali prose from the early 1800s.

Rammohan planned to preach the *Brahma Sutra* and so he wrote *Vedanta Sar* (essence of Vedanta) in Bengali, Hindi and English and added Sankar's commentaries. The Bengali version was published in 1815. He also published English and Bengali versions of four Upanishads by 1817. He distributed Bengali versions for free only to convince people that the prevalent customs of Hindus did not have any connection with original scriptures. He wrote *The Unitarian concept in Hinduism* in 1817, and a Judgmental book on *Sati* in 1818. He wrote the inner meaning, *Gayatri Mantra* in Bengali in 1818. His English translations of *Mundaka* and the *Katha Upanishads* were published in 1819.[9] Mr. William Adam, who had come as a Baptist missionary, was convinced by Rammohan's Unitarian ideas, but Joshua Marshman, one of the Serampore Baptist Missionaries, strongly objected to Rammohan.[10]

Rammohan wrote a series of articles in Bengali, Persian and English to convince the Government and his people that there was nothing religious in Sati, and strongly pleaded for its legal abolition. After consistent lobbying for about 15 years, Lord Bentinck became convinced of the arguments of Rammohan Roy and the missionaries. He was bold enough to overcome the orthodox resistance, and abolished Sati in 1829.[11]

Rammohan planned to start western education in Calcutta. David Hare, a self-employed Calcutta resident, was a good friend of Rammohan and they often discussed the necessity of English education for Indians. Rammohan also had trusted native friends with whom he assembled informally in his *Atmiya Sabha*. The main purpose of this Sabha was to promote new ideas, and develop reading and writing habits among its members.

In 1816 the members of this association together with David Hare decided to initiate an English school, and on the same day their member Baidyanath Mukherjee was dispatched to Sir Hyde East, the Chief Justice of the Supreme Court to communicate their proposal. Sir Hyde immediately called David Hare and Rammohan for further discussions, and engaged Baidyanath to gauge public sentiment on this issue.

A meeting was held at the residence of Sir East on 14 May 1816, where some other gentlemen were present. The meeting endorsed the proposal for an English college in Calcutta. But Rammohan was not included in this committee due to objections from Ramkamal Sen and Radhakanta Deb who opposed Rammohan's radical ideas. In the next meeting of 21 May, the proposal was finalized. Hindu College was established in 1817. This college produced many good students who fulfilled the dream of Rammohan Roy (Appendix 1).

Rammohan started his own English high school in 1822 under the patronage of the Calcutta Unitarian Association to teach all subjects including science and Bengali. David Hare and others assisted Rammohan in running this school. Raja Rammohan's son and Debendranath Tagore were students of this school. In 1826 he established Vedanta College for propagation of Hindu Unitarianism. Pandits were recruited to teach Sanskrit literature. Rammohan favored Sanskrit, but the College offered both Indian learning and Western social and physical sciences.

Rammohan opposed government policy that promoted only oriental learning (Sanskrit and Persian), but not western education. On 11 December 1823 he wrote to Lord Amherst that the Government had intended to keep the British subjects in ignorance. He wrote, "... if improvement of the British native population is the object of government, it will consequently promote a more liberal and enlightened system of instruction, embracing mathematics, natural philosophy, chemistry and anatomy with other useful sciences."[12] He also advocated for well-resourced college education, the supply of books, instruments, etc. and providing European teachers for instruction. His recommendation took twelve years to be effective after Macaulay made similar recommendations.

Apart from educational reforms, Rammohan promoted radical religious changes in Hindu society to promote monotheistic belief in God. He established the Brahmo Samaj based on the concept of Vedanta Sutra for promoting logical religious thinking. Dwarkanath Tagore, Kalinath Munsi, Mathuranath Mallik, and other Bengali elites supported his ideas. The Brahmo Samaj began officially in a rented house at Chitpur, Calcutta in 1828 with provision for Saturday evening prayers. The congregation was shifted to a custom built premise in 1830. The trust deed of the Brahmo Samaj depicted that this new building could be used by anybody irrespective of caste and creed, and that everybody would have liberty to pray to God. Idolatry in any form would not be allowed. Radhakanta Deb established the *Hindu Dharma Sabha* in Colootola - a parallel Hindu organization. But many students of Hindu College joined the Brahma Samaj defying their parents' dictates. Within a short time, the Brahmo Samaj attracted many educated persons (Appendix 1).

Apart from working against degraded orthodox society, Rammohan also protested against the Permanent Settlement Act. Knowing his own limitations, he wrote against zamindars, surveyors and revenue officers who took advantage of the Act. He suggested improving revenue collections by bringing wastelands into cultivation, and imposing tax on luxury goods. He then suggested replacing the official army with a people's militia to save expenditure.

He respected the laws, but appealed to consider public opinion before changing systems in administration and jurisprudence. He also wrote to restrict the denominations of the company's servants in the legislative councils by allowing natives to undertake administrative responsibility to restore their civil rights. Rammohan kept his faith in the British judicial system and ethics, and at the same time pointed out gross errors of government. He lodged several political protests which continued even after reaching England. He collected data from government papers to prove that millions of Pounds were being drained yearly from India to England as salaries and interest. He suggested replacing European officers with Indians.

He did not forget to criticize the ill effects of Christian faith in administration, and published articles on British insolence on public roads towards common people, and protested when the Anglo Hindu law of succession was set aside. He believed in democracy and free will and supported the independence movements in Spain and Portugal, expressed his pain over the defeat of Napoleon, and his concerns for Irish people under British dominance.

Rammohan favored European colonization, and encouraged free trade, breaking the Company's monopoly, and wrote in *Sambad Kumudini* and

Weekly Reformer urging for European support in the form of capital and advanced technology for improving the Indian economy. He wanted the British to continue but not for unlimited time.

His articles on the drain of Indian resources to Britain were not swallowed by the British. Lord Hastings planned to introduce press censorship in 1822. Rammohan protested this curtailing of press freedom. John Adam, a civil servant, who replaced Lord Hastings for some time, implemented the censorship and wrongly deported Mr. Buckingham, an assistant editor of a radical paper, to England. This ordinance of 1828 forced the editors to give undertakings to the Chief Secretary. Rammohan contested it in the court of law with support of Dwarakanath Tagore and Prasanna Kumar Tagore arguing that press restrictions would hinder the natives' mental improvement.* When their claim was subsided, Rammohan discontinued his Persian weekly saying that he felt dishonored for being asked for an undertaking. The *Friend of India*, published from Serampore, supported Rammohan's cause. His next appeal was to the King of England. It was received by His Majesty,[13] but dismissed by the Privy Council after six months of debate.#

After the Jury Bill 1826 was passed, Rammohan suggested Indians be appointed as Indian judicial assessors and judges – jointly with Europeans – and for defining codes of civil and criminal laws and separation of the executive from the judiciary. Charles Grant, a sympathetic member of the Court of Directors, helped Rammohan to settle his claim in early December of 1831 allowing Indians to act as Grand Juries. The bill was passed in June 1832 against opposition, and restored Indians' rights.

---

* Note: Lord Bentinck felt the need for freedom of press for a good government, but was forced to quit because of his bad health early 1835. He advised Lord Metcalfe, his successor, to restore press freedom, being convinced by Rammohan's arguments. Against administrative advice, Metcalfe dared to lift press censorship in September 1835.

Note: Saumyendranath Tagore in his book entitled *Rammohan Roy: His role in Indian Renaissance* (Calcutta: Asiatic Society, 1975), 75–76, quotes an extract of a letter of a Colonel written to Rammohan Roy which contained the Privy Council's judgment.

The Company's Charter was passed by Parliament in 1833 when Rammohan was in Britain to bring his views before the select committee of the House of Commons. He did not appear in person but submitted his views in the form of "Communications to the Board of Control." The *Bengal Spectator* wrote in 1842 that Indians were indebted to Rammohan for concessions in regard to the privileges contained in the 1833 Charter. After the bill was passed, Rammohan heartily rejoiced at witnessing the salvation of the nation.

Many newspapers like *The Reformer, India Gazette, Friend of India, Sambad Kumudini, Dikdarshan*, etc. supported Rammohan. He was opposed but never stopped and created outstanding advantages for the future. Within a hundred years of Rammohan birth, another great Indian soul, Narendranath Datta (1863–1902), continued his reforms by awakening youths to improve the fate of Indians who became impoverished due to the British drain. As Swami Vivekananda, he introduced a spiritual dimension to politics.

Fig. 20 Dwarkanath Tagore. Portrait Bengal Club, Calcutta, 1827 (Wikimedia).

2.4 Institutions and Western Education

Pre-British India did not have a formal educational system; there were no formal schools, no press and no printed books. There were a limited number of *toles* or *Pathshalas*, where pandits taught Sanskrit aided by *punthis* (handwritten manuscripts). Prose writing in Bengali did not begin yet. Initially, the EIC was reluctant to introduce something new. But a few British inhabitants of Calcutta thought about starting English education for natives. They arranged for printing school books and founded schools. Some local elites joined them with full support. They also began institutions of national importance.

From the time of Warren Hastings, Calcutta became the residence of several European intellectuals. One of them was Sir William Jones, a Supreme Court Judge who was also a philologist with profound interest in ancient Indian scriptures. He founded the Asiatic Society in 1784, which became a center for recovering the glory of India's ancient past. As stated before, oriental interests motivated Hastings to engage pandits to introduce ancient Hindu marriage and succession laws. The Asiatic Society focused on piecing together ancient history through oriental research, collecting archaeological data and publications.

Before Sir Jones founded the Asiatic Society, scholars – like J. Z. Holwell– published interesting *Historical Events* in 1767, Alexander Dow wrote a *History of Hindostan* in 1772, and Nathaniel Halhed published the *Gentoo Code* in 1776, and a *Bengali Grammar* – the first of its type– in 1778. Charles Wilkins published a translation of the *Bhagavad Gita* in 1785, and in 1816, Francis Whyte Ellis distinguished the South Indian Dravidian languages as a common group. Others like H. T. Colebrooke, and Alexander Campbell labored to reinvent India's past culture.

To train interpreters of Hindu and Muslim laws in law courts, the government's priority was to open the Calcutta Madrasa in 1781. Jonathan Duncan initiated the founding of Sanskrit College in Kasi (Banaras) with support from Warren Hastings in 1792.

In 1800 Lord Wellesley established the Fort William College at Calcutta to train young Europeans joining the civil service. They were taught Indian customs, history, and the vernaculars. The College also became a center for oriental studies and culture. Dozens of Indian scholars and experts in different vernaculars were recruited. In 1801 Wellesley appointed the Serampore missionary William Carey as Bengali teacher. He was aided by pandits for his translations of Christian scriptures into Indian vernaculars. Their collective efforts ultimately helped Indian vernaculars to replace Persian as the administrative and legal language. Fort William College had an academic atmosphere and became a center for cultural interaction between Europeans and Indians.

In 1800, William Carey and his Baptist colleagues established a press in Danish Serampore and started printing and publishing classical literary works as well as books on history, philosophy and botany. Carey used the Fort William College as a platform for initiating prose writing in Bengali, improving on Halhed's Bengali Grammar.[14] The Serampore Mission Press became an important press for printing prose in the Bengali language. It printed books for Fort William College, the School Book Society, and for schools of the Serampore Mission. From 1818 it began publishing *The Friend of India,* and Bengali news bulletins like the *Samachar Darpan* and *Dig Darshan*, instrumental for dissemination education and general knowledge in India.

Robert Kid was an army officer who established the Royal Botanical Gardens on the western river bank at Shibpur in 1786. After him, the Scottish surgeon William Roxburgh enriched its collection, and made an inventory of Indian plants. After his death, his findings were edited and published by William Carey as *Flora Indica* printed at the Serampore Mission Press (1832). Roxburgh also established an Herbarium. The Asiatic Society endeavored to establish an Indian Museum when Nathaniel Wallich, a Danish Surgeon and Botanist from Serampore, offered to donate his personal collection. In 1814, Wallich was honored with the position of founder and first curator of the museum. All these establishments needed Indian participation.

Charles Grant, India's great friend, was the first to propose systematic Indian education using the English language, which he recommended to the Parliament in 1793 during renewal of the EIC charter. But the Board of Control kept it pending. Wealthy city based natives were privileged to learn English through their association with British men or private tuition at home. Then Anglo-Indian communities in Calcutta opened a few English schools for boys of elite families. Dwarkanath Tagore (Fig. 20) was a student in a school opened by Sherburne at Chitpur Road.[15] Motilal Seal began learning English in a similar school opened by Martin Bowle. At the initial stage the students were taught to improve their English vocabulary only, without learning grammar. The brahmo intellectual Rajnarayan Bose's *Segal aar Eikal* (Now and Then), 1873, contains funny stories of how natives conversed with Europeans using broken sentences to communicate in workplaces.

From the early 19th century, some Europeans sought administrative consent to open English schools in urban areas to begin formal education. A comprehensive survey of Bengal (1807–14) by Buchanan-Hamilton recorded the grim state of native education. Village Pundits taught only Sanskrit grammar, giving no scope for infusion of basic knowledge. Lord Minto observed that teaching of traditional religious books or abstract science were in a progressive state of decay. In 1811 he suggested government's intervention to secure books and persons capable of teaching to increase the number of subjects. He recommended encouraging Sanskrit learning by opening new institutions in Nadia. Mr. Colebridge of Fort William College was included in the ministry in 1811 to advise the Governor-General. A small fund was also allotted for Sanskrit and Persian education.

But people's desire to learn English only increased. A few schools were opened by private efforts even in suburban areas. The British missionaries began schooling in western style from 1800 in Danish Serampore. Reverend Robert May, a missionary of London, opened a school in Chinsurah in 1814 with sixteen students. Mr. Forbes, Commissioner of Hooghly, arranged to shift the school to an abandoned fort when the student strength increased. He wanted to open more branches with a monthly grant of Rs 600, sanctioned by the government. Rev. May encouraged the Maharaja of Burdwan to start teaching English in his school. Jayanta Ghosal of Banaras donated a sum of Rs 20,000 to the London Missionary Society, which in the 1820s had residential branches to support English education in North India.

Mr. Adam, Mr. Hodgson, and Mr. Wilkinson encouraged the publication of school books to support English education. David Hare, along with a few native elites, founded the School Book Society in 1817 to publish school books to meet basic needs of formal education. Rammohan Roy's urge for English education, the success of the Hindu College, and demands for English schools, influenced the Government to rethink its policy to expand Sanskrit and Persian education. A public instruction committee was set up in 1823 with an allotted fund. This was partly spent on printing books in Arabic and translating Persian classics. But there were no buyers for those books. This alerted the committee members.

After the success of Hindu College in the 1820s (Appendix 1), the urge for western education increased. Rammohan's letter to Lord Amherst caused a part of the fund of the Public Instruction Committee to be diverted for constructing a building for Hindu College close to Sanskrit College. Furthermore, a special fund was allotted for Hindu College provided government' deputation of an inspector was allowed.[16] From 1830, the annual government grant for the Hindu College was raised to Rs 1,250. But the Board of Directors could not take effective steps for a comprehensive education policy, until Macaulay wrote in February 1835, "... English is better worth knowing than Sanskrit or Arabic... it is possible to make natives of this country thoroughly good English scholars; and to this end our efforts ought to be directed."[17] Macaulay's note, or Minute as it became known, influenced Lord Bentinck to reserve a fund of one lakh Rupees per annum for teaching English literature and western science. From then on, the Government discontinued their support of vernacular teaching, to the disappointment of the president and secretary of the Public Instruction Committee. They resigned as they disagreed with Macaulay. The students of Hindu College, however, supported Macaulay's Minute.

After Bentinck left, the Scottish missionary Alexander Duff aided Lord Auckland to modify Macaulay's Minute to overcome the public's objections. Duff was in favor of English education, but he recommended reintroduction of the vernaculars alongside English. To him, the assimilation of the vernacular and English were the better options for students. His formula helped the Bengali language to flourish rapidly along with English learning.

After the Educational Council was formed in 1842, more private institutions were set up with help of Company officials and well-wishers in individual capacity. Lord Hardinge passed the Despatch Law in 1844 which made provisions for natives to take government jobs. In 1854, preparations were made for starting Universities in the three presidencies. In 1857, universities were established in Calcutta, Bombay and Madras. Calcutta University became the largest university in the world in 1900, with 8,000 students.[18] It taught mainly Art subjects, which led to a neglect of teaching the sciences.

Hindu College became a model institution. Students of this college began promoting English learning through discussions and writing articles. David Hare founded a School Society for opening new schools. The Hare School of Calcutta – bearing his legendary name – was initiated in 1818 at a close proximity to the Hindu College. Calcutta University was later established close to the same campus along College Street. Hare took personal care for native boys of his schools and sent good students to Hindu College for higher studies.

The Serampore Missionaries who managed schools from 1800, founded Serampore College in 1818. It served students from all religious backgrounds. The facilities of Serampore Mission Press were used by School Book Society and Fort William College.[19] English and Bengali journals and newspapers, printed at Serampore contained material to educate the youth. Bishops' College was established in Shibpur, Howrah (now BE College), for the education of clergy by the first Bishop of the diocese of Calcutta in 1820. Later in the century the College was shifted to Calcutta.

Gradually many new colleges and universities were opened. In 1830, Alexander Duff founded the General Assembly's Institution in Calcutta. It was later named Scottish Church College. In 1836, Hooghly Mohsin College was established, followed by Nadia's Krishna Nagore College in

1846, and Berhampore K. N. College in 1853. Even an engineering college had begun. In Calcutta, through the initiatives of Rajendranath Dutta, Hindu Metropolitan College was established, sometime after 1836. D. L. Richardson (of Hindu College) was appointed as principal, when Hindu College refused admission to the son of a courtesan. This school did not continue long but produced some great students. St. Xavier's Colleges were opened in Calcutta and Ranchi in 1860 by the Catholics. Patna College was established in 1863. In East Bengal, Dacca school was founded in 1835 and elevated to Dacca College in 1841, through the initiatives of Dr. James Tailor Wise.

In Poona, Maharashtra, a Hindu College was begun to teach Sanskrit with funds available from Peshwas after its annexation in 1821. An English school which started in 1842 was merged with this Sanskrit College (later Poona College) and students' enrolment increased to hundreds. From 1835, in Madras, schools were opened for native education. The Madras Presidency School was opened in 1840 with direct support of Thomas Munro, Governor of Madras Presidency, and Mr. Cooper of Hooghly College (Bengal) who was transferred to Madras. He served the School from its inception until Mr. E. B. Powell, a Cambridge Wrangler, took charge as the principal. In 1854, a letter from London ordered the Court of Directors of the EIC to increase the scope of Indian education. The so called *Wood's Dispatch* advised to: a) create a separate Department of Education; b) establish universities and normal schools in different places in each province; c) maintain all established schools and colleges, and increase their number; d) establish new middle schools and initiate vernacular teaching with improved standards; and f) sanction grants for schools founded by the natives. By 1855 records show 47 English schools in India that were supported by this scheme.

In 1858 when the Crown took over from the EIC, new posts of State Secretaries for Education were created, following the Dispatch of 1854. A Director was appointed in charge of the Education Department as well, and posts for School Inspectors were formed. Normal Schools were established in different places to provide teacher training. In 1856, Madras

Presidency School was elevated to become Madras Presidency College. After 1857 this College was affiliated with Madras University. In North India, Higher education was gradually extended through establishment of Lahore University (1864), Aligarh Muslim University (1875), and Allahabad University (1887).

In cities, new English medium schools were instituted, and middle schools as well as vernacular schools were opened in rural belts. By 1882, the number of English schools increased from 209 in 1882 to 1,481 in 1902 – one third of the total being private but receiving government's subsidy. In 1902 students' enrolments reached 250,000, of which 20 % were female students.[20] In the early twentieth century, the educational budget was raised to 5,645 Pounds (about 0.5% of the total budget). But this was insufficient, as the literacy rate could not keep up with population growth.

Calcutta Medical school began in 1822. At the initiative of wealthy natives of Calcutta, a Mechanical institute was set up in 1839. In 1847, regular technical training was begun in a College of Civil Engineering in Roorkee (north of Delhi), and in 1856 Bengal Engineering College opened in Howrah at the premises of Bishops College, after it was shifted. In 1906, Bengal Nationalists began a Technical Institute, which later became Jadavpur University (see chapter 3.4).

Medical treatment for Europeans started in Calcutta by European doctors with help of hospital assistants sent from Europe. To get local assistance, a Native Medical Institution was set up in Calcutta in 1822 which taught names of some European medicines and their uses. Instructions on the fundamentals of Anatomy, Surgery and Medicine were given in vernaculars after translation. Sanskrit College had provision for teaching *Charaka* and *Sushruta Samhita* – indigenous medicinal treatments using herbal medicine. With increasing demands of doctors for European style of treatment, the government planned for a medical college in Calcutta.

Lord Bentinck set up a commission under Ramkamal Sen to collect public opinions on its feasibility. Following its recommendations, Calcutta Medical College was established in 1835 abolishing the old Native Medical

Institution on a plot of land donated by the Bengali merchant Motilal Seal. At the same time Seal donated twelve thousand Rupees for a female Hospital. Students were selected from Hindu College, Hare School, and General Central Assembly's Institution. Teaching started with 49 students who were given scholarships. The graduates practiced Surgery and Medicine, and were eligible for public service as native doctors. Four students of the first batch –all Bengalis– were sent to England with scholarships arranged by Dwarkanath Tagore. By 1912, 269 doctors of medicine passed from this College.[21]

The Calcutta College of Arts and Craft was established privately in August 1854 at Chitpur to teach British artistic traditions. It was taken over by the government in 1864 and renamed Government School of Arts. In 1892 it was shifted to a new location south of the Indian Museum. An Italian, Ernest Binfield Havell, as principal (1896–1906) introduced the Oriental School of Painting. Havell, being influenced by Indian culture, urged his students to infuse Indian traditional art concepts in their work to overcome western influences. Abanindranath Tagore (1871–1951) who attended this school in 1890, learnt new painting techniques, and introduced fusions of Indian traditional art-concepts.

Abanindranath's contribution to the Swadeshi (Indian-made) movement was significant as he painted the iconic *Bharat Mata* with a full body with four arms holding food grains, white cloth, book, and prayer beads, symbolizing the nationalized mother in 1905. It is said that Abanindranath was influenced by Bankim Chandra's work of 1870. Abanindranath officiated the post of principal after Havell. His disciples earned fame as modern Indian artists. His brother, the painter Gogonendranath Tagore (1867–1938), first introduced cartoons during the Swadeshi movement, while their nephew Rabindranath Tagore developed Bengali literature. The Ceylon born Ananda Coomaraswamy's philosophy also influenced Indian nationalistic art.

The Japanese scholar Okakura Kakuzo visited India from 1898–99 to foster pan Asian art, and engaged in dialogues with Abanindranath and Rabindranath, who were fascinated by Japanese artistic traditions. Okakura also inspired Abanindranath to found his Bengal School and sent his pupils Yokoyama Taikan and Hishida Shunso in 1903, who taught washing in art to Abanindranath's students. Abanindranath used to take lessons from Taikan, who in turn learned to paint in Indian style from Abanindranath.

Dwarkanath Tagore had introduced the first privately initiated library facility to Calcutta. In 1835 the Calcutta Public Library collection (with many of his books) was transferred to the newly built Metcalfe Hall. The Imperial Library, created by Lord Curzon in 1903 at Alipore, amalgamated with this library. Peary Chand Mitra was its first librarian. William Carey maintained his personal library at Serampore from the early 1800s.

Carey and Marshman established the Horticultural Society in 1820, with support of Lady Hastings for research on vegetables and fruit plants. She arranged for the society the lease of land in Alipore.[22] Some contemporary natives were members of this society. It was the first institution in India where William Carey encouraged experiments to improve vegetables, fiber (Jute), and Indian ornamental plants.

2.4.1 Girls' Education

Girls' education was begun in co-educational schools sharing the facilities with boys. This arrangement was promoted by the School Society in 1817. The Female Juvenile Society was then formed by a few influential ladies of the city to establish several girls' schools in Calcutta. Some of its members helped the British and Foreign School Society to create a fund and send a lady teacher to Calcutta. In 1821, Miss Cooke arrived in Calcutta, and the Church Missionary Society supported her stay.

Miss Cooke learnt Bengali, visited some co-ed schools and opened ten girls' schools within a short time, admitting 277 girls. She discontinued after two years. The *Bengal Ladies' Society* formed by Lady Amherst, established many girls' schools. This society even built a school building for which Raja Baidyanath donated Rs 20,000. From a government report it is known that about 19 schools were established in different places in remote districts accommodating about 450 girls in total.[23] Schools established by missionaries (e.g. Serampore BMS and LMS) were among those. Bethune School, founded by Groundwater Bethune in 1849, was secular in outlook. In 1879 Bethune School was upgraded to Bethune College – the first women's college in Asia. In Madras, Sarah Tucker College was established in 1895.

Hindu organizations did not favor girls' education. But Ramgopal Ghose, Debendranath Tagore, Ramtanu Lahiri, Peary Charan Sarkar, alumni of Hindu College, and members of Brahmo Samaj encouraged girls of their own families to attend school. They opened several schools in western and eastern parts of Bengal where girls remained confined at home (vide Appendix1). The Barasat Balilka Vidyalay was established in 1867 at the initiative of Peary Charan Sarkar and two brothers, Kalikrishna and Nabakrishna Mitra. The rate of increase of girls' schools was slow as the marriageable age of girls was low, but higher education of women increased rapidly. There were 5,000 female students in 1935, and about 500 of them graduated. In 1916 the first women's university, *Nathibai Damodar Thackersey Women's University* was founded in Maharashtra.

The Muslim community was reluctant to receive western education. Sir Syed Ahmed Khan, who was in government judicial service, wanted Muslims to be educated, but not to reject Islam. However, the Anglo Arabic College (Delhi College) which was founded in 1696 under the Mughals is supposed to be the first educational institution in India for promoting Islamic learning in Persian and Arabic. This institution started teaching English from 1828, and became Delhi College (now Zakir Husain College) after independence.

2.4.2 Effects of Western Education

Within a decade English teaching started, native society tended to change amidst conflict with prevailing orthodoxy. Among educated youths, political consciousness grew. Lord Ellenborough (1841–44) said to Dwarakanath Tagore, "'you know if these gentlemen succeed in educating natives in India to the utmost of their desire, we should not remain in this country for three months.' 'Not, three weeks,'" Tagore replied.[24] Youths with western education supported the growth of the Bengali language, published periodicals and journals, leading to a growth in the number of native presses.

The press supported the common people's reading habits and developed political consciousness. Journalism also worked against racism and discrimination. Educated Indians received opportunities to be recruited in educational, civil and Judicial services. English education caused the spread of Indian nationalism and created a native business community, especially in Maharashtra.

People living away from big cities in the north, northeast, northwest and central India were less privileged as facilities of universities were available only in three provinces. Even in the Bengal province, Biharis and Oriyas did not receive educational opportunities. Similarly, the Gujarati speaking people in the Bombay Presidency, the Telugus or Malayalees of Madras Presidency were under-privileged in comparison to people of the Marathi and Tamil speaking communities.

2.5 The Sepoy Mutiny

The insurrection or Sepoy Mutiny of 1857 is well documented because the news of the mutiny days was preserved in several Indian and British newspapers. It received a lot of attention. Only its salient features have been described here.

The Earl of Dalhousie realized a rising public resentment due to excesses committed through the Permanent Settlement. Many sepoys were from farmer's families burdened with high taxation.[25] When the wrong signals were perceptible in the army, Dalhousie reduced the tax rate. Also Macaulay's negative attitude against everything Indian, and growing missionary activities since the middle of the 1830s, hurt public sentiments. Sepoys' sentiments were further hurt when the Marshall law of 1855 brutally killed the Santhals who protested the revenue system by introducing their own law. Furthermore, white Indigo farmers tortured the Indian peasantry unopposed, considering themselves as superior human beings.

In 1856, the last year of Dalhousie, a new commander-in-chief joined the army, who treated sepoys badly. Newly recruited British officers bullyed sepoys who served faithfully for more than 20 years. In the army, the accommodation conditions were awful. Hindu sepoys of the 47th regiment at the army base at Barrackpore became agitated when they were forced to go to Burma crossing "black water," which was against their culture. Both Hindu and Muslim sepoys were offended when suddenly in 1857 new gun cartridges with a coating of cow and pig fat were introduced. The religious sentiments of both the communities were hurt. Those cartridges were manufactured at Barrackpore to fit in the newly introduced rifles. There was an official warning that the sepoys would refuse this change and that they were close to rebel.

The cartridge issue was transpired to Berhampore when some of the Barrackpore sepoys were transferred there in February 1857. The sepoys of Berhampore fought with their officers and were stripped of their uniform – a matter of great insult for a soldier, and dismissed following an order of Lord Canning. Some of the dismissed sepoys were from Awadh, and on their way back, they whispered about the incident publicly. The news reached Meerut. When some sepoys refused to use new cartridges on 6 May 1857, eighty-five of them were court-martialled and jailed.[26]

The severity of this punishment agitated the rest of the sepoys in Meerut, and they started a direct revolt at sunset on 9 May. The next day they released all in custody, looted the treasury, and occupied the armory. This mutiny commenced at Meerut, and the mutineers marched towards Delhi, killing Europeans on the way. On 11 May they took control of Delhi and reinstated Bahadur Shah, the last Mughal emperor, to the throne.

This mutiny, beginning from Meerut, with the first discharge coming from a certain Mangal Pandey of the Bengal regiment, spread over the entire country like an oilfire. About 30,000 sepoys violated every measure taken by the authorities. The incident provided opportunities to some civilians who were deprived of their dues by the government. Nana Saheb, Tantia Topi, a commander of Nana Saheb, and the Queen of Jhansi were among those who sided with the rebels. A Maulvi of Faizabad who was annoyed with the British after a Nawab of Lucknow was dethroned, instigated thousands of people from Awadh to join the rebellion.

The pension of Nana Sheb, the adopted son of Baji Rao, was dismissed by a new order. He stayed in Betur near Kanpur, confined in isolation being dissatisfied with British administration. When he was asked by the British force to protect Kanpur with 1500 Company soldiers, Nana used the facility to support the rebels, bringing Kanpur to the focal point. Men of Nana Sheb joined the mutineers and deceived groups of Europeans on boats and brutally killed hundreds of men, women, and children. The Queen of Jhansi who was in conflict with the British sided with the mutineers. A huge area from the northwestern region to Buxar, and the Arrah area along the Bihar border came under sepoys' control.

The Europeans in Bengal were panic stricken with the rumor that sepoys would loot their properties and kill them. Many British families took shelter inside Fort William. They advised Lord Canning to take drastic steps to crush the rebels. Canning favored a more measured response, some British newspapers like *The Times* dubbed him 'Clemency' Canning for his leniency. When the rebels were predominant in Awadh and the northern western provinces, the Bengal, Madras and Bombay Presidencies remained fairly calm.

Many historians wrote on this Mutiny of 1857, but rarely focused on how Indian civilians, and even the sepoys helped to control the insurrection. Sambhu Chandra Mukherjee, put forward evidence on natives' corporation to check the Mutiny.[27] He cited articles in the *London Times*, July 1857, that described the character of the revolt and how the Indian Empire was salvaged.

Sambhu Chandra, who was an eye witness, gave examples of the fidelity, aid, and advice the native people offered during the insurrection. His book reveals that people of Calcutta organized several meetings condemning the rebelling sepoys, and even vernacular translations of resolutions of meetings were circulated among the public beginning from May 15, 1857, to raise their support against the Mutiny.[28] People willing to help hungry fleeing foreign fugitives, held back only because they were afraid of insurgents' ire threatening to burn their villages. But much help came on humanitarian grounds.

A 19 year old man writing from Meerut, told his story thus: "It would be too long, my very dearest sister, to tell you of how for three days and nights we wandered in the jungles, sometimes fed and sometimes robbed by villagers, till at length, wearied and footsore, with shreds of clothes on our back we arrived at a village where they put us in a hut and fed us for four days, and moreover took a note from us into Meerut, whence an escort of cavalry was sent out, and we were brought safe here."[29]

Thus native fidelity played an important role to check the mutiny. The experience and candid admissions of Anglo-Indians recorded that the quick quelling of the Mutiny was due largely because of the fidelity coming from different native sources. Fidelity came even from the sepoys themselves, and many princely states like Kashmir, Hyderabad, Patiala, and others which virtually rescued Delhi. A liberal paper wrote, "the first signal of resistance risen against England, our rule in India might, perhaps, by great exertions and large expenditure, have been recovered, but we should only have recovered a population watching the next favorable opportunity for revolt and have re-established an empire on sand. It was the general good of the population which rendered the suppression of military mutiny both practicable and beneficial…"[30]

Soon after the Mutiny was brought under control. Delhi was recaptured by the end of September and Bahadur Shah was sent into exile; he was buried in Rangoon, Burma. Kanpur was taken back by mid-July. It took several months to bring Awadh and Jhansi under control. The after-effects of the Mutiny, retreated by the government, were also horrible. British soldiers avenged indiscriminately by killing Indian soldiers and civilians. After the strategic failure of Nana Sahib, native properties and villages were destroyed during their march from Allahabad to Kanpur. The state of post-mutiny trials and hasty judgments displayed the ruler's vindictiveness and cruelty. The Raja of Ballabgarh who was a quasi-loyal Prince, was hanged without trial, only out of suspicion of misconduct.

Sambhu Chandra wrote, "Governmental misbehavior only serves to embitter their affection, and deepen the difference of race."[31] According to Sastri, 800 natives were hanged in Allahabad alone.[32] Insurgency was crunched after nine uncertain months, but the Company remained responsible for murdering and hanging tens of thousands suspected rebels in many places lining the Ganges. This first major revolt against the British, the Great Rebellion, created a rift between ordinary Indians and the Britons resulting in social segregation that lasted until Indian Independence. It is believed that the Sepoy Mutiny ignited Indian nationalism and sowed future directions. The Mutiny failed, but its furore made the British nerveless, even though the majority of Indians were on their side.

This Mutiny also caused the peasantry to start a revolt against the Indigo planters and the zamindars of Bengal from 1859 (Appendix 1). These movements spread in different places including Maharashtra during the 1860s.

2.6 Trade, Economics, Industry and Infrastructure Building

The following paragraphs describe the economic interests of the British in trade and commerce and how the EIC improved the infrastructure, and started survey work that continued during the period of British India.

2.6.1 Trade and Economics

The East India Company began with trading spices breaking the Dutch monopoly. Then cotton, silk, indigo, saltpetre, and tea were added to its wares as major commodities. The high income earner Opium was incorporated once the Chinese market became available. Trade was mainly private under the protection of the EIC contributing to Britain's economy. Industrial growth began late and grew until the 1930s.

British investment in Bengal began with importing gold and silver to pay for goods to be shipped to Britain. When the EIC secured the right of revenue collection from 1765, imports of gold and silver ceased. It was the starting point of decline of the Bengal economy. The capital reaped from Bengal was invested mainly in textile industries, and British prosperity increased with their industrial revolution, fuelled by raw materials imported from India. But this led to de-industrialization of Bengal. Until the 1830s, India remained a major exporter of cotton textiles, which were popular even in the American market. But textile imports from Britain gradually increased from 25% in 1811 to 93% in 1840. Furthermore, the entry of Indian finished goods in Britain was restricted over time.

The economic exploitation of Bengal started from when Mir Qasim was on the throne. Company servants helped British merchants to dominate by alluring the producers to pay more than the usual market price. Also an illegal market was in operation by force. Clive's administration monopolized certain valuable commodities, and allowed EIC's employees to conduct business on the side. Producers were then brought under their control through personal contacts or often by force. This practice caused Company losses, and it at one point became bankrupt. However, EIC employees and traders dispatched an unaccounted sum of money to Britain as private earnings.

Initially, the rural economy of Bengal was not much affected as it was supported by cottage industries that produced woven cotton and silk textiles, as well as raw silk, salt, and saltpetre. These cottage industries provided rural employment. Food grains were also sufficient. There were practically no landless laborers until the Permanent Settlement Act 1793 was enacted.

The Permanent Settlement made the zamindars de facto rulers of rural Bengal. Most of them were wealthy people who lived in the town centers. The landlords were loyal to the government, though it asked for a major share of taxes in return. Their loyalty increased when the zamindars could seize lands of defaulting peasants. And so the farm production fell as landless laborers increased in number. The cottage industries also waned gradually with imports of cheap industrially British-made goods, during the industrial revolution. Capital amassed from land revenue and profits from their export market in India greatly increased British prosperity at home.

The new economy that emerged from the end of the 18th century resulted in the vanishing of local capital both in agriculture and cottage industries. It harmed the indigenous banking system, which flourished during the early years of the EIC, before the Pitt India Act came into effect (1784). The economic deterioration of rural Bengal reached its climax around 1859 when the occupancy right of ryots (tenant farmers who lost land ownership) was conceded.

British profits rose to about £20 million sterling at the end of the century. Many authors, old and new, claim that India was alienated through economic exploitation, especially in the middle of the nineteenth century.

From the time of Cornwallis, a social order grew discriminatory which indulged the white people to feel superior; and the centralized administration from the 1880s destroyed the Indian economy completely.

From the middle of the 1830s, the rural production fell further when the Company's trade of Indian opium in exchange for Chinese tea flourished. This system boosted opium cultivation considerably, reducing the production of foodgrains. When the opium trade optimized, the first Opium War began (1838–42) and China was compelled to hand over Hong Kong to the British. Forcible indigo cultivation by British mill owners also reduced food crop production. An increased rate of cash crop production served British interests, but the production machinery in rural Bengal was severely disrupted.

Tea cultivation began in Assam from the 1820s, following experimental research in the Calcutta Botanical garden. Its commercial production became effective through a committee set up by Bentinck in the 1830s. For this, private Chinese help was used to develop techniques for tea processing. The tea industry in India provided additional revenue to Britain. Agriculture did not suffer due to establishment of tea gardens as crop production was less profitable in hilly places. But like indigo cultivation, the labor forces were exploited by the European Tea growers.

The native population was economically down but had to pay high taxes. William Digby worked in different places as a government officer, and wrote a book on the financial condition of Indians during the Company's tenure by extracting year by year data from Indian Blue Books Data presented in his book depicts, "People became poorer and poorer. Average daily income of people in 1850 was 4 cent/ person, in 1882 it fell to 3 cent, and in 1900 it became less than 2 cent. Additional earnings gained by exploitation of poor people were used to support the high salaried Englishmen in Company service. The people without purchasing power were victims of famine." He also wrote, "there were 29 famines in a hundred years. Government's tax collection increased from personal taxation which was high. A person with an average income of 1£ 2s. 4d. ($6.00) per annum paid 3s. 3d. ($2.00) as tax. A Proportion of one-seventh. This was twice what people in England paid. Even common salt was taxable. "Prices were so high that average people consumed less salt than medically permissible." Net drainage, he estimated in the 19th century, was £4.2 billion.[33]

According to Esteban, major commodity imports from India to Britain included indigo, raw silk (more than half of total export), a variety of cotton goods, and superior grade of salpetre.[34] The economic drain from India was caused by excess exports for which there were no equivalent imports. The Indian opium and Chinese tea exchange trade, and the quantum of indirect diversion of Indian resources, which was quite high to Britain, remained unassessed.

Esteban, referring to works of different authors on the quantum of Indian drain (calculated considering different parameters), showed that the figure (though not consistent) of Indian drain was less than £1,000 million (in current prices) between 1775–1885. This figure was considerably lower than what which Digby projected. But he justified his data as they were sourced from documents marked confidential (unpublished), which he received from Mr. Bradlaugh, a Member of Parliament, as the House of Commons refused publication of those data.[35]

One of the major sources of drain were salaries paid to British officers, and their extra earnings not officially calculated. A colonel in garrison was paid £37+ per month, £25 in tent allowances, and £93+ as half allowances for affairs of campaign (*batta*). In addition, there were princely gifts for military officers and civil servants. Lord Wellesley received £4,000 for his capture of Seringapatam, and later from the siege of Bharatpur in 1826, one Commander-in-Chief gained £60,000.[36] There was additional expenditure for maintenance of European officers' residences which was not calculated.

According to Esteban, $38 million or £30.2 million were sent home from Bengal through private accounts before 1757, and 15 million between 1757–84.[37] He also found that net Indian transfers to Britain were made in the form of commodities, not bullion. In that case, the exact quantum of actual drain remains incalculable. In addition to dispatch in cash and kind, the Indian tax payers supported the entire military expenditure and expenses for British soldiers stationed in India which rose to about 40% of total revenue collection until World War II.

Bowen wrote that India was hardly an export market of Britain. He said that export of metal to India, as sometimes stated, was a gesture as there exist no record of such exports until the middle of the eighteenth century. But there is no doubt that Indian resources contributed to spectacular growth of Britain's economy.[38]

The EIC's annual earning after 1765 was partly plowed back as annual investment or purchase of Indian goods destined for Britain, and to China for tea purchase in remodeled trading activities.[39] In the latter half of the century there were exports to India of wool, iron, lead, and copper to meet European consumption. This commodity market in Calcutta was run mainly by British merchants of both India and England. The census of 1837 indicated that there were more than 3000 Europeans residing in Calcutta alone, and by the 1850s they formed "White Calcutta." European customers were affluent and were major consumers of imported goods. There was a surge of demand for British made cotton textiles. Exports to India increased to thousands of tons per year.

In this period, some Bengalis accumulated wealth through British traders, especially with the growth of the Calcutta Port. Some of them became trading partners of the Europeans, or secured lucrative jobs like interpreters, head brokers, suppliers of cash and kind, etc. These babus got privileges for inland trading, and obtained agencies in the ports, etc. The wealth they accumulated from Calcutta was invested in land, for acquiring private property and agricultural lands (after the Permanent Settlement). They lived in Black Calcutta. Some native tycoons like Hidaram Banerjee, Akur Dutta, Gokul Ghosal became fabulously rich with wealth earned from rural areas. Some became international merchants. Ramdulal Dey, for example, began trading with America. There were also Bengali ship owners and bankers, and some of them ran insurance companies in Calcutta.

Many Bengali traders made their fortune charging higher prices than native markets when demands for cotton, jute, silk, indigo, opium, sugarcane, etc. increased overseas. But, their monopoly was gradually lost with a growing number of foreign competitors, including the EIC (after its monopoly was abolished).

2.6.2 Industry

Apart from rural cottage industries, Indians were not engaged in industry, after the steel industry was destroyed, until the 18th century. Dwarkanath Tagore (Fig. 20) was supposed to be the first Indian who owned indigo factories, sugarcane plantations and sugar mills, mining, shipping companies, ship building, insurance companies, etc. He became Prince Dwarkanath. Lord Bentinck helped him to acquire a partnership with a European company designated as Carr Tagore & Co. Some large European firms like Gilmore, Homfray & Co., Alexander & Co., Andrew Yule, etc. began in Calcutta taking advantage of the Charter Act of 1833. At first, they mined newly discovered coal. Dwarkanath's direct association with some of them made him a leading commercial man between 1834–46. However, he suffered losses during the commercial turmoil of 1830–33, when the leading business houses collapsed due to capital scarcity.

In Bombay, from 1857, a business community rose who owned spinning and weaving mills. Driven by the Maratha War, Bombay saw an enormous increase of population migrating from Gujarat and Delhi areas and supported industrialization on the west coast. The first group of entrepreneurs were the educated Parsi community. Port facilities and railways supported the cotton industry which grew rapidly when the American supply of cotton to Lancashire stopped during the Anglo–American war. The shipping and port industry on the Coromandel Coasts was also busy. British traders utilized this facility for carrying thousands of quintals of pepper annually from Madras with the extension of the railways up to the port.

In eastern India, the railways facilitated a quick growth of jute, cotton, and mining industry, at the end of the 19th century. Andrew Yule was the largest coal producer in Bengal from 1908. The company had its base in Calcutta even after Indian independence. Companies like Balmer Lawrie, Gillanders, Bird & Co., Jardine Henderson, Macneill Barry, arrived each with better management and more capital. They pushed the Bengali businessmen back in the second half of the century. These British companies took over jute, tea, cotton, mining, and engineering industries.

From the 1830s, Bengal entered into the industrial age through European investments. Dwarkanath Tagore lamented that all natives' possessions, including liberty, were taken away by the European industrialists and merchants.

From 1813, the missionaries of Serampore set up ink and paper manufacturing facilities to support printing and publication of books from their press using a steam engine to meet the demands of Calcutta School Book Society, Fort William College, and their own schools. Christian scriptures translated into Indian vernaculars, and those from newly established Bible society were printed from this press. A monopoly printing business created employment for a few hundred. The natives also worked in the newspaper publishing unit (like the *Friend of India*, etc.).[40]

Rapidly growing opportunities in the mining sector demanded better communication facilities. It encouraged the establishment of the East India Railway Company (EIR) in 1845. Founded in London by a deed of settlement, its initial capital was raised in Britain. The Company officers and the Crown guaranteed the investors 4–5 % return risk free loan after 1858.[41] The Raj was responsible to pay back this loan with interest of Indian earnings.

The Company was incorporated in 1845. The Court of Directors of the EIC signed an agreement with EIR for a short experimental run to reach the coal fields of Raniganj area in Bengal in 1849. The first journey from Howrah station (present location), started in August 1854. In the west, Dalhousie built the firs railway from Bombay to Thane, which began in 1853. The Bombay, Baroda and Central Railway Company, incorporated in 1855, build a railway from Bombay to Surat. Operations from Madras began in 1856. The railways augmented trade and commerce and growth of ancillary industries, and provided facilities for transportation of goods, and the military.

From 1848 the postal services were extended. The first iron steamer plied on the Indian Ocean route at this time. After the Suez Canal was completed in 1869, travel time from London reduced greatly. The telegraph was introduced in 1852. From 1870, Calcutta Agra and Karachi were connected with London through the Indo-European Telegraph line, enabling easy communications.

To support the growing railway operations, a workshop came up first in Jamalpur, Bihar in 1864. Railways reached Northgate, Delhi in 1864, and Lucknow in 1867. In 1881–82 the narrow gauge Siliguri-Darjeeling line began operating, and in 1899 the Nilgiri Mountain Rail opened.

Calcutta became an industrial hub with improved infrastructure as well as technology. Bengali entrepreneurs were in banking, insurance, and steam services. Small scale industries grew up with the Swadeshi movements, but other small (cottage) industries were destroyed by that time. Calcutta was the hub of the British merchants who operated both import and export business to Europe and Southeast Asia.

In the middle of the 19th century, from before the EIC was terminated, Howrah and Hooghly districts were hubs of clusters of jute mills which demanded supply of raw jute fibres. Hooghly River traffic grew so much in 1855–56 that it caused disruptions to the ferry connection to Howrah. A committee was appointed to review the possibility of getting a fixed bridge across the river. The Mutiny shelved the plan, which got revived in 1868. The Port Trust was founded in 1870 and the operations from Howrah railway – terminal began.

With the passage of the Howrah Bridge Act 1871, the Lieutenant Governor of Bengal was empowered to construct a bridge under the aegis of the Port Commissioner. A contract was signed with Sir Bradford Leslie to construct a Pontoon Bridge with decks on two shores of the river (Fig. 21). The bridge was erected with an assembly line and spares coming from England. It was a floating bridge with provision for opening the halves locked at center to allow navigation. The bridge was completed at a cost of Rs 2.2 million and opened on October 17, 1874. It was about 2,000 ft. long and 62 ft. wide, with a 48 ft. wide road in the middle, with two footpaths each 7 ft. wide. The road narrowed down to 43 ft. at the shore span.

Fig. 21 Pontoon Bridge. By Johnston & Hoffman (Public Domain).

Later in 1906, a committee headed by R. S. Highest (Chief Engineer East India Railway) and W. B. Mccabe (Chief Engineer Calcutta Corporation) proposed a plan for a new 60 ft wide bridge with tram lines. However, when World War I broke out this plan was shelved. A new Committee headed by R. N. Mukherjee was formed to set up the New Howrah Bridge Commission in 1922. The New Howrah Bridge Act 1926 approved construction of a suspension bridge following a design made by Mr. Walton. The Braithwaite Burn & Jessop Construction Co. began construction work in 1936. The foundations on the two sides were completed by 1938. This construction was also delayed due to World War II. The new bridge was finally opened in 1943 as the world's 3rd longest cantilever bridge.

The industrial growth created ancillary business opportunities. There were demands for book sellers, drapers, couch makers, piano makers and tuners, hatters, hosiers, brewers, distillers, engine drivers, firemen, weaving masters, engineers in cotton and jute mills, etc. These technicians and craftsmen were brought from Britain. There were banks, and several tea companies, all run by British people. Europeans, numbering not more than 70,000, introduced a new culture to India. They were mainly city residents and consumers of British made goods.

2.6.3 Survey Work

The British traders began survey work to learn more about people, their habits and social practices. Some journalists also needed surveys on social issues. The first topographical surveys began when Robert Clive felt its necessity for military purposes in 1757. James Rennell made maps of Bengal and became the first Surveyor-General in 1765. The great Indian Geographical Survey began from the early 1760s. Then Rennell (1763–77) mapped parts of India in greater detail than done in many European countries. He is famous for his *Bengal Atlas* (1779) and *Memoirs of a Map of Hindoostan* (1782). The year before a survey school began in Madras in 1784 to train up Indians to continue Rennell's work, Warren Hastings, ordered the then district Magistrate of 24 Parganas to bring certain parts of the Sundarbans in order. Since then survey work began, and in 1828 a map of Sunderbans was finally completed. The map ascertained the *Dampier-Hodges Line* – indicating the northernmost limits of the estuarine zone affected by tidal fluctuations.[42]

From the tenure of the Earl of Mornington (1798–1805) more methodical surveys began for the census of people and societies, and village boundaries. Francis Buchanan and Colin Mackenzie categorized people and societies, their knowledge base and cultural activities. It was a colonial construction. They even surveyed some remote villages, and the census contained data on cultural remains, published in gazetteers for future administrative use.

In 1802 William Lambton, an infantry soldier with knowledge of survey work, began the Trigonometric survey of Mysore after Tipu Sultan's death. His work improved to a level that was sufficient to draw the details of surface-contours, slopes, river channels and mountain tops. This survey work in India is supposed to be the longest measurement project of earth surface to ever have been attempted.

When the survey work was in progress covering the subcontinent, Radha Nath Sikder, recruited from Hindu College and working with Sir George Everest, the superintendent (1823–43), innovated a technique that aided in measuring Peak XV, the tallest mountain top of the Himalayas. This peak was named Mount Everest in 1865, after Surveyor-General Sir George. Mr. H. W. Voysey superintendent of Trigonometric Survey (1818–23), made a geological map of Hyderabad, and in 1846 the Geological Survey of India was established to locate mineral deposits. Sir Gerald Ponsonby Lenox-Conyngham (1912–21) was the last superintendent of the Trigonometric Survey. Work of the Botanical and Zoological Surveys were also in progress. The Asiatic Society had already begun an Archaeological survey.

2.7 Observations

One of the main purposes of the EIC was to consolidate Bengal from their Calcutta base from 1765. The Company started territorial expansion using native sepoys but gradually adding British persons and their number in troops reached 25,000 by 1867. Growing European dominance in the military and their feeling of superiority ignored the sentiments of Indian sepoys instigating them to revolt.

The EIC began to westernize the administration for reforming it. In 1773 a council of four persons was entrusted to rule three provinces and this system changed gradually passing new acts. By the Permanent Settlement, revenue collection was increased exploiting the Bengal peasantry. The 1813 Charter allowed missionaries to start working, and through this Charter, the Company ceased to be a simple trading company. It allowed the EIC to become a political and administrative body on the Crown's behalf to govern civil and military affairs, giving the Governor-General sole power of legislation. In the Charter of 1853, major power was transferred to Parliament when one third of the total court directors were nominated by the Crown. Lieutenant Governors were appointed for the provinces where a legislative council with twelve officials formed the base of the administration.

British energy brought an extended geo-political territory into one unit which independent India inherited. This expanded territory, built from its Calcutta base, was a huge market of exports and a potential source of income for Britain in an undisturbed environment. However, this British ambition destroyed a vibrant Indian economy. Even the metallurgical industry which produced finest steel was shut down. The rural people became increasingly poor and subject to repeated famines, mainly because they lost purchasing power. This impoverishment began a gradual exodus of peasants to the town centers and cities.

The flourishing economy of the EIC created opportunities for the European population to grow. From the 1750s to 1852, European residents in India grew from about 6,000 (excluding army men) to 70,000. Non official residents distributed in large towns were engaged in commercial activities and provided a partial provision for natives' employment.

The EIC helped initiate western education at the urging of Bengali elites with private support of British residents of Calcutta. The Bengal Renaissance came into being in similar fashion as the 15–16th century European Renaissance, a cultural revival that aided Indians to develop intellectually. They became nationalists and struggled for Indian emancipation. The tenure of the EIC was good for the Bengali babus who earned their fortunes through British association. This period also gave rise to associations of landlords who supported the British ambition and benefitted from economic growth.

During the tenure of the EIC, Bengal (after the discovery of coal in Raniganj) experienced the beginning of industrialization. The Calcutta Trade Association formed in 1830, and the Calcutta Chamber of Commerce established in 1834 influenced the government to introduce railways and lift trade restrictions for both Europeans and Indians. However, heavy industries were restricted to protect the British market. Plantations were developed for producing jute, cotton, and tea from the late 1830s. The introduction of indigo and opium cultivation put enormous psychological pressure on peasantry and its ill effects integrated elite Indians to collectively oppose the British administration. The railways helped the coal industry to grow and provide improved distribution of imported commodities to hinterlands. At the same time, it caused harm to the surviving indigenous industries.

In 1859, Lord Canning announced that the Companies' Indian possession would be nationalized and would pass under direct control of the British Parliament. This decision was the result of an incomprehensible societal rupture by the Mutiny. Canning was the last Governor-General of the EIC. The British witnessed their golden period between 1765 and 1857. A few small-scale agitations erupted, but these were controlled by military power. The legal system was introduced but it did not adopt any tangible measures to check large-scale exploitation.

References:

1. Brendon Piers, *Decline and Fall of British Empire 1781–1997* (London: Vintage Books, 2008), 33.
2. David Gilmour, *The British in India: A Social History of the Raj* (New York: Farrar, Straus and Giroux, 2018), 34–35.
3. Sivanath Sastri, *Ramtanu Lahiri O Tatkalin Banga Samaj* (transl. Ramtanu Lahiri and Contemporary Bengali Society) 3rd edn. (Kolkata: Rubi Publishers, 1903, 2019), 6.
4. William Dalrymple, "The East India Company: The Original Corporate Raiders," *The Guardian*, 4 March 2015.
5. Barbara D. Metcalf and Thomas R. Metcalf, *A Concise History of India* (Cambridge: Cambridge University Press, 2005), 60.
6. Dalrymple, Ibid.
7. Brojendra Nath Banerjee, "Rammohan Roy an Educational Pioneer," *Journal of Bihar and Orissa Research Society*, Vol. 16 (June 1930), 154–175.
8. Sastri, Ibid, 46.
9. Saumyendranath Tagore, *Rammohan Roy: His Role in Indian Renaissance* (Calcutta: Asiatic Society, 1975), 16.
10. Barid Baran Mukherjee, *Serampore: Late Medieval and Colonial Era* (Kolkata: Ghosh Publishing, 2021), 227.
11. Ibid, 60.

12. Tagore, *Ram Mohan Roy*, 16.
13. Ibid, 76.
14. Mukherjee, Ibid, 174–75.
15. Sastri, Ibid, 59.
16. Sastri, 67.
17. Thomas Babington Macaulay, "Minute Upon Indian Education (1835)," in H. Sharp (ed.) *Selections from Educational Records Part I, 1781–1839* (Calcutta: Government Printing, 1920), 116.
18. James Lawrence, *The Making and Unmaking of British India* (New York: St. Martin's Press, 1998), 355.
19. Mukherjee, Ibid, 190.
20. Lawrence, Ibid, 344.
21. Ibid, 345.
22. Mukherjee, Ibid, 203.
23. Sastri, Ibid, 146.
24. Lawrence, Ibid, 347.
25. Haraprasad Chattopadhyaya, *The Sepoy Mutiny, 1857: A Social Study and Analysis* (Calcutta: The Author, 1957), 1.
26. Sastri, Ibid, 165.
27. A Hindu, *The Mutinies, the Government and the People* (Calcutta: D' Rozario and Co., 1858). Reprinted as Sambhu Chandra Mookherjee (A Hindu), *The Mutinies and the People, Or, Statements of Native Fidelity: Exhibited During the Outbreak of 1857–58* (London: Smith Elder, 1858).
28. A Hindu, Ibid.
29. *The Times*, 20 July 1857 quoted in Ibid.
30. *Edinburg Review*, No. 218, April 1858, Quoted in Ibid.
31. Mookherjee, *The Mutinies and the People*, xv.
32. Sastri, Ibid, 167.
33. William Digby, *Prosperous' British India: A Revelation from Official Records* (London: T. Fisher Unwin, 1901), 6–8, 22.

34. Javier Cuenca Esteban, "The British Balance of Payments 1772–1820: India Transfers and War France," *The Economic History Review*, Vol. 54, No. 1. (Feb, 2001), 65.
35. Digby, Ibid, xxii.
36. Gilmour, Ibid, 35–36.
37. Esteban, Ibid, 66.
38. H. V. Bowen, "Sinews of Trade and Empire: The Supply of Commodity Exports to East India Company during the Late Eighteenth Century," *The Economic History Review*, 55 (3) (March 2003), 466.
39. Ibid, 468.
40. Mukherjee, Ibid, 187–89.
41. Metcalf and Metcalf, Ibid, 96.
42. Aloke Kora, "Rakkahas Khalir Tamralipi- Bhumi Dan Sankranta Dalil" (Deeds for Land Allotment), *Udbodhan* 126 (February 2024), 58.

Other Literature consulted:

Michael Edwardes, *British India, 1772–1947* (New Delhi: Rupa, 1993).

Amit Kumar Gupta, "Defying Death, Nationalist Revolution in India," *Social Scientist* (Sept to Oct 1937), 3–27.

Ramesh Chandra Majumdar, *History of the Freedom Movement in India* (Calcutta: Firma K. L. Mukhopadhyay, 1971).

Samar Kumar Mallick, *Adhunik Bharoter Derso Bochor (1707 to 1857)* (one hundred and fifty years of Modern India) (Kolkata: West Bengal Publishers, 2003).

P. J. Marshall, *East Indian Fortunes: The British in Bengal in the Eighteenth Century* (Oxford: Oxford University Press, 1976).

P. J. Marshall, "The White Town of Calcutta under the Rule of the East India Company." *Modern Asian Studies* Vol. 34, No. 2 (May 2000), 307–331.

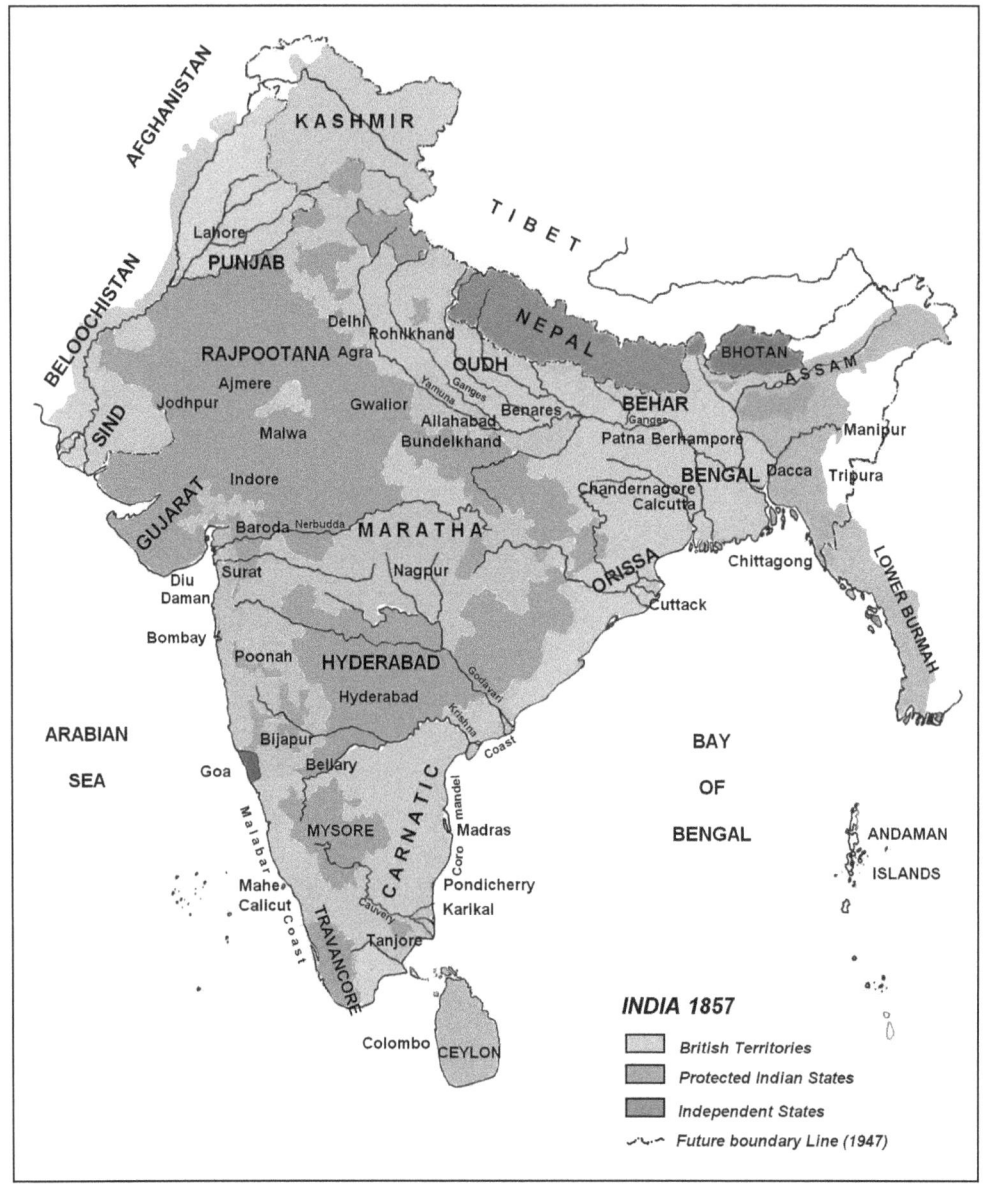

Fig. 22 **Map India 1857.**

CHAPTER 3

British Raj 1858 – 1919

After the Mutiny, Queen Victoria took over Indian affairs. With the Charter renewal of 1858, Company rule came to an end, and India's governance was effectively transferred to the British Parliament. However, the Queen did not formally assume charge until 1876, when she received the title Empress of India. The central Indian states of Gwalior, Rohilkhand, Lucknow, etc. which had rebelled were recaptured by early 1859. The costs of the campaign to submit rebellious states born by the British crown was extracted from Indian tax payers. This chapter describes the beginning of imperial rule with the formation of the British Raj and its administrative policies, the formation of Indian National Congress (Congress) and Muslim League. It explores how the nascent Congress politically matured through interactions with the administration, and how constitutional reformation initiated assigning Muslims political status.

3.1 Post-mutiny Administration

After renewal of the Company Charter, the administration in Britain watched with interest the mobilization of educated Indians, a process which had started in the early 1850s. In Calcutta, the British India Association was formed in 1851, which extended influence in Bombay and Madras. In Britain the rhetoric in favor of Indians increasingly rallied public opinion.

By this time the agony of the Mutiny alerted Parliament. India became a growing concern. To check its recurrence, governance over India was transferred from the East India Company to British Parliament through the Government of India Act 1858, making the Crown arbiter of India's destination. The purpose of the Act was to control India's domestic politics by increasing the power of the Governor-General and limiting the number of members in the Executive Council of Legislative councils. Several administrative reforms were introduced, and the drastic expansive policies adopted by Wellesley and Ellenborough severely curtailed.

From the early 1860s, Bengali educated youths began public protests against withdrawal of so called "Black Acts" drawn up to check the indigo planters' oppression on peasantry. They were ambitious to get more influence on Indian affairs. The Indian Councils Act of 1861, allowed two Indians to be nominated as members of the legislative council of the Bombay and Madras Presidencies. The executive council was transformed into a mini cabinet, consisting of five ordinary members each with responsibility for various portfolios such as home, revenue, finance, law and military. The sixth member was the military commander in chief. The Governor-General retained the power to overrule the council. As the Viceroy, he was also responsible for looking after the Princely States.

From 1862 onwards, Provincial Councils were introduced in Calcutta, Bombay and Madras with authority to frame laws. The number of members in the Central Legislative Council was increased from 6 to 12, including nominated members. Half of them were non-officials. The Indian government was firmly subordinated to Parliament under the Secretary of State. Administrative procedures were kept in check by periodic renewal of acts.

A few decades earlier, the EIC had reformed city administrations placing them under the Governor-General, his Council, and judges of the Supreme Court. In 1847 each city council was liberalized by appointing board members. Four out of seven members were elected by ratepayers. When city taxes were imposed in 1858, residents objected strongly, and agitations increased in 1868 when personal taxes on trade and profession were imposed. In 1861, The Indian Civil Service Act was implemented. Most Indian cities remained outside direct British control, but in Calcutta taxes were enforced by especially appointed collectors.

The new Municipal Act of 1863 offered Indians to participate in administration as board members. New bodies were formed with an elected vice-chairman, and different departments were created in cities. More reforms in municipalities began from the 1870s allowing Indians to be elected as members in the boards but with limited power. Measures were taken to check public agitations by involving Indians in local administration.

In 1870 a part of the educational budget was allocated to initiate mass education through the vernaculars. This measure limited English education. Educated youths, however, urged to increase funding for English education, while at the same time supporting vernacular education by curtailing funds ear-marked for the military and Home Charges.

From 1874, a new department called Public Works was set up (which in 1904 was renamed as Commerce and Industry Department). This change gave opportunities for Indians to utilise the funds raised from trade taxes (imposed from 1865) for local development through mass contacts. Until 1890 the civil administration remained undisturbed, barring the North Eastern Frontier.

3.2 Crown rule – Viceroys / Governor-Generals

During the transition period from EIC to British Raj, Lord Canning (1858–62) was acting as the Governor-General. He passed the 1861 Act, and the Municipal Acts of 1863 before he was replaced by John Lawrence (1864–69), following a short tenure of Lord Elgin. When the Russians invaded central Asia in 1865 and the Pathan tribal raiders became offensive in the northwestern territories, Canning and then Lawrence diplomatically pacified the Afghan hostility. To check these threats, the London office sent instructions to advance the Indian frontier beyond the Hindukush range. The Russian–British rivalry over influence in Central Asia became known as the Great Game.

Lawrence reduced taxes to appease the natives and safeguard British rule. He, however, could not prevent the Orissa famine of 1866 where about one million died. Lord Mayo (1869–72) favored creating the North Western Province to secure India against Afghan incursions. He decentralized finance for extending irrigation canals, roads, railways and forestry, and ordered for the census to be held (1872). Mayo's desire to secure and improve India came to an unexpected end. While visiting Port Blair in the Andamans to settle conflicts with convicts, he was assassinated by an Afghan prisoner in 1872. In the subsequent void, Lord Napier stepped in until London appointed Lord Northbrook (1872–76) to take over as Viceroy later that year. When the Russians advanced up to Turkestan in 1874, Northbrook was asked to proceed to Kabul, but he took a non-interventionist approach and resigned his office.

By promulgating the Laws Local Extent 1874 Act, Parliament took a radical decision to put the entire Indian system under British control. The Crown was authorized to appoint the Governor-Generals (Viceroys) and provincial governors directly, giving the British Raj an imperial character. By the Royal Titles Act 1876, Queen Victoria officially became the Empress of India. Further Acts empowered the Governor-General to decide on trade and business transactions.

After Northbrook's resignation, Lord Lytton (1876–80) became Governor-General, taking up the Afghan concern, counteracting Russian regional influence, and securing India's frontiers. When in 1878 he learnt that a Russian diplomatic mission was allowed in Kabul, he sent a rival emissary to Kabul as well. However, when this envoy was turned back at the border, Lytton launched a full scale invasion, waging the second Afghan War. He occupied Kabul in 1878 retaining control over the border. The campaign was expensive during a time when the great famine of 1877 took thousands of lives. In 1879 Lytton overruled the entire council for accommodating home demands by eliminating import duties chargeable for British made cotton goods, and ignored requests for monetary relief to famine stricken people.

Lytton's decisions to engage into an Afghan war and his neglect of starving people were criticized by the nascent but active native press. He secured the Princely States under the Queen through treaties. His most regrettable decision was the export of huge quantities of wheat to England when Indians were at the height of famine. Indian newspapers also criticized this action.

The Indian administration assumed that semi-Bengali babus writing seditious texts were a potential threat for future troubles. From 1876 Indian opportunities to serve in Civil Service were curtailed by lowering the age limit from 21 to 19 years to qualify to sit for ICS examination in London. Lytton promulgated the Vernacular Act of 1878 to prohibit public protests through newspapers. This decision spurred protests initiated by Surendranath Banerjee of the Indian Association. When a British diplomat was killed by Afghan rebels during Lytton's campaign, it partially contributed to the win of Gladstone's Liberals defeating the Conservatives in 1880. As a consequence, Lord Lytton resigned. At this time the French rivalry increased, especially when the French planned expanding towards the Indo-China border and establishing trade relations with upper Burma.

On Gladstone's return to power in 1880, the Marquess of Ripon (1880–84) replaced Lord Lytton. Ripon ended the Second Afghan War in 1882, and used his power to introduce a portfolio system. He nominated three Indians in his legislative council, and the provincial councils were empowered to look after the provinces. Political suppressions imposed earlier, were partially withdrawn in the 1880s. On the recommendation of Gladstone, Ripon introduced the Ilbert Bill in 1883. In its reform of the Criminal Code, the bill allowed Indian senior magistrates to trial British subjects with equal rights of British judges. The bill was opposed by European officers in cities, as well as Anglo-Indians.

Upon introducing the Ilbert Bill, Surendranath Benerjee organized the National Indian Union conference in the venue of an industrial exhibition arranged in Calcutta (1883). The majority of the delegates who were from Bengal desired to have a parliamentary government in India to resist white domination in administration. This conference of nationalist individuals provided a platform for Indian politicians. The Ilbert bill passed in 1884 in weakened form as a compromise where British residents were allowed to be tried by special juries. Ripon was thought to have weakened the British empire, but he built up the Commonwealth. He lowered salt tax, tried to stabilize land tax, and restored press freedom. His subordinates did not cooperate with him, so he resigned in 1884 and joined Gladstone's ministry in 1886.

Having gained much insight in international politics as British ambassador to Russia and Turkey, Dufferin was the ideal person to be appointed as the next Viceroy. Lord Dufferin (1884–88) improved relations with Anglo-Indian and Indian communities and like his predecessor pushed through great reforms. When George V visited India, Dufferin entered the Durbar on a horse back avoiding a traditional imperial elephant. He declared war against Burma in 1885. Thibow, who was in power, surrendered and Burma was annexed as a province of the British empire. Dufferin planned to improve local administration and tried to win the cooperation of conservative elements. At the same time, he attempted to control the educated youths passively.

Dufferin favored Indians getting a platform if it worked as Britain's mouthpiece similar to the British parliamentarians in the opposition. He promoted social reforms.[1] Mr. Allan Octavian Hume, a retired civil servant, who had similar ideas also took an active role in the overall improvement of Indian youths and students.[2] He addressed the guardians of the Calcutta University, urging them to organize cultural, social and political platforms. The Indian National Congress was founded in 1885 at his initiative.

The British public felt that the administration did not do enough for the lives of Indian subjects. The Liberals in the British Parliament were unsure of any real improvement of Indians. But infrastructure making was in progress. By 1887, the Jubilee Bridge over the Hooghly improved rail connections of Calcutta Port with the interior. Similarly, Bombay Port was connected with Gujarat and Rajasthan. Most of central India had the option to use any of these two ports.

After Dufferin's resignation, Lord Lansdowne (1888–94) took over as Viceroy and sent his secretary to Kabul to open discussion for delimitation of the border. On the eastern frontier, Manipur became a princely state after the Anglo–Manipur war of 1891. The next Viceroy, Lord Elgin (1894–99) sent an army for further punitive actions to the northwestern frontier where independent tribes caused trouble. To mark the Afghan border, the Durand Line was established in 1896, adding tribal territories along with Chitral and Gilgit to guard access to crucial mountain passes.

Though Ripon had promoted the view that Indians should be fully part of the administration, British conservatives doubted Indian qualities. Taking over the charge, Lord Curzon (1899–1905) focused on the troubled Northwest. He was not eager to accommodate the turbulent tribal area with Punjab province, and created a new North Western Frontier Province (NWFP) in 1901, following the guidelines of Mayo's proposal during his tenure.

During the turn of the century, as increased imports of Britain caused a decline of indigenous industries (mainly textiles) and increase of cash crop cultivation to support British industries, Indian laborers became redundant. Such surplus laborers were utilised to serve Britain's tropical colonies which faced a shortage of agricultural and industrial laborers. Some of them were deployed in the Indian army. The process of sending Indian convicts as laborers to other British colonies began from 1796. Indian money from south Indian banks was invested in agriculture in Burma and Ceylon with commercial interest. But the government neglected creating new opportunities for local employment.

With the founding of the Indian National Congress, Congress initially did not take any initiative to oppose the new European mercantile trade and recover indigenous production. In the late nineteenth century some effeminate Bengali Babus with poor moral standards were prominent in society. Their presence as products of the Bengal Renaissance in anglicized habits and style confused the political projections of a young Congress.

3.3 Genesis of Indian politics and Foundation of Indian National Congress

The pioneers of Indian politics were the products of renaissance, the immediate followers in the footsteps of Rammohan Roy. Rammohan was a lone pioneer to seek justice for the Indians through judicial and administrative reforms from the early 19th century.

The Derozians (vide Appendix 1) like Rasik Krishna Mallick attempted to persuade Rammohan's agenda from 1833 by writing against government's policies adopted during Cornwallis' Permanent Settlement of Bengal (1793). He also publicly advocated for revision of the Company's Charter to abolish policing powers given to the merchant companies. Similar sporadic public approaches continued at individual initiatives. But there was no collective approach to place demands effectively.

The *Landholders' Society* (or Zamindari Association) was formed in 1838 to look after landlords' interests. However, it demanded reforms in police and judiciary and an extension of the Permanent Settlement all over India. This was the first political inclination shown by an organization that addressed the government, even as it was motivated to promote landlords' interests only.

From the 1830s, indigo planters and factory owners increasingly used state machinery and forced the peasantry to cultivate indigo, replacing the cultivation of crop plants. Peasant farmers were discriminated against because the legal system allowed the European planters to remain beyond the jurisdiction of rural courts. Worse still, the courts indulged Europeans to escape criminal court cases even after committing crime. The indigo planters and factory owners applied pressure on the unwilling farmers to surrender to serve their interests.* The legal system provided a special privilege of immunity to the Europeans. Around 1849 such oppressions

---

* Note: From 1796, the Bengal peasantry started protesting against forcible possession of their land and forcibly plowing up half grown crops by the indigo manufacturers with legal protection. Haris Chandra Mukherjee, editor of Hindu Patriot, published a few articles on oppression of ryots by indigo planters. Mukherjee, was harassed and lost everything he had (Sivanath Sastri, *Ramtanu Lahiri and Tatkalin Banga Samaj* (1903), 216–17). When anti-indigo agitation intensified in 1859–60, the Indigo Enquiry Commission was set up to uphold the rights of the planters. Haris Chandra was influenced by Dina Bandhu Mitra's book, *Nil Darpan* (refer Appendix 1). Mitra was a witness of the misery of the peasants of different districts of Bengal and wrote this book published in 1860 from Dhaka. *Nil Darpan* was translated into English by Madhusudhan Dutta, but printed by Reverend James Long, which led to Mr. Long's imprisonment. Finally, with the availability of synthetic indigo from 1892, indigo cultivation became unprofitable and faded out.

became rampant in Nadia and Jessore districts, and subsequently in certain places in Bihar. At this lowpoint, public opinion pressured the government to change the law.

Mr. J. Groundwater Bethune, an administrator in the Governor-General's office, had legal expertise. He was asked to draw Acts countering this legal system. The four Acts that Bethune drafted in 1850 were: 1. Act for abolishing exemption from the jurisdiction of East India Company's criminal court; 2. Act declaring the privilege of Her Majesty's European subjects; 3. Act for protection of judicial officers; and 4. Act for trial by jury in Company's court.[3] The Acts abolished legal favor given to the Europeans, but caused the Europeans to start a collective and loud agitation as soon as the drafts were placed before the council. They designated these Acts as "Black Acts."

During a large gathering in Calcutta, Europeans collected a large sum of money, and took their case to the British Parliament. Following the direction of the British authorities, the draft Acts were removed from the government agenda. Then indigo planters became more oppressive. Bethune was popular among the natives after he founded the Bethune School for Hindu girls (1849). But the Europeans abused and cursed Mr. Bethune through papers edited by them. The hapless natives, on the other side, were waiting for favors coming from the administration. Neither they had any organization nor any media to ventilate their demands.

The Derozians – also known as *Young Bengal* – were against the withdrawal of the Acts. Ramgopal Ghosh, one of them, worked with Bethune when he founded his School. Ghosh was then well-known as a powerful orator and a good writer. When the Black Acts were dismissed and the peasants were left isolated and helpless, Ramgopal took their side to build up public opinions by delivering fiery public speeches. He also published articles, printed a pamphlet, and wrote in the *Bengal Spectator* supporting the Black Acts. He led the first direct public protest against British policies. The Europeans had their demand already fulfilled, and Bethune died in August of 1851. They did not appreciate Ramgopal's vocal protests and he was eventually forced to resign from the Agri-Horticultural Society.

Ramgopal did not stop though he was alone. He was a fan of George Thompson who awakened the natives' political thoughts and founded The British India Society. Ramgopal, becoming one of the members of this society, learnt from Thompson how to deliver political speeches. But, his failure to reinstate the Black Acts, and his insult of being removed from the Horticultural Society became a sentimental issue among the learned natives of Calcutta. They realized that Ramgopal's failure was because he stood alone, and the Europeans were successful because they fought collectively. The natives then became inclined to lodge collective protests.

Sambhu Chandra Mukherjee was a practicing journalist imbued with liberal views in favor of the efficacy of political moderation. In 1860 he wrote a pamphlet criticizing the British move for imposing income tax upon Indians by quoting the American dictum, "No taxation, without representation." He edited journals and campaigned for creating opportunities for employment of youths. He also supported Ramgopal Ghosh's public protests in favor of Black Acts. Free press Journalism had been put under restriction by Wellesley in 1799, and from 1808 all forms of publication were brought under government control. Even the editors of the *Bengal Gazette* and *Calcutta Journal* were sent back to London for criticizing government policies.

The *Landlords'* or *Landholders' Society* which patronized wealthy Indians, lost its edge but continued. Also there was the *British India Society* functioning actively with young participants. Ramgopal took initiative to amalgamate these two associations into a strong single unit as the *British Indian Association* which was born on 31 October, 1851. A sixteen-member committee was formed with Radhakanta Dev as the president and Debendranath Tagore the secretary. Ramgopal Ghosh, Peary Chand Mitra, Kali Krishna Dev, Prassana Kumar Tagore amongst others, were members. It was the first indigenous association formed to support the Indian causes and oppose administrative injustice. The Europeans realized that an elite native society was waking up and it would be difficult to ignore them. Natives felt that they were no longer isolated.

Several decades later, Sambhu Chandra formed the *India League* (1875) with support of Anandamohan Bose and Durgamohan Das to ventilate domestic grievances. Next, Surendranath Banerjee formed the *Indian National Association*, along with Anandamohan Bose in July of 1876, with the objective to bring together Hindus and Muslims to form a united front towards the British. They opposed the outcome of the Ilbert Bill, and claimed in the early 1880s an extended jurisdiction of Indian judges. It raised the issue of appointing Indian members in the Viceroy's Executive Council. Lord Ripon listened to them. About 25 years after Rammohan Roy's complaint against British policy in Britain, the Parsi Dadabhai Naoroji in 1865 actively propagated Indian concerns in Britain. From the 1870s several vernacular and English dailies were published throughout India to raise awareness of the plight of India's masses.

Naoroji, born in 1825, was one of the first generation Indians who received western exposure. He was a social worker and a journalist. He taught mathematics in Elphinstone College Bombay during the 1850s but soon moved to London to start a trading company. He also became associated with the *London Indian Society* and the *East India Association*, with the sole purpose to work for Indian political and social issues. From 1866, he actively tried to move related issues before the British Parliament. When the Indian National Congress was established he took a short break and visited India. He then returned to London to continue with his political agenda. In 1892, Naoroji, the first person of Indian origin, was elected in the British Parliament representing the Liberal Party and used his position to look after the Indian causes.

Just like Rammohan Roy had attempted, Naoroji analysed the economy of colonial India to prove that an estimated £200–300 million earned as revenue from India drained to Britain and never recirculated. He urged for British investments in labor and capital in their Indian colony. His drain theory was supported by Prafulla Chandra Roy's work *The Poverty Problem in India* (1895), Mahadev Govind Ranade, *Essays on Indian Economics* (1899), Romesh Chunder Dutt's *Economic History of India Under Early British Rule* (1902), and G. Subrahmaṇya Aiyar's *Some Economic Aspects of British Rule in India* (1903).

Even some British officers ventilated poor Indian conditions in foreign media. The newly elected Liberal British Prime Minister Gladstone recognized the needs of Indian subjects, and in 1877 he urged the Indian administration to work for the benefit of all their subjects and give due respect to the educated elites. This was a time when hostilities were instinctive among many white officers, even as moral issues tended to be liberal in the face of continuing demands.

The natives were working for Indian integration in a right forum. From the early 1860s when Debendranath Tagore, secretary of the British Indian Association, collected data at different levels when Indians took administrative offices. A rising print media supported this effort. The *Bombay Samachar* was in publication from 1822 and gradually vernacular newspapers and journals proliferated from the 1860s. Their editorials shaped the build-up of national concepts among the public. By 1885, there were 319 vernacular publications with a total circulation of 150,000 and 96 English language papers with a circulation of 59,000.[4] Apart from several from Bengal, hundreds of such newspapers were in circulation in Allahabad from 1860, Bombay from 1861, Madras from 1866, Lahore and Orissa from 1870, actively venting news on Indian matters, and campaigning for political and economic equality for all Indians. Such concerted propaganda by the Indian press influenced the development of mass political consciousness at a time when the educated classes were avid newspaper readers.

The flourishing journalistic writings helped establish communications at pan India level and growth of local organizations promoting political nationalism. It was further facilitated with the progress of railways, telegraph, and postal services. The British Indian Association, identified ten specific issues bringing them to the notice of the government in the late 1860s. Those were to, 1. establish agricultural banks; 2. reduce military expenditure; 3. develop irrigation systems; 4. develop education, health care, and sanitation; 5. appoint Indians in higher government positions; 6. open technical and professional training facilities; 7. separate the judicial system from administration; 8. scrap the Arms Act. passed by Lord Lytton;

8. approve a larger number of elected representatives in administration; 9. ensure security of people and resources; and 10. approve Indian representation in the council of London. Such a radical approach was unexpected and was not easily swallowed by the government.

When repeated requests and prayers of this type failed to impress the administration, people felt the need of a platform to seek broader and national consciousness, involving the masses. Bankim Chandra Chatterjee's hymn "Vande Mataram" (Ode to the Motherland) written in 1870, was published in his novel *Anandamath* in 1882. This book drew large public attention and gained wide popularity throughout the country. The Vande Mataram became a powerful tool to evoke mass nationalism as this song aroused mass sentiments by accepting India as the mother goddess.*

With passage of time, elite Indians became more determined to form a national platform to promote native issues more effectively. Several rural based issues needed attention as Indian villages were victims of cash crop farming (mainly opium and Indigo). Local industries were destroyed for the benefit of Britain. The post-industrial revolution conditions of Britain were not good either. In the 1880s the Social Democratic Federation reported that a quarter of London residents lived below the breadline. Other survey reports also indicated that the conditions were worse; 30 percent of the Britons could not afford to buy bare necessities, and some lived in extreme distress.[5] How could it be that the home of the great empire could be associated with the wretched corner of an Indian colony?

The British middle class, who had benefited from the industrial revolution, pressured for reforms, but the political power was swayed largely by wealthy industrialists. The policies of the Indian colony were controlled

---

* Note: Initially, the entire song *Vande Mataram* was felt to be suitable as the national song. Part of the song emerged as a national slogan to awaken patriotic feelings. But in 1937 when the Muslim League was defeated in an election, they refused to accept *Vande Mataram* because of its religious connotations. Ultimately, at the suggestion of Rabindranath Tagore, only the first stanza of the song was adopted as the national song in pre-independent India.

by the Lancashire industrialists who influenced politicians to exploit Indian markets. Indian students staying in England for higher studies knew how British politicians were biased. Some of them, like Surendranath Banerjee and Anandamohan Bose returned home imbued with ideas of liberty and nationalism. They had high expectations as well as political skill. They were well off, led administrative and political careers, and were even associated with academic institutions. They comprised an embryonic political class and endeavoured to be united for a common cause.[6]

3.3.1 Preparation for Indian National Congress

As alluded to, educated youths were working to be united. In 1868, Sisir Kumar Ghosh of Calcutta published *Amrita Bazar Patrika*. From 1876 this nationalistic newspaper used to analyse the national problems, their origins, and provided suggestive ideas. Lytton introduced the Vernacular Press Act in 1878 when Indian papers criticized his Afghan campaign and his neglect of famine-stricken people.

In 1879 Surendranath Banerjee bought the *Bengalee* which was in publication from 1862. He began lecturing on liberal politics and Indian history. After the Indian Association was formed, Surendranath convened a national conference in Calcutta in 1883 to consolidate opinions in favor of the Pitts Act opposed by Europeans. Major vernacular newspapers like *The Hindu, Tribune, Kesari*, etc. were regularly published from different Indian regions supporting Indian causes. Also several organizations were established in the contemporary period to promote national issues.

The National Indian Association finally merged with the Indian National Congress. *Madras Mahajan Sabha* was founded in 1884 and *Bombay Presidency Association* came into being in 1885 with a common aim to integrate the pan Indian national feelings through cultural and political activities. Even an *Arya Mahilah Samaj* (Arya Women's Society) was set up in the 1880s in Maharashtra, advocating for womens' rights.

Groundwork was in preparation, but the situation was not ripe enough to build a national platform. It was more of an illusion. Suddenly an opportunity arose when Allan Hume got involved in establishing an organization for Indians. Mr. Wedderburn was another Britisher who supported Hume's efforts. There were a few British like him who were friends of India, and some scholarly British officers stayed and worked in India without taking part in politics (Appendix 3).

Hume's interest was ignited when he was in civil service. After retirement in 1882 he freely worked to unite Indians in a platform. From secret police reports he knew that poor and middle class educated youths were becoming more and more dissatisfied and agitated because the prosperity of natives was reduced to the lowest human level due to economic drainage.[7] The reports hinted at the possibility of a revolt. To avert its outcome in a bigger form, Hume advised Indians, "…The remedy is not petitioning but boycott... prepare your forces, organize your power, and then go to work so that they cannot refuse you what you demand."[8] Hume witnessed the Mutiny of 1857, as well as agrarian riots in Deccan and Bombay caused by administrative neglect. He proposed and advised Indians to form a common platform and push for a benevolent administration.

A decision was taken to establish an all-India forum, and the convenors of the ensuing organization published their first manifesto in March 1885 designating it as *The Indian Union*. They gave a call for its first convention to be held in Poona. But the venue was shifted to Bombay, and the date was fixed on 28–30 March 1885. The Bombay Presidency Association was the host. Seventy-two delegates at all India levels assembled on the first day, and they proposed that the name of the organization would be changed to the *Indian National Congress*. This convention was presided over by W. C. Bonnerjee, a renowned Calcutta High Court barrister.

Bengal was the birthplace of domestic political activities, but in the first meeting only four Bengali delegates were present. Of a total 72 delegates, 38 came from Bombay, and 21 from Madras, and remainder from Punjab, Northwestern Provinces and Awadh. This first convention ensured that all political programmes would be coordinated throughout the country, but they did not have any specific agenda. Surendranath Banerjee himself could not attend this meeting. Perhaps he was busy with his Indian Association. Since 1885 the Indian National Congress convention meets every year at the end of December.

The constitution of the Indian National Congress was made democratically accessible to anyone provided one abided by its prescribed regulations. These were flexible and open for change. Every member had provision to be an executive. From this time, the Indian National Congress became the dominating nationalist political party at an all India level for every Indian irrespective of caste, creed, or religion. It initiated freedom movements. It was composed of moderates who wanted India to be like Canada or Australia, and radicals who wanted complete freedom. Everyone, no matter their background or ideology, was encouraged to work together.

Meanwhile, Lord Dufferin worked out a plan for the overall development of India and proposed to enlarge the provincial councils enhancing their status. He also partially introduced elective principles and liberalized the political institutions. He desired educated Indians to be conversant with the British Parliamentary Government and English constitutional systems so that they could inspire their countrymen to cooperate with the rulers. However, he left India before the scheme was implemented.

Though Congress was founded for all Indians to forge nationalism, with the popularity of the Vande Mataram as its (unofficial) mantra, and the dominance of Hindu delegates, some Muslims became concerned that there would be little room for their views. In 1868 Syed Ahmed Khan, an educated Muslim philosopher and educationist, proposed to separate Muslims from Congress, and founded *United India Patriotic Association* (1888) to check the Congress propaganda for spreading nationalism. He attempted to unite Muslim nationalists to support British rule. However, during the 1888 Congress Session still about 15% of the delegates were Muslim.

3.3.2 Congress in its early days and the Administration

Dadabhai Naoroji presided over the second Congress Session of 1886, held in Calcutta. He advised members to take the Indian issues to the government immediately.[9] A ten-point demand list, the same actionpoints Debendranath

Tagore in the 1860s identified, was placed before the government. This approach was moderate, and shaped like prayers. But the Government remained silent. The moderate members, dominant from Congress' inception, were cautious against agitation. It is said that the moderates avoided Surendranath Banerjee's presence in the inaugural session in Bombay apprehending him as a sedition monger. However, during the Calcutta session of 1886 differences were resolved and his association merged with Congress.

During his tour in India, Naoroji met with the people suffering under colonial India. As a Member of British Parliament, he tried to influence the lawmakers to give relief to poor Indians burdened with shouldering the cost of the military postings for protecting the empire beyond Indian borders. Gopal Krishna Gokhale and Lokmanya Tilak, two outstanding leaders from Maharashtra, became associated with Congress between 1889–90 through Naoroji's influence. Gokhale was moderate and Gandhi accepted him as his mentor. Gokhale even went to South Africa at the invitation of Gandhi.

Tilak, known as the "father of Indian unrest" was an uncompromising nationalist, an educationist, and a social worker. Before starting his political career, Tilak co-founded an English school and initiated the formation of an educational society which began the Poona Fergusson College where he was a teacher of Mathematics. He was conservative on Hindu customs and unsympathetic to social reforms, but popular among the Marathi youths as he opposed moderate approaches of Congress. As the first radical nationalist he appealed to Indian youth to sacrifice themselves for the motherland. Tilak prepared the youth to claim self-rule, and wrote an article in *Kesari*, a Marathi newspaper, criticizing British rule. He was influenced by Swami Vivekananda from 1892 when Swamiji rested in his Poona house for a few days as a wandering sannyasin.

Lord Lansdowne executed Dufferin's reforms by passing the Indian Council Act 1892 empowering the councils of both the center and provinces, as well as the local bodies to frame rules for themselves with concurrence of the Governor-General. The Governor-General's council was also extended to include 16 members. The 1892 Act, for the first time allowing Indians members in the council, opened their participation in administration. They took part in pre-budget discussions and asked questions on the floor, but without voting rights. In 1893, the English writer and activist Annie Besant joined the Theosophical Society which was founded by Madame Blavatsky in Madras in 1886.

Tilak was arrested in 1897 under "sedition" charges for a public speech delivered during the Shivaji Festival. He quoted the Gita to inspire people to fight against evils, and published an article in *Kesari*. He was imprisoned for eighteen months. Tilak's prosecution was prompted by the assassination of two British officers shortly after the Shivaji Festival, and one of them was an officer who behaved excessively towards the people while executing a plague-control program.

Tilak's punishment was heavy for a simple cause. The nation was in tears. Surendranath Banerjee, a civil servant, declared Tilak innocent, and took his side. At the end of the 19th century when educated youths were expected to fulfill imperial aspirations, Tilak's radical expression directed against the government was understandable. He became exemplary to his people. His outlook was radical but he never participated in violent activities. While imprisoned his adopted slogan was "Swaraj is my birthright," which inspired a younger group to participate in anarchist movements.

The famine of 1896–97 caused large-scale casualties in rural areas and aroused widespread public agitation. For the first time the moderates in Congress rebuked the government to reduce land revenue, impose taxes on imports, and stop the drainage of wealth. This approach encouraged a pro-swadeshi movement causing a decline in foreign investments, which naturally caused alarm in London. This incident, at the beginning of the 19th century, influenced London to decentralize the administration to remote towns and villages, introducing an elaborate bureaucracy with central connection. Influential landlords, representing the District Boards, were put in the chain of bureaucracy. London consolidated its power bringing the village administration under direct control of Parliament. The system kept remote areas out of political influence.

The Bengal Renaissance produced a creative intelligentsia. Not all educated elites were in politics, but all were nationalists. They advised Indian leaders to be self-confident and claim rights instead of begging. Lala Lajpat Rai who was critical of its leadership, criticized Congress as an organization for holding annual national festivals. This passivity in Congress leadership was the cause of growing radical nationalism from Bengal. British intelligence concluded that Bengalis were politically conscious and leading the Congress, and that Bengal was a center of political unrest.

The turn of the century was a critical time in world history, as the South African Boers fought against the British, the Japanese were fighting Russia, and Russians were opposing the Tsar to get liberty. In India domestic forces also rose to challenge the imperial government. All this became fertile ground for anarchism, which started from Bengal.

3.4 Lord Curzon – Bengal Partition and Consequences

Lord Curzon came to India in 1880 and 1890. He loved India –being fascinated with Indian heritage and culture– but his opinion of Indians was very low. He subscribed to the idea that India was the "White Man's Burden." That the Empire was to do good, but would also receive benefits. At a dinner party he said, "The East is a University in which the scholar never takes his degree," by which he justified the British presence more or less forever.[10] In 1899 he was appointed Viceroy, replacing Lord Elgin (1894–98). Elgin was sympathetic to the victims of the great famine of 1896–97, which he failed to control. He admitted that some 4.5 million people died of starvation. According to another estimate, 11 million died.

Curzon favored British investments in India.[11] He brought the Northwest under control by creating North Western Frontier Province (NWFP), and initiated a mission into Tibet. He introduced changes in administration by separating the police service and creating a department of Commerce and Industry. He arranged repairing old monuments, establishing new ones, and began the Archeological Survey of India. He also reduced taxes but took steps to limit higher education.

Curzon believed that Indian nationality would not pose any danger to the British, but was enraged with a growing educated class who were politically conscious. He passed the Municipal Adjustment Act 1899 to limit elected members in the Calcutta Corporation. Then the Indian University Act of 1904 that reduced autonomy of universities, and limited private entrepreneurship in higher education. He curbed freedom of press in 1904 to reign in nationalists. Finally, he planned for partition of Bengal along religious lines to split the politicalized Bengali speaking population. Until Curzon's arrival, Congress politics were moderate.

In this tense environment, the Indian National Congress was gaining public support, and Curzon knew that Lytton's administration did not trust educated Bengali babus. He found that Dufferin's administration had made maps necessary to upscale the military operations in Burma. He believed that the administration was not equipped to manage the large Bengal province which suffered famines in the 1860s and 1890s.

The government had planned to trim the Bengal province during the previous century. Assam and Sylhet were already separated from Bengal as a Chief Commissioner's province in 1874. Commissioner William Ward, had moved to make a separate administrative circle by transferring two districts of East Bengal to Assam. The next move to transfer more districts of Bengal to Assam was resisted by Sir Henry Cotton, the next Chief Commissioner of Assam. In Orissa, language centered movements unified Oriya speaking people into one territory. And so Sambalpur was shifted from Central Provinces to Bengal as the inhabitants speak Oriya.

Banerjee-Dube refers to a note of W. B. Oldham (Commissioner of Chittagong) recommending the creation of a new province with Malda, Rajshahi, Dacca, Chittagong divisions, Hill Tipperah and Assam, each with high concentration of Muslim, to reduce political threat posed by Hindu majority intelligentsia in undivided Bengal.[12] Perhaps Curzon was influenced by Oldham's note. Several historians believe that the Bengal partition was a political move only to break the unity of Hindus and Muslims. Undoubtedly Bengal (united Bengal) housed over 78.5 million people residing in a 490,000 km^2 area, but its administration ran without constraints.

Curzon silently planned a new scheme in 1903 for creating a separate region of East Bengal with Dacca as the capital. He was opposed by H. J. S. Cotton. But Curzon promulgated the Bengal partition on July 19, 1905. The partition of Bengal became a sentimental issue and shocked many educated elites.

The Bengal Partition for the first time integrated the masses on a political cause. Anandamohan Bose, Surendranath Benerjee, Gurudas Banerjee, Rashbehari Ghosh, Rabindranath Tagore, Maharaja Monindra Nandi, and others from Calcutta, and Abdul Rasul, Aswani Kumar Dutta, Brahmabandhab Upadhyay, Nawab Atikulla, Liakat Hassain and others from East Bengal, united to form the *Anti-Partition Committee* on 16 October 1905. Rabindranath Tagore, broke his silence writing a song, "Banglar Mati Banglar Jol Ek Houk, Ek Houk…" (let the soil and waterways of Bengal be integrated) which fuelled the national sentiment. *Rakhis* (bracelets) were tied on the wrists of Hindus and Muslims to show their solidarity. An evening mass meeting of 16 October resolved to founding a Federation Hall in Calcutta.

During the period of apparent peace until 1890, anti-British sentiments increased. The famine of the 1890s took millions of lives due to administrative inactivity. In the Madras Congress meeting of 1898, Bipin Chandra Pal demanded the repeal of the Arms Act 1878, restricting Indians to possess arms. Then a police firing near Vizagapatam (then under Madras) killed several agitating hill-men in 1900. These incidents aroused anger so long suppressed among masses. Being frustrated with an indecisive Congress leadership, the *Anusilan Samity* was formed in 1902 in Calcutta. Its members planned to start an arms struggle against the British. When in 1905 the Bengal Partition was executed, public outrage became widespread.

The turn to the new century was significant for Congress politics. Bal Gangadhar Tilak called the nation to work for Swaraj in a united territory. Congress became polarized on methods for lodging protests, and a strong radical group emerged under the leaderships of Tilak, Lajpat Rai, and Bipin Behari Pal. Surendranath Banerjee had a strong personal opinion (he differed moderates on civil disobedience movements, and supported the

Montagu-Chelmsford Act of 1919), but he was not associated with any of the groups in Congress. Surendranath took the lead in protesting the Bengal Partition.

The events of the early twentieth century were important. Swami Vivekananda, who inspired the youths to rise, passed away in 1902. Organized youths turned radicals from 1902 and became offensive against the British. On the 50th anniversary of Sepoy Mutiny in 1907, Punjab witnessed a widespread riot. Hemchandra Kanungo set up a bomb manufacturing unit in Muraripukur in Calcutta in early 1908, and in the same year Khudiram Bose attempted to assassinate Kingsford. The Mayor's house in Chandannagar was bombed. The following year Lord Minto was the target of the anarchists and Madanlal Dhingra killed Curzon Wyllie in London. In 1912 Lord Hardinge narrowly escaped in Delhi when a bomb exploded very close to him on the occasion of the shift of the Indian capital from Calcutta to Delhi. Police framed it as the *Delhi Conspiracy Case*. Rash Behari Bose, said to be the leader of this conspiracy, absconded, and afterwards fled to Japan.

Aurobindo Ghosh entered politics in his early 20s from Baroda (1904–05). His formative life of 14 years was spent in England. He enriched himself with European culture, but retained his obligation for the land he was born. He returned to India in 1904 with knowledge of British administration accumulated while preparing for the Indian Civil Service examination in Cambridge.

Aurobindo read Indian classics and ancient Indian philosophy. He wrote a series of articles on the current Indian political situation as *New Lamps for Old* in a Bombay Weekly, writing that the approach of Congress leaders was not in the spirit of sincerity and whole-heartedness. He found their methods wanting, and Congress leaders were not right to be trusted as they broke with the political base. He campaigned for a mass-awakening following Vivekananda's preaching. Then he was only 21 years old.[13]

Aurobindo visited different places with a mission to establish links with different secret organizations working for liberation. He had discussions with

Tilak, and asked Jatin Banerjee (Niralamba Swami) and his own brother Barin Chandra Ghosh to organize revolutionary work from Bengal. In the Surat Congress of 1907 Aurobindo supported Tilak. Finally, he left Baroda for Bengal and joined Bengal National College, Calcutta, in 1907 which was established for teaching Indian philosophy backed by nationalist control.

Satish Chandra Mukherjee had founded this college with donations offered by Subodh Chandra Mallick, Raja Surya Kanta Acharya Chowdhury, Brojendra Kishore Roychowdhury and others, with an aim to create a National University in Bengal that would challenge British education policy by introducing a nation-building curriculum which the Calcutta University ignored. Lord Curzon's University Act 1904 restricted the scope for natives' higher education.

A meeting of 10 December 1904, in presence of more than one thousand delegates, including Rabindranath Tagore, resolved for *The National Council of Education*. It was formed in 1905 and the Bengal National College became affiliated with it. Rashbehari Ghose was the first president and Aurobinda Ghosh was the first principal of this College.

In 1910 the *Society of Technical Education* founded to promote education in technology, and a *College of Engineering and Technology, Bengal* was established purely on nationalistic views. Deshbandhu Chittaranjan Das, as the mayor of Calcutta Corporation, arranged a piece of land in Jadavpur in 1924 to house this College. It later became the Jadavpur University.*

Aurobindo was a regular contributor to *Jugantar*, an organ of Bengali revolutionaries, and *Vande Mataram*, a periodical started by Bipin Behari Pal. Both papers encouraged nationalist movements. Aurobinda also edited his own paper *Karmayogin*. All such arrangements intrigued nationalists to prepare themselves for a long term movement.

---

* Note: In the 1940s this college was virtually functioning as a university until it became Jadavpur University after independence. Jadavpur University has historical obligations to the nationalists.

3.5 Swadeshi Movement

The *Swadeshi Movement* was officially inaugurated at a public meeting of 7 August 1905 at Calcutta Town Hall to protest the Bengal Partition. Surendranath Banerjee read a pledge to boycott foreign goods taking Bipin Pal and Aurobinda Ghose by his side. Many meetings and demonstrations were organized which campaigned for rejecting foreign goods. The movement infused nationalistic feelings and self-reliance among Indians, and generated a new idea of emancipation. Later Gandhi also adapted the swadeshi concept in Sabarmati.

The message of Swadeshi reached the Maratha speaking people from Bengal. Tilak, one of the sublime figures of the day, became fully engaged and became the idol of Bengal. The Punjab Kesari Lala Lajpat Rai became also directly involved in this movement with a large influence among Punjab peasantry. Tilak's popularity increased through his involvement in boycott movements. He received support from the labor class, and the circulation of his *Kesari* increased. The Ganpati festival in Maharashtra was revived from 1905. He was arrested again in 1908. Involvement of Tilak and Lajpat Rai with Bengal strengthened the Swadeshi, making it a pan Indian movement.

The movement inspired Punjabis to boycott water tax that was increased in canal irrigated areas. Their leader Lala Lajpat Rai was exiled and all his meetings were banned. Bipin Pal took this movement to Telugu speaking Madras (Andhra Pradesh) from where the students participated with full energy even after facing oppressions. Here they founded national schools. An agitated group became violent and attacked British establishments in Kakinada.

The natives built new establishments as indigenous production centers. The wealthy natives donated money and dedicated lands to rural based production all over the country. Even Swadeshi banks were established starting from Punjab. Swadweshi rejuvenated the Congress. The moderates also joined the movement boycotting foreign goods. Gokhale recognized Bengal as the birthplace of Swadeshi. He once remarked, "what Bengal thinks today, India thinks tomorrow." Output of Indian goods increased so much that the British trade in India languished. The Bombay spinning mill owners benefited. Swadeshi also influenced the working class to become self-conscious. From 1905, the workers of Burn Company, of jute mills, railway workshops, government presses, etc. started movements against discriminatory authorities to secure better working conditions.

Swadeshi, however, remained limited mostly to the middle class, and bypassed the peasants. It developed as an internal force which drew apolitical men into political banners at the leadership of Lala Lajpat Rai, Bal Gangadhar Tilak and Bipin Behari Pal (LaL- BaL- PaL). Swadeshi was not new in Bengal but it was revived this time. The original concept was introduced in the late 1850s through Rajnarayan Basu's prospectus entitled, *A Society for Promotion of National Feelings Among Educated Natives of Bengal.* The booklet inspired Nabagopal Mitra in 1868 to organize a *Hindu Mela* (or *Chaitra Mela*) for instilling a sense of national pride through exhibition of swadeshi art and recitals for mass awareness at the patronage of the Tagore family. Gaganendranath Tagore, in his inaugural speech, advised Indians to become self-reliant and independent and not to long for help coming from the British.

Rabindranath Tagore established Swadeshi Bhandar (1887) and campaigned for *Palli Sanskar* for the reconstruction of villages. His extended work for making the villagers self-sufficient led to the establishment of Sriniketan in 1921. Acharya P. C. Roy founded Bengal Chemical (1893), Jogesh Chandra Chaudhuri started Indian Store (1901), and Sarala Devi opened Lakshmir Bhandar (1903). Tagore converted Shantiniketan to a model school based on the concept of "ancient ashrams" in 1901. He aimed to impart real man-making education and to promote unity of people of different world-cultures.

A culture of artwork, literature, music and science was promoted. Abanindranath Tagore's typical artworks with swadeshi subjects (e.g. Bharatmata) were unparalleled creations of this period. National feelings grew stronger from the last quarter of the 19th century through Jyotirindranath Tagore's musical dramas. His dramas based on Indian history evoked mass patriotism. P. C. Roy, being a leading scientist, said that if necessary, students would come out leaving test tubes in the labs, that science might wait but not Swaraj. Roy was treated as a revolutionary in the disguise of a scientist. J. C. Bose's work on *Responses of Plants to Physical Stimuli* started in 1906, which was hailed to be of national importance.

Lord Minto, successor of Curzon, planned to educate Muslims and bring them into politics. But he blamed the swadeshi leaders as foolish and impolite, perhaps because British trades declined. He restrained all political movements, and even curbed press freedom. Tilak asked the government to dissociate itself from the commercial aspirations. Activities of Indians in this period coincided with the triumph of Japan over Russia in 1905. It was a threat to the west and indicated the rise of Asian powers. John Morley joined as Secretary of State for India and immediately aimed to win back Indian support by introducing liberal policies. Minto started an advisory council to be backed by the Indian Princes, to return to a durbar style of governance.

Let us return to the Bengal Partition. It became effective on 16 October 1905. A couple of months before that, Lord Curzon engaged in a personality clash with the commander-in-chief of the Indian army, who was in league with H. S. Cotton, who opposed the partition. Curzon resigned because the cabinet did not take part. His resignation was accepted by King Edward VII in August, 1905.

In the 1906 election the liberals came into power. Lord Hardinge became the Viceroy from 1910. He believed that the issues which limited the British imports, originated from the Bengal Partition. He was a liberal and tried to improve British relations with Indians by annulling the Partition, and Curzon's order was revoked during the King's visit to India in 1911. But on 12 December that year, the capital was shifted to Delhi, as a more centrally located and more historical capital. The new capital was constructed to the south of the old city as *New Delhi* according to plans made by Sir Edwin Lutyens and Sir Herbert Baker.

In 1914, Hardinge established the North Eastern Frontier Tract (NEFT) through a tripartite conference (1913–14) in Simla. Participated by plenipotentiaries of Britain, Tibet and China after separating three tracts viz. Ballipara, Laknimpur, and Sadiya in 1912 upon consultation with the local people. China refused to sign the final agreement; but the *McMahon Line* was created separating Tibet and India in 1914. Presently parts south of this line are disturbed due to hostilities between India and China.

3.6 Trends of Congress Politics (1906 – 1914)

The Congress session of 1906 was held in Calcutta. At Tilak's initiative Dadabhai Naoroji came over from London to preside over the session. He proclaimed the "Swaraj" or self-rule in his presidential address. This session changed the direction of Congress politics. Congress urged the government to induct more Indians in executive posts and Indianize both the domestic and foreign subjects. The meeting also approved starting movements for self-rule. Motions for promotion of Swadeshi and boycott of foreign goods were also passed. But moderates like Gokhale and Madan Mohan Malvia could not accept all the resolutions. However, the boycott movements did not stop. Simultaneously, anarchism continued its spread through North America and Europe until 1915.

In 1907 the groupism in Congress widened when the venue of the Congress session shifted to Surat from Poona to avoid Tilak's influence. Rash Behari Ghosh became Congress president with moderates' support, and he was re-elected in 1908 at the Madras Congress. Henceforth the radical composition of Congress tended to decline. Aurobinda Ghosh resigned from politics, and other Bengal members were dispersed after the Alipore Bomb case. Tilak also remained imprisoned until 1914.

At the Allahabad Congress of 1910, moderates proposed writing a constitution of post-Independent India after the British model, and proposed a steady administrative reform. It was resolved to foster intellectual, moral, economic, and industrial development, and secure Indian's rights and responsibilities in administration. By 1911, Gokhale vocalized his demand for developing democratic institutions. The moderates were rejuvenated to become proactive against the administration. During this period the government became occupied restraining anarchism. The Minto-Morley Reform was on its way.

3.7 Anarchist Movements

The subject of anarchist activities is well researched by Manmath Nath Gupta, Hem Chandra Kanungo, Nalini Guha, themselves being revolutionaries. Of late Jesse Cohn, Peter H. Marshall, Maia Ramnath and others wrote books on Indian anarchism. The following paragraphs present only a synopsis of its beginning, and refer to 'police documents' which are not much known. Anarchism was organized in two major phases and is important for Indian history as it caused the British administration to change policies.

The *Anusilon Samity* – the pioneer organisation of the anarchists, was established in 1902 under the leaderships of Pranatha Mitra, Satish Chandra Basu, Jatindra Nath Banerjee, Sarala Devi from Calcutta, and Pulin Behari Das of Dhaka. At some point the Dhaka Samity grew even larger than its parent organization in Calcutta.

The inspiration for starting such an organization came from Bankim's *Vande Mataram* and Swami Vivekananda's *Works*. Aurobindo Ghosh became its mastermind. His brother, Barin Ghosh, and the brother of Swami Vivekananda, Bhupen Dutta, formed a secret organization known as the *Jugantar Group* which was thought to function as the inner circle of the Anusilon Samiti. Even some female members like Sarala Devi gave her support by opening a gym in Ballygunge, and Sister Nivedita who was a patron in disguise.

The term "jugantar" means the end of an era and the beginning of a new one. This new era was famous as the *Agni Yug* (Age of Fire) and became significant in their time by activities of a conglomerate of youths with no less than 40 members. The youths were believers in violence, plundering, and murder. Their purpose was to harass and terrorize the British administration. Barin Ghosh was a front line leader of a group composed of Khudiram Bose, Prafulla Chaki, Jatindranath Mukherjee (Bagha Jatin), and Bipin Behari Ganguly, among others. At the advice of Aurobindo Ghose, a newspaper called *Jugantar Patrika* was first published in April 1906, with the purpose to disseminate the ideology of the Jugantar and spirit of nationalism to help build up a strong national sentiment among masses.

3.7.1 Major Activities in Bengal

Jugantar created a bomb manufacturing facility in a garden house at 32, Monohar Pukur Road, then under Maniktala Police Station, Calcutta within the jurisdiction of Alipore police headquarters. Two days after Khudiram Bose and Prafulla Chaki attempted to assassinate Kingsford, a British Judge, their Muraripukur garden house was raided. Khudiram was only 18 years old when he was hanged on 2 May 1908, and Prafulla Chaki committed suicide. In the Muraripukur raid police arrested 34 members of Jugantar, and put them in Alipur Jail as convicts. They were tried under the Alipore Bomb Case.

One of those arrestees, Naren Goswami of Serampore (not related to the Goswami Raj family) turned out to be an approver, and was subsequently assassinated by his comrades, Kanailal Dutta and Satyendra Nath Bose. As this topic will not be elaborated here, only a part of the story concerning how Narendra Nath Goswami was assassinated has been outlined as follows and based on a Confidential Report dated 31 August 1908.

The arrestees were required to present their witnesses before the judge as and when required. Narendra was assassinated because he revealed the names of Barin Ghosh and Ullaskar Dutta from the witness box, identified Shanti Ghosh involved in bombing a train when the Governor was on board in Chandannagar rail station, and connected the bomb outrage at the Mayor's house, Chandannagar with Charu Chandra Roy – the mentor of Kanailal Dutta, another arrestee. Next day, Naren mentioned names of Aurobindo Ghose and Subodh Chandra Mallick linking them with ongoing anarchist movements.

The following is an excerpt of this report which was compiled by F. L. Halliday, the Police Commissioner, for submission to the Chief Secretary, Government of Bengal. It reads:

> This morning at 7 am undertrial prisoner named Narendra Nath Goswami who had turned approver in the prosecution of some 34 persons pending trial before the Session Judge of Alipore, was shot by two undertrial prisoners named Kanailal Dutta and Satyendra Nath Bose in the jail hospital of Alipur Central Jail.

Narendra, who was kept separate from other prisoners and confined in a European ward, was brought to the jail hospital by an European convict named Mr. Higgins. Narendra had apparently previously arranged to meet at that time with two fellow prisoners in hospital who were there as patients. They were Kanailal Dutta and Satyendranath Bose. It is said in the report that Narendra was apparently approached by the second of the prisoners who had pretended that he also wished to make a statement, and his visit was really in order to get the statement. It was evidently part of the plot to get Narendra in striking distance for it appears that almost immediately on Narendranath's arrival on the landing at the head of the staircase leading to the second story of the hospital, these two persons opened fire on him with two revolvers which they secreted on their prison … Narendranath was shot several places… Narendra fled down the stairs … Kanailal persuaded him to shoot fatally through the back.[14]

The report also mentioned, "Kanailal Dutta is a native of Jantipara, Serampore." Satyendra Nath Bose a native of Midnapur designated as the head of the National volunteer group. Kanailal was a student of Charu Chandra Ray in Chandannagar Duplex College. Narendranath was assassinated with approval of the menters of the Jugantar group.

The police discovered works of Swami Vivekananda almost in all houses during the raids. The British intelligence became engaged to compile secret reports on the Ramakrishna Mission to know why Swamiji was so popular among the anarchists. Dr. Sankari Prasad Basu published some documents of a secret police report in his book entitled, *Vivekananda O Samakalin Bharatbarsha* (Trans. Vivekananda and Contemporary India).[15] Recently Jayanta Sanyal published an excerpt of reports with documents.[16]

Jatindranath Mukherjee, Taraknath Das, Rishikesh Kanjilal, all part of the core group of Jugantar, escaped arrest. Jatindranath went underground and became chief commander of Jugantar. Tarak Das fled to the USA, and

Rishikesh absconded and was later arrested and sent to the Andaman Jail. Rash Behari Bose also left Bengal to shun the bomb case trial, and took a service in Dehradun Forest Research Institute. He was involved with Ghadar movements during the first world war.

3.7.2 International Activities

Following the punitive actions in Bengal, the anarchists were dispersed to England, USA and Germany and worked in coordination with the Bengal group. The following paragraphs highlight how an officer of British India was assassinated in London, with details of Gandhi's Hind Swaraj, and the Second Christmas Day Plot.

An overseas Indian organization was set up as *The Indian National Organization* which was housed at India House, London from 1905. Madan Lal Dhingra, an engineering student in London, assassinated W. H. Curzon Wyllie, an officer, on 1 July 1909 by opening fire from close range. Mr. Wyllie was walking along with a doctor, Cowasji Lakaka. Mr. Lakaha, who tried to thwart the shooter, also died on the spot.

The British government was suspiciously watching the activities of India House, and targeted the organization. It caused many members of the organization to move out of London. A group went to San Francisco from where Mr. Har Dyal founded the Ghadar Party in 1913 with help of Tarak Nath Das. Virendra Nath Chattopadhyay moved to Berlin, and founded the Berlin Committee in 1814. Later the Berlin committee changed its name to the *Indian Independence Committee*. Also, a Paris Indian Society was formed to be used as a training camp for the Indian activists. These organizations worked with close understanding and full coordination with the remnants of the Jugantar group in Calcutta. It was the World War I period, and the Indian organization in Berlin used to receive official support from the German government.

Mr. Mohandas Karamchand Gandhi (Gandhi) came to London in 1909 with a South African Indian delegation when Madan Lal Dingra was on trial after he committed the assassination. Gandhi joined a meeting of the anti-imperialist activists working for clemency of Madanlal who was executed on 17 August 1909. At this time Gandhi was drawn to a long discussion with V. Savarkar, in charge of the Indian London Office. The discussion was about the *practical effectiveness of revolutionary activities*. The discussion affected Gandhi and he was deeply engrossed with the London violence connecting similar incidents happening in India. This thought process helped him to develop arguments against the use of violence as a means to achieve political ends.

During Gandhi's return to South Africa from London, he thought more on the consequences of violence. The ongoing violent activities stirred Gandhi, and influenced him to write some imaginary but argumentative dialogues between himself and an imaginary person. These dialogues concluded that the practice of non-violence and love would be more moral and powerful than any type of violence even if it was for good causes. He also decided not to adopt the western civilization for Indians. Gandhi turned home to become a different person.

Gandhi put his thoughts down in *Hind Swaraj*, which outlines the principles of Gandhism. In chapter 17 he elaborated the concept of passive resistance (albeit *Satyagraha*) for securing rights through personal suffering. He was convinced that soul-power was more powerful than might, even when defeated. And since non-violent resistance originates from self-chastity and practice of truth, it should be free from fear. Gandhi carried forward this conviction for the rest of his life. His view was, however, intellectually debated.

As alluded to, Indian anarchism spread internationally and was linked to the outbreak of the First World War when Germany tried to weaken British power. The Germans did not hesitate to offer help to Indians with arms, money, and even war expertise. Tarak Nath joined the Berlin committee from the USA, and stayed back in Germany. Jitendra Nath Lahiri of Serampore, when he was student at Berkeley, was a friend of Dhan Gopal Mukherjee, a cousin of Jatindra Nath Mukherjee also a student at Berkeley. Lahiri came in contact with the Jugantar through Dhan Gopal.

A plan to instigate a mutiny among the soldiers at Fort William, Calcutta, with overseas help was chalked out. This was *The Second Christmas Day Party Plot* after the first plan foiled. To materialize a second plan, the Ghadar

Party and the Berlin group worked harmoniously. The plot is referred to in several works. The present story is based on the works of Majumdar,[17] Puri,[18] Hopkirk,[19] Hoover,[20] and Gupta.[21] Majumdar writes that this plot was foiled due to the betrayal of some comrades of the Jat regiment.

The Plot aimed to capture Calcutta taking control of Fort William on the Christmas holidays of 1915. Jatindranath Mukherjee was the coordinator. The Governor of Bengal arranged a gala on Christmas day in presence of the Viceroy and high dignitaries. The planners approached the 10th Jat Regiment stationed at Fort William who were engaged for security to participate in their operation. The plan was made well in advance, and necessary Arms and ammunition were procured from the USA at the courtesy of German officials. German interest was to use Indian rebels against the British and Indian rebels used the German support, Britain being their common enemy.

A pan Indian mutiny covering the Andaman Islands to Madras to the United Provinces was also planned. This plan was made jointly by the German military, the Ghadar Party, and the Berlin Committee. Arms would be procured from the USA. The Berlin Committee strategically modified the original plot and the arms shipment was rescheduled to the east coast of India for the Calcutta operation only. The Jugantar group was responsible for collecting the arms from the ship. A German representative reached Calcutta to enquire about the local situation. After discussion with Jatindra, the emissary recommended the German Government to provide support. The War was on. In 1914 Satyen Sen went to the USA to meet Dhan Gopal and establish contact with the Ghadar party. Jitendra Nath Lahiri was inducted as one of the operators in the plot.

From Berlin, Virendra Nath went to Washington to negotiate the arms purchase along with a German military attaché posted in Washington. Spending about $200,000, small arms were collected, and the Ghadar party arranged for the shipment of the arms via San Diego, Java and Burma to the coast of the Bay of Bengal. Shipment was carried by the *S. S. Maverick*, an oil tanker. Jitendra Nath Lahiri was recruited as the link man to release the cargo on the coast of the Bay of Bengal sometime in March of 1915, keeping contact with key persons in Calcutta.

After the *Maverick* passed San Diego, Mr. Karl Helfferich, the German representative, was asked to wait in Batavia. With prior information that the consignment would arrive soon, Jitendra Nath Lahiri proceeded to meet Mr. Helfferich in Batavia along with Narendra Nath Bhattacharyay. They were assigned to escort the ship to the coast at Raimangal (a large river in the Sunderbans) near Calcutta. The ship arrived at Batavia and Jitendra and Narendra were on board to guide the ship. Unexpectedly the news of the arms shipment was revealed to the British embassy in Batavia, and the whole plot fizzled out. Jitendra and Narendra went underground and escaped arrest.

Another plan was made for a mutiny in North India in 1915, making Rash Behari Bose the coordinator. This plan was also leaked. Rashbehari, who had remained underground since the Delhi Conspiracy case of 12 December 1912, escaped to Japan and remained there.

Jatindra Nath Mukherjee who was waiting at Balasore to receive the consignment sent in the Maverick, died there in an encounter with a police force in 1915. The incident was widely circulated thereafter. Aurobindo Ghosh already retired from revolutionary activity after he was acquitted from the Alipore Bomb case of 1909, and Barin Ghosh remained imprisoned in the same case. Jugantar became a leaderless organization, and the remaining anarchist activists went underground. Gandhi's participation in Indian politics would change the direction of the Indian freedom struggle.

3.8 Muslim League

Muslims attempts to come closer to their British rulers began in Bengal from 1855. The British were initially reluctant to Muslim causes suspecting their role in Mutiny and their connections with the Afghans. But Muslims were brought closer to restrain growing nationalism. According to Gilmour, some British administrators were leaning towards Muslims and preferred them to Hindus.[22] Muslims, like the British were a conquering people, and like Christians they had a monotheistic religion.

In 1871 Mayo increased grants for Muslim institutions to promote education and train suitable Muslim men for administration. In 1875 Northbrook went a step further, providing additional privileges through the Education Commissioner. Abdul Latif Khan and Syed Amir Ali, with a western background, who wished Muslims to be educated, later founded the Mohammedan Association in 1877 to take care of Muslims' education and bring them into the political sphere. This was resisted by the orthodox Islamists.

Dufferin also allowed communal class character in administration. To get British favor, Syed Ahmed Khan, founded the Aligarh Mohammedan Anglo Indian College (later named as Aligarh Muslim University) to educate Muslims and keep them aloof from Congress. Badaruddin Tyabji of Bombay was a liberal Muslim with a blend of eastern and western culture who did not discriminate between Hindus and Muslims. He joined Congress and presided over the Madras Congress session in 1887. He also pleaded for Muslims' education.

In 1893 Syed Ahmed Khan formed the *Mohammedan Anglo–Oriental Defence Association to promote* English and Western Sciences for Muslims, thus restricting it for Muslims and Englishmen only. This association received royal favor, but the government had no plan to choose class representation. In 1897 the government of India notified for increasing the proportion of Muslims in subordinate services.

During his tour of eastern Bengal in 1904, Curzon sensed a Muslims' support for partition. Aga Khan in 1906, for the first time, formally appealed for a separate representation of Muslims. To protect Muslim interests, he founded the Muslim League in 1906, restricting the members among Muslims only. Lord Minto indirectly favored establishing the Muslim League. In 1909 the Government allowed a separate electorate for Muslims, though Lord Morley, Secretary of State, initially opposed this arrangement.

Mohammad Ali Jinnah, a Bombay lawyer, joined Congress around 1912. He had studied law in England. He later took interest in the Muslim League when he got disconnected from Congress after Gandhi launched his non-cooperation movements, and eventually became the leader of the Muslim League.

Lord Morley proposed constitutional relaxations in the western sense with a liberalized administration, expecting that it would ameliorate domestic tensions arising from the Bengal Partition to ensure an uninterrupted financial supply. He announced a scheme in 1906 which took shape as the Morley Reform Act which was passed in 1909.

3.9 Minto – Morley Reform Act of 1909

This act allowed limited representation of elected members from Congress, Muslims, and other classes in central government and provincial councils, while keeping the provision of relaxation of the limit for Bengal. Out of a total of 60 seats in Bengal, the British officials retained 33 and the remainder were for elected members including eight from Muslim quota. Nominations in the provincial legislature were allowed to those with clean political backgrounds.

Muslim representation was based on a quota in territorial constituencies, but only larger provinces had separate Muslim representation. The Governor-General was empowered to nominate non-officials from the quota. Only Bengal was allowed a clear elected majority, and four of the elected members were fixed from the European community. Indians were barred from interfering in Army affairs and the Princely States. The provincial councils contained additional quotas for landlords, business communities, and the universities.

This Act provided the first step towards self-governance. It allowed autonomy to provinces keeping the overall power of the central government in the hands of the Governor-General. Lord Crewe, then Secretary of State, said that the bond between India and the British Parliament would be stronger. The Act also made provision for an Indian nominee in the Viceroy's executive council. Sir S. P. Sinha from Bengal was the first Indian to enjoy this privilege. Elections were held with restricted franchise, and Indian members in the extended executive council were given responsibilities but no power. They were allowed to ask questions during the budget session, but only after it was settled.

The Minto-Morley policy allowed constitutional relaxation in some form, but introduced a communal character for the first time. This Act became applicable to entire India with one set of laws, and it provided an opportunity for nationalist politicians to build up a common strategy at all India levels. Congress denounced this reform after seven years during the Lucknow session (1916). The conservatives in British Parliament kept the progress of the Act pending at the advent of War.

3.10 During World War I

In 1900, there was a consolidation of the United States, several major European nations, Russia, Turkey, and Japan that were recognized as imperial powers though they were not united. These nations made treaties to maintain balance of power and ensure peace and prosperity. Colonial powers, in any case, were driven more by economic ambitions growing with advanced technology than by ideals. At the turn of the century, the rivalry among these nations increased, triggering an arms race. A small state in southeastern Europe became a place of tension, when its heir to the throne was assassinated, an event which became the catalyst of the first World War.

After news of the declaration of war reached India in July 1914, the Indian government sought cooperation from Congress and Muslim League. There were pan Islamic anti-British feelings because of Britain's neutrality in the war between Italy and Turkey over Tripoli in 1911, furthermore Indian Muslims were unhappy for annulment of Bengal Partition. But Muslim League finally agreed to cooperate with the British, just as Congress did. A fraction of Congress radicals, however, were against making a commitment for cooperation because Britain kept Indians as dependents even though they claimed to fight for democracy of small nations.

In the Lucknow Congress session of 1916 radicals and moderates came to an understanding and agreed to accept Muslim representation in the provincial legislature. The Muslim League also agreed to participate in Congress led movements for autonomy. Tilak on behalf of Congress signed the pact, and Jinnah representing Muslim League played a key role for this agreement. Thus both the parties obliged the government hoping for further reforms.

The World War reached a critical phase in 1917. Indian soldiers, well over a million, were inducted in the war especially serving the Middle East and partly at French warfronts. Nearly 70,000 of them were engaged in

Mesopotamia against the Ottoman Empire and thousands died in the trenches of France and at Gallipoli due to Churchill's mistaken planning. Their sacrifice was enormous. They fought with so much courage in unfamiliar lands that demands for Indian soldiers rose in every war field. But ultimately Indian soldiers were discriminated against, their efficiency was not rewarded, nor they were given the status they had earned.

Political activities remained suspended to oblige the government. This War demanded excess expenditure from the Raj's coffer as maintenance of the troops was the Raj's responsibility.

Home Rule League: Annie Besant, a sari-clad convert Indian nationalist of 66 years, joined Congress in 1913 from her Madras base. When political activities were kept suspended, she formed the Home Rule League in 1915 after the Irish one, and demanded self-rule for the Indians like for those in Canada and Australia. In addition, she planned to reform Indian society from superstition, the caste systems, and untouchability. She revived political activities by the planned publication of two newspapers - *New India*, and *Commonwealth* as announced in a public meeting. When she was pressed to pay security deposits on her papers under the revised Press Act of 1910 she refused to pay it and was arrested.

Tilak was released in 1914 after six years of imprisonment, and became interested in the Home Rule League movement as it was similar to his Swaraj. He joined the Bombay Provincial Congress of 1916 in Belgaum forgetting earlier disagreements and campaigned throughout Maharashtra with a pledge for the Home Rule to control the purse. Gokhale died in 1915. But Tilak's efforts lasted only for the next two years.

Many Congress members joined Annie Besant's programme. Her arrest in June, 1917 along with B. P. Wadia and George Arundal, instigated thousands of farmers and laborers to agitate for her release. Gandhi saw for the first time that the common masses were united for a national cause. He advised Sankarlal Bankar and Jamnadas Dwarkadas to initiate a signature campaign condemning Annie Besant's arrest. Tagore wrote that Annie Besant's mode of actions were more effective than begging for freedom. Subsequently the Ghadar party extended their base in Punjab.

That year, Edwin Samuel Montagu (1917–22) became the new Secretary of State. Viceroy Lord Chelmsford (1916–21), suspected that disgruntled soldiers were supplying arms to the revolutionaries. Montagu announced that Indian soldiers would be treated as an integral part of the empire, and their cases would be considered. He rejected the 1909 Act, and convinced the cabinet, including Lord Curzon, to further constitutional relaxation to gain Indian cooperation.

Montagu announced his plan to the House of Commons on 20 August 1917, and proceeded to India to examine the Indian situations with His Majesty's permission. Some conservatives in the Parliament advised the Indian administration to make the government an arbiter and objected to including inexperienced Indians in the administration as they did not represent all sections of society.

Montagu along with Lord Chelmsford toured India and received deputations to form political, communal, and liberal bodies before publishing a joint report in July 1918. This Montagu-Chelmsford Report became the Government of India Act 1919, and will be discussed in the next chapter. The war with Germany was won for now.

3.11 Observations

The British Raj began its journey by obliging the EIC with a loan of about £50 million required to restore normalcy in areas disrupted by the mutineers, by deploying troops. The Raj then decided to strengthen the military bases to secure protection of the northwestern border. Different Governor-Generals adopted different policies on border issues. All Viceroys did not follow Queen Victoria's proclamation of 1858 that declared offering a responsible government for the welfare of Indians citizens.

Victoria's declaration was first violated by Lytton. He ignored Indian needs during famine time and in 1876–77, sent Sir Richard Temple (who during 1866 famine in Orissa had imported rice from Burma for relief) to Madras with instructions not to reduce the cost of commodities as relief measures for saving government money. One of the purposes of Lytton's press census was to stop the circulation of news that people were dying of hunger. Shashi Tharoor quotes Henry Nevinson who spelled in 1908 that Curzon had disregarded Indians' feelings in the partition of Bengal and intrigued unrest in India, his speech on Indian mendacity dishonored Indians, and he excluded Indians from public positions.[23]

In this situation Congress set out on a journey without a clearly formulated goal. But the partition of Bengal helped the party to become better organized and become nationalist. It matured through the swadeshi movement which also helped spread nationalist feeling and culture among the non-political middle class. Alongside, an extremist group sprang up with plans to subvert British rule using violence. Though political agendas were diverse, the common goal was to achieve self-rule.

The constitutional relaxation announced was to tame domestic politics. But Indian Muslims were given political identity for the first time to split Indian unity. In the pre-colonial period Hindus and Muslims lived intertwined with a bit of cultural difference which became hardened through this Act. The policy of dividing Hindu-Musolman was a colonial construction, and this policy of divide-and-rule was felt necessary because the soldiers of both communities cooperated so well during the mutiny of 1857.

To mitigate the Afghan problem and safeguard the northwestern border additional combatants and non-combatant troops were recruited following instructions of the London office. All service benefits of the troops were supplied by Indians. Starting from the 1880s, besides protecting the border, the Raj was also committed to bear military expenditures beyond the Indian border to protect the Gulf countries, East Africa including Egypt, and Siam. Military demands consumed many funds. Furthermore, revenue earning declined after the withdrawal of import duty from the late 1870s at Lancashire pressure.

In 1890 when the silver standard was introduced there was loss of exchange, and the drain of money accelerated with the slump of Indian exports for exchange difficulties. The swadeshi movement also constrained British imports. While military expenditure increased at the neglect of human suffering from famines. Thirty thousand troops were prepared in 1902 at the Defence Committee's suggestion.

The military quota was further raised to 300–400,000 apprehending the Russian involvement with the Afghans. When Russian mobility increased from 1904, the Raj's military budget was increased to £2 million per year for 1904–09. (It was scaled down later). In the first year of World War I, Indian revenue supported 80,000 British troops and 230,000 Indians (combatants and non-combatants). Over the war period 1914–18 India provided 800,000 combatants and 400,000 non-combatants. The Raj's expenditure rose from £20 million (1913–14) to £30 million (1917–18). The cost of the war and its preparation destabilized the Indian economy. The imperial government sanctioned credit but remitting money from Britain to India was not possible. In 1918–19 the government of India's commitment rose around £140 million including home charges but excluding the £100 million taken as loan in 1916.[24]

When political activity was suspended during war time, the Raj neglected making long term plans to augment domestic productions including agriculture. R. C. Dutt's recommendations to change land policies were ignored by Curzon. The Indian cotton market in Britain decreased when the American supply was restored after the Anglo-American war. But the declining Indian cotton industry was not protected, only the tax base was increased. A report of the Industrial Commission published in 1918 indicated that India produced raw material but not manufacturing goods. Extension of roads and canals, and improvement of literacy rate necessary to match the growing population were neglected making military expenditure a priority.

The agrarian production was monsoon dependent. Its failure caused famines due to a damaged economy and loss of people's purchasing power. Revenue offices ran with a utilitarian doctrine backed by lack of efforts to increase the domestic economy. Also, the rise of a new political culture directly affected developmental work. Recommendations of the Famine Commission made in 1880 and 1901 were not seriously implemented. Agricultural departments were established up to provincial levels, and a research institution was established in Pusa for improvement of crop yield, but extension work was neglected even having a few elected representatives who gave more attention to political agendas.

The government had to float loans in London to make up the deficit by 1907–09. Minto increased tariffs by 10% in two instalments on industrial output in 1909. In 1910 conditions were better with better exports and a stronger Rupee, but the military expenditure increased speculating a Russian approach.

Apprehending future problems, the government of India (British Raj) asked London in 1916 to decide a definite goal accepting the endowment of British India as an integral part of the Empire.[25] Domestic revenue was raised to 16% in 1916–17 to meet the war time expenditure, it was raised 14% again in 1917–18 and further by 10% in 1918–19 to repay debt. In addition, the government minted vast numbers of silver rupees. But the purchasing power of Indians fell unexpectedly.

The Swadeshi movement put pressure on Raj's coffers. Internal trade declined when the railways were reserved for military purposes. Industrial growth increased with demand for war supplies. But the failure of monsoon in 1918 coupled with excess food requirement for the troops caused famine and epidemics. In this crisis period the Raj needed Indian collaboration in finance and administration to create new sources of earnings at provincial level in order to bring a balance between income and expenditure.

Foreign and domestic investments were restricted to protect British imports. Commercial establishments owned by British traders in Calcutta remained unaffected even after the capital was shifted from Calcutta to Delhi in 1911. J. N. Tata initiated domestic industry at Nagpur in 1887. Cotton manufacturing units picked up in western India. But jute, tea and mining industries remained concentrated in Bengal. At the end of World War I, Bengal accounted for 43% of Rupee capital of all joint stock companies, and 73% of paid up capital of Sterling firms. Bombay was the competing city which was holding 17% of Rupee and Sterling when it was 40% in Bengal. Up to this period the control of manufacturing and the companies were under British directors. Almost all joint-stock tea companies had British directors, and all fifty Jute companies were under British management. Also about 87% of major collieries were under control of British agencies.

Those industries run by British merchants were stable due to better management. But capital from those sources did not percolate to the native population and their purchasing power could not be improved. This period witnessed an inclination of the masses towards the anti -British campaign. A grim financial situation forced Britain to relax the constitutional process again in 1919 to woo Indian cooperation.

References:

1. W. C. Bonnerjee, *Indian Politics. With an Introduction by W. C. Bonnerjee* (Madras: G. A. Natesan & Co., 1898), 7.
2. B. L. Grover, *A Documentary Study of British Policy Towards Indian Nationalism 1885–1909* (Delhi: National Publications, 1967), 181.
3. Sivanath Sastri, *Ramtanu Lahiri o Tatkalin Bangosamaj* (Kolkata: Reprint Rubi Publishers, 2019), 147–48. (first published in 1903).
4. James Lawrence, *Raj: The Making and Unmaking of British India* (New York: St. Martin's Press, 2019), 356.
5. "The 20th Eventful Century: Forging The Modern Age 1900." II Series *Readers Digest* (Pleasantville, NY: The Reader's Digest Association, 2000), 99.
6. James Lawrence, Ibid, 349.
7. G. K. Gokhale, G. A. Natesan (ed.), *Speeches of Gopal Krishna Gokhale* (Madras: G. A. Natesan, 1916), 929.
8. Devaprasad Goswami, *Twelve Great Men of Hindustan* (Kolkata, 2020), 156.
9. R. S. Mehrotra, *The Emergence of the Indian National Congress* (Delhi: Vikas Publications, 1971), 11–12.
10. Refer https://www.newworldencyclopedia.org/entry/George_Nathaniel_Curzon.
11. George Nathaniel Curzon, *Speeches of Lord Curzon of Kedleston*, Part 1 (Calcutta: Government Print, 1900), 34.
12. Ishita Banerjee-Dube, *A History of Modern India* (Cambridge: Cambridge University Press, 2015), 225.

13. A. B. Purani, *The Life of Sri Aurobindo* (Pondicherry: Sri Aurobindo Ashram, 1958), 37–42.
14. Confidential report No. 1876-C, dated 31st August 1908, preserved as *Assassination of Narendra Nath Goswami* in the Bengal Government file on *Assassination*. Refer: *Documents in the Life of Sri Aurobindo*. https://incarnateword.in/documents/assassination-of-naren-goswami
15. Sankari Prasad Bose, *Vivekananda O Samakalin Bharatbarsha* (Kolkata: 1955) (Transl.: Vivekananda and Contemporary India).
16. Jayanta Sanyal, "Goyenda Report O Ramakrishna Mission, Kichu Aprakasita Tatta," *Udbodhan*. No. 8 (2021–22), Swami Krishnananda Ed., 635–43. (Transl.: Ramakrishna Mission in Confidential Report-a Few Unpublished Documents).
17. Ramesh Chandra Majumdar, *History of the Freedom Movement in India* (Calcutta: Firma K. L. Mukhopadhyay, 1971), Vol. II: 281–82.
18. Harish Kumar Puri, "Revolutionary Organization: A Study of the Ghadar Movement," *Social Scientist* 9, no. 2/3 (1980), 53.
19. Peter Hopkirk, *On Secret Service East of Constantinople* (Oxford: Oxford University Press, 2001).
20. Karl Hoover, "The Hindu Conspiracy in California, 1913–1918," *German Studies Review*, 8 no.2 (1985), 245–261.
21. Amit Kumar Gupta, "Defying Death: Nationalist Revolution in India, 1897–1938," *Social Scientist* 25 no. 9–10 (Sept–Oct 1979), 3–27.
22. David Gilmour, *The British in India: A Social History of the Raj* (New York: Farrar, Straus and Giroux, 2018), 404.
23. Shashi Tharoor, *An Era of Darkness: The British Empire in India* (New Delhi: Aleph Book Company, 2016), 86.
24. B. R. Tomlinson, "India and British Empire 1880–1935." *The Indian Economic & Social History Review*, 12 no. 4 (1975), 350 (337–380).
25. S. D. Waley, *Edwin Montagu: A Memoir and an Account of his Visits to India* (Bombay: Asia Publishing House, 1964), 132.

CHAPTER 4

British Raj 1919 – 1926

Two controversial Acts were passed in the same year. One of those being repressive resulted in a massacre in Punjab. This chapter tells the story how Gandhi used the tragedy to enter into national politics and how he organized Congress into a mass organization while avoiding holding any political office. It also depicts how the Swaraj Party was formed and continued with its political agenda bypassing original Congress resolutions, and describes how anarchism returned during this period.

4.1 Government of India Act 1919

A new Act, proposed by Edwin S. Montagu and Lord Chelmsford, came into operation after the report on Indian Constitutional Reform was placed before the Lower House in summer of 1919 which passed in Parliament in December 1919 as the Government of India Act, 1919. This Act introduced a dyarchy (co-rule) in provincial administration. At the executive level, councillors were selected by the Crown, and at a popular level, ministers were chosen by the Governor from elected Indian members. Crucial portfolios like police, justice, land-revenue and finance were reserved to executives, while departments such as local self-government, education, public health, and public works were administered by elected Indian members. The purpose was to improve the involvement of Indian associations in different branches of administration. It ensured that apart from Hindus, minorities such as Muslims, Sikhs and Christians could also take part in the legislature, but only a maximum of 250 Indians per province had the right to vote. The Viceroy was given authority to nullify votes, if required. Montagu said that this Act was necessary to increase liberalization,[1] and constitutional reform. At the same time, the government retained the Rowlatt Act passed in March 1919. This decree —which gave government powers to make arrests without any trial— led to the Amritsar massacre. In the preamble, the colony (The Raj) was renamed as British India to segregate the Princely States at the convenience of the Parliament to legislate the States separately.

The Government of India Act 1919 for the first time gave liberty to provinces for better management. It empowered Governors to appoint ministers and abolished formal division of power between the center and the provinces. This allowed provinces to earn revenues. Depending on their net earnings, each province would then contribute 40–60% of their annual income to the center. This decentralized system allowed a much needed expansion of the tax base.

The proportion of elected members was raised to 70% in some provinces (Bengal had as many as 139 elected members). Provinces were given authority over education, agriculture, excise, and local self-governments by recruiting ministers from elected members in legislative council and removable by vote by that council. Departments like police, justice, finance were placed under administration of the Governor's Executive Council to be appointed by His Majesty's government. The Act included an apparent parliamentary system but the administrative power of the governors effectively increased. An election was scheduled in 1920.

Instead of making a single electoral list for all Indians, Muslims electorates were extended, and seats for Sikhs, European and Anglo-Indian, native Christians were reserved. Furthermore, a provision was included for nominated representatives of the depressed class. For the Madras and Bombay Provinces, non-Muslim seats were reserved for non-Brahmins to satisfy the Justice Party, which was dominated by the Nairs who opposed Annie Bessant's connection with the higher caste people. The ultimate control was retained by the Secretary of State.

The post of Statutory Commissioner was created with responsibility to evaluate the performance of this scheme. In 1927 a Royal Commission was appointed under chairmanship of Sir John Simpson to ascertain direction for the next stage of constitutional advancement.

The Congress resolution in the special Bombay session of 1918, presided over by Syed Hasan Imam, criticized the proposed introduction of this Act because it was inadequate for self-rule and for its hybrid nature. Congress opposed the introduction of social divisions and demanded the end of the Bengal Partition. It opposed giving Muslims a separate electorate as it advocated a united India irrespective of caste and creed. The retention of the Rowlatt Act was also opposed.

4.2 Hindu Mahasabha

Some Congress members were urging for the protection of Hindu rights after the Bengal Partition and for giving Muslims a separate electorate. The Hindu issue was placed before the Allahabad Congress of 1910. A skeleton of Hindu unity existed as *Punjab Hindu Sabha* from 1909. In the next few years similar Hindu Sabhas came up in UP, Bihar, Central Provinces and Bengal. Following some preparatory sessions, the *All India Hindu Sabha* (Hindu Mahasabha) was established at the Kumbh Mela at Haridwar in 1915 where influential Congress members like Madan Mohan Malviya (founder of the Banaras Hindu University), Navin Chandra Rai, Lala Lajpat Rai and others, participated. They made provisions for its function as a unit within Congress, and the special Congress session in Lahore (1921) called for education and economic development of Hindus.

From the late 1920s, Mr. V. D. Savarkar, a critic of the secular outlook of Congress, became an influential figure in the Hindu Sabha. He had been jailed with his brother in the Andamans for his involvement in various conspiracies to overthrow the government. After his transfer to Ratnagiri Jail he developed his thoughts around Hindu Rule (*Hindutva*) which was published just before his release in 1924. He opposed the Lucknow Pact between Congress and Muslim League of 1916, and discontinued his Congress membership. Savarkar gave a new identity to this Hindu organization when he became its prime leader over the next decade by proposing *Hindu Rashtra: the Hindutva*. He influenced the formation of *Rashtriya SwayamSevak Sangh* (RSS) in 1925 which developed into a nationwide network as an apolitical organization. In Congress those who were believers of a composite culture continued to be in majority and the younger generation did not favor any special right for Hindus.

4.3 Gandhi and the Indian National Congress

Gandhi returned to India from London in 1891, trained in Law from the Inner Temple. He was shy and not a fluent speaker. His London circle was among middle class theosophists like Edwin Arnol, the former principal of Deccan College, Poona, who needed Gandhi's help in translating the Gita from Sanskrit. Gandhi also met Annie Besant, member of the Theosophical Society. Back in India he could not settle in law practice either in Rajkot or Bombay, being insulted by a white court agent. He realized that the Englishmen in India hated the natives.

He then sailed for Natal, South Africa in 1893 with a job with an Indianized firm. Gandhi became a well-known political figure in South Africa (1894–96) for his activism against the discrimination of non-white people. Gandhi was also imprisoned in Natal along with hundreds of Indians in 1913. After twenty years in South Africa he returned to India in January of 1915. At that time the anarchist movement was in decline. During the First World War, Gandhi cooperated with the British. He even helped collect funds and recruits for the army. Now in India, he was shocked to experience that Indians were victims of the high price of food grains which was beyond the reach of poor people. The War caused the price index to almost double between 1913 and 1918. The peasantry became extremely impoverished, and many farmers were oppressed by European Indigo planters.

Out of his tiresome labours in South Africa and bitter experience in India, Gandhi set up Sabarmati Ashram in his home state near Ahmedabad. It became the experimental field of his theory of *Hind Swaraj* – a place to practice a simple lifestyle based on vows of truth and non-violence using indigenous consumables. He taught *Buniadi* education in a model school for versatile training of rural people to make them suitable for self-employment.

Gandhi also initiated a national education programme in the vernacular. Alongside he developed programmes on animal breeding, agriculture and textiles, along with preaching *satyagraha* —non-violent resistance— based on ancient Indian culture and Buddhist thought. During 1917–18, he used the unique technique of producing hand-spun and hand-woven clothes from natural fibers (*khadi*). Each resident of the ashram was required to participate by performing manual labour.

Gandhi traveled to Indian core-regions to meet peasants and industrial laborers to learn of their real condition, and to survey the land. Government was skeptical, but allowed his tours. During 1917–18 he was involved with the indigo farmers' movements in Champaran (Bihar), small farmers' movements of Khedia (Gujarat), and a labor movement in Ahmedabad. Gandhi got some dedicated and educated followers like Rajendraprasad from Bihar, J. B. Kripalani from Andhra Pradesh, and Mahadev Desai, Sankarlal Bankar, and Vallavbhai Patel from Gujarat. They surveyed and collected data on the 8,000 farmers oppressed by indigo planters in Champaran, and convinced the appropriate authorities that the peasants were being oppressed. The Indigo planters were forced to quit their malpractice.

Gandhi also became involved with the labor movements in an Ahmedabad mill owned by one of his friends. He started fasting in sympathy with the starving laborers. It was his first and experimental hunger strike in India. He arranged for tribunals to end the laborers' exploitation, and helped them in their demands for an increased bonus to compensate for inflation. These initial experimental movements were kept limited in small places.

Annie Besant's Home Rule movement —which had grown strong through the involvement of many Congress members— attracted Gandhi, but he did not get involved directly. However, he did arrange to collect funds to support her movement through innovative ideas. Until then Gandhi had only limited access to Indian politics.

The purpose for which the Rowlatt Act was promulgated shocked Gandhi, and he proposed to oppose this Act by organizing satyagraha at an all India level. Without being certain of its outcome, Congress approved his proposal. In his first major political undertaking Gandhi was cautious to limit the extent of the movement. The date was fixed on April 6, 1919 – which was a Sunday. His was a call for a *hartal* (strike) only for those who would work on Sunday.

4.4 The Rowlatt Act and Amritsar Massacre

The Rowlatt Act of March 1919 allowed certain political activists to be tried without juries, and permitted internment of suspects without trial. Press-freedom was also curbed and mass assembly restricted. As a new entrant, Gandhi lodged protests against the Rowlatt Act, which he called a draconian ruling. He started the satyagraha movement as stated before. It gave the future direction in his political career.

Gandhi was new but this movement covered a wider area. Though his first major experiment with public involvement –the Rowlatt Satyagraha– was unsuccessful, it was identified as the largest anti British protest after 1857 and it was typified as non-violent. Even after Gandhi's persistent efforts to attract people from the main cities, only a few organizations like his own Samity in Bombay, a group from the Home Rule League, and a small Muslim organization participated in the hartal.

His non-violent protest was a call for suspending all business matters for 6 April, which created an unprecedented situation for the administration. This Sunday strike received support in limited areas in Delhi, Bombay and Lahore. Simultaneously at a few places mass fasting began. In any case the movements were not adequately organized, its participants were freshers and few in number, and not properly trained. Gandhi later admitted that calling upon people with 'insufficient training' was a blunder. Two nationalist leaders, Dr. Saifuddin Kitchlew, a Muslim, and Dr. Satyapal, a Hindu, who addressed meetings on 9 April responding to Gandhi's call in Amritsar were arrested, and interned at Dharamsala the following day.

Their arrest triggered a mass agitation in Amritsar. Punjab, was already under special surveillance prohibiting mass assembly because of the Ghadarites. Large areas were under Martial Law with a military presence. On 11 April some 600 troops arrived to quell the agitation. Abiding by a proclamation of restricting any assembly, the city was apparently peaceful.

On 13 April, being unaware of the prohibitions, some 10–15,000 people from the surrounding villages assembled in Jallianwala Bagh, Amritsar, to observe Baisakhi day festival. They were in a festive mood. The place had only one main exit with three sides blocked by buildings.

Brigadier General Reginald Dyer, without knowing the reason for this assembly, ordered to block the only main exit by deploying Indian armed forces, and to start firing indiscriminately on the gathering without warning. People could not escape. About 380 of them were killed (an accepted figure), and thousands injured by some 1600 rounds firing in just 10 minutes – an extraordinary shoot rate. It was a deliberate brutal killing and confirmed that the colonial ruler failed to consider the value of Indian lives.

Though there was widespread outrage everywhere, the administrative inquiry of this massacre was ineffective. British cabinet was reluctant, and the punishment of the commanding officer was nominal. His dismissal was upheld by the House of Commons. Dyer never showed remorse while describing his actions before an enquiry committee. Even some British people honored the officer. *The Morning Post* on 9 July opened a fund for Dyer as reward for his stern measure (Lawrence, 1998)[2] in which Indian donations also flew. The brutality of the subsequent martial law caused mass upheaval throughout India; people responded to the action with anger. Rabindranath Tagore renounced his knighthood.

The Rowlatt Act was not implemented thereafter. Jawaharlal Nehru on behalf of Congress went to Amritsar to meet the public and enquire about the incident. Portions of his diary recorded the presence of 67 bullet marks on a part of the wall; and the conversation of Dyer, overheard by Nehru while he was traveling back in the same compartment, was also recorded. Nehru wrote that "he (Dyer) felt like reducing the rebellious city to a heap of ashes, but he took pity on it and refrained."[3]

The Congress session that convened in Amritsar in December 1919 condemned the brutal massacre, lodging a strong protest against the administrative indefectibility. Gandhi was unanimously accepted by seniors in the party. In the meeting a group of Congress members favored the

1919 Act viewing that its harmful clauses could be rejected. Others were suspicious about the possibility of any real reform. This meeting could not decide on a specific resolution and future directive. The party had to be reorganized from the level it was running during the swadeshi movements.

4.5 Congress becoming a mass organization

During these troubled times, in a special session at Calcutta in September 1920, presided by Lala Lajpat Rai, Congress resolved to non-payment of taxes and *triple boycotts* of the legislature, law court, and educational institutions. The next Congress session of December 1920 held in Nagpur brought together many leaders like Motilal Nehru and C. R. Das, Mohammad Ali Jinnah, Bipin Behari Pal, Lala Lajpat Rai, Madan Mohan Malaviya, Maulana Abul Kalam Azad. Some Europeans like A. O. Hume and some British Labor Party members were also present. At Nagpur, Gandhi was projected as a future leader. Chittaranjan Das, as the president of Bengal Congress, also joined hands with Gandhi.

Gandhi took responsibility to rewrite the Congress's constitution. The new constitution aimed to take the party to the masses. A four ana (quarter of a Rupee) membership campaign started to woo the people and raise party funds. Congress was decentralized down to village level. For the convenience of separate linguistic groups, the organization of Madras was split into Tamil and Telugu linguistically. The Congress Working Committee (CWC) became the supreme decision making body with 15 members recruited from the regions to overcome the tendency of Bengal and Bombay to dominate. The most significant change was that the immediate goal of Congress was set to establish Swaraj, cutting all ties with the British, and rejecting earlier provisions for self-government within the British empire. When asked for clarification, Gandhi said, "Swaraj was self-government within the empire if possible and outside if necessary." Another resolution pointed out that the scope of reform in the new Act was inadequate. This meeting also criticized British attitudes towards Turkey.

When Indian Muslims started the Khilafat movement in protest against liquidation of the Turkish Empire, Gandhi advised Congress members to stand by the Muslims and support their cause. Gandhi's gesture attracted all communities to support Congress movements. Meanwhile the elections of 1920 had begun, and Congress resolved to boycott legislation. Non-cooperation movements, however, continued campaigning on the Jallianwala Bagh issue.

Surendranath Banerjee defied the election boycott, and his men won many provincial seats in the provincial elections. Muslim League remained neutral. Some regional parties in Madras and Punjab emerged successfully. Also a reasonable section of Congress, including Motial Nehru and C. R. Das was not in favor of boycotting the legislation as they had a different strategy to be in the councils.

The plan of Gandhi was to paralyze the administration from within the constitution, using non-violence, satyagraha, and demonstrations. Not all agreed that non-violent protest was the way ahead. M. A. Jinnah called satyagraha a political anarchy, and left Congress in 1920, though he apparently accepted constitutionalism. From 1915 to 1920 Gandhi gathered a large number of followers, especially from the peasantry. Many lawyers from the main centers Calcutta, Bombay and Madras, supported Gandhi for his focus on the inclusion of the masses. Tilak expired in 1920.

In March 1921 the khadi campaign helped collect about one crore Rupees as donation in the Tilak Swaraj Fund following a resolution during the Vijayawada conference. About fifty lakhs of Indians took Congress memberships. From then onwards, khadi-made clothes became a symbol of the Indian freedom movement. In Madurai, Madras, Gandhi received complaints that khadi clothes were costly. He then started using his khadi attire of optimum lengths, which he maintained for the rest of his life.

The strength of Congress increased everywhere, however the response in Punjab and Madras was relatively less. A galaxy of lawyers joined Congress and a good number of them were whole timers giving up their professions. They influenced their practicing colleagues in British law courts. From this time, litigations were settled by arbitration under Congress control, resulting in the government losing the court fees. Campaigns for mass-scale temperance reaching remote places caused a fall of earning in excise. It became so bad that some provincial governments like Bihar began promoting liquor sales to boost provincial income.[4]

During the post War period, when the majority of Indians were pushed below the poverty level, Gandhi appealed to ten million Congress members to create a fund of ten million Rupees to meet expenses under various heads for a relief campaign. Students and women joined the campaign reaching remote villages to promote khadi to help rural people to be self-employed by boycotting foreign textiles. Making the villagers self-sufficient through the khadi industry, and bringing men and women under Congress umbrella was Gandhi's great contribution from the start. Many students left government aided schools to enrol in nationalist schools opened in Nagpur, Poone, Calcutta, Dacca, Patna, Banaras, and many other towns.

After the Champaran movement in Bihar, peasants rallied behind the non-cooperation movement from the early 1920s. These movements spread to the United Provinces, Gujarat, and other places. Rajasthan's Bhil movement, the Mahishya peasants' movement in Midnapur, Bengal, and Orissa's tribal movements extending to Guntur in the South, were all most remarkable. In most places people boycotted oppressive landlords and union boards demanding reduction of taxes. *Kishan Sabha*, an organized forum, was established at the end of the 1920s. Even people from the Princely States like Alwar and Baroda organized movements, though Congress was reluctant to intervene in these States until 1938.

A younger generation started joining Congress in the 1920s. Future leaders like Jawaharlal Nehru, Sardar Ballavbhai Patel, Subhas Chandra Bose, among others joined. Jawaharlal Nehru, a student of Harrow school and Trinity College in Cambridge, was not comfortable with his profession as a lawyer and decided to join politics. Soon after, in 1920, this radical young man became a prominent leader. On 21 May 1922 he was imprisoned in Lucknow jail for 21 months. Jawaharlal was a voracious reader, and he finished six (out of seven) volumes of Gibbon's *Decline and Fall of the Roman Empire*, while in custody in Lucknow.[5]

Subhas Chandra Bose was keenly watching Aurobindo Ghosh's freedom struggles as a school student. After going through the works of Vivekananda he was motivated to engage himself for the service of his motherland. As a student of Calcutta Presidency College he was punished for lodging a protest against a teacher who had an anti-Indian feeling. Bose was one of the toppers in his ICS examination, but gave up his career and responded to the call for freedom of his motherland. He joined Congress as a leader of the youngsters' wing in Calcutta in 1921.[6]

Vallab Bhai Patel, raised in the countryside of Gujarat, was a practicing lawyer. Later, he became Bar-at law. He emerged in political life when he won an election in 1917, led a no-tax campaign in 1918, and joined Congress at Gandhi's influence abandoning his professional life. Along with many other dedicated workers this trio was significant for India's freedom struggle.

Let us back to the main text. On 30 July 1921, *The Bombay Chronicle* advertised, "Boycott Foreign clothes – Bonfire of Foreign clothes" on the front page. It was an open public invitation to attend the meeting at the Elphinstone Mill, Bombay, where Gandhi would raise money in the Tilak Memorial Fund. People were asked to come in khadi attire and bring foreign clothes for a bonfire. This really took place on 31 July 1921.

Edward the Prince of Wales, came for a tour of India in an unusually fraught time, in October, 1921. Upheaval in Punjab had not died down. Setting out from Bombay, the Prince was due to visit Calcutta, Madras and Karachi. He arrived on 26 October accompanied by his cousin Lord Louis Mountbatten, a naval commander. (It was purely coincidental that Mountbatten in August 1947 would terminate the British rule). On the same day Gandhi spoke before a huge gathering in Bombay. All the streets were empty and all establishments were closed. Foreign clothes were burnt publicly.

Anglo-Indians and several of the Bombay Parsi community who were loyal to the Raj, assembled to welcome the Prince got engaged in a clash with nationalist youth. Sixty persons died during the police firing that followed. Gandhi fasted for three days to ameliorate the situation. The reception of the Prince in Bombay and other places was clearly not favorable.

The Prince read the message of the King, "for years –it may be for generations– patriotic and royal Indians have dreamed of Swaraj for their motherland. Today you have the beginning of Swaraj within my Empire and widest scope and ample opportunities for progress to the liberty which my other dominions enjoy."[7] This message was the practical inauguration of the shift of British policy by a British authority by pronouncing "Swaraj" (self-rule) for the first time. From 1921 Gandhi conducted a series of meetings asking the government to ease poverty, end untouchability, and to allow self-rule.

Early 1922, when Lord Reading was the Viceroy (1921–22), a cabinet meeting in London apprehended that Raj was falling apart, and expressed worries about the Bombay government's reluctance to arrest Gandhi to control the disorder. Gandhi was arrested on 10 March 1922 on sedation charges for his article published in *Young India*, and imprisoned for six years. However, he was released early in 1924 for a much needed surgery.

4.6 The Chauri Chaura incident

From 1921 the administration was unexpectedly confronted with non-cooperation movements, Khalifat issues, widespread communal riots during Muharram celebrations, and police firings. There was the Muslim Moplah's revolt in Kerala in August killing hundreds of Hindus, and some violent outbreaks were not uncommon in that period. Specifically, the Chauri Chaura incident of Gorakhpur in the United Provinces, turned out to be an undisciplined expression of mass commotion in 1922.

On 5 February 1922, non-cooperation movements began in Gorakhpur following the pan India Congress programme. The participants, mainly farmers, clashed with police who opened fire. The farmers became so violent that they burnt alive 22 policemen in their camp. This was understood to be a mass retaliation against the Amritsar massacre. Gandhi was deeply ashamed of this brutality and he unilaterally suspended all movements. Pan-Indian movements had spread over the tribal belts and rural areas, created laborers' movements against the Railway authorities in 1921–22, and peasants' movements who agitated against the zamindars from eastern Bengal up to Awadh. A section of Congress opposed Gandhi's unilateral decision to call off the movements, just as non-cooperation was gaining momentum. Even non-political leaders did not accept this decision. The Khalifat issue also lost significance after Mustafa Kemal Pasha was brought to power in Turkey.

At the Gaya Congress of December 1922, at the presidency of Chittaranjan Das, the issue of withdrawing the movements was discussed. From his prison Gandhi refused to rescind. It led to immediate segregation of extremists in the party. They set up a revolutionary party, called the *Hindustan Republican Association* under the leadership of Jadu Gopal Mukherjee and Sailendra Nath Sanyal. The second phase of the rise of anarchism was led by this association. The Hindu Mahasabha unit in Congress was already dissatisfied with the Muslim quota. They opposed the Lucknow Pact. Gandhi reasoned that he did not want to continue movements with masses who were not trained.

Furthermore, some liberal moderates who opposed the Congress agenda of boycotting legislations, formed the Swaraj Party within Congress in 1923. Led by Chittaranjan Das (C. R. Das) and Motilal Nehru, the Swarajists proceeded with an alternative agenda defying Congress resolutions. Supporters of the Swaraj Party were the *pro-changers*. On the other side stood men who were close to Gandhi, like Rajagopal Acharya, Rajendra Prasad, Sardar V. Patel, Maulana Abul Kalam Azad, who supported boycotting the legislature. They were called the *no-changers*. The pro-changers gained prominence while the no-changers were silenced without an agenda during Gandhi's imprisonment.

4.7 The Swaraj Party

The Swaraj Party planned to enter into provincial and central legislative councils to bring changes, or boycott it from within the legislature if they failed. Chittaranjan Das, a relic of the Bengal Renaissance and the sitting Congress President, resigned on moral grounds as he defied the Congress agenda. He was a lawyer with nationwide popularity because he successfully advocated for the release of Aurobindo Ghose from the Alipore Bomb Case. However, both the "no" and "pro" changers were against the dyarchy (of the Act 1919). The pro-changers advocated an agenda to strategically amend the clauses of the Act 1919, if elected, or boycott from within the legislature as alluded to. Lajpat Rai, M. M. Malviya, M. R. Jayakar, some men from the South, and Tilak's followers openly supported the pro-changers. In 1923, both the fractions merged by adopting another resolution that permitted willing Congress members to enter the administration.

At their Allahabad conference (Dec 1822 to Jan 1823), the Swarajists proposed their constitution. C. R. Das became the president and Matilal Nehru secretary. They restarted mass contacts for political, constitutional, social, and economic reforms and to bring communal unity, and promised to reframe the laws from within the council targeting the *dominion status*. However, they adhered to Gandhi's non-violence and non-cooperation. Their goal was to take the constitution beyond 1919 by winning elections in the Legislative Council and Assembly.

The Swarajists won with a sweeping majority, and gained control over the government. They captured 42 seats out of 101 in the Central Legislative Council and absolute majority in Central Provinces. In Bengal, Assam and UP, they did fairly well, and emerged as a distinct group within Congress. The Swarajists also formed a coalition with moderates and Muslim nationalists in Bengal.

To keep their election promises, the Swaraj Party reduced salt taxes, and excise duties on salt and cotton were repealed. The railway fares were lowered, and provincial contributions to the center reduced. They helped national industries by imposing taxes on imported goods. No-changers also performed well in local self-governments of major cities. They kept promises, and played fair roles in assemblies where they won. The campaign for khadi and tax imposition on foreign goods continued, which caused the British market to languish.

In Bengal the Swaraj Party allowed Muslims a proportional representation in the Council. In a joint meeting with no-changers this pact was replaced by the Indian National Pact (graft). Another pact was made with Muslim League of Punjab in 1924. These agreements were made to strengthen their fight while retaining communal harmony, though over time these ideals failed.

When the administrative accomplishment in several provinces was found unsatisfactory, the funds to pay the salary of ministers of those provinces were withheld by the center. This caused resentment in the "diarchy" of the Central Provinces and Bengal. The Swaraj Party was unable to work autonomously and the authority of elected members was limited to the overriding certifying powers of Viceroy and the Governors. A plan of C. R. Das, then Mayor of Calcutta Corporation, for improving living conditions of the slum dwellers of Calcutta by setting up a municipal bank, was blocked in 1927. C. R. Das also failed to take action when Subhas Chandra Bose was arrested without trial in 1924.

The double administration of co-rule clearly failed to solve India's governmental problems. Motilal Nehru later called an all party conference to amend the 1919 Act and to promote the idea of *dominion* as a regular constitutional status. He received support from the Muslim League. Some British parliamentarians also conceded that giving India dominion status might be a better option. An enquiry committee was set up to find out the defects in Act 1919 that inhibited the dominion. Motilal Nehru was included in this committee, but he declined. The Government concluded that the overall performance of the Act was satisfactory, and the new Conservative government of 1925 declined to make any new promise on reforms for the next ten years.

Subhas Chandra Bose, returned from England and joined C. R. Das in politics. He became Deputy Mayor of the Calcutta Corporation, and formed the *Bengal Volunteers*, an organization to attract a new generation to national politics. It prospered among the youths of Bengal. A fraction of the Dacca group planned for the *Writers' Building Mission*.

When Gopinath Saha was arrested in Calcutta (see below), the administration requested C. R. Das to help end the terrorism. He agreed to cooperate with certain conditions, but died suddenly in 1925, and the government reverted to meet any demand. The Swaraj Party also suffered with his death when some leaders left the party pursuing other engagements.

In July 1925, Lord Birkenhead, Secretary of State, rejected the claims of nationalists. He stated that India as an entity was as obscure as Europe, the nation was never united nor would be in the future; whether there would be any nation only time would tell. However, at the same time he urged critics to draw up a constitution that would satisfy general Indians. Motilal Nehru accepted this challenge as the leader in the Central Legislative Council.

In September 1925, he agreed to work on constitutional amendments and administrative reformation of government in consultation with other Indian parties. He received support from all parties, including the Muslim League. Elected Muslim members also supported his earlier amendments for calling a Round Table Conference of delegates to recommend a scheme for establishing a responsible government in India as a dominion.

Gandhi had taken political retirement between 1924–28, because Congress popularity declined after withdrawing the movements. Several phased communal riots broke out for minor and unwarranted causes. After the demise of C. R. Das, the Congress took over the responsibility of the Swaraj Party's agenda. Otherwise, between 1923 and 1925 Congress activities were restricted to Vallabhbhai Patel's *Borsad Satyagraha* in Gujarat against taxation to cover police expenses, and the *Vaikom Satyagraha* organized in the Princely State of Travancore to oppose growing untouchability. Patel also initiated the *Bardoli Satyagraha*, in 1928 when taxes were increased by 22%. He succeeded in reducing taxes utilizing trained Paridar participants. During the Calcutta Congress of 1928, *Purna Swaraj* was demanded by young members. Gandhi was encouraged to return to politics.

4.8 Anarchist Movement – Second Phase

The second phase of anarchists' activities was begun by Gopi Nath Shah in 1924 and continued through 1926 during the tenure of Lord Irwin.

4.8.1 Gopi Nath Saha

Born in 1905, at Serampore, Hooghly, West Bengal, Gopinath (according to another source he was born at Santipur, Nadia) came in touch with local anarchists as a school student, and left the school to join them. He became associated with the Hindustan Republican Association and began working in different places. He was assigned to assassinate Charles Tegart, an infamous police officer posted in Bengal. In 1923 Tegart was the head of the detective department of the Calcutta police, and involved in rounding up a revolutionary group working under the leadership of Jatindra Nath Mukherjee at Balasore in 1915. He shot Jatindra in the encounter who died the next day.

Gopinath was prepared to assassinate Tegart, a cruel and uncompromising officer. But Gopinath had never seen him before. He only knew that the officer was a red headed Irishman. Based on information Gopinath was waiting outside the police headquarters on 12 January 1924 for Tegart's arrival. Soon as he saw a red headed man passing near the headquarters, he shot him erroneously. The victim however was another red headed white man, Mr. Ernest Day, whom he mistook for Tegart. Gopinath was arrested and tried.

When asked to defend his case, he answered in defiance, "I do not seek any mercy; I wish that the court will give me the death penalty because the action will further intensify the movement; and every drop of my blood will sow seeds of revolutionaries in every house." He confessed he wanted to kill Tegart. When hanged in March, 1924, Gopinath kissed the knot with a smile.

Subhas Chandra Bose, then Deputy Mayor of the Calcutta Corporation, was impressed by Gopinath's fearless devotion, and his final words touched him deeply. When Gopinath's clothes were sent from the jail after his final rites, Subhash first touched those.[8] He subsequently moved a resolution in the Provincial Congress meeting in honor of Gopinath's martyrdom. A portion of the resolution read "... it's respectful homage to the patriotism of Gopinath Saha...," he was made to rewrite, because Gandhi disliked the word "patriotism" qualifying Gopinath. Gandhi's strong anti-violent sentiments in Gopinath's case disillusioned a section of the party, and as the amended resolution was put to vote, Gandhi's supporters won by only a few votes. Soon after Subhas was arrested on 30 April under the false charge that he was connected with the revolutionary party. He was deported to Burma until 1927. A police search found no evidence of his involvement with Gopinath.

4.8.2 Benoy, Badal and Dinesh

The trio, Benoy Krishna Bose (1908–1930), Badal Gupta (1912–1930), and Dinesh Chandra Gupta (1911–1931) were born near Dacca, who became members of the Bengal Volunteer Force formed by Subhas Chandra Bose. They attended the Calcutta Congress of 1928 where the resolution for complete independence was moved. When Benoy was a student of Mitford

Medical College, Dacca, he shot and killed a police inspector visiting the campus and fled to Calcutta, living in a shelter at Bangalakshmi Cotton Mill of Mahesh, Hooghly. Badal was born in a family which had connections with the Jugantar Group and two of his uncles were involved in the Alipore Bomb Case. Dinesh was a writer and also trained in using firearms.

Benoy led the party of three plotting Operation *Freedom* after his success in Dacca. It was a terror attack on the Writers Building (the Calcutta Secretariat) to shoot Mr. N. S. Simpson, Inspector General of Police (Prisons). They entered in European attire, and shot dead Simpson, while three others were injured in the ensuing battle on the 30th December of 1930. Ultimately as they were overpowered, Benoy shot himself, Badal consumed Potassium Cyanide to commit suicide, and Dinesh shot himself but survived. After his recovery and trial, Dinesh was hanged on 7 July 1931 at Alipore Jail.

4.8.3 Bhagat Singh

Bhagat Singh was a leader of the local Punjab unit of Hindustan Revolutionary Association, which had connections with the Gadar Party. In December 1928, Bhagat Singh, Chandrasekhar Azad, Sukhdev Thaper, and Shivaram Rajguru (or Sukhdev), planned to assassinate James Scott, the then police superintendent of Lahore. This to retaliate the death of Lala Lajpat Rai who died due to the police attack supervised by Mr. Scott. Due to misfiring Scott was saved, but two other policemen were killed. The group escaped and absconded for some time.

The party had instructed Bhagat Singh to refrain from shooting operations to avoid his capture, because in 1928 they found him a young student, an efficient organizer, and a leader with convictions. He read Marxist literature though never not professed to be a Communist. He was a writer too. Bhagat Singh identified himself as an anarchist and justified his stance by writing that anarchism defied a ruler, and that did not mean the absence of law and order; ultimately the goal of anarchism was complete independence from religious dogma, money and all worldly desires, – there would be no chain on. In a next daring move, Bhagat Singh and Batukehswar Dutta exploded two bombs inside the central legislative assembly of Delhi, while showering pamphlets to the public and instantly surrendered to police. All were tried. Bhagat Singh, Sukhdev Thaper, and Shivaram Rajguru were hanged on 31 March of 1931. In his last letter Singh wrote, "I have been arrested while waging a war. For me there can be no gallows. Put me into the mouth of the cannon and blow me off…"[9]

4.8.4 Chandrashekhar Azad

Originally born in a Tiwari family, Azad went to Banaras in 1921 to study Sanskrit. When the Hindustan Revolutionary Association was formed during the Gaya Congress, he associated himself with it. He used to collect funds by robbing government cash. Azad was the leader of the *Kakori Train Robbery of 1925*. He was also behind the attack on Viceroy Irwin's train in 1926. Rajendranath Lahiri and two others were sentenced to death in the 1925 train robbery case, but Azad, Keshab Chowdhary and Murari Mohan Sharma escaped. In 1928, Azad was in Bhagat Singh's plan. Someone known to Azad committed treachery by aiding police to encounter him in Allahabad. Azad challenged the police force on the spot, but he succumbed to their bullets on 27 February 1931.

Their deaths created sensations among nationalists. Subhas Chandra Bose wrote, "Bhagat Singh had become a symbol of new awakening among the youths; Nehru wrote, "Bhagat Singh's popularity was leading to a new national awakening." Gandhi wrote in *Young India* of 29 March 1931, "Bhagat Singh did not want to live. He refused to apologize, nor even filed an appeal. Bhagat Singh was not a devotee of non-violence, but did subscribe to the religion of violence. He took violence due to helplessness and to defend his homeland… But, we should not imitate their act in our land of millions of destitute and crippled people … Though we praise the courage of these brave men, we should never countenance their activities…"[10] Gandhi principally disagreed with violent death and once said, "I cannot in all consciousness agree to anyone being sent to gallows. God alone takes lives, because he alone gives…" The Congress, while disapproving their violent actions, pleaded to stop their execution but failed.

It resolved, "Triple execution was an act of wanton vengeance and a deliberate flouting of the unanimous demand of the nation for commutation."

4.9 Observations

During the post World War I period, people suffered from poverty and expressed their dissatisfaction of British rule by supporting the nationalists against the administration. The Government of India Act 1919, intended to give greater freedoms to the people was passed to pacify public outrage, while at the same time the Rowlatt Act gave extraordinary judicial and police powers to suppress popular dissent. This ambiguity caused the Amritsar Massacre. The modalities of the Rowlatt Act provided Gandhi the opportunity to rise to leadership at national level. He protested the administrative means of suppressing agitations by initiating an experiment on non-violence and non-cooperation, and rose to become a public figure in certain political circles. He was so much trusted by senior Congress leaders that they entrusted him to rewrite the Congress' constitution. He did it by taking the party down to the grassroots level involving rural masses, including youths and women, and resetting the ultimate goal of Congress as complete freedom for Indians.

Gandhi's decision on suspending the movements and boycotting the legislative process was not supported by senior members like Motilal Nehru and C. R. Das. He faced a temporary setback when the main body of Congress became unpopular while the Swaraj Party increased significantly due to its administrative efficiency. He accepted his responsibility and retired from politics temporarily.

The Swaraj Party efficiently ran the administration rising to power; and helped people by properly utilising the positive sides of the Act 1919. They even advanced the claim for dominion status as the first step to complete freedom. The Prince of Wales understood the Indian situation and hinted on possibilities of awarding dominion status for the first time.

Revolutionary activities continued and spilled over right up to the tenure of Lord Irwin. Women's participation in national politics received an injection after Annie Besant became the Congress President in 1917.

Sarojini Naidu became the second female to preside over Congress in 1925, and there were several women volunteers who took part in direct anarchism. The spirit of nationalism in Congress allured several British trained younger groups to join Congress politics as well.

Apart from this political side, the economy of India took a downturn as additional expenses made during war time could not be compensated even by allowing fiscal autonomy and increasing the tax base through the Act 1919. Between 1920–23, when domestic politics resumed with new leaders, there was a positive balance of trade as there was no exchange crisis, and no dearth of Rupee demand to pay for Indian exports. Also the price of silver grew high during war time.[11] This temporary and transient betterment was not utilized for improving the domestic manufacturing sector though war boosted industrial growth. Raw materials remained unutilized. Neither any attempt was taken for boosting crop production by developing irrigation systems.

The London office took the decision to partially share the military responsibility to ease financial liabilities of the Raj. British exports to India were reduced during the swadeshi and khadi movements. However, until 1930 India remained the largest purchaser of British goods.[12] In this period tariff policy was flouted by imposing tariffs on Iron and steel. The cotton excise was also abolished in 1926. But all these measures failed to augment people's income steadily declining since the middle of the 1920s. With the Great Depression looming, the financial condition deteriorated further at the end of this period. The economy of the Raj declined further when a community of landlords rejected the peasantry's attempts to become a part takers in agricultural business, leading to further impoverishment.

References:

1. S. D. Waley, Edwin *Montagu: A Memoir and Account of his Visits to India* (Bombay: Asia Publishing House, 1964), 135.
2. James Lawrence, *Raj: The Making and Unmaking of British India* (New York: St. Martin's Press, 1998, 2019), 479.
3. J. L. Nehru, *Jawaharlal Nehru: An Autobiography* (London, New Delhi: Oxford University Press, 1936, 1982), 43.

4. Subhas Chandra Bose, *The Indian Struggle 1920–1942* (New Delhi: Oxford University Press, 1997), II: 50.
5. Piers Brendon, *The Decline and Fall of the British Empire 1781–1997* (London: Vintage Books, 2008), 376.
6. Parveen Bhalla, *The Life and Times of Subhas Chandra Bose* (Kolkata: Prabhat Prakashan, 2016).
7. Quoted in Hansard (1803–2005), 5 November 1929 Vol. 75, 397. https://api.parliament.uk/historic-hansard/lords/1929/nov/05/india-the-viceroys-statement.
8. "Gopinath Saha" in *Marxist Indiana: An Encyclopaedia of Freedom Fighters in India in Alphabetic Order*. Blog Post No. 188 (November 23, 2013) https://radhikaranjan.blogspot.com/2013/11/gopinath-saha-1901-1924.html.
9. Quote from Bhagat Singh's last letter, published by Gandhi in "Young India," 29th March 1931 after Bhagat's martyrdom on 23rd march 1931. http://www.rrtd.nic.in/bhagat%20singh.html.
10. Ibid.
11. B. R. Tomlinson, "India and British Empire, 1880–1935," University of Cambridge, *Sage Journal* Vol. 12, no. 4 (1975) (published online, 2016), 355.
12. Ibid, 357.

CHAPTER 5

British India 1926 – 1938

This period witnessed how domestic politics intensified and sporadic instances of anarchism appeared. Gandhi secured an unchallengeable position in the national arena, facing a more aggressive administration. In Britain, the economic depression resulting in increased domestic pressure, forced Parliament to introduce a major constitutional relaxation. This chapter also describes how the Congress movements influenced the 1937 elections, and how the Muslim League's consolidated position caused Indian politics to become much more complex. Internal conflicts in Congress led Subhas Chandra Bose to establish the Forward Bloc.

5.1 The Simon Commission and after Effects

In 1926 Lord Irwin (1926–31) replaced Lord Reading. To evaluate the progress of the 1919 Act, Irwin set up a Statutory Commission with Sir John Simon as the chairman and seven other members representing different British Parliamentary parties. The Commission did not include any Indians. Clement Attlee was one of the committee members who later became the key person to terminate British rule. Domestic parties boycotted the Commission in November 1927 when it became clear that their demand for dominion status was not being considered.

Following the Madras resolutions of 1927, Congress organized demonstrations in Delhi and Lahore on 17 November. Lala Lajpat Rai and Jawaharlal (the son of Motilal Nehru) were lathi charged. Lajpat Rai was severely injured and died shortly after. Early 1928 Indian parties held conferences in Delhi and Bombay to urge for early solution of the dominion status. To draft a future constitution, the Nehru Committee was formed with Motilal Nehru as the chairman. This draft, known as the *Nehru Report*, recommended a two tiered parliamentary system similar to dominions of Canada and Australia having central and provincial subjects, and universal adult franchise. The report published in August 1928, at a specially convened All Parties Conference, contained a provision for the Princely States to be included in a future free state.

During the next All Parties Conference, this report was rejected by the smaller parties who preferred negotiating with the Simon Commission. At another such meeting in December 1928 held in Calcutta, Jinnah submitted a list of 14 demands while considering the dominion status. The list was unacceptable to the majority of parties as Muslims wanted to exclude the Hindu Mahasabha from the national agenda. To avoid any more complications, a younger group in Congress preferred to aim straight for Purna Swaraj (full independence). By this time some Muslim leaders accused Jinnah of maintaining affiliation with Congress. He took a break in politics and moved to London, after attending the first Round Table Conference (RTC) (from 1930 to 1935). The Congress, however, unilaterally planned to proceed with the Nehru Report.

a) Fate of Nehru Report: Together with young Congress members, Jawaharlal Nehru and Subhas Chandra Bose as Joint secretaries, formed the *Independence of India League* that proposed to aim for complete freedom during the Calcutta Congress of 1928. This radical stance allowed them to bypass the question of dominion status promoted in the Nehru Report. Their proposal was rejected by the Congress Working Committee (CWC), but a consensus was reached with a commitment that Congress would accept this proposal in the next session of December 1929 if dominion status was refused. The Nehru Committee's proposal was sent to the government for approval. The Calcutta Congress resolved to start non-cooperation movements to revive the morale of workers lost after Congress had split.

b) Lord Irwin and dominion status: Lord Irwin went to London and consulted different politicians like Secretary of State Wedgwood Benn, ex-prime minister Baldwin, the new prime minister Ramsay MacDonald, and others before the formal declaration of India's dominion status. Irwin received a mixed opinion. Some of them argued that "dominion status" was a fluid term in need of a better definition. Back in India on 31 October 1929, and against the conservatives wishes, Irwin decided to declare India's dominion status because it was committed in the 1919 Act. This became known as Irwin's October Declaration. It was rumored that through this (rather vague) declaration Irwin intended to placate increasingly vocal nationalist leaders.

Lord Irwin also announced that the British Government would invite British India, the Princely States, and political leaders to address Indian problems and ascertain the constitutional status. However, a section of conservative British Press condemned the Viceroy's decision on dominion and some Parliament members even questioned India's ability to run the administration. Thus awarding the dominion status to India remained disputed. Taking this opportunity, Congress youths prepared to move for complete freedom at the 1929 Lahore Congress.

c) Return of Gandhi: Gandhi returned to politics, and was entrusted to lead the non-cooperation movements. He encouraged the younger group to take leadership. On 4 March 1929 he was again arrested in Calcutta for organizing a public bonfire of foreign clothes, defying a police order. On 23 December, an attempt was made to blow up the Viceregal train with Lord Irwin on board. This action received condemnation from all sides. Parliament immediately curtailed the Indian administration. Gandhi, after his release, condemned the action and made a courtesy visit to Irwin. During the conversation, Gandhi asked Irwin to commit to dominion status.

After the Simon Commission's report was published, Irwin announced a Round Table Conference (RTC) to discuss a future constitution. This was unexpected. It prompted Motilal Nehru, Gandhi and Malviya to meet Irwin to inform him that Congress would meet at the table, provided Congress' representation was in majority, and the dominion status was included in the agenda. They also asked for amnesty of political prisoners. But Irwin could not give any assurances.

d) Jawaharlal Nehru and Subhas Chandra Bose in Congress leadership: Gandhi moved Jawaharlal's name to preside over the Lahore Congress session, 1929, overriding the opposition of some state Congress committees, but rejected Subhas Chandra's proposal for a parallel government and tax boycott. The session of 1929 was significant because the resolution for Complete Independence was passed, even though Motilal Nehru favored dominion as a first step of reform.

Jawaharlal and Subhas Chandra jointly proposed a socialist type of plan for restructuring future India at the 1929 Congress. Instead, Gandhi was in favor of making 60,000 villages of India self-sufficient in agriculture, village industry, and khadi. Clearly, there were fundamental differences between the younger group and Gandhi followers. Lahore Congress scrapped the possibility of attending the RTC of 1930, and resolved to boycott the legislature, unless constitutional progress was committed. Gandhi took responsibility for planning the movements. Congress asked Indians to celebrate Independence Day on the 26th January of 1930. This day continued to retain its significance for Indians when on 26 January 1950, the Government of India became the Republic of India by adopting a new constitution.

5.2 Fate of the Simon Report

The report published on 10 May 1930 superseded Irwin's October Declaration of 1929. The Commission declared that, 1) provincial diarchy would be abolished; 2) ministers would be given power; 3) provisions made for direct elections to reconstitute the central and the provincial governments; and it promised that, 4) the central legislative assembly would be renamed as Federal Assembly, retaining power of the Governors intact. It was also noted that the recommendations would not be implemented until Burma was formally separated.

Meanwhile, a report of the *Indian Central Committee* was presented opposing Simon's recommendations. The Simon Report was killed when Lord Birkenhead, Secretary of State, suddenly called for a RTC. He did not want to foster British supremacy, and overruled the possibility of dominant self-government as India was unfit for it. The Muslim League participated in the RTC with Jinnah and opposed a strong center (in absence of Congress). The RTC decided for an All India Federation including the Princely States. His Majesty's government, in principle, recognized the responsibility of the executives in the legislature except the defence and external affairs which rested under the Governor-General.

Meanwhile, Gandhi called for a civil disobedience movement against oppressive state-laws. But other parties were not prepared for it. This time the government wanted to avoid political disturbances. On 31 January 1930, Gandhi produced a list of demands to the government. Some of those were old, like curtailing military expenditure. New demands were for restoration of the Rupee value that was adjusted recently, reduction of land revenue, and abolishing the salt tax as it was easily extractable. Irwin showed no inclination.

On 2 March 1930, Gandhi announced that Congress had planned to begin civil disobedience against the Government's reluctance on Indian issues, and he would agitate against the Salt Act of 1882 that established the British monopoly on salt extraction and trade, denying access to Indians. This was the start of Gandhi's Salt Satyagraha. Access to cheap salt, Gandhi reasoned, was as important an issue for all Indians as the right for air and water.

5.3 Salt Satyagraha (Dandi March) and Outcome

Gandhi set off on his march for peaceful salt extraction on 12 March 1930, from his Sabarmati Ashram. With dozens of his followers he proceeded to Dandi, a coastal village in Gujarat, covering a 240-mile trek over 24 days.

With thousands of people who joined him, he reached Dandi on April 5 (Figs. 21 & 22). Next morning Gandhi walked to the beach encrusted with salt crystals. When the police forestalled him he became an overreacher to collect a lump of salt, as a symbolic act of civil disobedience. The administration was unprepared as it thought that Gandhi's experiment would become a fiasco.

The mass upheaval of the Dandi march became world news. The *New York Times* of 6 April, 1930 wrote, "Never was there a more forlorn setting for drama than the tiny struggling village of Dandi, perched on hummocks above the beach and long rollers of the Arabian sea…" By picking up a handful of natural crystals from the beach Gandhi crystallized an exemplary and unprecedented protest against the British Raj. The Salt March catapulted him into international limelight for the first time.

At the same time on the eastern border of India, the antagonistic approach was revived. On 18 April 1930, Surya Kumar Sen who was originally a Gandhist, chose an anarchist route with his followers such as Ganesh Ghosh, Loknath Bal and others. They ventured looting two armories of Chittagong (now in Bangladesh) and built up an armed force with local revolutionaries. A total of 303 rifles and other arms were snatched after occupation of the armories, but failed to procure basic ammunition.

Absconding in hilly tracts, Surya Sen with his followers encountered a large police force causing multiple casualties on both sides. Sen escaped and the government announced an offer of Rs 10,000 on his head. Being tempted, some Netra Sen facilitated in Sen's arrest, when he had found shelter at his betrayer's house (1933). After trial, Surya Sen was hanged on 12 January 1934. Netra Sen was assassinated in revenge. Surya Sen had inspired the formation of women cadres too. One among them was Pritilata Waddedar who dedicated herself for the cause of her motherland after graduating from Bethune College Calcutta. After she was caught during the attack of Pahartali European Club at Chittagong, she consumed Potassium Cyanide to end her life.

Another young student activist, Bina Das, attempted to shoot Stanley Jackson, Governor of Bengal on 6 February 1932 in the Convention Hall of the Calcutta University. A special tribunal sentenced her to nine years of imprisonment.

The Chittagong Armory raid of 1930 proved that anarchist radicalism was gaining popularity even after the execution of Gopinath. The attacks organized by Benoy Bose, Bhagat Singh and others were discussed in Chapter 3. Anarchism reached remote places of Midnapore district also. The Government promulgated emergency acts for Bengal arresting hundreds without trial. Many anarchist prisoners adopted Gandhi's policy of fasting in the jail.

Gandhi was arrested on 7 May before he could reach Dharsana (south of Dandi) to resist a raid of the picketing government salt workers. His arrest triggered a mass outrage. Abbas Tyabji, a 76-year old nationalist Muslim who replaced him was also arrested. After him Sarojini Naidu led the movement. On 21 May 1932 a crowd offering no resistance, was indiscriminately lathi charged. These new tactics of nonviolent protest inspired innumerable people from Bengal, Behar, UP, and Punjab to the south of India, to participate in Gandhi's satyagraha. In defiance to government orders, millions of Indians began illegally collecting salt. These movements were unchecked until August, and became the first massive anti-British mass mobilization.

The police responded forcefully. Crowds stoned the police who sometimes remained silent spectators. Gandhi was particularly impressed with women who joined the protests (Fig. 23). In the 30 April issue of *Young India*, he appealed to them to leave their homes and join the processions. They learnt to picket before the liquor shops, boycott foreign clothes, and how to spin khadi to earn a livelihood. Responding to an address by G. D. Birla, the business community donated funds. Jawaharlal Nehru and other leaders were imprisoned. Subhas Chandra Bose was already in prison after being arrested on false grounds. The agitation did not stop until Gandhi was released. In total about 60,000 people were arrested. Salt

Satyagraha became the biggest continuing movement in the subcontinent. Inspired by the example of one person, the entire episode of nonviolent protest became exemplary throughout the world. Gandhi as an inspirational leader became irreplaceable.

Led by Rajagopalachari, this movement helped Congress to gain political footing in Madras and southern regions for the first time in the mid-1930s. South Indians had been politically aloof up to then. People collected salt on the Tanjore coast. After the salt movement, Congress replaced the Justice Party. E. V. Ramaswami Naicker, however, set up a militant organization known as *Self Respect*.

Among other parties, Communists were busy with rail workers' strikes in Calcutta and avoided the salt movement, and the majority of Muslims, barring "Frontier Gandhi," the Pathan Khan Abdul Ghaffar Khan's (Badsha Khan) and his people in North Western Frontier Province (with majority Muslim population), did not participate. Khan sympathized with Gandhi accepting the non-violence mantra, and preaching non-violence caused the Pathans to become peace loving.

The satyagraha movement was a warning for the administration, both in India and in Britain. The Viceroy sought to reconcile with Gandhi and negotiate a pact. They released him early in January 1931. Gandhi's release disgusted Churchill, a conservative Member of Parliament, who said British withdrawal from India would be "a hideous act of self-mutilation, astounding to every nation in the world."[1] The Indian situation during 1930–31 was so tense that the British people thought it, "the beginning of the end of the power."[2] India was Britain's biggest export market, "the nucleus of British economy as well as the fulcrum of its empire."[3] So valuable, they said, "the astonishing gold mine we have discovered in India's hoards has put us in clover."[4] Up to the Great Depression of the 1930s, the Indian market paid enormous dividends, and the British were keen to retain it. But India was fast becoming a declining asset.

British India 1926 – 1938 **175**

Fig. 23 Salt March 12 March - 5 April 1930 (Rue des Archives. citeco.fr).

Fig. 24 Salt March 12 March - 5 April 1930 (Wikipedia).

Fig. 25 Gandhi's Quit India Speech, 8 August 1942. (navyuvaz.blogspot.com).

5.4 The Gandhi – Irwin Pact

Upon Gandhi's release, the Gandhi – Irwin Pact was signed on 5 March, 1931 agreeing that, 1) all ordinances and prosecutions would be withdrawn; 2) peaceful picketing at foreign liquor and clothing shops would be allowed; 3) confiscated properties of satyagrahis would be restored; 4) all curbed activities of Congress would be lifted; 5) persons residing near the seaside would be permitted to collect salt; and 6) all prisoners, except those arrested on charge of violence, would be released. In turn, Gandhi agreed to suspend non-cooperation and civil disobedience movements. The Pact strengthened the position of Stanley Baldwin, the leader of the Conservatives.

The Karachi Congress of March 1931 demanded a *Constituent Assembly* that would enable Indians to write their own Constitution considering all castes and creeds. Congress also reiterated complete independence, and passed socialist resolutions claiming civil rights of industrial laborers by fixing wage levels, and improving their working conditions with assurance for protection in their old age. This meeting approved of the Gandhi–Irwin Pact, but condemned the violent activities of anarchists. However, energetic younger groups in Congress like Nehru, who entered politics through opposing the Simon Commission, denounced the Pact, calling it a 'sell out'. They urged for movements to continue. This meeting also condemned the execution of the anarchists.

Second Round Table Conference: The Gandhi–Irwin Pact enabled Gandhi to join the RTC in London, scheduled on 7 September 1931. He went to Britain representing the Karachi resolution mainly to claim an early self-rule and oppose the separation of electorates. He was prepared to return empty handed. When the minority issue was raised, Gandhi emphatically said that Congress, representing the entire Indian population including the Muslims, would accept only one constitution and one electorate. Gandhi also tried to neutralise disagreements with the Muslim League, but failed. The Second Round Table Conference was unsuccessful (Fig. 26)

Fig. 26 Second Round Table Conference, London Sept 1931 (British Library Archive).

Ramsay MacDonald continued as PM in a Conservative coalition government. He made commitments to save the minority rights and retain British control on defence and external affairs. He also reminded Indians about financial obligations of the government of India. Lord Willingdon (1931–36) replaced Lord Irwin. On 18 April, at his last speech at the Chelmsford Club, Irwin said that he could not do more for India due to reactionary forces that were working against him in India and England.[5] Irwin sincerely tried to do good for Indians but the officials in Delhi opposed him.

During Gandhi's absence in Britain peasants of the United Provinces, Bengal, and the North Western Frontier refused to pay agricultural tenancy, and so Jawaharlal Nehru and Abdul Ghaffar Khan were arrested. The government had passed a series of ordinances to crack down Congress activities that instigated political upheaval in 1919, 1920–1 and 1930, engulfing entire India. These arrests again became commonplace. Reacting to this, the CWC urged for a public inquiry committee on the validity of these ordinances, threatening to restart civil disobedience. The British decided that negotiations had no effect and so on Gandhi's return in December, Nehru was again arrested for breach of ordinance while he went to Bombay to meet him. Gandhi's arrest followed on 4 January 1932 along with sweeping arrests of Congress workers who were protesting the ordinances of 1931. More than 15000 workers were in custody up to February. The government became revengeful. Congress had no choice but to suspend all programmes.

Lord Willingdon introduced intermittent but strict censorship through issuing identity cards, and imposing heavy fines. The measure was strictest in Bengal, especially in Chittagong and Midnapore. Free movements were restricted, and all kinds of assemblies curbed. Subsequent police atrocities instigated the people to murder three successive magistrates in Midnapore. Many Congress volunteers were put in custody. Nehru remarked, "the subcontinent had turned into a vast prison of human spirit."[6] From jail, Gandhi advised to avoid confrontation, but Nehru disagreed. After his release Gandhi resigned from all activities, though his command in national politics remained strong.

In August 1832, McDonald awarded separate electoral quotas for the Hindu Depressed Classes, Muslims, Sikhs, European, and Anglo minorities. Gandhi denounced the policy of separating the Depressed Classes from the main Hindu body, as it would strengthen communalism, and began a hunger fast from 20 September. Dr. Ambedkar (who chaired the constitution making committee for independent India) emerged as the leader of this Depressed Class. He helped to reach an agreement through a pact known as the Poona Pact of 1932, which allowed Scheduled Castes (SC) to increase their seat allocation, and it redressed the community as special at par with Muslims. The Poona Pact was supported by Rabindranath Tagore, but the Bengal Congress opposed it as 10% of reserved seats were accorded to the SC (in Bengal only 0.01% population), reducing Hindu Caste seats while the Bengal Muslim representation was large.

Madan Mahan Malvia left Congress when the quota system could not be abolished. Class quota allotment for Depressed Classes and Muslims were seen as a British ploy to divide Hindu vote-banks and keep Congress at bay. He and others argued that Muslims, Sikhs, and Princely States were segregated only to drive a wedge in national unity. Prime minister Attlee later said that the British Raj lacked the power to raise untouchables as their position and status were determined by the Hindu social system.[7]

When peasants in the United Provinces organized a land tax boycott movement from March 1932, Congress organizations were declared illegal, and their funds were seized. However, civil disobedience ran at provincial and district levels disobeying police orders. Their activities slowed down gradually, but the movements continued until 1934. Ultimately the government felt that Congress had weakened. Also, younger groups in Congress thought that the party needed to change direction to stay relevant. Gandhi felt that left-minded leaders were in favor of continuing non-cooperation movements, and in September 1933 he wrote to Nehru that Indians were advancing following the right path. At the Patna Congress of 1934, the CWC came to terms with the left inclined Swarajists who were still prominent in certain places.

5.5 Economic Instability

During the economic depression of 1893–96, the Indian Rupee, isolated from international exchange, was barely affected. Commodity prices were relatively stable. At the close of the 19th Century, the Rupee was linked to the gold exchange, and it became connected to western economies. During World War I, like elsewhere, prices grew rapidly. During the 1920 prices stabilized. But the next depression affected the Indian economy so much that the price of Indian staples fell by 40% from October 1929 to December 1930. The Rupee was clearly overvalued. This situation improved slightly from 1932 after abandoning the gold standard in 1931. But the price index of export items like cereals, jute and cotton fell by 46% and that of imported items fell by 25%. The slump caused by large stocks, hoarding and over-production meant prices slumped, affecting many jute- and cotton growers.[8] The resulting hardship caused repeated political uprisings. Confused administrators failed to make policy decisions other agricultural nations were making, even as British business in India languished.

Lord Irwin had imposed taxation on British imports to stabilize the Indian economy as he knew that the strength of Congress was increasing. He attempted to minimize financial pressure on Indians to restrain public agitations. The economy dwindled from the end of the last century causing a deficit in Raj's treasury due to war efforts, and slowly recovered during the next seven to eight years after fiscal adjustments.

According to Tomlinson, 40% of gross expenditure of the Raj was spent for maintenance and training of Indian troops recruited in a ratio of one British against three Indian soldiers.[9] The commissioned officers were only British. The Raj had to pay for the maintenance, training and pensioning of the troops and for their employment in imperial roles as per provision in the Act 1858. In addition, the Raj repaid the annual interest on loans received with guarantees from the Home Department in London for Indian railways, and subsidies. These compulsory payments were a huge drain of the exchequer. Also a part of the British capital was withdrawn due to swadeshi pressure, worsening the cash flow situation.

In 1880, India's army comprised of 1,30,000 Indian sepoys and 66,000 British troops. India functioned as an army barrack from which Britain could draw any number of sepoys. These troops were required against requisition to maintain Indian frontiers safe from the Afghan tribes, and to be posted beyond borders. They served in Afghanistan (1878), Egypt (1882), Burma (1885), Nyasa (1893), in Mombasa and Uganda (1896) and Sudan (1896–97) without any British compensation.[10] Additional resources consumed for imperial services were enough to destabilize Raj's economy.

The expenditure under committed heads was 40% of total revenue earned from India. The remaining 60% of revenues was mostly spent for administrative staff, European and Indian, their salary, and pensions. The leftover amount was not enough to carry out all recurrent and capital expenditure for developmental works. Natural disasters, such as famines, consumed additional funds. Finally, the treasury reached rock bottom during the Great Depression of 1930–32.

This situation was apparently overcome by currency adjustment and Rupee devaluation. The domestic force opposed the increase of direct taxation and urged to stop resource mobilization to England. The Raj's commitment to maintain a balance between income and expenditure was disrupted. Also the currency exchange did not work in India's favor from 1880 to 1930.

Debates had begun when Ripon abolished the import tariffs in the 1880s. Since then no effort was being taken to maintain parity between Indian exports and excise duties. Indian production stagnated from before World War I, as no policy existed to augment revenue from alternative sources. Mayo, Ripon, and Lord Irwin were more sympathetic and rendered concessions towards the Indian causes on humanitarian grounds. Irwin ignored strong imperial pressure to relax tariffs on British imports.

Ripon made provisions for native employees in local government to enhance revenue collection, and Mayo tried to increase provincial collection of taxes from forests, excise, stamp, license, and registration. Other Viceroys were reluctant to locate alternative income sources when the economy took a downturn and war expenditure increased. The constitution was further relaxed to appease politicians, but this measure did not aid the economy.

In 1930 the deficit reached the bottom, and Irwin tried to collect extra revenue by increasing import duty on cotton textile from 11 to 15%, and again to 20% in January 1930, overruling the Lancashire pressure and imperial threats to stop the constitutional process. Irwin had full knowledge of the strength of Indian opposition. He said that Indian tariff policy must be decided in India's interest alone and warned that any concession to British interest would only increase the effective boycott of British goods. The Cabinet ultimately backed down.[11] The single positive exception was mining. Net income from minerals including coal mining, grew from 89 million Rupees in 1920 to 192 million Rupees in 1929.

In September 1931, Irwin increased cotton tariffs again by 5% to balance the budget, irking the Lancashire group. British Conservatives enjoyed the support of 60 MPs from the Lancashire belt and it became difficult to overcome their lobby. Gandhi on 31 November 1931 condemned the fixing of the currency ratio at 1s.6d in a meeting of the federal structure committee during the RTC.

Samuel Hoare, the new conservative secretary, asked Irwin to nullify the effect of the high tariffs. The Viceroy reminded him again that any dictation from London on Indian tariff policy would cause a drastic rise of political temperature in India, and three of the Indian and two of the British members of his Executive Council would resign if the Cabinet's proposal went through.[12] Irwin accepted Congress as a considerable force and always believed that a liberal attitude might facilitate restoring economic and political stability. He was firm in his resistance to London's attempt to interfere.

After the political surrender of Congress in 1932 to Viceroy Willingdon, British trade received an impulse by an Indo-Japanese trade agreement at the interest of Japanese and British capitalists. It also served the interest of the Indian textile industrialists. However, no single economic measure could deal with the urgency of the question of India's political future.

To mitigate this situation, the cabinet finally passed the Government of India Act 1935, which basically favored India's advancement towards self-rule.

5.6 Final RTC and Government of India Act, 1935

The final RTC of November 1932 allotted 33.33% seats for Muslims in the central legislative council; and Sindh –a predominantly Muslim province– became a separate province. In early March 1933, the Government published a white paper depicting that a Joint Select Committee would draw the Constitution of British India incorporating Princely states in the constitutional machinery, and the Reserve Bank of India would be established for financial management. This white paper excluded provisions of fundamental rights for Indians.

Congress activities were subdued, but it initially opposed the White Paper, demanding an elected Constituent Assembly with authority to write the constitution, while rejecting the communal agenda. Neglecting objections of Congress the White Paper was approved in 1933, and a bill was passed in December 1934 in both houses. It was finally made law as the Government of India Act 1935 after Royal assent was obtained on 4 August 1935. A synopsis of the Act is as following.

The Government of India Act formed British India as a federation with a provision for automatic accession of the eleven provinces, and the Princely States were formally incorporated in it. The Governor-General, as the Crown representative, was empowered to look after the Princely States. One third of a total of 375 seats in the legislative assembly were kept for elected members. The Princely States were allocated 260 seats which were nominated. The Government of India was given more financial autonomy by transferring fiscal control from London to New Delhi.

The central government retained the federal subjects like defence, external affairs, finance and the tribal areas. The provincial governments were given autonomy in criminal and civil laws, welfare, land, factories and labor, education, etc. But major guiding principles common to all provinces remained to be laid down by the central legislature.

The Viceroy was given special powers to check financial and political instability, protect the minorities, and promulgate ordinances. A dyarchy was introduced at the center accommodating both the council of ministers and the Governor-General's executive committee. The Government of India was put under the control of the Secretary of State, representative of the British Crown. The relation between the Government of India and the provinces was strictly federal; and His Majesty (through decisions made in London) was empowered to appoint provincial governors with a tenure of five years who would act with assistance of a council of ministers in respective provinces.

The number of elected seats in the provincial legislative assembly was based on population estimates in the 1931 census. Women were given special franchises relating to seats allotted to different communities. The upper chamber was made a permanent body. The provincial governors remained accountable to the Secretary of State on some issues. Because provinces were given more autonomy, there was provision for a federal court to settle issues on trespassing when the center interfered in the province's domain or vice versa. Burma was separated from India in this Act, and Sindh was separated from Bombay as a Muslim dominated province along with North Western Frontier Province (NWFP). The status of Bihar and Orissa was also changed. This Act formed the basis of the constitution and parliamentary institutions.

More than half of the Princely states disagreed to be in a federal structure. Congress also disagreed with this Act because, 1) it was drawn up without consulting Indians; 2) it kept no provision for protecting the rights of the Indians, and there was no promise for self-government; 3) a provision for more than one dominion might break national integrity; 4) special powers given to the Governor-General on issues of the minorities and the Princely States defied the instrument of accession in treaties between Crown and the States; 5) democratic rights of the people of the Princely States were denied by offering them 30–40 % of the nominated members in central legislature; and 6) because the Act restricted the possibilities of Congress to be in majority and its access in power in central legislature. This Act was written unconventionally without any preamble. What irritated Congress was that India was not identified as a single secular unit, and several departments did not have power. The Muslim League opposed the Act because it allowed a majority rule which would dominate them.

The Muslim League got an impression that they represented the entire Muslim community even when a large section of Muslims were nationalists and Congress members. Allotting a Scheduled Caste quota was against Congress policy. Congress wished to reduce untouchability and keep all Hindus politically united.[13] The constitution was inoperative as a federation was not established, and was suppressed until 1937. Government suspended it again in September 1939 due to the outbreak of War. Viceroy Linlithgow (1936–43), who had overseen the writing of the White Paper, was against some important clauses of the proposed constitution. Nehru said of the 1935 Act, "The Act is a machine with strong brakes and no engine, … a charter of slavery."[14]

Congress rejected the Act. The Princely States were against it because they lost autonomy. Though minority interests were preserved, Muslim League also refused to accept the Act. Indian Christians demanded a common electorate.

The positive sides of the Act were that it, 1) introduced direct elections, and increased the number of members in the provincial council, and kept scope for a majority-rule, 2) promised a federal system and federal court (which was not introduced), and 3) for the first time proposed a written proposal for Dominion Status. Above all the Act kept all current operations as existing, and made a provision of making changes if required. This advantage of flexibility was smartly used by the last Viceroy to execute the transfer of power.

5.7 Period of Political Stalemate

From the 1920s, Congress movements were limited to swadeshi and civil disobedience. Between 1935 and 1936, Congress activities were confined to minor agendas as most of its members were under arrest. Jawaharlal Nehru along with Subhash Chandra favored forming the *Congress Socialist*

Forum to introduce left inclined characters, but forming a minority in the CWC, they could not push it through. For a considerable period, both Nehru and Bose were in custody, making them inactive.

Coincidentally both of them were released from jail and encouraged to visit Europe on compassionate grounds. Subhas sailed to Europe in 1933 for recovery from his illness on recommendation of Lt. Col. Bouley, who had been treating him. He needed a break from his long confinement. Nehru too was released to go to Europe to visit his ailing wife.

5.7.1 Subhas Chandra and J. L. Nehru in Europe

While in Europe, Subhas began campaigning for Indian causes. He also remained by the side of Kamala Nehru who was in Germany for treatment of Tuberculosis. Nehru, still imprisoned, was also suddenly released in 1935 to rush to his ailing wife. When he arrived in October, his wife was on death bed and passed away a few months later in front of her husband, daughter, and Subhas. The families of Nehru and Subhas were closely connected and built up mutual trust and understanding while working together.

Nehru was not in a mental state to pursue political activities in Europe. But while staying in Germany, he visited England and France, and completed his autobiography which was much appreciated in Europe. He had to back India by March of 1936 with the commitment to take over the Congress presidency which he continued up to 1937.

Subhas negotiated with different European national leaders. From 1933 he met Labour Party members in the British Parliament to effectuate Indian freedom. He went to Geneva to work with the League of Nations hoping he could utilize them for India's cause, but was disappointed to learn that the organization was controlled by Britain and France. From Geneva, he published a bulletin on India in French, English and German, in collaboration with the International Committee on India. Vithubhai Patel, a senior brother of Sardar Patel, was in Europe for medical treatment, took a liking to Subhas. Vithubhai jointly with Subhas issued a memorandum for the international campaign against Britain. Subhas had to take a break in 1934 to visit Calcutta when his father was on the verge of expiry, but he was detained at the airport.

He returned to Bombay in April 1936 to attend the Lucknow Congress session though he was warned in writing by the British government (through the British consul in Vienna) that he would be arrested if he returned.[15] Subhas had consulted Nehru on his decision to return. During his stay in Europe, he was regularly shadowed by agents of British Embassies.[16] Subhas was taken to Bombay prison, the moment he set foot on Indian soil.

5.7.2 Nehru as Congress President

Nehru as the Congress president rejected the Act 1935 outright, and demanded a Constituent Assembly. M. N. Roy, who was once associated with the anarchists, who became a Marxist and one of the founders of Communist Party of India, suggested the formation of a Constituent Assembly in 1934 for the first time.* In his two term presidency, Nehru strove to rejuvenate the party and accommodate new faces as Congress officials developed socialist policies.

Nehru along with left wing associates refused to participate in the forthcoming election of 1937 as a token of protest against the 1935 Act. James Grigg, a Finance Member in the Viceroy's council and Churchill's aid was not in favor of the Act either. He remarked, "If England wants to keep India, it will have to be at the point of sword; a reconquest followed by autocracy."[17] But Britain pushed ahead and elections were held in 1937 following the provision of the 1935 Act. Congress participated in the elections when Gandhi overruled Nehru and his left wing.

5.8 Elections of 1937 and Post-Election Incidents

Some 30 million (one sixth of the adult population), voted in the first major provincial elections held in the winter of 1936–37.[18] After the results were declared in February, all arrested politicians were released including those who were in the Andamans. The election results changed the political scenario in the entire country, as Congress won most of the seats taking control of 8 provinces.

---

* Note: Again in 1939, Rajagopalachari demanded for a Constituent Assembly based on adult franchise, which was finally approved in 1940 and the first election for a Constituent Assembly took place in 1946.

People rejoiced in Congress' victory, and the national flag flew over public buildings. Congress, a mass movement organizer, emerged as rulers. The salt movement, and repression of Willingdon since 1932, integrated the masses to stand behind the Congress leadership. The professionals, many businessmen, industrial laborers and peasants were united in their support of Congress. The business community in Madras, who were dependent on government support, did not favor Congress. Even down south Congress soundly defeated the Justice Party and other minor parties.

Muslim League's performance was unsatisfactory in North Western Frontier Provinces, Punjab, Sindh and Bengal. All these were Muslim majority provinces. The result dismissed the League's claim of being the sole representative of Muslims. The Krishak Praja party of Fazlul Huq, with class based economic issues, defeated the Muslim League in eastern Bengal. Similarly, Sikander Hayat party owned overtaking the League as it worked for the improvement of agriculture in Punjab jointly with Hindus. In Punjab and Bengal regional parties came to power with Muslim support.

Jinnah, who had miscalculated the power of regional parties, cried, "Islam in danger" and tried to regain Muslim identity. Jinnah himself though was not was not a true Islamist in the sense that he had tasted alcohol and ham sandwiches while in the West.[19] Jinnah threatened that Muslims must think about their own interest, and urged for separation of the Urdu speaking states. At this time Jinnah was suffering from acute tuberculosis, but never disclosed it. He astutely pursued his goal to fight for a separate homeland for Muslims.

After the elections, Congress agreed to take office, provided the administration would not interfere. The governors, instead of making any promise, agreed to accept ministerial advice. When some left-minded Congress members refused to take office, Linlithgow assured them that the responsibility of the governors did not entitle them to intervene in ministerial administration, and appealed to all to take advantage of the Act.[20] Gandhi also insisted Congress members to take their offices during the interim period.

During the election campaign in the United Province, Congress disapproved of the League's request for a coalition. But Congress failed to secure Muslim seats there. This attempt by Congress to manoeuvre Muslim votes in UP caused its rift with the League. Otherwise relations between Congress and the League were good until Jinnah's return in 1934. Since the performance of Muslim League in the elections was not satisfactory, Jinnah became determined to project the League as a distinct party. In the same year, the Central Legislative Council passed the Shariat Implementation Act, that regulated all matters relating to Muslim family affairs. Jinnah attempted to consolidate Muslims at national level, and his services for ulema, motivated the student community to be involved in the Leagues' politics.[21] Muslim integration increased further after the resignation of Congress ministers in 1939. The League and Congress grew increasingly apart. Jinnah celebrated *Deliverance Day* to rejoice over the exit of the Congress government on 22 December that year.

Nationalist Muslims succeeded in some provinces against the League's opposition. When Congress wanted their Muslim representatives to be in responsible positions, Jinnah urged that Muslims other than those elected only under the Muslim League banner would not be in the legislation. Gandhi, Subhas and Jawaharlal jointly insisted on the authority not to recognize Muslim League as the representative body of the entire Muslim community.

Congress governed provinces were generally free from communal problems as the governments maintained a secular character. But the Bihar government initially suppressed peasant's movements against the landlords. Down south, Rajagopalachari arrested left-wing Congress members in Madras. Congress was obliged to safeguard the peasants and industrial labourers as promised during the Faizpur Congress Session, although being constrained by the Center under British control all promises could not be fulfilled. Furthermore, there was pressure on Congress from the industrialists, professionals and wealthy peasants. Zamindaries could not be abolished to the extent as promised, but the UP government brought the peasantry of Agra and Awadh under the Ryoti system. The Bihar government restored lands to poor peasants evicted during the depression; and in Bombay and Orissa illegal levies imposed on tenants were abolished. Generally, people were satisfied and Congress membership increased. Congress had learned to take responsibility for people.

Being in power, Congress governments aided industries, especially textile mills, to recover the indigenous markets due to the fall of exports. Until then Congress did not have a clear laborer policy at all-India level; and so some labor leaders failed to stand up against influences of European controlled merchants or domestic factory owners.

Congress had founded industrial labor organizations from the 1920s. In the All India Trade Union Congress (AITUC), Lala Lajpat Rai was president. Even communist minded leaders like S. A. Dange was associated with AITUC. Nehru appealed to trade union leaders to support Congress candidates in elections. Rajagopalachari influenced AITUC to make way for Congress. The new government supported trade union activities. A National Federation of Trade Unions (NFTU) was also formed to coordinate the different unions. Each left and the right fractions in Congress who ran unions, took efforts to consolidate industrial laborers.

Mr. V. V. Giri, the Industrial and Labour minister in Madras, introduced mutual settlement methods to solve disputes and avoided strikes or closings. G. D. Birla threatened to shift their base from Bombay to nearby Princely States when union activities intensified. The Congress ministry introduced the *Bombay Industrial Act* in 1938, ignoring opposition of Congress-man Gulzarilal Nanda and S. A. Dange, a communist trade unionist. Nehru or Subhas Chandra, working with labor unions and left-wing members, did not oppose the Act. They suggested modifying clauses and solving problems.

5.9 Subhas Chandra as Congress President

We have noted how after the 1937 elections Subhas Bose was released in March from internment in hospital. In December 1937 he arrived at his favorite health resort in Bad Gastein, Austria. The following month he went to England and learnt that he had been elected Congress president for 1938.²² There he met with Indian sympathisers such as Mr. Attlee, Mr. Arthur Greenwood, Sir Strafford Cripps, Mr. Harold Laski, among others, before he returned to India.

Fig. 27 Jawaharlal Nehru and Subhas Chandra Bose (Public Domain).

In his first term as the Congress president, Subhas and Nehru (Fig. 5.27) jointly drew developmental plans for future India through a national planning committee. They accepted industrial development as the foundation of the economy in post-independent India. Both of them were believers of Fabian socialism in England. On the contrary, Gandhi with some of his ardent followers favored a rural khadi based India as Gandhi was a critic of "machine civilization."

On 18 December 1933 Gandhi, Nehru and Subhas made press statements and disclosed their political likings.²³ Gandhi expressed his dislike of fascism preferring to communist ideals but excluding its methods of orthodox approaches. Nehru said that if Congress was given the option to choose between some form of Communism and some form of Fascism, he was all for the former. He abhorred Fascism and Capitalism, both being brutal. Subhas, however, believed in the possibility of synthesis of Communism and Capitalism. He said that experiments of such a synthesis were possible in Indian conditions, as another of Gandhi's experiments had aroused profound interest. Subhas further stated that both Communism and Fascism believed in supremacy of the state over the individual, and were therefore prone to dictatorships. He wanted none of the two by themselves, but believed in planned reorientation of India if possible by synthesis of the two. Nehru, as the Prime Minister of India accepted this idea of synthesis, and adopted a mixed system for planning.

Though three frontline leaders in Indian politics were in favor of socialism, the blind followers of Gandhi, the majority in the CWC, were right inclined and opposed the socialist programmes of Subhas. This disagreement widened from the end of 1938. In a CWC meeting held after the Munich crisis of September 1938, and one year before World War II broke out, Subhas wanted to start a national campaign to prepare its people for a radical struggle which would synchronize with the coming war in Europe. But his every move was opposed. The group in opposition would tolerate Subhas only as a puppet president, to which he would not accede.

When Subhas planned to induct progressive minded people into the CWC to work for postwar reconstruction, Gobinda Ballav Pant supported by the majority insisted on retaining the older group, casting the leaders of the Congress Socialist Forum out. Gandhi, however, advised Subhas to select persons of his own choice.[24] This advice was a challenge for Subhas and he did not accept it, and rather wished Gandhi gave his leadership accepting the leftist agenda. Gandhi declined that wish. Gandhi believed in a strategic contradiction between non-violence and left minded agendas. He wanted to practice both nationalism and non-violence. But Subhas was an ardent nationalist with a single minded goal to free India. It is not that Subhas did not accept Gandhi, but he did not accept Gandhi's non-violence as the only weapon against the British.[25]

To strengthen the party base Subhas intended to induct socialist minded people, but those who came from the communist party did not support him as they preferred a more conventional leadership. Moreover, the left inclined Congress leaders who worked for Subhas to be re-elected in 1939, failed to resist the opposition which jeopardized Subhas's second term.

Even P. C. Joshi, a communist leader, accepted the national movement under Congress as the biggest class struggle. Subhas faced the political challenges alone, and when he could not work in peace he realised he came to a dead-end. He resigned on 29 April 1939 and immediately formed the *Forward Bloc* as a progressive group within Congress by assembling those who still remained by his side.

Subhas planned for making Forward Bloc stronger and capable to act on its own to face any major problem, and take preparatory approaches to win freedom. He had assessed that war would begin soon, and Forward Bloc sprang up in response to "a historical necessity," as Subhas said.[26] Subhas believed that an approach of non-cooperation might paralyze the administration, but could not throw out the government; more drastic measures were needed.

At this challenging juncture, Nehru –who patronized the left group himself being left minded– chose not to be on the side of Subhas when he needed him most. Nehru remained neutral.[27] He apprehended, and even expressed personally to Subhas in April 1939, that his step might split the Congress,[28] and for the greater interest of the party, he urged Subhas not to resign.[29]

Nehru's neutrality in this particular situation was painful for both of them. Nehru was in two minds over the issue and wrote that he was "in very low spirit and it was difficult … to carry on without a breakdown."[30] When Nehru spoke about unity in Congress, Subhas said that one would distinguish between the 'no unity' which led to more effective action and 'unity' which resulted in inaction.[31] Subhas wrote to Nehru expressing his disappointment at Nehru's silence. Within a few days Nehru wrote to him, "… glad I am that you have written to me fully and frankly and made it clear to me how you feel about me… frankness hurts often …but it is often desirable, especially between those who have to work together… Your letter is helpful… and I am grateful to you for it."[32] In 1939, Nehru, in an address before Congress Committee, said that he kept himself neutral to avoid disunity that would have eventually weakened the party, and to tether the freedom struggle.[33] Nehru was honest with himself.

The influence of Subhas was unquestionable, and when he was Congress president, Congress became so popular that its membership surged to a record number of 4.5 million. The formation of Forward Bloc might be an undesirable ending, but it paid future dividends. Indians will ever remember the sacrifice Subhas made, and the boldness he showed. The unprecedented move of the Azad Hind Bahini unnerved the British administration more than the non-cooperation movement could do.[34]

5.10 Observations

Congress activities emerged above the ground after a pause during Gandhi's absence. Through the Salt-march movement the organization established a mass contact at pan India level. It brought back fresh energy among party members and Congress gained confidence to organize future movements on a larger scale.

From the turn of the century, growing political tensions made the Raj uncertain about its capacity to comply with imperial commitments using Indian resources as the economy was dependent on the political situation which was getting more and more complex. Busy tackling political situations, the Raj could not ascertain whether their economic policies during the period was matching their capacity to control Indian resources favorably.

During this period the recession grew deeper. Irwin understood how complex the situation was, but could not convince the Cabinet. He deviated from imperial policy by overruling the warnings of London only to oblige Indians. He took precautions because he knew that an increasing strength of nationalists was working against imperialism over the last two decades, and that Indian radical incidents coincided with those in South Africa and Russia in 1905, and Ireland in 1920–21.

There was a sign of economic improvement during the wartime which was not sustained even after the Raj's commitment to cover military expenses was relaxed. The Cabinet's decision of 1923 to transfer the responsibility of Indian troops from the Viceroy to His Majesty's Government was commendable, as well as their share in the expenses for modernization of Indian troops before World War II.[35] But the tax burden of Indians was not reduced sufficiently, causing mass participation in politics to surge in the 1930s. Government brutally retaliated to thwart all opposition. Anarchists were executed and large numbers of activists were arrested to suppress Congress. But this policy indirectly caused both nationalism and communal passions to thrive, which prevented a stable environment for a stable economy. That the government was ultimately pushed towards withdrawal was perceptible when the Act 1935 was passed.

During the interwar period, the economy of Britain was too weak to sanction additional support to the Raj when the Indian economy, suffering from unfavorable exchange rates, lost international confidence. The Government of India Act 1935 was a virtual surrender of the government to Indian hands, which began with the handover of land revenue collection to the provincial governments to increase the tax base and buy political peace.

The government did not formulate any policy to combat political tensions. Even when the financial crisis was less acute, the Raj was reluctant to improve the Indian economy by developing alternative sources of earning necessary for poverty alleviation. Expenditure on irrigation was barely one-ninth of that spent on railways. Shashi Tharoor refers to William Jennings Bryan's comment that ten percent of army expenditure applied to irrigation would complete the system within five years.[36] Even the taxation rate could not be increased on a level which was already high. Overstretching the military expenditure and inept finance management led the government to reconcile for political expediency.

Policies of stiffening the administration and to divide and rule, adopted after replacement of Irwin, only increased the strength of Congress, bringing it to power after the 1937 election. Congress was given the opportunity to control the administration and the Raj remained to engage in more wars. Even the Princely States, after being incorporated under federal provision, became more nationalist in character. However, Congress, even though it was in power, could not deliver all its promises, because the provincial governors and the majority of permanent civil service officers were British.[37]

The results of the 1937 election helped revive the Muslim League to become significant in Indian politics. After his return from his London exile in 1934, Jinnah wished to work together with Congress by honoring the Lucknow Pact. They both accepted the communal quota agreed upon in Lucknow. But other Muslim leaders aggravated problems by their regional stance. When during the election campaign in the United Provinces, Nehru attempted to woo Muslim voters in favor of Congress, a major and irreparable rift between two parties emerged.[38]

Jinnah then took over the reins and affirmed the League's stake in the political arena. The League was encouraged by the British to stick to the minority quota after Gandhi failed to convince the cabinet that Muslims were Indians and they would be part of a common voter list.

The Congress party itself split, giving rise to the Forward Bloc for which people close to Gandhi were responsible. Subhas, however, admired Gandhi by writing that for twenty-two years he had built up organization spanning the country including the Princely States, and awakened political life even in remote villages. The masses learnt how to counter the most powerful enemy through weapons of passive resistance. But Subhas had reservations to accept that a passive force would be sufficiently effective to expel an imperial government.[39] Instead, he wished that strength of mass support be suitably used to build up post-independent India.

The question remains whether the Forward Bloc in unison with Congress could be strong enough to counter the great powers which Subhas proposed. Gandhi, later in life realized that a wide gulf had always separated him from his followers, though they submitted to his authority. He also realized that slave-driving might be an agreeable pastime and great source of strength, but it did not pay in the long run. Perhaps this realization was his retrospection of indirectly indulging the right inclined wing in Congress who opposed the left, socialist agenda of Subhas Chandra Bose.

References:

1. Carl Bridge, *Holding India to the Empire: The British Conservative Party and the 1935 Constitution* (Burlington, VT: Vantage Press, 1986), 73.
2. Piers Brendon, *The Decline and Fall of British Raj 1781–1947* (London: Vintage Books, 2008), 384.
3. Brendon, Ibid., 246.
4. Neville Chamberlain, Robert C. Self, ed., *The Neville Chamberlain Diary Letters: The Heir Apparent*, Vol. 3. (Farnham, UK: Ashgate, 2000), 311.
5. Subhas Chandra Bose, *The Indian Struggle 1920–1942* (New Delhi: Oxford Press, 1964), 236–37.
6. Bose, Ibid, 366.
7. Alan Campbell-Johnson, *Mission with Mountbatten* (New Delhi: AICO Publishing House, 1951), 29.
8. N. Shivam, "History of Prices in India during Different Periods." https://www.economicsdiscussion.net/india/history-of-prices-in-india-during-different-periods/21260.
9. B. R. Tomlinson, "India and the British Empire, 1880–1935," *Sage Journal*, Vol. 2, Issue 4 (1975), 337. Published online 26 July 2016.
10. Ibid, 342.
11. Ibid, 366.
12. Ibid, 367.
13. Bose, Ibid, 347, 365–66.
14. Ibid, 365; J. L. Nehru, S. Gopal (ed.) *Selected Works of Jawaharlal Nehru*, Vol. 7 (New Delhi: Nehru Memorial Fund, 1975). Where this famous dictum appears in *Nehru's Works*, I have not been able to verify. Compare, "The Government of India Act of 1935, the new constitution, stares at us offensively, this new charter of bondage which has been imposed upon us despite our utter rejection of it..." *The Fazipur Congress*, 605. "A Charter of slavery is no law for the

slave. The slave who would be free can only tear it up and fashion for himself a new charter of freedom..." *Message to the Bombay Chronicle*, in Selected Works, Vol. 7, 183, 408.

15. Bose, Ibid.
16. Bose, Ibid.
17. Brendon, Ibid, 387.
18. Barbara D. Metcalf and Thomas R. Metcalf, *A Concise History of Modern India* (Cambridge: Cambridge University Press, 2005), 103.
19. Brendon, Ibid, 391.
20. John Glendevon, *The Viceroy at Bay: Lord Linlithgow 1936–43* (London: Harper Collins, 1971), 119.
21. Sekhar Bandyopadhyay, *Constraints in Bengal Politics, A History of Modern India* (Hyderabad: Orient Longman, 2004), 340.
22. Bose, Ibid, 370.
23. Bose, Ibid, 351.
24. M. K. Gandhi, *The Collected Works of Mahatma Gandhi*, Vol. 69 (New Delhi: Government of India, Publication Department, 1999), 98.
25. Shashi Tharoor, *Nehru: The Invention of India* (New Delhi: Penguin, 2007), 113.
26. Bose, Ibid, 377.
27. Bipan Chandra, M. Mukherjee, A. Mukherjee, S. Mahajan, K. N. Panikar, *Indian Struggle for Independence 1857–1947*, 2nd Ed. (Kolkata: K. P. Bagchi, 1994), 214.
28. Bose, Ibid, 375.
29. J. L. Nehru, *Jawaharlal Nehru: An Autobiography* (London, New Delhi: Oxford University Press, 1936, 1982), 192.
30. J. L. Nehru, S. Gopal, *Selected Works of Jawaharlal Nehru*. Vol. 1, 1889–1947 (New Delhi: Oxford India, 1976), 280.
31. Bose, Ibid, 375.
32. J. L. Nehru, Ibid, 329.
33. Eric Sevareid, *Not So Wild a Dream* (New York: Simon and Schuster, 1946), 241.

34. Jock Colville, *The Fringes of Power* (Guilford, CT: John Lyon Press, 2002), 583.
35. Ishita Banerjee-Dube, *A History of Modern India* (Cambridge: Cambridge University Press, 2015), 388.
36. Shashi Tharoor, *An Era of Darkness: The British Empire in India* (New Delhi: Aleph Book Company, 2016), 262.
37. Bose, Ibid, 378.
38. Banerjee-Dube, Ibid, 371.
39. Bose, Ibid, 360.

CHAPTER 6

British India 1939 – 41. World War II, Phase 1

This chapter describes the quickly changing scenario of the Indian political atmosphere beginning from 1939, after the War against Germany had been declared. Congress, Forward Bloc, and Muslim League were arguing with the Viceroy on participation of Indians in the war. It describes issues relating to the Defence Council Act, the Pakistan Resolution, and Britain's inclination to the minority community. This chapter ends with the escape of Subhas Chandra and the publication of the Atlantic Charter.

6.1 Beginnings

The Second World War broke out on 1 September 1939 with Germany waging an unprovoked attack on Poland. Along with France, Britain declared war on Germany two days later. On the same day September 3rd, Viceroy Linlithgow issued an ordinance suppressing all political activities in India and declared India to be at war. He called for immediate Indian support of Britain in the war efforts.

Subhas Chandra Bose made contact with Gandhi, Jinnah, and the Princely States to outline a strategy on the Indian stand. Gandhi himself expressed sympathy for Britain, which astonished Indians who were waiting for self-rule from 1917. Immediately after the war began, the Forward Bloc started a campaign to convince Indians to remain neutral.[1] One of the largest rallies Subhas addressed was on the beach of Madras on 3 September, the day the ordinance was issued.

At the Wordaha Congress, 8 September 1939, Subhas Chandra, Acharya Naren Dev, and Joyprakash Narayan were invited to participate in discussions on war affairs. Subhas clarified that Indian freedom struggle would begin at once, as Britain's difficulty would become India's opportunity, and Forward Bloc was free to act for the best interest of the country.[2] This meeting radically resolved that self-determination was a democratic right of Indian people, and they might seek mutual defence along with other nations. Viceroy Linlithgow was asked whether Britain's fight was for the extension of democracy and if so, she must end imperialism first. He was also asked to declare the government's aims in war. Congress had planned for a national government at centre and announced that if independence was promised after the war, it would support Britain. Muslim League agreed to support Britain only if Indian Muslims got protection against Congress dominance, and the League was allowed the right to veto in case of a future change in constitution.

Next, the Defence Council Act 1939, passed on 25 September was enacted. It was effectively a martial law. Britain's interest swiveled more to war as it remained busy with commitments in the Middle East and Southeast Asia. Congress was automatically acting as the alternate British Raj with responsibilities in central and provincial administrations.[3] However, from the turn of the century, Congress had slowly drifted away from Britain. Nehru said that a government run by Congress would bring a new order. He was committed to counter imperialism since he had attended the *Congress of Oppressed Nationalists* in 1927 in Brussel. Congress as the Indian national party supported anti-imperialist movements of some Asian and African countries since the 1930s, and at the same time sympathized with people suffering in Spain, Ethiopia and Czechoslovakia.

From 11 September, the Act 1935 was suspended, and a week later the Viceroy promised to appoint a consultation that included Indians as his adviser. He requested Gandhi on 26 September to support Britain. Gandhi, in response, asked the Viceroy for the declaration of a concrete policy. The Viceroy declined to make any concessions on further reforms until communal problems were solved and the war would end. Gandhi pressed him to satisfy Indians by giving them some hope.

The Viceroy then met with Rajendra Prasad (then Congress President), Nehru and Patel on 2 October at Gandhi's request, for further discussions. They urged him to allow the Constituent Assembly, or else they would not attend any future all-party meeting. The Muslim League and other minorities, when requested to participate in the war effort, asked the Viceroy to declare Britain's plans. The Viceroy evaded all questions, but agreed to modify the Act 1935 as might seem desirable.

On 14 October 1939 the Viceroy released a White Paper promising India's dominion status and an extended Executive Council with more Indians. He informed that the British would not transfer responsibility to anybody who might be challenged by opponents, but he agreed to form an advisory committee with Indians. Congress assumed that colonies would not survive the holocaust of the war, and the CWC on 22–23 October rejected the White Paper, and reaffirmed they were unwilling to extend any support to Britain before domestic issues were clarified. Nehru said that Linlithgow was "... slow of mind, solid as a rock and with almost a rock's lack of awareness."[4] Muslim League urged the Viceroy to satisfy their demands first. On 29 October CWC advised the state ministers to lay down their office. Provincial legislature adopted resolutions following the CWC's September model. Congress relaunched the civil disobedience movement.

The House of Commons agreed to expand the Viceroy's Executive Council on a temporary basis during wartime, but reinstated white dominance in the center which was lost after the 1937 election, and refused to commit to a federal structure. Congress refused to accept any transitory offer and asked the ministers to resign by 31 October, and postpone all political agendas – even plans for a national government at the center.

With ministerial resignation, the respective Governors of eight Congress ruled provinces assumed administrative control by appointing advisories following the provision in the Act 1935. Bengal, Punjab, and Sindh remained unaffected as Congress was not in majority. Jinnah rejoiced at the Congress departure designating the 22 December 1939 as *Deliverance Day*, gathering more Muslim members in the League.

Because the Executive Council was extended without considering the federal structure, Gandhi asked the Viceroy to create a common ground for further discussions to be profitable, and in early 1940 he requested him to reach an understanding through applying moral strength by each Congress and the government. He also said that if Britain could not recognize India's legitimate claims, it showed Britain's moral bankruptcy. The Viceroy then sought Congress' help to end minority problems.

Jinnah was afraid of the return of Congress enforcing stability of the dominion status. He expressed his dislike of such engagements between the Viceroy and Gandhi. Linlithgow offered the League to form a government in North Western Frontier Province as Congress ministers had resigned. But Jinnah declined to go into dominion status, and threatened to begin a civil war if Congress returned.

On 28 February 1940, Congress planned for civil disobedience to press for a federation using the provision in the Act 1935. The League however, opposed unilateral enforcement of any constitution and self-rule. Jinnah assumed that the British were preparing for withdrawal by handing over the control to a Hindu Raj. The Forward Bloc observed an *Anti Compromise Conference* on 23 March 1940 in Ramgarh demanding for transfer of power. The Congress Working Committee also had a meeting in Ramgarh to discuss future plans, as the party did not have a wartime policy. Subhas said that by suspending the movements, Congress gave the Government the impression that it talked more than it did in actual practice. His remark provoked Gandhi to write to the Viceroy to assign India the dominion status immediately in terms of the statutes of Westminster.[5]

At the Lahore session of Muslim League, Jinnah on 23 March 1940 announced that the social order in Islam was different from Hinduism and two communities could not share a common nationality. Muslims should have their own home land. He proposed that the provinces in east and west numerically dominated by Muslims should be grouped to constitute a sovereign independent state. This was the *Lahore Pakistan resolution*. Muslims expressed that Bande Mataram as the national song, the Tricolor flag, and choosing the Hindi language instead of Urdu were contradictory to their culture. Meanwhile, Forward Bloc proposed to observe *National Week* from 6–13 April to spur civil disobedience nationwide.

In the European Spring, Germany suddenly invaded Norway, Denmark, Holland and Belgium, causing these nations to surrender. With the change of war scenario, the Secretary of State declared in the House of Lords on 18 April 1940 that eighty million Muslim subjects of His Majesty's India would not be imposed a form of constitution under which they would not live peacefully. In May 1940 the British cabinet changed leaders when Winston Churchill, a strong supporter of imperialism, was elected Prime Minister. The Secretary of State for India was also replaced. This period in the 1940s was crucial because British aspirations were directly opposite to Congress, and both sought the advantages of the war time crisis.

After British forces were withdrawn from Dunkirk, France also capitulated on 22 June 1940, leaving Britain's prospects against the German might unpredictable. Subhas took this opportunity to talk to Gandhi in June (Fig. 28) requesting him to actively resist Britain with the support of Forward Bloc. Gandhi wanted to wait, but did not discourage Subhas to proceed with his plan. Gandhi thought that the country was not prepared for a direct encounter with Britain, and that it could put a future peaceful changeover in jeopardy. He encouraged Subhas saying that he would be the first person to congratulate Subhas if he succeeded.[6]

Fig. 28 Gandhi and Subhas Bose (Public Domain).

To Winston Churchill the protection of Britain and keeping India as a colony were equally important for retaining Britain's supremacy. As the war situation worsened, Linlithgow was instructed to convince Indian leaders to join the Viceroy's executive council and support the war. Gandhi was assured of a dominion within a year or after the war, and for that the Viceroy had planned to draft a new constitution. Naturally his priority was safeguarding defence and Britain's commercial and other interests. Gandhi asked him to initiate exploratory processes to quickly meet the pending issues after the war. Jinnah sent a memorandum asking the government not to oppose the two nation proposition.

In an emergency meeting of 3–7 July 1940, the CWC wrote to request for elections to ensure a national government at the center with transitory measures, and to enable the pending Constituent Assembly without delay. An appended note stated that if issues were resolved in time, Congress would participate in the defence of the country. Gandhi, however, opposed any involvement in war.

In the next resolution adopted in Poona on 27 July, Congress offered direct cooperation with Britain on condition independence was promised. Understanding what might happen in Poona, Gandhi excused himself from this meeting, keeping himself away from war, and planned to retire. But he returned on 15 September after Congress decided for fresh agitations in lieu of war participation.

Given emergency powers because of the war, the Viceroy restricted freedom of speech, public meetings, and enforced imprisonment without trial. All Congress ministers were arrested. Subhas was already in jail. In July 1940 hundreds of supporters were imprisoned without trial. Gandhi announced that freedom of speech was necessary to establish the right of existence, and opposed Viceroy's oppressive order by launching the *Individual Non-Cooperation movement*. Some business communities were not in favor of major movements. Vinoba Bhave, who inaugurated this movement on 17 October 1940, was the first to be arrested. Nehru was put in jail from 31 October for four years. Thousands of volunteers were also arrested. When Nehru was asked for a trial, he said, "not him, the British empire was on trial before the bar of the world." From jail, Nehru wrote to Indira, his daughter, that he "retreated into the mighty Maginot line" (meaning he was relaxing in custody). Nehru received an early release.

As the Viceroy's extended Executive Council remained inoperative, the new Secretary of State made another appeal for India's cooperation. He justified the claims of Muslims and indirectly encouraged Jinnah's Pakistan. As this news was ventilated in the press, the Secretary reverted and said that he was talking about integration of parties to prevent any external attack. Gandhi's call for individual non-cooperation now lost its edge. Restrictions were imposed on publicity and press. Abul Kalam Azad, Congress secretary, was arrested in early January of 1941.

6.1.1 Escape of Subhas Chandra Bose

The direct support of Mr. H. V. Kamath of Bombay, Sardul Singh Kaveesher of Punjab, and Satyaranjan Bakshi, and Sarat Chandra Bose from Bengal were the strength of the Forward Bloc. On 2 July 1940, just a few hours after he finished a meeting with Rabindranath Tagore, Subhas Chandra was detained and was put in the Presidency Jail for publishing an article in *The Forward* and his public lectures blaming the British. He was not a person sitting idly in prison, but he would not be released either! He started fasting until death protesting his illegal detention. When his health deteriorated Subhas was sent to his Calcutta residence in Elgin Road, where he remained under house arrest. Then, on the night of 16–17 January 1941, he escaped to Germany in disguise.

His nephew Sisir Kumar Bose, drove him up to the Gomoh rail station (presently called Netaji Subhas Chandra Bose station in Jharkhand) from where he reached Peshawar. He then escaped to Kabul with the help of Akbar Shah of NWFP. On 26 January 1941, his escape was made public. Aided by the Italian embassy, Subhas left Kabul in the middle of March and arrived in Germany early April via the Soviet Union.

Henceforth the government of India became ruthless. Many leaders were put in custody and all political movements were stopped. The non-political Indians were appointed members of the Executive Council. In February 1941 Muslim League proposed two Muslim states, Bengal–Assam in the east, and the western states including Punjab and Delhi.

After the fall of France Subhas became convinced that Britain would lose the War but would not release India, and so the Indian struggle would continue. Subhas was therefore inclined to collaborate with Axis powers (i.e. British enemies) for India's advantage.[7] On 2 April 1941 he reached Berlin and immediately issued a memorandum for setting up a *Free India Government in Exile*. He received support from Germany to carry on anti-British propaganda from *The Free India* Centre in Lichtensteinallee. The broadcast was to exhort Indians to rise up against the British. Till then the British government was in the dark about Subhas's whereabouts.

Leo Amery, the new Secretary of State for India (1940–45) was working on an expanded Executive Council in India in 1941. He remarked that two major Indian parties who always differed were united on the issue of the Executive Council. Gandhi defiantly answered that,

> Mr. Amery insulted Indian intelligence by reiterating *ad nauseam* that Indian political parties have but to agree among themselves

and Great Britain will register the will of a united India. I have repeatedly shown that it has been the traditional polity of Great Britain to prevent parties from uniting. 'Divide and Rule' has been Great Britain's proud and ill-conceived motto. It is the British statesmen who are responsible for the divisions in India's ranks and the divisions will continue so long as the British sword holds India under bondage.[8]

6.1.2 Atlantic Charter and aftermath

France surrendered to Germany in June 1940. The war situation took a serious turn as Axis forces invaded Norway and advanced to Yugoslavia and Greece, and occupied the islands in the Aegean Sea. Britain fought Germany alone, but its prospect in war was bleak when Germans occupied an extended area from the Mediterranean to Norway between 1940–41. The progress of the German army towards Russia was uncheckable until August and it was halted at the end of 1941. Bandyopadhyay wrote that Hilter made a blunder by invading the USSR on 22 June because he lost the chance of bringing Britain under Control.[9] In 1940 the British foreign secretary felt that the existence of his country was dependent on US assistance. From August she was bankrupt with the possibility of losing her position as an independent power. Britain had no alternative to sell some top-secret British inventions, sophisticated weapons to the USA. About a quarter of her wealth was exhausted due to an over-extended military expenditure in the raging war.

British prime minister Winston Churchill lamented that Britain was flayed to the bone. In August 1941 he met the American president Franklin Roosevelt in Newfoundland to discuss the financial crisis of Britain. Their opinions on imperialism differed. President Roosevelt was in favor of colonial emancipation, but Churchill was still hoping to preserve the empire.

Churchill reluctantly signed *The Atlantic Charter* in August 1941 with Roosevelt that set out their goals for a postwar world, which include a clause aiming to restore the sovereign rights for those who were forcibly deprived of that. Britain was fighting war against Hitler's fascism but her attitude towards India was still imperialistic. Roosevelt said, "I cannot believe that we can fight a war against fascist slavery, and at the same time not work to free people all over the world from a backward colonial policy."[10]

It was Churchill's task to recover Britain from the financial crisis, and he had to sign the charter that pledged "to respect the rights of all people to choose the form of government under which they would live." This joint declaration of 14 August 1941 was initially violated by Britain's refusal to accept it for the entire empire. A surprised Roosevelt pressured Britain to accept the Charter as universal. Nehru exchanged letters with Roosevelt expecting his support but he received none. Nehru felt, "almost alone America kept the torch of democratic freedom alight."[11]

In the House of Commons, Churchill initially said that the Charter did not apply to the empire, but finally he declared that the process for constitutional governments in the British Empire including India was advancing, that India was already pledged to obtain their partnership in the British Commonwealth, and his government agreed to maintain British responsibilities for her people. With an apparent change of British policy, the Indian controlled Legislative Assembly formally demanded the full enforcement of the Charter. The people of Britain also wanted the British to modify her policy and bring India back in the War.

By October the formalities for an expanded Executive Council were complete. Nehru, Azad and other satyagrahis were released, and the Congress members who had resigned from office, came back to power. At the suggestion of Jinnah, a Defence Council was formed in lieu of the Executive Council. In 1941, when the question of parity was raised again, Jinnah did not receive support from this Defense Council.

Meanwhile, Japan gained prominence by attacking Pearl Harbor in December 1941. The Japanese also progressed to Malaysia, Philippines, Indonesia, and coastal China. The British forces were pushed into retreat from Rangoon by 15 February 1942. Britain was forced to come into alliance with America, China, and the Dutch. This Alliance made surprising advances overpowering Japan.

In May 1940, the leftist Stafford Cripps, returned from his Moscow assignment to join the British War Cabinet then under Clement Attlee. Churchill proposed a policy declaration (not discussed here) which was later amended. At Attlee's request, Stafford Cripps travelled to India to look into the Indian demands and give India a status similar to that enjoyed by Canada. Cripps reached Delhi on 22 March 1942 to solve Indian governance issues and secure immediate war cooperation. He intended to Indianize the Executive Council and approximate a ruling cabinet.

6.2 Observations

Congress refused Indian participation in the war, rejecting the Viceroy's call, and urged for the immediate declaration of the Indian federation following the 1935 Act. At a certain stage, Congress agreed to support British war efforts with certain conditions, though Gandhi was against any involvement in violence, and Forward Bloc had campaigned not to support Britain.

After France's surrender to Germany, Subhas suggested Gandhi to take radical steps and use this difficult period in Britain to further the Indian cause, but Gandhi wanted to wait. The Raj administration became increasingly oppressive, using the Defence Council Act 1939, by curtailing human liberty and denying the constituent assembly. This repressive Act caused the conflict between imperialism and nationalism to intensify. Congress was planning for a national government when they were the *de facto* ruler of India, but suddenly Congress ministers resigned in 8 provinces to protest against the government's denial of a constituent assembly. Gradually the Raj became fully engaged in war issues.

Muslim League rejoiced in the Congress departure, and opposed participation in a dominion with a single constitution. The Lahore Resolution of March 1940 announced the creation of Pakistan for the first time. British conservatives, to dominate the nationalists and preserve imperial control, restrained the progress on a constituent assembly, and showed inclination towards the Muslim League. At the same time the Muslim League demanded a separate constitution instead of participation into a Constituent Assembly as a minority.

During this period of political turmoil Subhas Chandra escaped to Germany and sought international cooperation from British enemies. After France fell, Britain lost its superiority and became financially weak. It needed American support. Churchill reluctantly yielded to the shift from imperialism at American pressure. In this period Japan attacked Pearl Harbour and forced the British to retreat from Rangoon. The alliance among Britain, America, Dutch and China changed the war scenario.

References:

1. Subhas Chandra Bose, *Indian Struggle, 1920–1942* (New Delhi: Oxford Press, 1964), 382.
2. Shyamal Chandra Bandyopadhyay, "America's Rise & End of an Empire," *The Statesman (Durga Puja Special)*, Calcutta (2011), 45.
3. Subhas Chandra Bose, Ibid, 381.
4. Piers Brendon, *Decline and Fall of British Empire 1781–1997* (London: Vintage Books, 2008), 390.
5. Subhas Chandra Bose, Ibid, 383.
6. Ibid, 397.
7. Ibid, 387.
8. "Mahatma Gandhi's Statement." *The Indian Annual Register*, Vol. 1 (April 1941), 327.
9. Bandyopadhyay, Ibid, 46.
10. J. L. Nehru, S. Gopal (ed.), *Selected Works of Jawaharlal Nehru*, Vol. 2 (New Delhi: Nehru Memorial Fund, 1948), 371.
11. Ibid, 379. Quoted from the *The Atlantic Monthly*, Vol. 165 (April 1940), 455.

CHAPTER 7

British India 1942 – 45. World War II, Phase 2

This Chapter outlines the Cripps' Mission that opened the possibility of the Constituent Assembly so long suppressed, and discusses how Congress and especially the Muslim League reacted to it. This chapter also focuses on the Quit India movement and its consequences. The war situation with the approach of the INA – Japanese aggression in eastern India provides the context.

7.1 The Cripps' Mission and Responses

Cripps' plan: The aim of this mission was to secure Indian support for the war effort. It proposed to resolve communal unrest by forming an Indianized constitution and to ascertain a post-war successor of British India. Cripps collected information through his discussions with the Viceroy, members of the Executive Council, concerned officers and advisors, and with different parties. He talked to Europeans, Anglo Indians, and the Princely States, and drafted a conditional scheme which outlined the possibility of transfer of power to Indian hands. In a press conference of 29 March 1942, Cripps announced that:

1. The Constituent Assembly would be set up before the declaration of independence.* India would be free to leave or to remain within the Empire, and would have freedom to decide whether they wanted a Governor-General or not.
2. The concept of 'British India' would no longer exist after India was awarded independence, and the Princely States would have the option to be represented in the Constituent Assembly or not.
3. During the interim period of war, the defense of India would be the priority, and so a formal transfer of power would be delayed.
4. This scheme would be like an interim constitution with provisions for the Executive Council to function like a cabinet within the existing framework. There would be a provision to improve this scheme by adopting a better arrangement in the future.
5. This commission would have options to elaborate this scheme which would either be accepted or wholly rejected.

Cripps also declared that:
The Indian union would be like a dominion associated with the United Kingdom with the exception of domestic and external affairs. The elected members would indirectly elect the Constituent Assembly for writing a new constitution, and His Majesty's Government would implement it.

If any province refused to accept the constitution for a dominion, this non acceding province would follow the status quo. It would have provision for future accession, and liberty to frame their own constitution with full status of the Indian union/dominion and build up relationships with other members of the British Commonwealth.

---

* Note: After more than five year negotiations, the Constituent Assembly was formed on 9 December 1946 at the suggestion of a Cabinet Mission. Members of this assembly were indirectly elected by the members of the Provincial Assemblies elected in early 1946. It had a Congress majority. Early 1947 representatives of Muslim League and the Princely States joined the Assembly.

Until the final procedure was completed, the core task of defence and related matters would be carried by His Majesty's Government, and military matters and material resources would be under the Governor-General of India who would function with the usual cooperation of the Indian people.

Responses: The Congress Working Committee in its resolution of 11 April 1942 opposed the clause giving 'liberty' to any state or territorial unit to form its own constitution (which meant the province would enjoy the option to secede from the Indian union). After much discussion, they rejected the entire scheme in the CWC meeting on 1 May* and stated in a separate resolution that the Indian public was not interested in war, and in case of any foreign invasion, Congress would not cooperate. In another resolution, Congress stated its disagreement with the positions allotted for the Indian Defence members. The meeting concluded that the scheme was ludicrous as it would accelerate a division of the country instead of forging it in a single unit, and it was drawn up without a clear-cut promise of self-rule.[1]

Muslim League opposed the scheme as nothing was maintained about the formation of Pakistan. Thus, the two major parties refused to accept Cripps' proposal for opposite reasons.

Relegating the award of self-rule for the interim period, and participation in war, Gandhi wrote in the *Harijan Weekly* of April 1942 that India was living in a state of ordered anarchy. And if it would revert to complete lawlessness with the British withdrawal, they were prepared to take risks. Hereafter, Cripps and his team left India.

In the Wardha meeting of July 1942, Congress discussed some social issues like wartime price hikes, the scarcity of salts, and prolonged military occupation of land which caused public suffering. The CWC through a formal resolution urged the government to resolve the issues with immediate effect, threatening that pending movements would be resumed.

---

* Note: Gandhi did not attend the 1 May meeting, but had sent a draft stating that the "Japanese quarrel was not with India… if India were free, her first step would probably be to negotiate with Japan…" But Nehru excluded mentioning Japan or Britain in Gandhi's draft.

Jinnah interpreted Cripps' approval of one Constituent Assembly, excluding the option of a partition, as evidence of Congress' insensitivity to the League courting the British for a system that would transfer the power to Congress to establish a Hindu Raj. He recommended all Muslims to refrain from joining any movement under Congress.

The official mouthpiece of the Labor Party in London criticized Congress for pressing for demands at a crisis point and accused Congress for its petty standard of nationalism. Colonel Louis Johnson, President Roosevelt's personal envoy and head of the American Technical Mission, visited Delhi to push the Indian government towards conciliation. With the commission's permission, he amended Cripps' scheme to make it more acceptable. The CWC also amended the terms of the scheme. But all amendments were rejected in London.

The Secretary of State said that Congress precluded all agreed cooperation and that the government would not allow a constitution at the advantage of the majority party. His comment incited the minorities to reject the Constituent Assembly outright. Thus the high officials in Britain, and indirectly Cripps' scheme itself, encouraged the prospect of a future divided India.

At this stage Britain's real intention to part with its power over India became questionable. Later, Churchill, in a speech of 12 December 1946 in the House of Commons, made it clear that His Majesty's Government had not been willing to support Sir Stafford Cripps to the extent to which he himself was preferred to go.[2]

7.2 Quit India Movement

This movement began in the tumultuous period of Japanese advances. Singapore had fallen on 15 February, Rangoon was invaded on 8 March; Subhas Chandra met Hitler in May; Japan entered India in the east, and people were leaving Calcutta as the city was sporadically bombed; the Cripps' Mission had failed; and Indian public frustration heightened with the growing inflation. For some time, the Japanese pitched tents in the Khidirpur area of Calcutta (remnants of their houses are still found in

Khidirpur today). The imperial power apprehended that Congress might welcome the German - Japan axis with Subhas acting as a fifth column. This was a real possibility as he had pressed Gandhi to use the war situation against Britain.

Congress did prepare to take advantage of the times. After a prolonged CWC meeting in Wardha on 14 July 1942, Gandhi moved the resolution of a *Quit India Movement*, a passive direct resistance on the principles of satyagraha. Later in a press meet on 26 July he indicated a possibility of lawlessness. It was opposed by Rajagopalacharya and even Nehru and Moulana Azad were apprehensive of the consequences. Hindu Mahasabha and Muslim League rejected the call. But Joyprakash Narayan and other faithful supporters of Gandhi were in its favor. Gandhi began the call inviting all nationalist minded people to embark on the movement with the slogan, *Karenge ya Marenge* (Do or Die).

The All India Congress Committee approved the Quit India Movement at the Bombay Meeting on 8 August 1942, and Gandhi in a ninety-minute speech intimated his determination to fight to the end even if he stood alone against the whole world.[3] Gandhi called Indians to act as the citizens of free India, disobeying government orders, through non-violence and non-cooperation.

The meeting ended on the evening of 8 August with an appeal to start the movement right away to demand immediate British withdrawal. For Gandhi this was the first time his patience ran out, and so he took an ultimate step. The authorities responded swiftly. The Police Commissioner of Bombay arrested Gandhi the following morning of 9 August.

Gandhi's call spurred massive civil disobedience (Fig. 29). Though intended to be non-violent, the insurrection went out of control in several places. Government houses were burnt and communications disrupted. Forgetting their affiliations, people from all over India participated in it, except supporters of Muslim League and Communists. Movements spread to Delhi, Bombay, Calcutta. Between 9 to 14 March 1943, Patna witnessed marches of huge Indian crowds towards the Secretariat to hoist national flags. Common people including students in Banaras, parts of Gujarat,

Orissa, Karnataka, eastern UP, and so on, participated in the movement with support of city based business leaders, and landlords in rural areas. Residents of Princely States opened their doors and traders in Baroda took leadership to organize strikes. This momentum of public outcry did not stop, but continued in phases. The movement ended only in 1945 once all detainees were released during the Simla Conference of Wavell.

Fig. 29 Civil Disobedience Bombay, 1942 (G. G. Parekh, orato.world/2023/05/09).

According to Hutchins,[4] *Quit India* used different techniques to pressure the government. In north-eastern Bihar, guerilla warfare was waged under leadership of Joyprakash Narayan. Where Aruna Asaf Ali and Suchta Kripalini were in lead, the movement was clean and non-violent in Gandhi fashion. Even some Congress enclaves set up local governments. The most prominent of those were under Pabitra Pradhanran of Talchir, Orissa. He was a leader of Praja Mandal, a rural based Congress set up. Ajoy Kumar Mukherjee, who was Chief-minister of West Bengal, formed a self-government in Tamluk. The Talchir government was short-lived, but that in Tamluk continued for a number of years by the Congress led peasantry class. Parallel governments functioned while defying police orders.

The movement soon produced its martyrs. On 29 September 1942, Matangini Hazra, a khadi clad 72-year old veteran, remembered as *Gandhi Buri*, was shot dead while she was marching with her women squad to besiege the Tamluk police station to hoist the national flag. She was a Gandhi follower since the days of salt satyagraha and involved in many movements for which she was arrested multiple times.

The Government deployed troops to retaliate. Police sometimes opened fire causing many deaths, and thousands were injured. Surprisingly, some policemen supported the agitators. Many CWC members were arrested on 9 August as well. All leaders were put into custody for three years. Congress committees were declared as unlawful associations. From his custody in Poona, Gandhi wrote to Viceroy that the Government had goaded the people to the point of madness, and if its attitude would not change, he would resort to the law and start fasting.

The leaders of small parties requested the Viceroy to allow them to meet Gandhi and release him. When the Viceroy refused to make an exception for Gandhi when many others were detainees, they resigned from the Viceroy's Executive Committee. Gandhi began his fast from 10 February which lasted until 3 March 1943. In absence of Congress, Muslim League's power was consolidated by inducting some smaller Muslim organizations outside the League who favored a separate Muslim identity. In the political vacuum, the Communists also built up their organization.

The governor facilitated the ministry of Sindh to merge with Muslim League. In Bengal, Fazlul Huq was forced to resign.[5] A similar situation occurred in Assam and in the Northeastern Province. Viceroy Linlithgow was blamed for siding with Muslim League with support of the cabinet. Trans-Atlantic public opinion went against the intransigence of Churchill who had just signed the Atlantic Charter for liquidation of the Empire.

7.3 The Penultimate Viceroy

In September 1943, Viscount Wavell, who, as the Commander-in-Chief was responsible for suppressing the Quit India movement while keeping the Japanese at bay, replaced Linlithgow. Claude Auchinleck became the new Chief. Lord Amery, the Secretary of State, announced that existing policy would remain unchanged. In 1943, the tide turned in favor of the Allied Forces, and the end of the war was in sight. It became difficult for Wavell to hold up the transfer of power because the cabinet was nearly committed to withdrawal.

Through a radio broadcast, Wavell appealed for harmony to all communities including the Princes, and welcomed new proposals (better than Cripps had offered) on constitutional issues. He also pressed for Indian cooperation in war affairs. Sir Tej Bahadur, a leader of all minor parties (also known as Non-Party), apprehending the rise of communal tensions in absence of Congress, urged the Viceroy to release Gandhi. However, Gandhi was not released until 6 May 1944, when his health deteriorated.

After his recovery, Gandhi agreed to withdraw movements if a clear promise on self-rule was made. He also hinted at the possibility of Congress ministers coming back to office. The Viceroy did not respond, but in December, the Secretary of State announced that India was at war, and no agreed future constitution was yet decided upon.[6] In September 1944, Gandhi finally yielded to Jinnah for the post-independence partition of India on the basis of the League's Lahore resolution of 1940, which rested on Muslim majority states.

Jinnah also agreed to proceed for partition, but before independence contradicting Gandhi's proposal for the partition on a majority vote after independence. The League then stated their objections to the central legislature to function. In the midst of these domestic complications, Indian politics took an unprecedented turn with INA's move from outside India.

7.4 Subhas Chandra Bose, Azad Hind and Indian National Army

From 1942 Subhas had begun broadcasting on the German sponsored Azad Hind Radio in Berlin, in cooperation with the Indian Legion. This consisted of released prisoners of war from North Africa (POWs captured by German-Italian forces). Subhas was kept waiting in Germany for a number of months to meet Hitler. In November 1942, he founded the German Indian Society and selected the present "Indian national anthem" to be sung in its inaugural meeting. The Germans failed in Stalingrad and their plan to attack India with the Afghan army was terminated.

Subhas's Europe visit in 1933 had coincided with the Nazis coming to power. Hitler was a racist and opposed to linking Germany to "inferior" races like Indians. He had mocked Indian nationalists and closed the Indian Information Bureau established by Nehru. He even supported India's enslavement. Once the Germans retreated from Russia, and helped by Galeazzo Ciano, the Italian foreign minister, Subhas could meet Hitler on 29 May 1942. Hitler advised Subhas to go to Japan and fight from a place nearer to India, and provided him a submarine (U180) for travel. Subhas was then married and waited for his wife to give birth.

After his meeting with Hitler, Subhas wrote that he had become disillusioned with Germany, and that Hitler was "raving mad."[7] Subhas was criticized for his alliance with the fascist Nazis. But his only desire was to liberate India, accepting British enemies as friends. Indian revolutionaries had also taken German aid to execute the Christmas Day Plot during World War I (see above).

Subhas left the harbor of Kiel with his aid Abid Hassan in 1943, and transferred to a Japanese submarine in Madagascar to reach Tokyo, where he met Hideki Tojo, the Japanese Prime Minister. He met him on 10 June 1943, when the Quit India Movement was at its height. Tojo committed to cooperate. Singapore was then occupied by the Japanese. In 1942 Captain Mohan Singh with help of a Japanese major had already formed the Indian National Army (INA) in Singapore. INA consisted of Indian POWs who were captured after the Japanese occupation of S. E. Asian countries. Rash Behari Bose, who took residency in Japan after escaping from India, was in charge of INA until Subhas reached Singapore in 1943.

Subhas pronounced the formation of a Provisional Government (the *Azad Hind*), in Singapore in October 1943, and INA was placed under its aegis with her own tricolor flag, currency, postage stamps, court, and independent code of conduct. The Azad Hind Government was immediately recognized by the Axis powers. Subhas then proceeded to the Andamans and hoisted the tricolor at Port Blair on 30 December 1943. The freed Andamans and Nicobars were renamed as the *Martyrs Islands* and the *Freedom Islands* respectively. The INA had three brigades, successively named after Gandhi, Nehru, and Maulana Azad. The women's squad was named the Rani of Jhansi Regiment. People of Indian origin joined INA being recruited with Japanese help. The strength of the army surged to 85,000, and it emerged as a military ally of the Japanese Imperial Army. Subhas gave up civilian clothing and took to a military uniform. Subhas now became famous as *Netaji* (leader).

The Japanese–INA force encountered the Allied forces targeting the eastern frontier of India, the Indo-Burma front comprising the Imphal (Manipur)–Kohima (Nagaland) sector. Subhas intended to send a part of the army to Bengal with a plan to carve out Bengal as a liberated enclave, but this was opposed by the Japanese. Instead Chittagong was selected as the first target for invasion.

A special force breached the army defences in Kohima. The invasion started in the first week of March 1944. It succeded in reaching Morang, which is within the mainland of India. The tricolor was hoisted again in Morang. Soon after Imphal (Manipur) and Kohima (Nagaland) were seized by the Gandhi and Nehru brigades.

However, despite these successes, Netaji's strategy to appeal to the Indian army of the British regiment to revolt and join him, failed. An untimely rain bogged down their approach, and supply lines from Burma were cut. As a result, the British alliance force overpowered them ultimately causing the Japanese–INA alliance to retreat to Burma. Kohima became the turning point.

The battle, which took place in phases between 4 April and 22 June 1944 in Kohima, changed the course of the Second World War in Asia. This encounter, though initially not very well known, was so important historically that it became a subject of intense research.*

---

* Note: Publications of several authors like, James Antony Brett, *Report My Signals* (Hennel Locke, 1948), William Slim, *Defeat into Victory* (London: Cacassel, 1956), David Rooney, *Burma Victory: Imphal and Kohima, March - May 1944* (London, Cacassel, 1992), Louis Allen, *Burma, 1941–45* (1984), Fergal Keane (2010) are significant. Original papers were not consulted.

The Axis forces in this battle field were encountered by a strong British Indian Army joining from different parts of India and abroad. Among 49 infantry battalions, 16 were from the Gurkah regiment. The British alliance was supported by air powers contributed by the U.S, Canada, New Zealand and Australia. They also provided all out support on the ground, including life support systems in the mountain area, and forced the INA – Japanese troops to retreat.

According to Krishna Bose, the INA force was under-equipped and starving.[8] The Gandhi Brigade under major Abid Hassan fought from the southern section of Manipur. Major Garewal betrayed their cause and supplied maps and charts showing the INA's locations to the enemy camp. Ultimately, even after the INA position was rearranged, they were bombed from above, devastating the troops. Mid-July, Abid Hasan received an order to retreat. It was a long trek in the rain through forests. These returning troops had no food supply and many Indian soldiers perished on the way.

There were thousands of casualties on both sides. Many INA soldiers were killed in action, others surrendered, and the remainder died of disease or were invalided. The defeat resulted in a flood of dissertations to the British, marking INA's end. The Anglo – British troops had won. The last struggle was fought in April 1945, when Rangoon was reoccupied by the British. Thereafter the whereabouts of Subhas Chandra remained a long lasting mystery. Japan ultimately surrendered on 15 August 1947.

7.5 Final days of Subhas Chandra Bose

For many years it was rumored that Subhas was a victim of a plane crash in Taipei. But in May 1956 the Taiwan government sent a report to the UK government stating that there was no plane crash on that particular day. The destiny of Subhas Chandra is still a subject of much debate. Some printed records alleged that radio message recorded Netaji's (Subhas) voice being broadcasted on 26 December 1945, 1 January 1946, and early February of 1946. Independent India set up commissions to trace Netaji's ultimate fate. Their conclusion was that Subhas died in Taipei hospital after suffering from heavy burn injuries due to his plane catching fire on the runway.

James Lawrence, referring to the Public Record (Office WO 208/3819, 212, 297, 319), claimed that a British spy (agent 1189) accompanied Bose and his closest followers on his final journey.[9] This agent revealed that the party flew from Bangkok to Saigon, and on to Formosa (Taiwan). They then left for Tokyo in an aircraft which suffered engine trouble and crashed near Taihoku on 18 August, a few days after Japan's surrender. Bose, who had extensive burns to his head, thighs, and legs was semi-conscious. He was then taken to a nearby hospital, where he fell into a coma, and died within four hours. His body was cremated.

Krishna Bose describes the last journey of Subhas as well.[10] She was the wife of Sisir Kumar Bose, a nephew of Subhas Chandra Bose and a member of Parliament in India. While working on Netaji from the mid 1970s, she visited Taipei, and her last visit was in 2005 when she went there to deliver a talk in a conference on Democracy. On the last pages of her book she describes Netaji's end on 18 August 1945, depicting her own experience of visiting these sites. She refers to reports of Khosla and Shah Nawaz Commissions, a book by Harin Shah – *The Gallant End of Netaji* (1956), the testimony of Habib-ur Rahman, and Juichi Nakamura's statement on Netaji's death, and his last rites. She concluded her book with Netaji's final days based on Habin-ur Rahaman's testimony and Nakamura's observations. They claimed that both were with Netaji until his last breath.[11]

Habib-ur Rahaman's testified that he (Habib) and Subhas came to Bangkok from Singapore and planned to fly to Saigon. They boarded a plane destined for Tokyo on 17 August, two days after Japan's surrender and stopped overnight in Danang. On 18 August their plane landed in Taihoku airport, Taipei, for refueling. Soon after the plane took off the plane's propellers got detached, and a fire set out. After the plane came to a halt, when he and Subhas were attempting to leave the front exit, fuel spilled over their military uniforms and they caught fire. Habib helped Subhas to reach the ground on the runway. Both of them were taken to a Japanese military hospital in Taihoku where they laid side by side. When cutting away his tightly fit uniform, it became evident that Subhas was badly burnt, and collapsed in front of Habib. Habib's testimony also included Subhas's final words saying, "go back and tell my countrymen that I fought for freedom till my last breath, and they must continue the war; Indians would be free; no one could enslave her more."[12]

Juichi Nakamura, an eyewitness of Subhas's demise, told Krishna Bose that Subhas' mind was quite clear till his death. He and other Japanese chanted Buddhists mantras, while Netaji's body was cremated. Krishna Bose also visited the shrine where Netaji's remains carried by Nakamura were preserved.[13]

What Lawrence wrote was not much different from that concluded by Bose. Both records concur with the reports of the two Commissions.

7.6 After Subhas

When the news of Netaji's death broke, the entire nation was in shock. Nehru said, "The death of Subhas Bose has shocked me, it has given me relief that in the struggle for the cause of India's independence he has given his life and has escaped all those troubles which brave soldiers like him have to face in the end… although I personally did not agree with him in many respects… nobody can doubt his sincerity." In January 1946, he again said, "Netaji Subhas has set an example of courage and passionate devotion in the cause of Indian freedom, which will live long in Indian history…"[14]

A part of the speech Nehru delivered on the 49th birthday of Subhas goes,

> … some people ask me why I am now praising Subhas Bose when I had opposed him while he was in India. I want to give a frank reply to this question. Subhas Bose and I were co-workers in the struggle for freedom for 25 years. He was younger to me …Our relations with each other were marked by great affection. I used to treat him as my younger brother. It is an open secret that at times there were differences between us on political questions. But I never for a moment doubted that he was a brave soldier for the struggle for freedom. I do not expect there would be unanimity on every issue when we have achieved freedom. There will always be differences in the outlook of the people who

belong to a healthy race. ...The manner in which Netaji faced the crisis inspires admiration. Perhaps I might have done the same thing if I were in his position.[15]

Political opinions of Gandhi, Subhas and Nehru were different, but their personal relationship was strong. Subhas accepted his political debacle as the Congress president. It was painful for him, but he was great enough to accommodate the names of Gandhi, Nehru and Moulana Azad to identify different INA brigades. Gandhi in 1942 called Bose, the "prince among the patriots." Nehru expressed himself frankly and so did Gandhi on their political differences. They all had enough self-confidence and respected each other's opinions. Above all they were self-sacrificial patriots of high esteem. The appearance of this trio in the tapestry of the Indian freedom movement at this particular time might have been a simple coincidence, but it was essential for the future nation of India.

7.7 Calcutta Famine

During the tenure of the Conservatives in Britain during the early 1940s, the Indian situation was exceptionally sensitive. Eric Sevareid, an American war correspondent, wrote that Delhi's atmosphere was sick and was not unlike what he had experienced in Nazi Germany. No compromise within the framework of imperialism could ever put this country on the road to health. The Calcutta famine of 1943 was a result of utter neglect and reluctance of the administration at central and provincial levels. Churchill, the conservative War Prime Minister knew about peoples' sufferings in Calcutta, but did not show a minimal gesture of humanity when people were dying. He rather made ruthless comments and even declined to send relief.

During this war period a special food stock was created for the army as granaries dwindled due to a poor harvest. Supplies from Burma also dried up after the Japanese invasion. But the flow of refugees from Burma continued. Bengal witnessed hoardings, black-marketing and dishonesty by politicians. The Bengal government was reluctant. The economic depression was not over, common people were penniless and many of them starved to death in the districts. Many villagers started marching to the cities and towns crying for alms. Malnutrition and disease caused the death of thousands on the streets. Central government was busy with war, while the provincial government did not make any emergency arrangements to manage the unfolding disaster.

When Gandhi lay ill in prison, the London office was only curious about his health. Archibald Percival Wavell, the Viceroy, in his diary revealed that Churchill sent him a telegram asking "why Gandhi had not died yet?" Wavell wrote that Churchill had a Hitler-like attitude for India for which he got a first class rocker.[16] He also wrote, "Churchill had wished Bret Harris, his private secretary, to send some of his surplus bombers to destroy the famine stricken people in Bengal."[17]

7.8 The Simla Conference, 1945

When during the War the power balance shifted towards America, Churchill was keen to keep India under control. Britain, however, had committed to ending imperialism, as soon as the war would end and India was preparing to get an interim government in June. But the conflicts of interest between Congress and Muslim League were escalating. Also the elections in Britain were well overdue. Wavell wished India to become a free country within the Commonwealth. His proposal to hold a conference in Simla materialized with concurrence of Leo Amery and support of provincial Governors. Churchill also agreed to this proposal for, 1) he wanted a majority of the Britons, waiting for an early solution of the Indian issue, to stay by his side, and 2) he was sure that Jinnah would stick to his principle.

The London office instructed the Indian administration to retain 'parity' and 'veto power' of the Viceroy, as the new council members, that included Indian representatives, were due to be selected for interim government. The Simla conference was called on 25 June, restricting the invitation among executives of all the parties and the government. Only Gandhi, who had no portfolio, was specially invited expecting his influence might be needed to control Congress. Prior to Simla, the CWC members were released from jail.

The Viceroy began his negotiations with Gandhi to resolve the 'parity' issue before any council member was selected. Gandhi asked Viceroy's plan for the selection. "It would be paneled," Wavell replied. Gandhi clarified beforehand that Congress stood for Indians as a whole, and that the CWC would be ready to depute a non-Hindu representation. Moulana Abul Kalam Azad was ready to represent Congress. When Wavell raised the issue of Hindu-Muslim parity, Gandhi answered that it was a question of parity between Congress and the League, and not between Hindu and Muslim. Gandhi agreed to cooperate with Wavell, but not at the cost of his principles. He also said that he would advise Congress to participate only if the word 'parity' was withdrawn.

Jinnah said that the Muslims would not tolerate infiltration of non-League stooges. He even asked to postpone the conference. He again urged for the rights of Muslim League to nominate Muslim representation only from the League. The Viceroy told him that the League did not have the right to deny Muslims who wished to stay outside the Muslim League.

On 25 June Moulana Azad said that the fight of Congress was for self-rule for all Indians irrespective of any specific community, and it would be superfluous to discuss Hindu - Muslim parity. The deliberations in the Simla conference continued until 29 June. A separate meeting was also arranged between Congress and the League to patch up differences on communal quotas, parity and veto power. The meeting failed to reach an agreement and was adjourned till 14 July, but Jinnah did not change his opinion, nor was he ready to make any compromise.

Gandhi agreed to stay in Simla. He advised Viceroy to make his decision at the right time, not to impose any settlement on anybody, and help the council to work peacefully once it was formed. On the final day of the conference, when agreement between Congress and the League could not be reached, the Viceroy said that his government was to work against Japan's aggression and maintain law and order. He indirectly asked for Indian cooperation. Thus the last viable opportunity for agreement failed, leaving partition as the only remaining alternative.

7.9 After the Second World War

The surrender of Japan accelerated after the first atom bomb was dropped on Hiroshima on 6 August. To everyone's surprise, Churchill had just been defeated in the general election. On 26 July, Clement Attlee, representing the Labour Party, became the new Prime Minister. Indians welcomed the new government in Britain. Japan surrendered on 15 August.

7.9.1 New Elections 1945 – 46 and Other Issues

In India the time was ripe for fresh elections, as the last election was held in 1936–37. Cripps who had joined Attlee's cabinet, offered to work on a permanent settlement of communal problems fully aware that the League's push for partition was advancing.

The election procedures were under process. Congress was disorganized, many leaders were in Jail, the party had no funds, and properties were sequestered. Though unprepared, Congress finally agreed to fight the election. Muslim League also agreed. At the urge of His Majesty's Government, elections were announced for the end of August. But unexpectedly the army intelligence instigated to arrange for the trial of three ex-INA commanding officers.

7.9.2 INA Trial

A court-martial of three officers who joined the INA after their imprisonment in SE Asia, Major General Shah Nawaz Khan (Muslim), Colonel Prem Sahgal (Hindu), and Colonel Gurbaksh Singh Dhillo (Sikh), was arranged to be held between November 1945 and May 1946. Congress had agreed to cooperate and shouldered their defence. Jawaharlal Nehru was one of the advocates along with Bhulabhai Desai, Asaf Ali, and Tej Bahadur Sapru.

This news of the trial ignited patriotic sentiments that led to a public outcry. During the riots in Calcutta alone, 35 persons died and hundreds were injured. Headlines of newspapers demanded INA men to be considered as patriots. INA week was observed from 5–11 November. Anti-European feelings increased so much that Indian shops boycotted the European customers.

At Deshapriya Park, Calcutta, Sarat Chandra Bose, Nehru, and Patel spoke before lakhs of people. The Congress and the Muslim League became unanimous in a nationwide protest forgetting communal divide. Everybody was respectful to Subhas Chandra, his Azad Hind and the INA. The trial began in a tense atmosphere, while thousands were waiting outside.

The trial room was rocked when Bhulabhai Desai argued that

> ... it was not a case of three individuals waging war against the King, but it was the right of the Indian National Army (INA), - an organized army of a duly constituted provincial government of India to wage war for India's liberation ... the provisional Government controlled the territory of the Andamans for eighteen months, and Manipur and Bishnupur areas for four months; and when Japan took over the countries of S. E. Asia, ... the bond of allegiance of INA soldiers to the British was broken, and the British handed over the soldiers to the Japanese... Their bond of allegiance on part of the subject people would be tantamount to perpetuation of their slavery, since the provincial government controlled the territories for months together. It had legitimacy in declaring war.[18]

When the legality of the trial was questioned and the masses (especially from provinces that provided the largest number of soldiers) rallied in protests, the trials were withdrawn. All three army men were acquitted from murder charges and set free on 3 January 1946. This, however, was not the end.

When asked about the decision to hold this trial, the Viceroy said that the INA trial was arranged because the detained Indian prisoners of war were dying every day in disease or starvation, and their release was necessary.

7.9.3 Consequences of the Trial

Airmen of the Royal Indian Air Force, the number which increased a few fold during the War, began controlled strikes on 22 January for better pay.

The sailors of the Royal Indian Navy (RIN) whose number increased from 1.5 lakhs in 1930s to 3.5 lakhs in 1945, started a revolt in February for better food and shelter. These revolts were fueled by patriotic sentiments arising out of the INA trial.

On 18 February 1946, Sailors of RIN, engaged both on ships and on land, revolted in Bombay which quickly turned into a mutiny. They received support from the communists. At Bombay, Vallabhbhai Patel was trying to end the impasse. But the sailors of Calcutta, Karachi, Madras, and many other establishments gave direct support to the Bombay call after the news spread through the wireless. With deep respect for Subhas Chandra Bose, the soldiers shouted Jai Hind slogans while marching with his portrait through the city streets. On the 19th, the 'tricolor' (Congress flag) was hoisted on most of the ships. The mutineers took possession of Butcher Island where ammunition for Bombay was stocked.

Local police supported the uprising, making the situation vulnerable. The Viceroy himself as a military man witnessed the revolt with political sympathy, but this had gone too far. The mutiny was suppressed on 20 February with the help of Royal Navy warships and British troops at the Prime Minister's initiative. A few sailors and officers died in the encounter. But this revolt made the British extremely nervous about uncontrolled native soldiers who were in the majority. Losing trust in the Indian army was disastrous for this government's survival. About 500 sailors were discharged.

British history scholars identified that the internal condition of the Navy was the main cause. The weekly intelligence summary issued on 25th March 1946, admitted that the Indian army, navy, and air force units were no longer trustworthy. The recommendation for the army only was, to make day to day estimates of steadiness.[19] According to Child, the situation was deemed to be at "a point of no return."[20]

Congress leaders tried ending this situation being concerned over the soldiers' psychology that might contaminate a future military of free India. They concentrated on generating trust through sound constitutional reforms. In any case, the INA trial ignited fervent Indian nationalism and a united stand against the British from 5 November 1945.

7.9.4 Parliamentary Delegation and interim Government

Elections were deferred ignoring the formation of the Constituent Assembly that was kept pending since December 1945. Several British Parliament members were sent to Delhi to discuss forming an interim government. Congress members continued to exercise their faith in non-violence by forbidding the destruction of public property. Jinnah claimed for two separate constitution-making bodies. He said that the League would not take part in the interim government unless the government agreed to declare Pakistan along with 'parity' in legislation. He, however, accepted Pakistan within the Empire. Nehru said that if Pakistan was declared there should have to be a plebiscite in border districts. Amidst controversies, Viceroy conveyed his final decision that a new Executive Council would be formed from the elected members with power to bring about the constitution making body (the Constituent Assembly) by the end of January 1946.

7.9.5 Elections and after effects

The deferred Central Legislative Assembly election was rescheduled and the result was declared at the end of December 1945. Congress secured more than 90% of caste votes in non-Muslim constituencies. Muslim League was in second position winning the Muslim majority states.

The Pakistan issue had consolidated the Muslim voters polarizing the nation. In Bengal, the influence of the Krishak Praja party had declined from 1943 by an increase of League members during the coalition government, which was put on hold during the INA-Japanese approach in the East. Fazul Huq had resigned from Muslim League due to personality clashes with Jinnah, when as a member of the Defence Council, Huq opposed Jinnah's claim for 'parity.'[21]

Congress was the largest party at the center, winning 57 seats out of 102 (they gained 34 seats in the 1937 election), and won in all provinces except Bengal, Sindh and Punjab. Muslim League won 30, Independents 5, Akali Sikhs 2, and Europeans 8 making a total of 102 elected seats. Muslim League secured most of the seats allotted for Muslims at the center, and out of five provinces they claimed to include in Pakistan, League formed ministries only in Bengal and Sindh with Europeans' support. In the remaining three provinces coalition ministries were formed. The League won 442 (of a total 509 Muslim seats) in provincial elections. Hindu Mahasabha was routed, and the Dalits got only 2 out of 151 seats reserved for them. This happened because during the Quit India Movement the dalits and non-Brahmins worked in unison with Congress.

Violence erupted during the election days. In Calcutta dozens of people were killed. The Viceroy assumed that Jinnah would refuse the interim Central Government. Also the Labor government in Britain was uncertain about the formation of a constituent assembly when it was essential to effectuate the transfer of power.

Britain herself needed several post-war reformations. With growing American influence, the nation took a second seat and lost its capability to bear the cost of her over-expanded empire. The post-war situation compelled them to approve a three-member ministerial deputation to India by 24 March 1946 with Stafford Cripps as the head. It was the Cabinet Mission which aimed to help the Viceroy to reach an agreement between Congress and the League.

7.10 Observations

The Raj was under severe pressure generated by the Quit India Movement and the INA-Japanese attack at the eastern borders. The surrender of Japan in August 1945 brought some relief, but Britain was forced to reduce its military forces along with the Indian administration, to adjust to the declining economic post-war situation.

Incidents of post INA trials proved that native soldiers were no longer trustworthy. The security of the British presence became uncertain. The situation was made worse by the disastrous Bengal famine due to administrative inefficiency. Even Churchill was reluctant to send relief for the dying people. Wavell's Simla conference failed and the communal tensions increased when the constituent assembly was approved. These were the major incidents that influenced Britain to decide on withdrawal just after the British cabinet was replaced by the Liberals. The new government, however, was keen to form the Constituent Assembly and a caretaker government who would be the formal successor of the Raj; but this plan remained uncertain as the League was increasing pressure for a separate constitution for the Muslim enclave.

Britain was tired fighting the War and lost its international superiority. Her first priority was to reconstruct Britain and pay back American loans. The Labour Party was committed to India's independence since the 1935 election, and so the liberals' view on withdrawal was firm. With sending a Cabinet Mission, Parliament affirmed the formation of an Indian successor to British India. With reduced manpower and an unreliable army, the government lost its grip on aggravating communal tensions.

References:

1. Subhas Chandra Bose, *Indian Struggle, 1920–42* (New Delhi: Oxford University Press, 1964), 388–89.
2. V. P. Menon, *The Transfer of Power in India* (Princeton, NJ: Princeton University Press, 1957), 167.
3. Bose, Ibid, 386.
4. F. G. Hutchins, *Spontaneous Revolution: Quit India Movement* (New Delhi: Manohar, 1871), 250–251.
5. Ishita Banerjee-Dube, *A History of Modern India* (Cambridge: Cambridge University Press, 2015), 415.
6. Menon, Ibid, 186.
7. Krishna Bose, *Netaji Subhas Chandra Bose's Life, Politics and Struggle* (New Delhi: Picador India, 2022), 64.
8. Ibid, 151–155.
9. James Lawrence, *Raj: Making and Unmaking of the British Raj* (New York: St. Martin's Press, 1997), 575.
10. Krishna Bose, ibid, 155.
11. Ibid, 314–23.
12. Ibid.
13. Ibid.

14. S. Gopal (ed.), *Selected Works of Nehru*, Vol. 14 (New Delhi: Nehru Memorial Fund, 1984), 371.
15. Ibid, 373.
16. Pendon Moor (ed.), *Wavell: The Viceroy's Journal* (Oxford: Oxford University Press, 1973), 78; Gopal, Ibid, 371.
17. Jock Colville, *The Fringes of Power* (Guilford, CT: John Lyon Press, 2002), 563.
18. Prasenjit K. Basu, "How The British Raj Ultimately Fell to INA Trial," Dailyo.in dated 16.06.2017. https://www.dailyo.in/arts/subhas-chandra-bose-ina-trials-british-raj-empire-azad-hind-fauj-19004.
19. J. L. Raj, *Making and Unmaking of British India*, Abacus Publication Office, London War Office, 208/ 761A, 1997.
20. David Childs, *Britain Since 1945: A Political History* (London, New York: Routledge, 1979), 28.
21. Banerjee-Dube, Ibid, 367.

CHAPTER 8

British India 1945 – early 1947

This chapter deals with issues that arose from the Labour government's decision to withdraw from India, keeping it undivided. London sent a mission to create a congenial situation before the transfer of power. The text describes the Cabinet Mission plan, the reasons for the Mission's return, and the replacement of Lord Wavell, the penultimate Viceroy. The majority of information presented here comes from Menon's work.

8.1 Cabinet Mission Plan and Outcome

Britain wanted a single independent constitutional entity as the successor of British India. This would enable her to use India's geographical position as a base for operations from Egypt to the Far East, so crucial for maintaining a military presence with an undivided army during the interim period. A congenial, agreeable atmosphere was therefore necessary to be maintained before the transfer of power.

From February 1946, a team of three Cabinet members –Pethick Lawrence, Sir Stafford Cripps and A. V. Alexander– interacted separately with Indian leaders, including the Dalits and Princely States to discuss a common agenda, reporting back to the Viceroy and his officers. They ascertained that Congress was in favor of a united India with a strong center and a federation with more power allotted to the provinces.

But Jinnah was still insisting on a separate constitution for Muslims, arguing that India was never united before, and that the communities culturally differed, living in different quarters. His demands were for Muslim sovereignty in Sindh, Balochistan, NWFP, Punjab in the west, and Assam and Bengal in the East.

On 16 May the Cabinet Mission and Viceroy Wavell formally announced their plan for a Constituent Assembly which would draft the constitution. As early as August 1940, Linlithgow had promised Indians to draft their own constitution. During the War, its execution was suspended. Six years later a proposal for the formation of an interim government and constituent assembly was ready to carry out the British intention.

The Cabinet Mission Plan proposed that the Constituent Assembly in the Center would be formed by an indirect election by those members elected during the 1946 election in the provincial councils. It was a single transferable voting system of proportional representation. The election was completed by the end of July. The Constituent Assembly was formed with a total 389 seats, of which 292 representatives were from provinces of British India, 93 from Princely States, and 4 representing the Chief Commissioners of Delhi, Ajmer–Merwara, Croog and British Baluchistan. This Assembly, in similar fashion, was retained until the Indian constitution was implemented in 1950. Congress won 208 seats in the provinces, becoming the majority party in the election. Muslim League secured 73 seats. The election result ultimately enabled Congress to form an interim government, but only after the Cabinet Mission left India, unable to complete its aims.

The Mission Plan proposed a complex scheme placing the national government at center and provinces distributed over two territories, Muslim dominated and non-Muslim dominated states within it. The national (central) government would be formed with equal representation from Congress and the Muslim League, in the form of one or two federations, linked to a united center. Each would have a small military force. Princely States under the Center were given the option to choose their own representatives.

The Plan that was announced on 16 May was further elaborated by fixing three Provincial groupings, a) the Hindu majority provinces from Central India to South India; b) Punjab, Sindh, Balochistan, and N-W Frontier province (NWFP) in the West, and c) Bengal and Assam, including Shylet in the East.

The interim government would be a coalition of different parties with proportional representation, but the issue of the Constituent Assembly was left to be befitting to all groups. It was proposed that a Constituent Assembly would be decided by the newly formed provincial assembly for drafting the constitution first at the union level (center), then to split it in three sections (groups a, b, and c). Then after the constitution was completed at all levels, a province would have the option to opt out and join a new group, but everyone retained its place under the central union. After the procedure was completed, the interim government would take responsibility to help in the transition, and decide on India's admission to the Commonwealth.

The center of the new government at Delhi would control defence, currency, foreign affairs, and communication, with powers to raise finance for each sector. The Governor-General would have veto power in case of controversy. The Executive Council was planned to function as a ministry, while the elected prime minister would be designated as the vice president, and the Viceroy as president.

In short, the Indian nation would be a Union under an authority to be formed with elected representatives from provinces, and nominated representatives (not elected like other states) of Princely States; and all departments, except those concerned with the Union, would be under the control of the provinces. The provinces were to appoint executives and pass legislatures of their own, and allowed to form groupings among themselves. The groupings laid in the scheme were mandatory, but allowed provincial separation after the constitution was drafted.

Outcome: Congress rejected the plan for allowing provincial groupings, and felt the center was too weak. It also opposed the parity and veto power for the League or the Viceroy, and the policy of denouncing the people of Princely States for self-expression. Congress also pointed out that there was no specific promise for self-rule. However, in a meeting of 6 July, Congress gave conditional support for the long term aims of the Cabinet Mission. Nehru's speech of 10 July rejected the Plan's proposal that the provinces would be obliged to join a group, and said that Congress was not bound or committed to the plan. He agreed to participate in the Constituent Assembly and begin writing the new constitution as Congress had demanded for a number of years.

Throughout the month of June, before Nehru's 10 July statement, the Viceroy hosted discussions and debates between Congress and Muslim League regarding joining the interim government and accepting the constituent assembly. The League had always pushed for Pakistan, parity in some way or another, and opposed the representation of Muslims outside the Muslim League. On 25 June Congress wrote to the Cabinet Mission members that Congressmen never gave up their national aspirations. They vowed to keep a provision for Muslim representation from outside the Muslim League. They could not accept any artificial grouping, unjust parity, or agreement to veto power of communal groups. They also felt that the Plan kept the central authority limited in its power, and that the system of grouping provinces weakened the whole structure. Besides, Congress felt the scheme was unfair to Princely States and provinces like NWFP and Assam, as well as the Sikhs. Finally, Congress demanded formation of a representative and responsible provisional national government at the earliest possible date.

Jinnah initially endorsed the Cabinet Mission Plan and the League formally accepted it on 22 May. The provincial groupings signaled the possibility of forming Pakistan, and veto power was guaranteed keeping the provision of parity. But ultimately the League also rejected this plan, as it became clear that a sovereign Pakistan was unacceptable to the British. The Hindu Mahasabha, Dalits and Sikhs rejected the plan also. Jinnah suggested to His Majesty's Government to get rid of the impression that Congress had accepted a long term plan. On 18 July Pethick Lawrence in the House of Lords, and Sir Stafford Cripps in the House of Commons, expressed apprehensions that the provincial constitution of 16 May would be acceptable.

On 25 May, the Viceroy announced certain clarifications of the Plan, affirming that political parties would decide on the pattern of their representation, all portfolios including the War Membership would be allotted to Indians, and finally that the administration would move forward towards independence. He also clarified certain objections raised by Congress.

In response to Nehru's demand for absolute freedom of the interim government, the Viceroy informed the Cabinet about his plan for implementation of a 14-member strong interim government to be formed at the end of July, after the elections. Accordingly, on 16 June, he announced the setting up of the Executive Council with 14 members, following the allotted quotas for different parties. The Viceroy requested all parties to convey their acceptance.

Congress sent its acceptance. Muslim League initially declined, but agreed to join because the Secretary of States had decided to form the interim government even if a party refused to join. Sikhs initially refused, but finally agreed to join when Congress assured them of their full cooperation. This interim Government was given complete freedom. Congress secured the highest number of legislators in the 1945–46 election and they expected to reign in the interim government.

8.2 Interim Government

The Viceroy initially proposed the seat ratio in the Executive Council (ministry) as, Congress 5: Muslim League 5: Sikhs 2: remainder 2. Then on 16 June, at the suggestion of Congress, the ratio was changed by allocating 6 seats to Congress (one for depressed class Hindus): 5 to Muslim League: 1 seat each to Sikhs, Indian Christians, and Parsees. In total 14 members. The tenure of the interim government was extended to June 1948. But when the Viceroy refused to forgo his veto power, Congress opposed the proposal outright. The Cabinet Mission fell through completely.

After the Cabinet Mission went back in June, the Viceroy negotiated with Indian parties to convince them to cooperate and finalize the procedure for the interim government and the constituent assembly during the next 3–4 months to keep India united. The following is a synopsis of the events, following Menon.

The decisions on making the interim government and the constituent assembly, following the statement laid down on 16 May, were made final as it was agreed upon by all parties. Formation of the interim government was announced by the Viceroy with 14 members in the Executive council (as ascertained on 16 June). Congress, though objecting to certain points, gave formal acceptance to join the government. The Muslim League and Sikhs, though initially disagreed, finally accepted the scheme.

As decided earlier, the Viceroy formally informed Nehru on 6 August that he (Nehru) would be invited to form the interim government. He also informed the League of the same, and that this arrangement was made on the basis of their acceptance of the proposal on 29 July. The Muslim League, in response, argued that the comments of Congress on provincial grouping were not acceptable to them, and that they would reverse their decision to participate. In that situation the Secretary of State agreed that Nehru would form the government with the provision that Muslim League could join later.

On 14 August, Congress announced that the constitutional assembly had a sovereign mandate to function, and that it would draw up the constitution of India without interference from any external power. Nehru sought everyone's cooperation in drawing up the constitution of independent India, giving freedom and protection to all. Jinnah opposed the constituent assembly because of Congress' insistence on its sovereign character, and repudiated their stance on provincial groupings. They claimed a separate constitution for a Muslim state, and Jinnah gave the call for *Direct Action* to demand for a separate Muslim state on 16 August (see below), avoiding any further negotiation.

From August, the Viceroy continually attempted to convince the League to join the constitution assembly headed by Congress. However, the League, who continued to oppose the representation of Muslims outside the League, formulated their own interpretation on certain constitutional sections and provincial autonomy laid out in paragraphs 19 (v) and (vii) in the 16 May Mission Plan.

Following instructions from London, and the Viceroy's announcement of 24 August, the Interim government was finally sworn in on 2 September under Nehru's leadership. Congress had decided to resolve all existing disagreements, and Nehru invited all to enter the Constituent Assembly. Jinnah on 8 September in an interview to the *London Daily* stated that Congress' commitments were vague.[2] With the League effectively boycotting the Assembly, the Viceroy hesitated to let Congress' majority dominate, effectively allowing a one-party rule. The Secretary of State was inclined to give time to Nehru to renegotiate the demands of Muslim League.

On 16 September Congress finally called a meeting of the constituent assembly to implement the principles of the provinces and sections. On the same day Jinnah met the Viceroy and declined to join the assembly because he was aware that the League had a meagre majority in groups (b) and (c). He met the Viceroy again on 25 September and discussed his apprehension that other minorities might join Congress to act against the League on any discussion in the interim government. He requested that the post of the vice-chairman of the constituent assembly be made rotational. The Viceroy did not agree with him. Ultimately Jinnah agreed to accept this long term plan and on 14 October sent names of their representatives, one of them being a scheduled cast member of the Bengal ministry.

Congress withdrew their three sitting members to accommodate the League's representatives. Muslim League did not abandon *Direct Action*, and in the second week of October, Noakhali "hooliganism" began with an economic boycott of Hindus (discussed in subsequent paragraphs). They asked for the ministries of Home, External Affairs and Defence departments to which the majority members did not agree. The Muslim League took office on 26 October. Suspecting that the League might not join the constituent assembly, in the annual meeting of Congress in Meerut, many members urged the League to accept the Cabinet Mission Plan or quit the interim government. Nehru said that Congress' patience reached the limit.

When asked to join the constitutional assembly Jinnah showed a reluctant attitude, because of the communal violence in Bihar where many Muslims were killed, and asked for postponement of the assembly meeting. But the provisional date of the first meeting of the Assembly was scheduled for 9 December. The Cabinet called the Indian parties to London. Nehru insisted that there was no reason to reopen the case as the date of the meeting of the Constituent Assembly was fixed on 9 December. Nehru attended the meeting of 2 December after being assured of a fair treatment from Attlee. On 6 December a decision was taken to send the case to federal court as statements in paragraphs 19 V and VIII were conducive. Jinnah avoided federal court and stayed back in London. Nehru and Baldev Singh came back. The 9 December meeting was held as per schedule. Committees were installed on 20 January keeping provisions for the members of Muslim League.

8.3 Muslim League's Direct Action Day

Direct Action Day of 16 August started with violence in Punjab and Bengal before the interim government was sworn in. Both these provinces remained under the governor's administration. In Punjab, both Sikhs and the Hindus were targeted. During the lawlessness that followed, there were widespread murders, rapes and robberies. Many became homeless. Both the governors failed to protect the innocent. Many journalists who observed the Punjab riots wrote that in most places the Muslim police neglected their duties on the day. The Punjab atrocities were published in national and international media. Some books were also written. Direct Action helped the League to multiply its membership. Their supporters embarked with 'jihad' and slaughtered thousands. The number of (mostly innocent) victims increased over time.

The worst Bengal genocide that happened due to Direct Action, became known as the Great Calcutta Killings. Later riots broke out in different places all over North India from Bihar, Delhi to Punjab and continued until March 1947. The Noakhali riots in eastern Bengal persisted the longest. The following gives the events of the Bengal Riots.

8.3.1 The Great Calcutta Killings

At the 1946 elections, the Chief Minister of the Bengal government under Muslim League in coalition with the European representatives became Hussain Shaheed Suhrawardy. The majority of Bengal Muslims inhabited the rural districts of East Bengal. Western Bengal was Hindu dominated, and Calcutta, a cosmopolitan city of educated elites with a 70% Hindu population (as per 1941 census), was the provincial capital. The main business center, the Bara Bazar area, was dominated by Marwaris – a community migrated from Rajasthan, with a majority supporting the Hindu Mahasabha. The Congress and Mahasabha formed the opposition.

Suhrawardy was unpopular since he failed to control the 1943 Bengal famine. His political base in Calcutta were migrated Urdu speaking Muslims, mainly slum-dwellers of central Calcutta and Kidderpore. The majority of them were either rickshaw pullers, portworkers or industrial laborers.

When the government declared 16 August a holiday, the Muslim League called a general strike. The Congress-Hindu Mahasabha coalition opposed the strike and asked Marwaris traders to keep the Bara Bazar and other markets open on the day.

It is said that upon Cripps' announcement, that the Hindu population opted for partition of Bengal and believed that the Bengal government wanted to retain Calcutta under the League's command. The prospect of Muslim dominance caused apprehension among the majority of urban Hindus, which resolved to be prepared to encounter any unforeseen situation. As the day progressed, Calcutta was on fire, red with the blood of the slaughter of its inhabitants, with far reaching effects, especially in Noakhali district of Bengal.

Detailed information about the Calcutta riots being largely suppressed, we met available older people surviving in their nineties with vivid memories as sources of information. One of them was Ramkrishna Ghosh of Serampore (who died early January 2022, completing 100 years). The gist of their unanimous testimonies is as follows: 1) the Hindus were in favor of partition of Bengal; 2) Suhrawardy wanted to keep Calcutta under his Muslim rule; 3) on the 16th morning, there was a huge gathering of Muslims in a Calcutta meeting called by Muslim League; 4) a speech of Suhrawardy agitated Muslim sentiments; 5) he assured the gathering of government protection; 6) Hindu police officers posted in Calcutta were transferred from Calcutta, and 7) with remaining police looking the other way, Hindu-Muslim went totally beyond control.

An internet publication of the 1946 Report[1] of an enquiry commission, presided over by Sir Patrick Spens –the Supreme Court Justice of India– gives further information. Many eye witnesses were interrogated by the Commission, but its conclusion was never published. This report focused mainly on Suhrawardy's mass meeting at the Maidan, where he addressed an estimated 100,000 people stating that a) he had taken measures to 'restrain' the police; b) he afterwards positioned himself with his cronies in the police control room, and prevented the British Police Commissioner in charge of law and order, from attending to the troubled spots; and that c) Congress accused Mr. Burrows, then Governor of Bengal, because he did not restrain Suharwardy's interference with law and order; and finally d) the Prime Minister of Bengal hesitated too long to call in troops when the violence escalated.

An unpublished military report (1946) on the Calcutta Riots is also available. The reporter was in police service and his report was addressed to a Brigadier. The following 10 paragraphs are excerpts of the report:[3]

1. Refer to you my D.O no. 5706/3/c/csi (6) dated 8 Aug., para 4 regarding police morale and by DO no 7605/3/csi (6) dt. 15th Aug, regarding possibilities of a first communal class clash.
2. We are making out a full and detailed report …. the enormous amount of information has been collected. The trouble started in the early morning of the 16th and both sides were responsible. Hindus started putting barricades at Tala bridge and Belgachia bridge [in north Calcutta] to prevent Muslim processions coming in, and Muslim goondas went around forcing the Hindus to close their shops. In my D.O of 15th it was maintained that 'air was electric' and this caused crowds to gather, lathis were produced and in no time north Calcutta was a scene of mob riot. At 11.00 hours there were brick bat fights all over north Calcutta. During the fight for a few hours, students were taking a fairly prominent role, but by the afternoon they had realized that it was much more than

ordinary rowdy such as they had been indulging in for the past 9 months. The student elements then cleared out and went to their houses and homes and did little more than defend themselves and their families, if attacked.

3. By late in the afternoon the situation changed and persons involved on both sides were rickshaw pullers, tea shop wallahs, pan biri wallahs, cartpulers, cartman, goondas of the worst type. Soon after midnight of 16/17th they fought out desperate battles-murder, butchery of the worst type was going on in the side lanes, bylanes of north Calcutta. Round Vivekananda road, Central Avenue crossing about 50 Bihari rickshaw pullers were caught in a cul-de-sac and butchered. Further on central avenue round the temple which stands in the middle, a party of some 30 Mohammedans were killed. It was during the period of midnight 16/17th and 7.00 hours on 17th.

4. Our patrol was out but due to tremendous fighting, it was impossible to force our way into the areas in which main killings were taking place.

5. Police opened fire in Harrison Road at 11.00 hours on 16th Aug. '46, 2 rounds of buckshot and Barnes and Smith emptied their pistols into the crowd. Crowd dispersed, formed up in Bowbazar Street and a fight started between Hindus in Bow Bazar Street and the Muslims coming up from the Lower Circular Road. I was there at that time. Police finally dispersed the crowd with tear gas. By 12.00 hours there were fights at every street and alley from Sealdah to Shyambazar. Eastern command intelligence center jeeps dispersed some of these crowds without firing. But as soon as we had gone the fight started again. By 14.00 hours on the 16th, the Government was considering the troops but police had already fired the above mentioned number of rounds.

6. Apart from a few senior officers, police themselves were unwilling to open fire and I don't blame them. If they had done

so and succeeded in quelling the outbreak, but mind you they would only have succeeded if they had fired quickly and a very large number of rounds, they could have been blamed for unnecessary firing. During the whole riot until the army was called out and authorized to shoot, I met various police patrols and pointed out rioters and looters, but there were always some good excuses as to why they should not fire. Above is known to the army commander. I have given him a note which he has sent to the governor. It is not only myself who realizes that the police were hesitant, but any one who witnessed the riot, public confidence in police has been rudely shaken. The Governor told the commissioner of police on 16th, when the riot started, that he would back him in any strong action taken, but I think really this assurance was given too late for the information to be really absorbed by the subordinate ranks. If he could have given this assurance a fortnight ago, which of course was not of the question, the Calcutta police who have been a fine body of loyal constabulary, would have done their job much more successfully. I do not say that the whole riot could be quelled by Calcutta police without the aid of military support, but I am confident that if all ranks had known they would be supported to the hilt, nothing like the state of affairs which occurred would have taken place. There is no doubt that this situation will be put right in the very near future and I trust it would be an example to other provinces.

7. The most important was that Europeans were not attacked. No bricks were thrown at army lorries except in stray cases, or when they took an active part in dispersing mobs. In fact, both sides were only too pleased to offer advice on how to act and beat up the other side. From the time the riot started, every little blacksmith was working mad in his house manufacturing spears, rods, and knives. Iron rods used in reinforced concrete were stolen and sharpened at both ends and those crude

weapons were used for butchery. Men, women were slaughtered by both sides indiscriminately, and when Mallick bazar was burnt three Hindu children were thrown into flames.

8. The result of this riot has been complete mistrust between the two communities. Most of the babus do not go to their offices because they have to pass through Muslim areas, and they are afraid of being stabbed. Though the city is quiet, there are still stabbing cases and both sides are very frightened. The trams are resuming today (22nd). There are buses and taxis and the city is quickly returning to normal. We have cleared up practically all the corps, D.D.T. has been sprayed and everything has been done.

9. There is a lot of talk in the town that the army should have been called in aid of the civil power earlier during the riot. Personally I think it would have been mistaken if this had been done. It is the duty of the police to first try and quell a disturbance and only when they expand all the power they have, then should troops be called in.

10. There is hardly a person in Calcutta who has a good word for Suhrawardy, respectful Muslims included. For years he has been known as the king of goondas and my private opinion is that he fully anticipated what was to happen and allowed it to work itself up, and probably organized the disturbance with his goonda gang as this type of individual has to receive compensation every now and again. It is difficult to estimate the number of casualties, but I should say it is somewhere in the region of 2–3 thousands at least. There were corpses all over North Calcutta, they were in rivers and canals, side lanes, in fact everywhere. Number of shops looted and burnt must be somewhere in the region of 2–3 thousands. I personally think that killings on both sides were fifty, fifty or if anything, more Muslims than Hindus, but damage financially has been much greater to Hindus than the Muslims.

This report is fundamentally similar to the statement of the persons interviewed, or that published on the internet.[4]

The riot spread to the suburban industrial belts on both sides of the Hooghly. At the boundary of Serampore and Rishra (industrial suburbs of Calcutta) there is an extended slum area inhabited by Hindi speaking Hindu and Muslim laborers employed in two jute mills of Rishra. They still live side by side without prejudice. But the incidents of Calcutta instigated a riot in this slum, and an unknown number of both the communities were murdered with crude weapons. Serampore also has slum areas housing Muslim industrial laborers, and a good number of Bengali Muslims live there. Mercifully, this town remained free from violence. Sheikh Mujibur Rahaman, before becoming the first president of Bangladesh 1970–71, fled from Calcutta, where he was student, to his relative's residence at Serampore knowing it was safer.

Many of the Calcutta victims were Bihari migrants. Hindus in Bihar were enraged by the news and over the next few months the Bihar Riots were unleashed killing thousands of Muslims. Vengeance spread out further, extending to western parts- from Punjab to the North West Frontier, and Rawalpindi to Multan, Lahore and Amritsar. The cities were worst affected when riots went beyond control.

The effects of Calcutta and Bihar riots instigated the Muslim population of Noakhali, a rural district headquarter in East Bengal. The records of the riots of Noakhali included in the Proceedings of Bengal Legislative Assembly Vol. LXXII was not available to us. However, available evidence tells us enough of the sobering course of events.

8.3.2 Noakhali Riots

The Noakhali riots, described as a genocide, were ignited by a series of inflammatory speeches delivered by a local Muslim League leader. His speech of 10 October (an auspicious day for Hindu festivals) enraged the Muslim population living under 10–12 police stations covering about 200 square miles of area. The riot began with stray incidents of harassment of

Hindus by their majority Muslim neighbors. At the end of the day, the Muslim community embarked on genocide of Hindu minority who formed less than 20% of the population.

Mr. Mohsinur Rehman, a resident of Bangladesh, wrote an article quoting reports published on 16 and 23 October of 1946 by *The Statesman* and the *Amrita Bazar Patrika*, English dailies from Calcutta.[5] The following are quotes from two newspapers:

(a) *Amrita Bazar Patrika*, 23 October 1946,

> ...for the 13th day today. Around 120 villages in Raiganj, Lakshmipur, Raipur, Begumganj and Senbag thanas (police stations) in Noakhali district with Hindu population of 90,000 and nearly 70,000 villagers in Chandpur and Faridganj thanas of Tippera (Comilla) district remained besieged by hooligans. Death stares the people of these areas in their face and immediate rousing of supply to these areas with the help of the military, who alone could do it, would save the lives of these people most of whom have been without food for the last few days.

(b) *The Statesman*, 16 October 1946,

> In an area of 200 sq. miles the inhabitants surrounded by riotous mobs were being massacred, their houses being burnt, their womenfolk being forcibly carried away and thousands being subjected to forcible conversion. Thousands of hooligans attacked the villages, compelled them (Hindus) to slaughter their cattle and eat. All places of worship in affected villages have been desecrated. The District Magistrate and Police Superintendent of Noakhali took no steps to prevent it.

The Noakhali carnage took place due to Muslim vengeance on the (falsely rumored) Hindu attack on Muslims during the Calcutta Killings. But there were also deep seated grievances of muslim peasants suffering under local zealous Hindu Zamindars. Tensions had been rising over several weeks, when it ignited on a Hindu religious festival on 10 October 1946 with the rousing speech of Ghulam Sarowar, an ex-MLA of Muslim League at

Begumganj Bazar. His anti-Hindu speech couched in verses quoted from the Quran, exhorted the Muslims to kill the kafirs and idolaters and perform their religious duty. This inflammatory speech became the source of the riot, followed by violent assault on Hindu properties and killings.

On 18 October, Dr. Bidhan Chandra Roy (who later became the second chief minister of West Bengal), conveyed the Noakhali incidents to Gandhi who was at Sodepur near Calcutta. Gandhi came down to Noakhali on a peace mission and for four months roamed different villages appealing to cease all violence. His mission was only partially successful. When he was asked to go back, he said, "I do not want to die as a discredited or defeated man. I would rather die in Noakhali than go back as a defeated man."

Bina Das and Kamala Das Gupta, both former women anarchists, accompanied Gandhi and walked with him through the villages. They observed how many Hindus left Noakhali deserting their homes for an uncertain future. Gandhi said, "my heart bleeds, my brain is strained to think that the East Bengal Hindus who were in the vanguard in their struggle for freedom, will be deprived of their ancestral home and hearth." This Hindu exodus migrated to India, where they arrived as refugees.

Viceroy Wavell was so disturbed with the administrative failures to contain the riots that his hope to move forward evaporated. He lamented that he had responsibility, but without power.

8.4 Fate of Interim Government

The League ministers joined but created a separate block defying Nehru's leadership. Then Bihar was still troubled by rioters. Jinnah asked League members to start sectarian meetings. He also claimed autonomy and voting rights of the provinces to be clubbed in groups. Congress members opposed it. Thus problems started again and the Prime Minister Attlee, attempted to resolve the issues through the Federal Court, but failed. On 20 February 1947, Attlee announced before the House of Commons that the target date for British withdrawal from India was set for 30 June 1948.

Apprehending that NWFP would not participate in a group, and Assam would oppose the grouping, the Muslim League evaded the Federal Court.

The interim Government was left with the support of Congress and Sikh representatives only. As the Sikh representation was reduced on Congress' suggestion, they felt ignored even though they were the third largest community. The Secretary of State agreed to accept this Congress-led government, if it abided by the terms and conditions.

Backed by cabinet support, the interim government prepared itself to accept the charge of Indian administration by June 1948 (the proposed date of British withdrawal). The budget session resumed with chaos, and the League members were asked to maintain peace or resign. Vallabhbhai Patel said if the League members were allowed to disturb, the Congress government would be withdrawn.

During the riots, the power of the Nehru government became limited, and it became disillusioned through the uncertainty when their administration was being ignored and two provinces were transferred under the respective Governors. Gandhi, the lone savior of India, was roaming in Noakhali. The Viceroy, having supreme power but feeling powerless, had reiterated his secret *Breakdown Plan of 1945* (made after the failure of Simla) and was uncertain to continue much longer; and his British officials were thinking of retiring to a safer place, leaving the administration in Nehru's hand. At that somber situation the Home Department reacted strongly. It was not honorable for the British to give up now when the transfer of power was already declared.

The cabinet finally decided to withdraw Wavell, keeping the scheduled date of transfer unchanged. Wavell was replaced with Viscount Mountbatten. Churchill said this retreat was embarrassing for Britain. But Churchill admired Mountbatten for his success in war.[6]

8.5 Observations

The Cabinet Mission returned to London being unsuccessful in convincing Indian leaders to be united to enable the British Government to transfer power to a single unit. Their plan was complex and segregated the Muslim dominated areas at the advantage of those who urged for two constitutions. Opposing the one Constituent Assembly proposed by the Cabinet Mission, the Muslim League rallied their supporters with Direct Action for Partition, unleashing violence throughout the subcontinent.

The penultimate Viceroy attempted to establish an interim government as the successor of British India, but the League avoided his plans applying tactics and pressure. His tenure also witnessed increasingly disturbed situations, heightened by other issues like soldiers' revolts and the Calcutta famine.

The economic condition in India deteriorated further during this period. The Raj was running short of remittances even as the British government offered several concessions shouldering a part of its military expenditure. Also currency notes were withdrawn from circulation enabling the exchange from currency-reserves in London. But this measure caused capital scarcity.[7] From the early 1930s the economic depression severely affected the Indian market. During the late 1930s (before another War broke out), Lord Irwin attempted to stabilize the economy. He curtailed the workforce which resulted in a lack of adequate fiscal management when experienced personnel were withdrawn from India.

For undertaking the imperial defence during World War II, and the responsibility of military expansion by Britain, financial pressure on the British taxpayers was increased. London tried to reconcile political demands in India by reducing their dependence on external finance of the Raj, and allowed more constitutional power to the Indian finance minister responsible to the popular assembly. But he was not given authority to control external financial policy. Furthermore, in 1943, C. D. Deshmukh was appointed as the first Indian director of the Reserve Bank which was created in 1934 with power of financial management. Expected economic and political progress was still stiffened by 1945. Also the novel arrangement for financing India's participation in the War II had resulted in repayment of all old debt, and acquisition of a sterling balance four times as large.[8] No fruitful result could be achieved even by changing the rupee ratio.

The prevailing economic stagnation during wartime broke an established system of marketing and credit supply within India due to ineffective credit management. It caused dislocation of the domestic economy leading to increased discontent and protests, particularly when the mechanism of food and raw material supply from rural areas, and the exchange for consumer goods and bullion from the cities and the international markets, was disrupted. The logistics and transport costs rose sky-high during war time, as the railways were reserved for military transport.

During the final decades of the Raj, domestic commercial activities were transferred from Europeans to the Marwaris who rose from traders and money lenders to business entrepreneurs. From the mid-1920s they began investing in jute and colliery sectors, and by the 1930s they acquired more than half of the jute mills. About half the joint stock collieries had Marwari directors. From the 1920s, discriminatory protection was granted to British industries like Iron, textile, sugar, paper, etc. Income from iron and steel, cement and chemicals grew more than three times between the 1930s and 1946. But old Bengali business houses like Carr-Tagore failed to survive after the failure of the Union Bank in the 1940s. Mopping up capital from Marwari business conglomerates was not possible. Some Marwaris began pouring money into the Congress fund.

The post-war economy of Britain was too fragile to rescue the Raj. Lapierre and Collins wrote that the British had emerged victorious and the nation had received much admiration for her achievement in war, but the cost of this victory had almost vanquished the British.[9] The War caused their industry to cripple and the Sterling survived only by injection of American and Canadian dollars. The war had swallowed the finance necessary to pay up debt. Over two million Britons were unemployed, people were living with uncertainty of regular electricity supply, and for the last eight years they had lived under rationing of almost every consumable item. Britain needed immediate economic restoration. The great economist John Maynard Keynes said in 1946 that they were a poor nation and must live accordingly. Maintaining an Empire became a luxury.

Tomlinson concluded that the Raj administration was less sensitive to provide right leadership during war and post-war periods, which caused greater nationalist pressures and communal tensions.[10] People were suffering; the per capita income of Indians for the last fifty years of imperial rule showed no growth as population increased. The tenure of the penultimate Governor-General, muddled with famine, revolt in military, riots, etc. pushed the economy into an extraordinary remittance crisis and the Raj, being default, became a burden on the British government. Britain lost interest in India.

The British planned for an immediate withdrawal, but it was constrained by disruption of the interim government by Jinnah's Direct Action, and his evasive attitudes in joining the constituent assembly. It deferred the execution of the plan. Wavell's last mission to bring the parties together in a communal understanding had already failed at Simla. At the same time, Muslim League was given leverage during the riots by undermining the interim Congress government. The Cabinet Mission's Plan also favored the League's demand to segregate the Muslim enclave. All incidents happened following a period when the Raj administration was already disarrayed due to the Quit India movement, Japan-Azad Hind advancement, and revolts in the Navy.

When the interim government, the successor of the British Raj, became virtually non-functional, and Wavell's administration could not execute concrete policies for immediate transfer of power, Prime Minister Attlee was prompted to change the Viceroy immediately to work towards an immediate and permanent solution.

References:

1. "Calcutta Riot 1946: Mass Violence and Resistance." *Research NetWork* (Science pst), 8 November, 2007.
2. V. P. Menon, *The Transfer of Power in India* (Princeton, NJ: Princeton University Press, 1957), 306.
3. "Military Report, 24 August, 1946." (E. C. & Personal, No. 5705/3/CSI b) National Archives, 12 A.P.C. Road, Kolkata. Report No. 216/66.
4. See Reference 1 above.
5. Mohsinur Rehman, "The National Riots: Forgotten Noakhali Hindu Massacre," *Category History*, Noakhali, 14 August, 2014.
6. Andrew Robert, *Eminent Churchillians* (London: Weidenfeld & Nicolson, 1994), 63.

7. B. R. Tomlinson, "Political Economy of Raj: Decline of Colonialism," *Journal of Economic History*, Vol. 42, No. 1 (March 1982), 135.
8. Ibid, 136.
9. Dominique Lapierre and Larry Collins, *Freedom at Midnight* (New Delhi: Vikas Publishing House, 2003), 1.
10. Tomlinson, Ibid, 137.

CHAPTER 9

British India March – August 1947

This concluding chapter begins by tracking complications in the appointment of the Lord Mountbatten, the last Viceroy, and describes his untiring efforts and negotiations with Indian leaders for solving pending problems and finishing all formalities before handing over the charge to the successors of British India. It also discusses why partition became inevitable, even as it culminated with enormous tragedy and human carnage. Finally, it describes the issue of the Princely States and their accession.

9.1 Lord Mountbatten's Appointment

On 18 December, Prime Minister Attlee, starting his plan to dismantle the empire, insisted on Lord Mountbatten to succeed Wavell. Having signed up to serve as Rear Admiral in the Navy from April 1947 onwards, Mountbatten was initially not prepared to accept the offer. Taking time to study this unexpected proposal, Mountbatten confirmed his acceptance on 15 January 1947 after consulting the King. On 20 February, Attlee announced that Mountbatten would be entrusted with "the task of transferring power to Indian hands the responsibility for the Government of British India, in a manner that will best ensure the future happiness and prosperity of India."[1]

Lord Mountbatten, later wrote he agreed to the India mission on three conditions, that he would be given i) plenipotentiary power in handling complex and decisive discussions with Indian leaders; ii) authority to fix his own time limit to end his job, and iii) that he would be allowed to bring out staff of his own choice additional to the staff he would inherit from his predecessor, Lord Wavell.[2] He said that the political success of his assignment was bound up with the government's readiness to accept an earliest possible date for the transfer. He advanced the time limit from that scheduled in June 1948. The new Viceroy received a wide mandate and was assured that no British arbitration would be imposed upon him and his naval career options would be retained. Additionally, Mountbatten was tasked to keep India intact with an undivided military.

Mr. Attlee said that if the outcome of a unitary constitution failed from the representative constituent assembly by the target time, "British Government would 'have to consider to whom the powers of the central Government in British India should be handed over, on the due date, whether as whole to some form of central Government…, or in such other way as may seem most reasonable and in the best interest of the Indian people.'"[3] Though the decision to transfer was firm, the Prime Minister's proposal would still need the Parliament's approval. To get parliamentary consent was not an easy task and required two days of discussion.

During the Parliamentary debates of 5 and 6 March, the conservatives raised objections to the speed of the process and its fixed deadline. They felt it was a breach of faith. Churchill resumed the debate on 6 March and pressed for a personal statement from Wavell. He said that he feared that a swift British withdrawal would result in India's haphazard fragmentation and not just a simple partition. Churchill also stated that Indians were fictitious and expressed doubts on their capability.[4] Thus the approval of Mountbatten's deputation in India by "targeting the date of transfer" in the Parliament was uncertain. However, Attlee pointed to "the dangers of delay," and of the Indian impatience and frustration. Lord Halifax (formerly Lord Irwin), forgetting his party line, concluded the 5 March debate saying, "I am not prepared to condemn what His Majesty's Government are doing unless I can honestly and confidently recommend a better solution."[5] His statement helped the Prime Minister to push his plan on the 6 March debate.

On 6 March, Attlee, who had two years' experience in India as a member of the Simon Commission, in his concluding speech from the Treasury Bench, firmly rebutted the doctrine that a personal statement of Wavell was necessary. About the attack on Indian politicians by Churchill, he said, "A very grave fault of the reforms that we have carried out over these years is that we have taught irresponsibility instead of responsibility. All Indian politicians were permanently in opposition, and speaking with long experience, it is not good to be always in opposition."[6] This concluding speech was able to bring out politicians from the party line, and the Parliament gave the verdict in favor of the delegation of Mountbatten with 337 votes against 185 in opposition.

Lord Louis Mountbatten was a handsome –over six feet tall– 46 year old successful naval officer and a great grandson of Queen Victoria. Brendon describes him as a reckless, flamboyant, egotistical, outspoken, and astonishingly popular leader.[7] From his return of his position as Naval Commander, Mountbatten was a frequent visitor of Downing Street as a consultant of SEAC Command, and familiar to the Prime Minister.[8]

Mountbatten reached Delhi on 22 March 1947, and settled in the Royal Viceroy's House (presently the Raj Bhavan) with his wife Edwina and two daughters. At the time, the negotiations between Congress and Muslim League were deadlocked, causing sporadic communal violence. Lady Edwina was an attractive socialite and granddaughter of a millionaire.

Nehru had met Mountbatten in Malaysia and this prior acquaintance helped him to become a family-friend of the new Viceroyalty. Nehru even entered into a romantic relationship with Lady Mountbatten. Mountbatten's daughter, Lady Pamela Hicks, in an interview (after her visit with Hugh Bonneville, who acted in the role of Lord Mountbatten in the film *Viceroy's House* released in 2017), said, "Jawaharlal and my mother undoubtedly loved one another... but my father was never jealous. He could see that the relationship made her happier to be around."[9] Mountbatten and Nehru worked together in close collaboration.

Mountbatten could not keep all his promises. The subcontinent was partitioned, triggering a tragic mass migration – the largest in human history. The result was that political propagandas sprang up, giving rise to many questions like, was the Partition an evil, or a necessary evil, could Partition have been avoided, was the Congress leadership responsible for the final action, or whether it is a result of a diplomatic coup of the British?

Gandhi was assassinated shortly after independence by a person who opposed Gandhi's alleged involvement with the Muslim moiety. Mountbatten was personally charged in Britain for the tragedy that followed the Partition, accusing him of undue haste for his own career prospects. In the following pages these questions need to be addressed. History shows that communal conflict was the sole cause of Partition.

The previous Viceroys left much work unfinished. Mountbatten worked with full confidence and sincerity without wasting time. He drafted a number of plans which, after extensive consultations with all parties involved, were modified and redrafted to bring the conflicting units into the 'Heads of Agreement' before the transfer of power became possible.

The original documents dealing with India's partition are retained in the administrative files in London and Delhi. Research work helped disclose much information, but perhaps much more remains undiscovered. Two books – by Menon and Campbell-Johnson – provided the information to write this chapter. Menon served as a constitutional adviser to the Viceroy with responsibility of processing each file prior to transfer of power, and Campbell-Johnson acted as the press attache during Mountbatten's mission. Historians like Philip Ziegler and David Butler also worked on Mountbatten.

9.2 Mountbatten – Last Viceroy of India

9.2.1 London office

Mountbatten came well prepared to Delhi. The programme of his mission was chalked up in cabinet house on 13 March 1947 in presence of two administrative staff who would accompany him. Lord Ismay was the chief of the Staff and Sir Eric Miéville served him as principal secretary. The other two of his personally selected staff who accompanied him were Alan Campbell-Johnson, his press attaché, R. V. Brochman, the conference assistant.

Mountbatten went first through the Cabinet records to finalise the procedure. The date of transfer was changed from 30 to 1 June 1948. He himself added a new paragraph stating that India would remain a member of the British Commonwealth for Nations (which came into being in 1926) as a free independent member, and act as a close friend of United Kingdom, so that India's future relation with Britain would be maintained through a military treaty to be completed after the transfer of power.[10]

On 10 March, V. P. Menon from the India Office,* had suggested the Secretary of State in London in a memo, to reconsider the same clauses of the Government of India Act 1935 for the transfer. The clause of the Act would help recognise India as a Dominion, and another clause would enable the Interim Government to become the successor of British India. Menon's suggestion was endorsed in the meeting, but he was not taken into Viceroy's inner circle quickly. This meeting decided to transfer full power to the Interim Government without any concessions to the Muslim League. The London meeting considered the importance of making constitutions for the provinces and for the groups following provincial elections, and were considering a solution for the Princes. Mountbatten was handed over the resolution of the meeting, and was sent to India with a short statement that the new Viceroy was being sent out expressly to terminate the British rule by a specific date.

9.2.2 Delhi office

Lord Mountbatten landed in Palam Airport on 22 March evening and was in his Delhi office the following day along with his officers. The swearing ceremony was held on 24 March. The then interim coalition government –led by Nehru– was running with jurisdiction over all the country including the Muslim majority provinces. Soon Mountbatten learnt that the Punjab government had been toppled by the League. Muslim League was pressuring the Congress government in the North Western

---

* Note: The South Indian V. P. Menon headed the constitutional section of the Government of India, and later, during Mountbatten's time, he acted as the Reform Commissioner. He worked with previous Viceroys of India, and was quite knowledgeable on the Acts introduced in India since the 1930s.

Frontier Province (NWFP) for a fresh election; riots did not end completely; and the officers posted in senior army positions, the police force, and in government offices were all Indians. Mountbatten knew that the main control of government rested at the hands of the Viceroy and his staff; and he was well informed that the Delhi administration was running with a staff shortage.

Meanwhile, the CWC meeting of 6–8 March, urged for the transfer of power to a single unit, which coincided with what the British wanted. Mountbatten first interacted with the members of the interim government and resolved the disagreement between Nehru and Liaquat Ali Khan by asking Khan to lower taxes which were imposed on wealthy subscribers. Then he convinced Gandhi and Jinnah to help maintain peace throughout the country.

Aided by Ismay, Mievelle and Alan-Campbell. Mountbatten began his negotiations with the Indian leaders to bring them in agreement. Mountbatten knew that Gandhi was a major force to be reckoned with, so he first met with Gandhi to form a strategy to keep India united. Gandhi quickly suggested to Mountbatten to offer Jinnah to form the first government, but with certain conditions. Later Congress Working Committees did not agree with Gandhi's proposal. Mountbatten also requested Gandhi to convince Congress to accept the Cabinet Mission Plan.

Jinnah in his first meeting with the Viceroy agreed to enter into discussions, stating out-right that the Muslim League would not agree on a united India. The Viceroy was not prepared to accept conditional statements until he knew the reasons. Within three weeks of his arrival, the Viceroy had several meetings with Jinnah in which he argued, begged and even cajoled him to change his opinion. Finally, Mountbatten became convinced that any previously proposed solution would fail.

9.2.3 The Balkan Plan

Within the first four to five days of his arrival in Delhi, Mountbatten realised the gravity of the situation from his trusted sources and concluded that it would be his priority to develop strategic plans to bring Congress and Muslim League in agreement and hasten the transfer of power to a single successor. He wrote to Attlee that the situation was grim and everything needed to be done quickly to avert a civil war. After a discussion with Nehru, Mountbatten learnt that Nehru was in favor of unity, but not at the cost of coercion. Nehru said that no unwilling non-Muslim majority community would go to Pakistan if partition was unavoidable.

Mountbatten also asked Nehru to enter the Commonwealth after the transfer. Nehru said that he agreed to make a treaty with Britain, and if India entered the Commonwealth it would be for a short period because Congress had resolved to found an Independent Sovereign Republic. To continue in the Commonwealth would mean an incomplete dominionship.

The Viceroy was immediately required to create a favorable environment so that the Cabinet could decide on a successor. But what if partition could not be averted? He asked his staff to work on an experimental broad based plan focusing on the problematic states like Punjab, Bengal, Assam, and N.W.F.P. only. His priority lay with Bengal and Punjab as their communal composition was almost equal. He advised that the plan would aim at giving the right to the people of Punjab and Bengal to decide upon their partition prior to their options for India or Pakistan. It would be a plan for a partition within the partition. Considering the position of the rest of the provinces, Ismay was asked to draw a broad plan based on the Cabinet Mission Plan. Ismay's draft divided India into 12 to 13 provincial units giving them autonomy to participate in one of three groups (from the Cabinet Mission Plan), but with full rights to opt out.

The Governors of Bengal and Punjab were asked to call separate representatives from predominant Muslim and non-Muslim regions of their provinces and seek their opinion, and assess whether they would vote for partition of their province. The provinces would be partitioned only if they agreed. People of Sylhet district in Assam were given the option to join the Muslim province, while the people of NWFP would select a province by election. Ismay's plan giving autonomy to the provinces to choose one was named the *Balkan Plan* (after Europe's multi-ethnic Balkan region) to differentiate it from the Cabinet Mission Plan.

Non-Muslims of Punjab and Bengal opted for partition. The representative of the Bengal Governor, however, suggested keeping Bengal united. Some local leaders wanted Bengal to be a sovereign state. But the majority of western Bengal opted for partition. The Muslims of Bombay and United provinces claimed autonomy in areas they were dominant; the extremist Sikhs demanded Khalistan; and a group in NWFP claimed a separate Pathan state. The Balkan Plan influenced some of the most powerful Princely States to think that partition would mean they could opt for total independence. Mysore, Hyderabad, Rajputana, and Kashmir, had closed borders. Thus the Balkan Plan giving autonomy to all signalled possibilities for India to disintegrate.

9.2.4 Implementation

Based on his discussions, Mountbatten recommended the partition of Punjab and Bengal. The Cabinet Mission plan, which allowed devolving power to the provinces, was kept undisturbed. This decision resulted in communal outbreaks in places like Delhi, and the agitation intensified against the elected Congress government of NWFP. At the end of April, Mountbatten personally intervened to pacify the situation.

The Balkan Plan of Ismay was drafted without consulting V. P. Menon. When consulted later, he said that it was an attempt to break up India, and he would resign if the plan was retained. Menon, in his note sent to London, had already proposed to accept the clauses in the 1935 Act which had a provision for dominions. When Nehru was asked, he said that the provinces in the Balkan Plan should have the right to decide their fate, but he was against imposing any constitutional condition on any community that had a majority in a specific area. He proposed to create a strong center with a federal structure.

Mountbatten considered the suggestions of Menon and Nehru, and asked Ismay to redraft the plan by transferring powers to two dominions which would stay within the Commonwealth, and that each of these two states would receive not only the provinces which they would choose, but also appropriate areas of Bengal and Punjab. But he cautioned not to mention 'Pakistan' as such. Decisions relating to 'transfer of power' were kept in abeyance to retain the Viceroy's power unchallenged.

Mountbatten suggested to his secretary to place the draft plan and the Commonwealth issue in the meeting of the provincial Governors which was called on 15 April. Twelve of the Governors were of British origin and had a long experience in India.

9.2.5 Commonwealth Membership and Dominion Status

Mountbatten himself included the issue of India's membership in the Commonwealth in the draft made in London. However, it was noted that Nehru was not interested in having a long term relationship with the Commonwealth. Mountbatten requested Baldev Singh, the defence minister of the interim government, to influence the minorities and convince Congress to accept a permanent membership in the Commonwealth which Nehru had refused. Congress then agreed to become a member of the Commonwealth until the middle of the year after independence. A friendly defence arrangement was also made with Britain. On 17 April, Mountbatten, in a meeting with Krishna Menon, Nehru's close friend, requested him to influence the Congress to put the CWC resolution about the *Commonwealth and* Sovereign *India* on hold for five years to secure India's defence under the Commonwealth.

In turn, Krishna Menon asked to allow the dominion status before 1948. Mountbatten agreed to recommend it if Muslims would stay in India, but not to the interim government. Then Krishna Menon proposed giving dominion status for both India and Pakistan and the provinces, joining in in two dominions. Mountbatten intended to keep the defence in British hands in order to control a single army for two nations. Krishna Menon said that dominion status without an army was laughable.[11]

Mountbatten gave more thought to Krishna Menon's opinion and met him again on 22 April. Krishna Menon suggested that India could be given dominion status consisting of two parts: Hindustan and Pakistan. Then Mountbatten immediately proposed a transitional constitution amendment of the dominion adapted to Krishna Menon's modified plan, which had the provision for the partition of India before dominion status was offered. A modified plan was drafted on 22 April which was finally re-drafted by V. P. Menon on 1 May in the presence of Krishna Menon and others.

But this draft was opposed by Jinnah. Krishna Menon suggested Mountbatten go to Viceregal summer residence in Simla with Nehru in the hope that time spent in solitude together would provide a way out of the impasse. Nehru accepted the invitation.

Mountbatten sought a legal opinion on the feasibility of India's Commonwealth membership from his friend Sir Walter Monckton, who had legal expertise and was visiting India at the time. Also, Nehru discussed with Monckton on India's continuation with the Crown in some form.[12] But they could not agree on certain points. Monckton then consulted on the issue with the Attorney General in London. He opined that "status of members of the Commonwealth was a matter of decision by the members themselves, and India as a republic can join in some new form." This opinion enabled India to decide about the Commonwealth membership after independence.

9.2.6 The Simla Episode

Before the Simla meeting began, Miéville met both Nehru and Jinnah with the draft plan. Nehru gave assent, but Jinnah demanded the dismissal of the constituent assembly and claimed responsibility for the entire six provinces where Muslims had a presence. He gave a call for civil disobedience and called for fresh elections in NWFP, which Mountbatten agreed to. The CWC on 1–4 May accepted the essence of the partition plan, and the principle of self-determination for Punjab and Bengal; but criticized the decision of holding an election in NWFP. The meeting denounced any method (i.e. methods adopted by Muslim League to put pressure on administration) which would cause the administration to submit to terrorism.

This CWC resolution was leaked from the Congress office. *Hindustan Times* wrote on 3 May, "… holding an election might force Congress to change its attitude towards the British government… Mountbatten was not playing a fair game." The government threatened to withdraw the press privileges, but issued a fresh notice for holding a referendum before the election in NWFP.[13] Muslim League then suspended civil disobedience movements.

On 4 May, Gandhi announced that he would oppose any partition and asked for transfer of power by June 1948 either to the League or to Congress on the basis of dominion status.

When the partitions of Bengal and Punjab were opposed, Mountbatten reminded Jinnah that the Cabinet Mission plan was still valid. Campbell-Johnson wrote in his diary of 7 May that Jinnah aimed to keep the British in India in hope of obtaining more favor.[14] He deliberately prolonged bargaining to make it more difficult for the British to leave. Mountbatten reached Simla on 6 May. The conference could now begin. Congress at a meeting of 7 May demanded dominion status soon, enabling both the interim government and the constituent assembly, and a safeguard for the minorities.

Mountbatten included Menon in his Simla-team because of his experience as a constitutional adviser to Linlithgow and Wavell. He had also been part of the team which drew the India Government Act 1935, and the Cabinet Mission plan. Nehru arrived at Simla armed with the CWC resolutions which demanded power be relinquished as one unit to the central government by June 1947 and retain the provision for provincial groupings for those who wanted to opt out of the Indian union, but not before the constitution was finalized. The resolutions were endorsed by Abdul Gaffer Khan of NWFP.

This Simla session aimed to finalize a new constitution as well as the partition issues. Menon suggested that the time frame of June 1947, as Congress wanted, was not suitable for completing the procedure for partition of Bengal and Punjab. He also suggested starting the discussion with the proposal for a dominion status before going straight for partition. He argued that the frame of the dominion would have provisions to accommodate two central governments in divided India; and at the same time, Congress would get time to draw a separate constitution for the Indian part and build up India's own military and civil administration. He said that Sardar Patel agreed with this proposal.

But Mountbatten supported Nehru's formula to start with the Union of India, allowing the unwilling provinces to opt out. Nehru and Menon drafted a note following the suggestion of Mountbatten, but they indicated that the referendum of the NWFP would be done under the supervision of the Governor-General to enhance a quick transfer of power adapting the Government of India Act 1935. Mountbatten was also thinking about constitutional continuity to pacify Jinnah's claim for two nations.[15]

Nehru and Menon met again on 9th, and decided to give priority to having a united domain, and if it was unattainable, power should be transferred to two separate executive councils- one elected by non-Muslim constituent assembly, and the other by Muslim constituent assembly. Each assembly with separate areas under a joint council handling matters of common concern under one Governor-General serving both the successors.[16]

Nehru insisted that if partition was unavoidable, it would be made after the transfer of power to avoid the recurring problems that might be created in Muslim enclaves of Hindu dominated states. The next meeting was arranged on the morning of May 10. On the 9th evening, Patel called Menon and informed him that he would favor immediate division (before the transfer) to avoid any further delay. Patel's endorsement encouraged Menon to directly propose two states, the union of India and Pakistan in the meeting of 10th morning. Congress remained with no option but to accept the partition in this form.

The Congress planned to accommodate the Princely States into the Indian enclave after the British responsibility on the States would terminate. However, Nehru was still in dilema about the timing of the division as he wanted the partition be enforced ahead of the transfer of power and avoid the problem of the States that might opt out of India if the new Indian constitution did not suit them. Also Nehru was unsure of the future of Bengal where some leaders wanted it as a separate unit.

Mountbatten avoided further complications and came out with a final decision confirming that partition could not be postponed. Regarding Bengal, he said that if a truncated Bengal was conceded for the present, there was a chance of the parted Bengal to return later. The India committee in London had already changed the original version of the Balkan Plan. Even Nehru did not know about those changes. Mountbatten assured that if any problems arose during the partition of Bengal and Punjab, it would be taken care of with a strict hand.

Nehru agreed for immediate partition as Patel also wanted it. The next meeting of 13 May formalized the transfer plan as the *Mountbatten – Nehru Deal*. It was an amalgamation of Plan Balkan and Menon's appendix depicting the transfer of power to two successor dominions keeping limited scope for Muslim League to interfere. Menon was asked on 16 May to compile the contents of the deal, and he did it under eight following clauses.

9.2.7 Menon's Draft Plan

1) The leaders agreed to the procedure laid down for assessment; 2) in the event of the decision there should be only one central authority in India, power should be transferred to the existing constituent assembly of dominion status basis; 3) in the event of a decision that there should be two sovereign states in India, the central government of each state would take over the power with responsibility to their respective constituent assemblies on the dominion basis; 4) the transfer of power in either case should be on the basis of the Government of India Act 1935, modified to confirm the dominion status position (thus the plan deviated from the Cabinet Mission Plan); 5) the Governor-General would be common to both the dominions, and at present, a Governor-General would be appointed; 6) a commission should be appointed for demarcation of boundaries in the event the decision was in favor of partition; 7) the Governors of the provinces should be appointed on the recommendation of the respective provincial governments; and 8) in the event of two dominions coming into being, the existing armed forces should be divided among them.

The draft also recommended that the units of armed forces would be allocated according to the territorial basis of recruitment, and would be under the control of the respective government. In case of dispute, there should be a committee with the Field Marshal, the Chief of the general staff, and two defence ministers to act under the Governor-General and settle the disputes. This committee would dissolve automatically as soon as the process was complete. Though the draft kept the option for a united India open, the plan was finalized with the understanding that partition had become inevitable.

9.3 Post-Simla Agreements

9.3.1 The statement of His Majesty's Government (HMG)

The draft was shown to Nehru and Patel by Menon; and Eric Miéville took it to Jinnah and Liaquat Ali. Congress accepted the plan as a continuation of the Cabinet Mission Plan but inserted certain modifications to fit the existing situation. Congress also said that if there were two states during the interim period (interim Congress government was still on hold), the Governor-General should be common to both. Jinnah on behalf of the League was agreeable on principle, but refused to accept in writing. On 18 May the Viceroy formally approved the draft and left for London accompanied by V. P. Menon with a break in Karachi.

In Karachi, Mountbatten understood that the proponents of Pakistan wanted immediate transfer of power. The next day in London, Mountbatten had discussions with the Prime Minister and the India Committee of the cabinet. The plan was approved by the cabinet, and accordingly the HMG issued an endorsement, that "That the constitution will be framed by India and it would not be imposed upon those who were unwilling." Constituent assembly consisting of a specific area would decide where they would join. Once those were ascertained, HMG would determine to whom power should be transferred. For Bengal and Punjab, and Sylhet (if Sylhet wanted separation from Assam), only the provincial assembly members, excluding the European members, would meet in two parts with Muslim majority and the non-Muslims majority (in census of 1941) to decide by a vote (of the members of each party separately) whether they wanted partition, and if so, they would join the state as their favorite dominion.

Final demarcation of areas would be made by the Boundary Commission to be set up by the Governor-General. Opportunities were given to NWFP to reconsider their position after the Punjab partition; but a referendum would be made to the electors of the legislative assembly to choose the state. Once partition was approved, representatives would decide upon the nature of the constitution they would like to frame. In case of Bengal,

Punjab, and Sylhet, if partition was decided upon, it would be necessary to hold elections to have representatives for the constituent assembly on the scale of one to one million population.

9.3.2 Implementation of Nehru Mountbatten Plan

Jinnah was pressing for the corridor connecting the east and west regions of the proposed state of Pakistan. Mountbatten returned to Delhi on 1 June and called a conference with Indian leaders and explained the existing problems with the partition of Punjab having a haphazard demographic pattern. Then he proposed for immediate transfer of power on the basis of dominion status and in affiliation with the Commonwealth, to enable HMG to pass legislation in the next session. He had convinced Churchill to support the passage of the bill. Mountbatten also said that HMG's office had inserted minor amendments in the plan, and the new governments would have liberty to withdraw from the Commonwealth if they so desired.

Mountbatten then circulated the HMG's statement to concerned parties requesting all to convey their written approval by midnight on 2 June. Nehru affirmed that Congress would let him know by the evening. Jinnah said that the acceptance would come later. Mountbatten asked Jinnah to communicate it by midnight. Jinnah made a verbal report. The Viceroy affirmed his broadcast in All India Radio by next evening, and invited Nehru and Jinnah to broadcast immediately after him. The CWC conveyed their formal acceptance on condition that Muslim League would declare that no further claim would be put forward. Baldev Singh requested to look after the Sikhs' interest when laying the boundary line. Gandhi said, "if India was partitioned it would be over his dead body." Mountbatten then met with Gandhi to persuade him to agree with the plan.

Not getting any written statement from Jinnah, Mountbatten told him that Prime Minister Attlee would broadcast the outcome on 3 June. Jinnah insisted on a corridor and said that he would not accept a "moth-eaten Pakistan." When stuck again, Mountbatten told Jinnah, "if you press again you will lose Punjab for good, and power would be transferred to the Indian domain leaving an independent government outside the commonwealth for the Muslim majority area." He commented that Jinnah was a "psychopathic case."[17]

9.3.3 The Status of Bengal

During the last week of June, Suhrawardy opted for a dominion status of undivided Bengal (a third dominion) along with the Bengal Congress. Suhrawardy and Abdul Hashem did not want to be ruled from distant Punjab; and the Bengal Congress was hopeful of getting back the Bengal territory under Indian union later. At a press conference on 27 May in Mussoorie, Nehru, in presence of Kiran Shankar Roy – a leader and member of the Bengal Legislative Assembly, declared, "we agree to Bengal remaining united only if it remains in the union." Shyamaprasad Mukherjee, representing Hindumahasaba considered the proposal of united Bengal was nothing but a ploy by Suhrawardy to control the industrial west. The prospect of a united Bengal was already dismissed by the Indian committee in London saying that it should have to unite with either the existing or the new dominion.[18]

9.3.4 Third June Plan – Radio Broadcast and June 4 Press Conference

Before Radio broadcast and press meet on 3 June, Mountbatten appreciated Indian leaders for their cooperation. He reminded Jinnah to submit Muslim League's opinion and asked whether Attlee should go ahead with the Prime Minister's announcement. Only after Jinnah replied 'yes,' Mountbatten communicated to the Secretary of State that he received assurances from all parties.[19] The House of Commons approved the *3 June Plan*.

Radio broadcast: Attlee in his broadcast on 3 June honored Mountbatten for solving a pending problem. He announced that it was not possible to retain India united and its partition was an inevitable alternative, and that power would be handed over as soon as possible to the two governments, each with dominion status. The "3 June Plan" was the final announcement for Independence.

Following Attlee, Mountbatten in a radio broadcast, explained that the plan finalized the partition of India because Muslim League demanded it, and Congress ultimately had agreed upon. The Boundary Commission would finally determine the boundary line between two nations. He regretted that the whole plan might not be perfect, but HMG accepted that two states would emerge each with dominion status. The procedure of the transfer would be finalized following the Cabinet's approval of the Act of Transfer of Power.

In his broadcast Nehru said that certain areas seceded from India, but it was a big advance towards complete independence. It was with no joy in his heart that he commended those proposals, though he had no doubt that it was the right course. Jinnah said that the plan did not actually meet the Muslim League point of view, however, so far he felt that the reaction of the League in Delhi circle had been hopeful;[20] and Mountbatten had worked with fairness and impartiality.[21]

Press meet: With Vallabhbhai Patel in the chair on 4 June, Mountbatten said everything was done hurriedly at the consent of the Indian leaders. Both parties wanted to speed up the transfer, but he felt that the forthcoming governments would formalize their constitution following the modified 1935 Act. For clarification of the dominion status which was a confusing term, he explained that dominion status was absolute independence in every possible way,[22] with the sole exception that the members of the states were linked together voluntarily and looked to support one another, based on mutual trust. Different administrations were at liberty to opt out of the Commonwealth as they pleased. On NWFP, he said that there was a Congress government, but the minorities were only 5% of the population, and the final decision would be taken after a referendum.* About the corridor issue, he simply said that it was not in the plan. Finally, Mountbatten announced that transfer of power could be done on about 15 August 1947.[23]

---

* Note: Abdul Ghaffar Khan and his brothers of NWFP opposed the partition and boycotted the referendum, but the fate of this state was settled through a people's referendum.

Mountbatten went to Gandhi who was in his usual prayer meeting. Gandhi told the public that the British Government was not responsible for the Partition. The Viceroy opposed it, but was left with no choice. Many Congress members were unhappy as they dreamt of keeping India united, but certain parts gave in.

9.3.5 India's Independence Act

The Independence Act passed in the Parliament on 18 July (some historians say that the date was 15 July, a month before power was handed over) enacted the partition, and abandoned the British Suzerainty over the Princely States, leaving them free to choose one of the new dominions. With the declaration of this new Act the British withdrew their responsibility of offering protection as previous treaties had done. So the States needed to join a dominion for a shake of security.

9.3.6 Consequences of Third June Plan

Gandhi said that if both Hindus and Muslims could not agree upon anything else, then the Viceroy was left with no choice. Congress members were not happy because they were attached to the entire land and fought for it for so long. They accepted the separation only for peace and a strong Indian government free from internal interference, and were happy as the historic name "India" was retained. The League in their New Delhi meeting of 10 June passed a resolution in favor of the scheme, being satisfied that the Cabinet Mission Plan was abandoned. Hindu Mahasaba opposed the partition and urged to restore the ceded areas. They observed Anti-Pakistan day. The communists said that the dominion status would enable Britain to sustain their control over India.[24] The American press praised Attlee and Mountbatten.

9.3.7 Independence Bill

V. P. Menon, assisted by a team of four persons including the law secretary, drafted the bill adopting the Government of India Act 1935. The bill included twenty clauses and three schedules.[25] After receiving the consent of all the parties, the documents were sent to London. This draft was finalized as a bill in HMO's office and introduced in the House of Commons on 4 July. The Secretary of State announced that on the 15th August India would achieve complete Independence, and would have a new status as a member of the Commonwealth, equivalent to other members, with all advantages of mutual cooperation. After the Bill was passed, elections were arranged in the disputed provinces. The India Office ceased to operate and the Secretary for Commonwealth Relations was responsible to look after the new dominions. Because the name "India" was retained, she, as a dominion, was able to continue as a member of the United Nations organization.[26]

9.3.8 Settlement of Bengal and Punjab

On 20 June the assembly members of the disputed provinces - Bengal, Punjab (and Sylhet) voted to decide on partitions. Members of western Bengal, and eastern Punjab opted for the Indian union, and those of eastern Bengal and western Punjab joined Pakistan. Sylhet wanted to stay with East Bengal. A referendum was held in NWFP on 17 July, in absence of Congress, as Khan Abdul Goffor Khan boycotted the process. It was included with Pakistan. Afghans encouraged people of this state to claim an autonomous Pathanistan. The HMO rejected it. The new states included in India i.e. West Bengal and East Punjab, were required to elect new representatives for their Constituent Assemblies.

9.3.9 Re-appointment of the Governor-General

Lord Mountbatten was accepted as the Governor-General of both domains. But the Muslim League selected Jinnah as the Governor-General for Pakistan, supplanting Mountbatten and bypassing the June 3 plan. Problems arising out of this situation were tactically avoided by withdrawing all portfolios allotted to the League members in the interim government, keeping Congress in power as a single unit and Congress was enabled to accept charge of all the affairs of the dominion of India.[27] The League representatives made their own arrangements to take charge of Pakistan.

Until Mountbatten accepted the position of Governor-General of India he acted as the Chairman of India and Pakistan, keeping provisions for each domain to deal with their business separately. He had options to consult with each for common issues. A complete separation of India and Pakistan was feasible immediately after India accepted Mountbatten as her Governor-General. A communique announcing the fresh arrangements was issued by Mountbatten. As his first priority, he appointed a boundary commission to determine the new border.

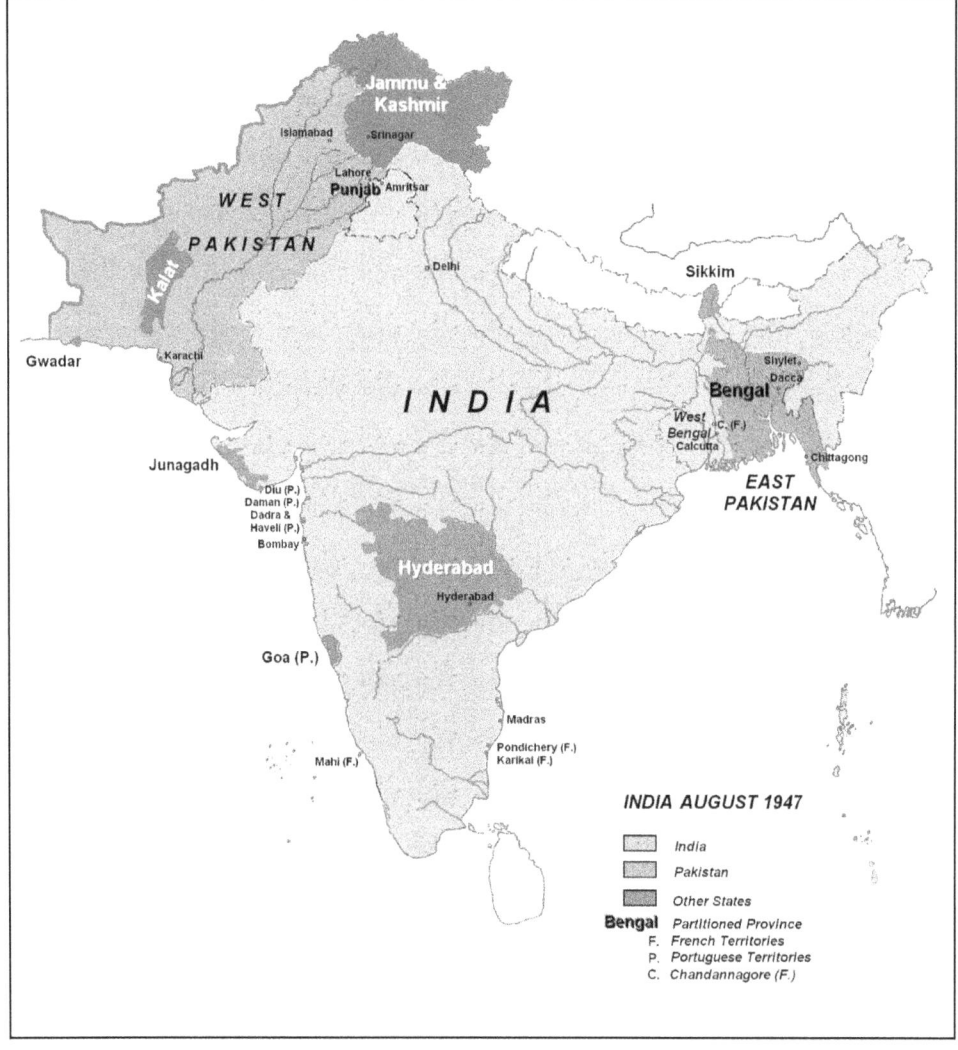

Fig. 30 Map India Partition August 1947.

9.4 Boundary Commission – Partition and Boundary Line

Sir Cyril Radcliffe, a barrister, was called from London to act as the chairman of the joint border commission with responsibility to draw the demarcation lines separating the domains. Two separate commissionerates were formed for Punjab and Bengal to work out demarcations independently of each other.[28] Radcliffe was given five weeks' time to complete the job by 15 August after his arrival on 1 July. He did not know India's topography and demography. The time frame was too short for Radcliffe, and he was given the leeway to decide on border lines. His private secretary, Christopher Beaumont was, however, familiar with Punjab.

Radcliffe was a man of great intelligence and probity, and he withstood enormous pressures with resilience while he was working on the field.[29] From 8 July he started consulting the 1941 census, and maps to locate the population, the positions of villages, and the river-courses along the proposed border. When he faced anomalies he had no alternative map to verify and decide.[30]

He had to consider many aspects like water sources, natural boundaries, communication patterns, socio-political aspects, and the majority-minority basis of the population of the border towns before deciding on the demarcation.[31] Punjab is a land of five rivers and their canals. The population distribution in Punjab was haphazard, without a clear line to divide Hindus, Muslims, or Sikhs. It was a much more complicated state to make a clear demarcation. He visited Lahore and Calcutta, and talked to the commissionerates there. Each of the two major parties had equal representation in the provincial commissions. Radcliff worked with absolute neutrality keeping distance from the Viceroy. Sometimes both parties responded with arrogance when they failed to solve the problems by themselves. In that situation Radcliff used his authority to make final decisions.

Places like Lahore, Amritsar, and Gurdaspur were complicated and mutual agreement was needed. Radcliff initially placed the Muslim majority city of Lahore in the Indian domain, but later he awarded it to Pakistan as it was not allocated any large city. In Gurdaspur, the Muslim population was found to be 51% but they used to pay only 35% of the total land revenue, and in the 1901 census the Muslim portion had dropped to 49%.[32] Furthermore, he observed that Gurdaspur retained the headwater of the canals that irrigated Amritsar, the holy place of the Sikhs. He considered all such issues to include Amritsar and Gurdaspur in one administrative unit suitable for India. In addition, Amritsar was the sacred place of the Sikhs, and Gurdaspur provided the land corridor for connecting Jammu and Kashmir later included in Indian dominion. In 1946 Lord Wavell decided Gurdaspur and Amritsar had to be kept together.[33] But Shakargarh tehsil of Gurdaspur district, which was situated on the other side of the river Ravi, was included with Pakistan. In cases of controversy over fixing the demarcations in Punjab, Radcliffe strictly stuck to his decision.

The border line was finalized by 9 August, but it was kept secret for two or three days. Part of a land east of Sutlej canal housing an army depot (presently the Firozpur Cantonment) remained undecided, but after 9 August it was transferred to Indian domain considering that the land contained the head water of the canals that irrigates Bikaner of Rajasthan. All statements of this project were finally approved by Radcliff.

Gossip had it that Nehru and Patel knew of the plan on 9 August, and someone was rewriting the original document of Radcliff before his final approval.[34] Liaquat Ali Khan, at the midst of controversy over Ferozepur, categorically said that he did not doubt Mountbatten's probity over the partition line.[35] In actuality the 1941 census recorded the Muslim population in Firozpur only at 45%.

The Bengal Partition was a more straight forward process as distribution of two communities were more or less equally divided. Muslim population of East Bengal had a majority in 15 districts, while the Hindus were majority in 12 districts of West Bengal. But controversy arose with the Chittagong Hill Tracts at the extreme southeast corner of East Bengal where more than 95% of the population were non-Muslims (majority being Buddhists). They opted for their inclusion with India. But they had no representative to plead for them. The Commission decided to retain Chittagong in East Pakistan as the town was its only harbour on the Bay of Bengal.

Calcutta was included in West Bengal after a bargain. In Malda and Murshidabad, the Muslim population was the majority. But those two districts were included in West Bengal only to retain the main waterway (the Ganga) which connects Calcutta Port. Pakistan however, was compensated by including the Hindu majority district of Khulna with East Pakistan. Bengal partition caused economic problems in both the areas. East Pakistan was the place for commercial production of raw jute, while all jute mills were established around Calcutta. Most of the boundary demarcations were finalized by 9 August. Radcliffe said the line partitioning Sylhet and Assam was not completed; he also said that he would hand over the complete package on 13 August.[36]

The map for redrawing partitioned Punjab was based more on logic as Radcliff had no other data available to him. The line of separation of Punjab was sentimentally unacceptable to thousands of folk whose forefathers established homes where they grew up and cultivated their land. But these peasants would have to leave their land forever. Villages whose Muslim inhabitants were exalted with the birth of Pakistan would be scheduled to be Indian and vice versa. Sikhs and Hindus begged their custodians to send them to India after being evicted. They would be welcomed in the other nation as refugees. They were shocked but had to accept the reality as there was no alternative.

People lost their senses, became vengeful and embittered, failed to control themselves, and landed in carnage. Punjab burnt. In the Lahore streets Hindu homes, like many other smaller towns, were ablaze. Neighbors who lived side by side for generations forgot their humanity, and engaged in frenzied murder. Irregular slaughter continued for six weeks. Muslim troops and police stood by watching.

Bengal was safe due to Gandhi's presence. Suhrawardy came to stay with Gandhi at Beliaghata, to quell the riots. His partnership was constrained initially as stray snagging continued. Gandhi began a fast that he would only stop if people's sanity returned. Both the communities attended Gandhi's prayer meeting held in the Maidan. Calcutta remained peaceful.

Every asset of the British Raj – from armed forces to its furniture and even stationery – were divided proportionally between the two domains, and the process was completed by the Joint Defense Council by 1 April 1948.

The Viceroy would be in Karachi for the Independence Day celebration of Pakistan. At last on 16 August, the leaders of India and Pakistan were summoned to hear details of the Partition.[37] The plan of separation of the domains was put on hold until 17 August. Withdrawal of British troops from India started from 17 August and continued until 28 February 1948 – the day the last light infantry left the shores of India.[38]

9.5 Announcement of Independence Day

The formal announcement of transfer of power to India would be on 15 August. The time of the occasion was fixed precisely at midnight, as according to the astrologers the day was not good for a new nation to begin with. The red– white– blue Union Jacks that flew for two centuries would be taken down forever at dusk, and the British monarch would screen off the Coat of Arms in the Durbar Hall. Its name would change at the stroke of midnight.

Nehru said, "... a moment comes, which comes very rarely in history when we step out from old to new… soul of a nation long suppressed finds utterance… long years ago we made a tryst with destiny, and now the time comes… At the stroke of the midnight hour, while the world sleeps, India will awake to life and freedom."[39]

9.6 Gandhi in Calcutta with Suhrawardy

Mahatma Gandhi arrived on 13 August in Calcutta at a crumbling building in Beliaghata– the Hydair House standing with dirty surroundings, but being just repaired for his stay. A Hindu mob, mainly the victims of the Direct Action Day, were waiting for his arrival. They were angry. Some of them threw stones at his old car. The old frail man of 77 got down and told, "You wish to do me ill. I have come to save Hindus and Muslims alike. I am going to place myself under your protection…I have nearly reached the end of my life's journey…" He asked, "I am Hindu by birth, a Hindu of Hindus, Hindu is my way of living, how can I be an enemy of Hindus?"[40]

His simple approach surprised the masses. Gandhi invited a few from them for conversations. Suhrawardy, who had been the head of the state and whom Hindus hated, would stay with Gandhi at his invitation. When the crowd was told about Suhrawardy, some of them were so agitated that they threw bricks and broke windows of Hydair House.

India's long march to freedom would end within a few hours. Seeing Suhrawardy inside the house, a mob moved towards Gandhi in anger. For the first time after returning to India, he experienced such treatment from his own people. Suhrawardy, though a seasoned politician, felt nervous. He knew his past credentials – why was he unpopular? Just a year back, on 16 August 1946 he acted as a faithful soldier of Muslim League in Calcutta itself instigating the riots.

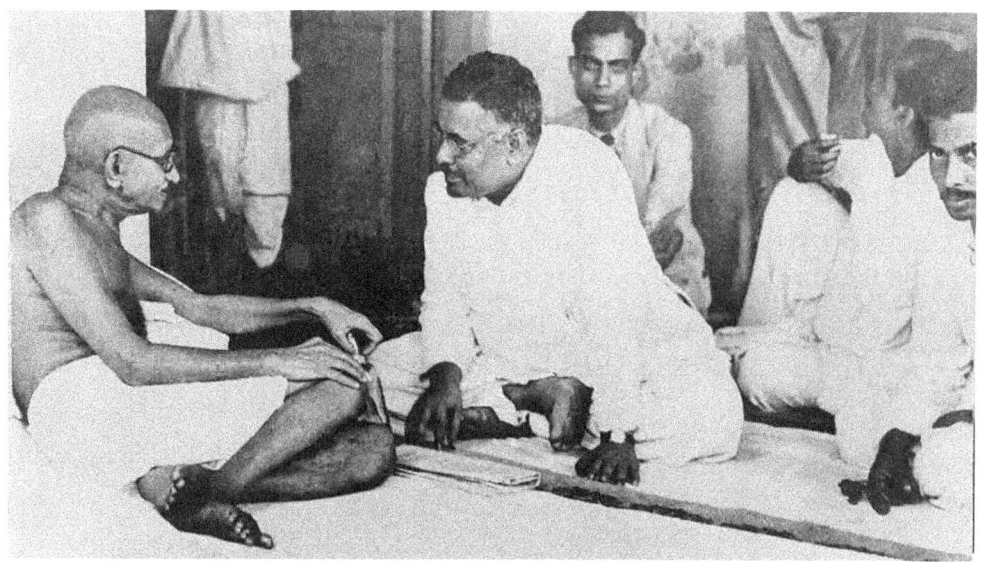

Fig. 31 Gandhi and Suhrawardy in Beliaghata, Calcutta, September 1–4, 1947 (Public Domain).

Sitting inside a house, encircled by the crowd, Suhrawardy asked Gandhi how long he would be there? Gandhi said that he would continue as long as needed, he would wait to see Calcutta as safe (Fig. 31). Gandhi asked him to stay with him knowing fully well that people had become fanatical. There was no-one to protect them.

Butler wrote of Suhrawardy,

> When he had held the power in Calcutta, he made sure that the city police force was mainly recruited from Muslims, now half of them had fled… Independence meant that there would no longer be any British troops empowered to keep the peace. Hindus were building themselves up to take terrible vengeance for the day of Direct Action. Now, with the anniversary at hand, they were at boiling point. Only Gandhi's presence in the Moslem quarters was preventing whole scale slaughter, and even so, Suhrawardy wondered how strong the old man's hold over his people might remain.[41]

Gandhi pacified the angry crowd when they enquired about Suhrawardy. "I assured him safety," Gandhi said. Suhrawardy admitted his responsibility for Direct Action Day. Gandhi asked the crowd not to stain their hands with blood for the cause of those children who would lead the nation. Power of his words silenced the crowd. Gandhi assured them on 14 August that a new spirit would radiate from Calcutta.

Gandhi had his final prayer meeting under the British Raj from 5 pm and people joined him. He said that from the very next day India would be delivered from bondage, and that the nation would be partitioned at midnight. He announced the 15th would be a day of sorrow, and if Calcutta maintained a brotherhood, entire India would be saved. He asked, "if flames of communal strife envelop the whole country, how can our new born freedom survive?"[42] He asked everyone to observe India's Independence Day by fasting, praying, and spinning.

9.7 Pledges and India's Obligations

The Pledges were taken in Delhi on the night of the 14th and the morning of 15th August. Lord Mountbatten was sworn as the Governor-General of India by the Chief Justice, and the cabinet headed by Nehru was sworn by the Governor-General. Power was transferred to India on the 15th, but the Partition was implemented from the 17th (Fig. 32). India lost large territory after the partition, but its identity as a state remained unchanged and India's obligations as a free nation were established automatically on 15 August 1947.

Fig. 32 News of Independence Friday August 15, 1947 (The Statesman).

Lord Mountbatten promulgated the Indian Independence order 1947 on 14 August. It was an international arrangement on the basis of which India obtained the right to enjoy memberships of all international organizations.[43] India continued in the United Nations with all rights and obligations of membership. Also, as the Governor-General, Mountbatten introduced certain changes in the Commonwealth paradigm to enable India to be part of it with the termination of its dominion status. The flexible statutes of the Commonwealth easily accommodated India.[44]

On 15 August 1947 the new Indian President Dr. Rajendra Prasad, paid tribute to Mountbatten on behalf of the Indians, and said that the British domination over India ended, and India's relationship with Britain would rest on the basis of equality, mutual goodwill and mutual profit. Then the National Flag of India was unfurled over the Council House.

This Friday, the 15th August of 1947, was a glorious moment in Indian history. But Gandhi was in Calcutta. Mountbatten and Gandhi maintained respectful relations with each other, and used to enjoy intellectual conversations, often full of humor (Fig. 33). Mountbatten stated, "At this historic moment let us not forget that India owes to Mahatma Gandhi- the architect of her freedom through non-violence. We miss his presence here today, and would let him know how much he is in our thoughts."

About Nehru he said, "... your first Prime Minister, Jawaharlal Nehru... His trust and friendship have helped me beyond measure on my task... India will now attain a position of strength and influence, and take her rightful place in the comity of nations."[45]

Fig. 33 Gandhi and Mountbatten, one week before Independence (Public Domain).

9.8 Princely States – Accession to India

The Princely States, about 562 in number, collectively covered about 40% of the area outside the direct command of the British Raj, and were distributed within Indian territory with partial dependence on Britain by a treaty (Fig. 34). To do away with complexities that might arise following implementation of the Indian Independence Act, it was Mountbatten's duty to accede those states before the paramountcy expired, and see that the States merged with India surrendering their wishes of individual independence. Mountbatten had committed to George VI that he, as the Governor-General of India, would see fair play for the Princes and create an integrated India establishing friendship with Great Britain.[46] Mountbatten also committed to Nehru to help their merger into Indian territory, and on 25 July he offered them accession to any one of two dominions. As a part of Indian administration he adopted all means, even through cajoling or bullying, applying his authority to merge the States with India by offering preferential terms.

As per the plans made with V. P. Menon, Mountbatten met the Princes with Vallabhbhai Patel in the chair. He first talked to the States that were landlocked, and offered them a chance for reconciliation with promises for protection and providing communication facilities. He assured that India would scrupulously respect their existence. He suggested all Hindu states to prevail upon to join India immediately.

Patel started negotiations, but he met with much resistance as most of the Maharajas, Rajas, and Ranars could not but lament to append their signatures to a document breaking the alliances their ancestors had made with the British, some of which had existed for centuries. Most of the Princes actually wanted autonomy, which was undesirable. As Patel dealt with opposition, Mountbatten firmly convinced the States to effect the accession.

When Maharana of Dholpur refused to accede, Mountbatten asked him to join before 14 August, or else the state would become completely isolated in the center of an indifferent India. When the princes showed indifference, he simply told them that His Highness asked them to sign the instrument of accession.[47] His strict attitude incited most of the states to accede to India. The remaining unwilling twenty-two princes were called again, and they agreed to join on August 1st. But problems remained with Bhopal, Jodhpur, Indore, Tanjabhore, Junagadh, Hyderabad, and Kashmir. A few states in Pakistan took more than two decades to accede.

Ultimately all of the Princes agreed to join in time except Junagadh, Kashmir, and Hyderabad. Maharaja Hari Singh was the Hindu king of Kashmir with more than 90% Muslims, and the Nizam of Hyderabad and Nawab of Junagadh (Gujarat) were Muslim rulers in Hindu-majority territories. These three States vowed to continue with full independence.

Soon Kashmir became involved in the problem between India and Pakistan. Pakistan was inclined to accept Hyderabad and Junagadh when they refused India. The Kashmir issue, in particular, needed further discussions as its status remained uncertain. Further details of accession of these three States has been narrated in Appendix 2.

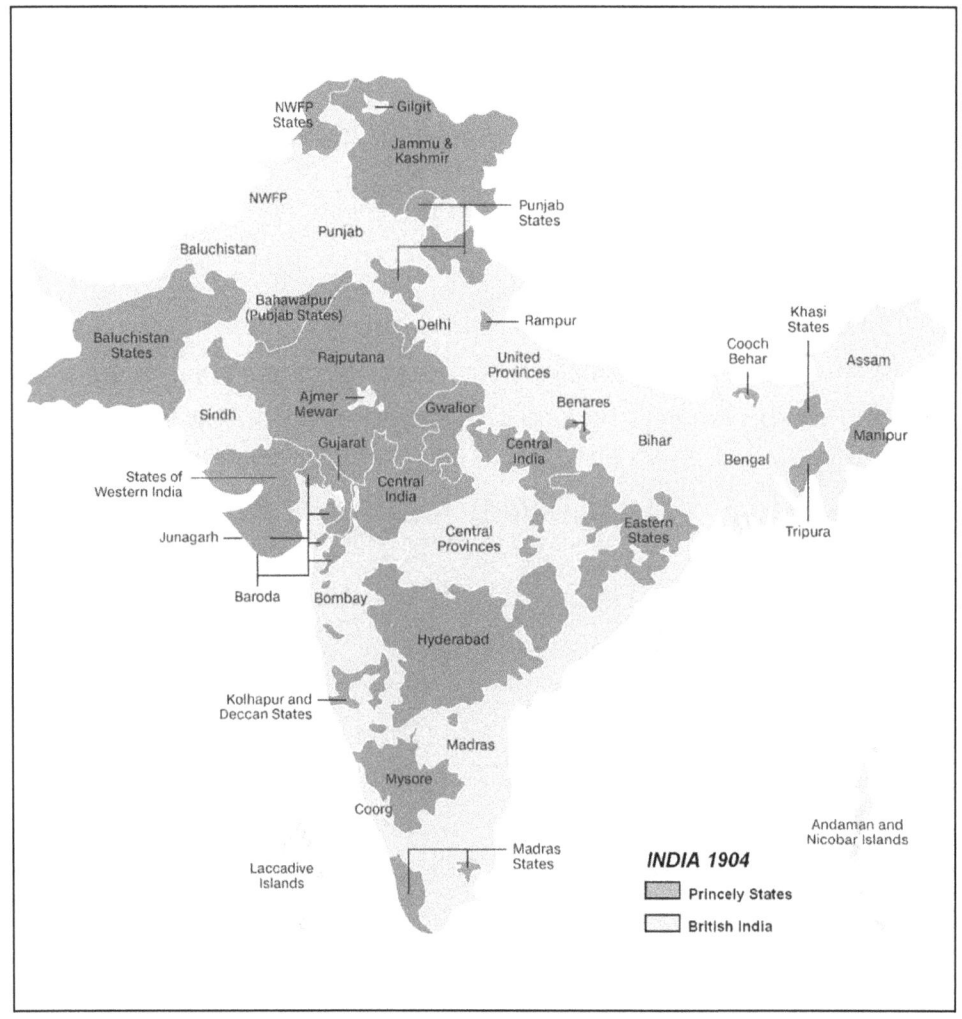

Fig. 34 Map Princely States 1904.

9.9 Observations

From discussions in previous chapters we know why and how the economy of Raj became disarrayed being affected by two wars, two economic depressions, imperial demands, inefficient management of resource mobilization, while keeping India under control. Tomlinson explains that after the 1920s, when the Raj paid in (London sourced) Pound Sterling, became an intractable problem for British policy as India was unable to pay back interest and Home Charges that would satisfy the bond- and tax-payers at home.[48] World War II became a financial drain for Britain. Post-war Britain was severely weakened to maintain its globe spanning empire looking after 560 million people. In this situation, we have seen why Lord Wavell was hurriedly replaced with Lord Mountbatten.

The decision to appoint Lord Mountbatten and to set a fixed date for transferring power to Indians was challenging for the Prime Minister Attlee to pass through Parliament. Churchill tried to put an embargo on these matters during the parliamentary debates in March 1947. After much discussion, reminding the members that India's independence was inevitable and better be executed quickly, Mountbatten's Viceroyalty was approved. Mountbatten was sent with plenipotentiary powers to terminate British India keeping India united and retaining an undivided army for an interim period. When Mountbatten joined, India was marred by violent riots and acute communal disagreement on the issue of selecting a successor of British India.

With advanced planning and an experienced team, partly thanks to the work of his predecessors, Mountbatten could successfully terminate the British Raj before the deadline. However, he could not keep India united due to Jinnah's iron will demanding a separate Muslim nation. Mountbatten did not know that Jinnah was dying from tuberculosis, otherwise he admitted afterwards, he would have awaited his death.[49]

Lord Mountbatten was appreciated nationally and internationally for his success. He was criticized too for being in haste (as some believed for personal benefit), and responsible for the huge carnage caused due to partition. He was undoubtedly in haste, but he was able to avoid indecision and uncertainty. Independence caused lots of self-searching. Congress leaders were questioned about their real intentions. Gandhi was accused and assassinated for neglecting Hindus. The administration was also blamed for being unprepared and lacking vision for making an advanced plan for those people displaced during partition. Why Partition was the only possible outcome has been narrated in the text, and remains open for readers to judge. Mountbatten's sincerity and tenacity was beyond doubt. The volume of his work was compiled as documents in some 2,800 pages.[50]

Jinnah's ambition for forming an Islamic state was fulfilled, and the Muslim League succeeded in securing Pakistan; but his nation survived only by giving up its democratic institution to autocratic forces. Gandhi's wish for a free India with morally responsible individuals forming *Ram Rajya*- an Ideal state built on equality, justice and truth no matter people's religion, was vanquished by the malady of corruption. Mountbatten's death was not different either; he was also tragically assassinated.

It is a historical irony that a man whose grandmother had been proclaimed Empress of India with power and sovereignty (who wished Britain to reign its territory forever), became the key person to terminate her dream. As a responsible representative of the British Government, Mountbatten kept himself away from sentimental attachments and did what was right for the people of Britain. Congress reluctantly accepted a truncated India instead of waiting for an uncertain future. The people of Punjab and Bengal were hapless victims of Partition. They found themselves in a situation of which they were not responsible.

References:

1. Hansard, India (Government Policy) Vol. 447: debated on Monday 10 February 1947 https://hansard.parliament.uk/commons/1947-02-10/debates/3017c227-daba-4a2b-b025-c5ecf6171d72/India (GovernmentPolicy)
2. The Earl Mountbatten of Burma, in his foreword (June 1972) of Alan Campbell-Johnson, *Mission with Mountbatten* (New York: Atheneum, 1985), 9–10.
3. Campbell-Johnson (1985), Ibid, 22.

4. Ibid, 28.
5. Ibid, 26.
6. Ibid, 29.
7. Piers Brendon, *The Decline and Fall of British Raj, 1781–1847* (London: Vintage Books, 2008), 411.
8. Dominique Lapierre and Larry Collins, *Freedom at Midnight* (New Delhi: Vikas Publishing, 1983), 5.
9. Susan Springate, "Lady Pamela Hicks on the Real Story Behind Viceroy's House." *The Telegraph*, 25 February, 2017. Pamela Hicks, *Daughter of Empire: My life as Mountbatten* (New York: Simon & Schuster, 2012), 110–159.
10. R. J. Moore, "Mountbatten, India and the Commonwealth." *Journal of Commonwealth and Comparative Politics*, Vol. 19 (1) (1981), 1–4. (Publ. online in 2008).
11. David Butler, *Lord Mountbatten: The Last Viceroy* (New York: Pocket Books, 1985), 15.
12. Vapal Pangunni Menon, *Transfer of Power in India* (Princeton, NJ: Princeton University Press, 1957), 367.
13. Menon, Ibid, 437.
14. Campbell-Johnson, Ibid, 86.
15. Menon, Ibid, 378.
16. Philip Ziegler, *Mountbatten* (New York: Alfred A. Knopf, 1985), 18.
17. Brendon, Ibid, 403, 409.
18. Moor, Ibid, 35.
19. Campbell-Johnson, Ibid, 103.
20. Menon, Ibid, 378.
21. Campbell-Johnson, Ibid, 107.
22. Ibid, 109.
23. Ibid, 106–108.
24. Menon, Ibid, 380.
25. Ibid.
26. Ziegler, Ibid, 408.
27. Butler, Ibid, 151.

28. Menon, Ibid, 383.
29. Ziegler, Ibid, 406.
30. Butler, Ibid, 151.
31. Ziegler, Ibid, 410.
32. Ibid, 447.
33. Menon, Ibid, 400.
34. Antony Read and David Fisher, *The Proudest Day: India's Long Road to Independence* (New York: W. W. Norton and Co., 1999), 483.
35. Zulfiquar Ali Sialkoti, "An Analytical Study of the Punjab Boundary Line Issue." *Pakistan Journal of History and Culture*, XXXV, Vol. 2 (2014), 98–99.
36. Butler, Ibid, 164–170.
37. Ziegler, Ibid, 241.
38. Menon, Ibid, 406.
39. Nehru's "Tryst with Destiny" Speech on 14 August 1947. Brendon, Ibid, 409.
40. Lapierre and Collins, Ibid, 294–295.
41. Butler, Ibid, 349.
42. Lapierre and Collins, Ibid, 303.
43. Ziegler, Ibid, 169–170.
44. Menon, Ibid, 406.
45. Butler, David, Ibid, 249.
46. Ziegler, Ibid, 410.
47. Ibid.
48. B. R. Tomlinson, "The Political Economy of Raj: Decline of Colonialism," *Journal of Economic History*, Vol. 4 No. 1 (March, 1982), 133–137.
49. Lapierre and Collins, Ibid, XVII.
50. Campbell-Johnson, Ibid, 11.

Conclusion

This book tells the history of modern India – a period of over 300 years – depicting the establishment and withdrawal of British rule, focusing on the Indian emancipation to achieve self-rule. It is a story of conflict between the British retaining their authoritative power and the growing consciousness of Indians asserting their right to rule their own country. It was difficult to write about all and sundry events that happened during this long period. The following is written as a summary and conclusion to incorporate some information not narrated in the story. My hope is that some loose ends in the text will be tied up.

A British merchant group, the EIC, initially came to India with the primary and direct interest in pursuing commercial ventures. The success of their initial venture influenced the British to increase their hold over the Indian subcontinent, taking advantage of India's unique geographical position to protect their empire using the Royal Navy which dominated from Libya to Turkey and the Indian Ocean. Over the years, the British annexed Mauritius, a French Naval base, and Dutch trading posts in Ceylon and on the Malay peninsula and posted distant battalions between 1810 and 1820 from their Calcutta base. India also became a source of military personnel during two World Wars. India was not only a gold mine but also a crucial strategic territory for military operation.

British aspiration of commercial gain was achieved by exploiting Indian resources using unethical means, taking advantage of ignorant Indians. The British King accepted the Magna Carta in 1225 as the Charter to provide liberty to his subjects, but for Indians this norm was flouted. The British did not select India as an extension of home as they did in Canada, Australia and New Zealand or America, each nation with plenty of vacant space. The exception was a few Britons who came in the eighteenth century, stayed back, worked for the benefit of Indians, and died on Indian soil.

The British did not preach Christianity among Indians like Spain attempted in Latin America. Neither did they spread western culture. They made India a dependency and tried to westernize India to protect their commercial activities, the easy extraction of Indian wealth which steadily increased in volume.[1] The Companies' bonds in London surged, breaking all time records. Indians lost their strength being victims of prolonged foreign rule. They became impoverished and had to tolerate and give in to British oppression and exploitation for hundreds of years.

In the pre-colonial period, the Indian economy was vibrant, having best quality manufacturing shops for cotton, silk goods, rugs, Kashmiri shawls, Dhakai Jamdani, pottery of Scind, jewelry, metal work, lapidation work, gems, and spices. These commodities captured large markets in Asia, Europe, and North Africa. British traders forcibly exploited native manufacturers and enriched the British economy. Acquiring access to both cotton and coal in course of time, the EIC exported those raw materials to Britain for supporting their Industrial Revolution producing cheap textiles which in turn completely destroyed the Indian economy. An extended area acquired gradually by military operation until the middle of the 1850s was used to support industrialization in Britain with legal provisions made by the Supreme Court that helped to control the tariffs dispatched to England. This legal system did not have provision to protect Indian peasantry and manufacturers.

When Robert Clive returned home with his loot, Bengal was the richest state.* In the pre-British period 85% of people were peasants and self-sufficient to feed themselves. The Permanent Settlement ensured

---

* Note: William Hodges was in India at the end of the 18th century and wrote that the welfare of British dominion in India ultimately depended on the prosperity of Bengal and the Indian administrators did everything to encourage its traders which might improve its revenue (William Hodges, *Travels in India during 1780–83* (New Delhi: Munshiram Memorial, 1794, 1999).

eighty-nine percent of land revenue to the government's share. Agriculture supplanted by cash crops fed the British Industry causing a food shortage and repeated famines. Cotton production in India increased during the Anglo-American war but later Indian cotton imports were restricted without giving protection to the farmers. But Britain had Corn Laws that guaranteed protection of their own agricultural market.

From his experience in India, W. S. Lilly wrote a book entitled *India and Its Problems* (1902),[2] stating that Indian famines broke out because the peasants, affected by a massive exploitation, lost purchasing capacity. He maintained that during the first eight years of the 19th century 18,000 people perished through famine; in 1816–17, one fourth of the population in Bellary perished; and a year after the Crown assumed control, some 5,000,000 people in southern India starved to death (1858). Just before Warren Hastings was recruited as the first Governor-General of Bengal, one third of the Bengali population died or left Bengal due to a famine.

Lily witnessed unburied human corpses and wandering skeletons, peasants who would not make the following day. Millions died of starvation between 1801 to 1900, even as monsoon rains did not fail once for over a hundred years, and an extensive railway connection to transport food grains was being established. And yet, the majority of people lived on the edge of starvation. Government was reluctant to mitigate people's sufferings. Lytton in 1877 instructed his officer not to reduce prices for famine-affected people in Madras, and Churchill during the Bengal famine of 1943 declined to send relief.

Rammohan Ray early on in the nineteenth century, and then Dadabhai Naoroji, and Romesh Chunder Dutt analyzed the trends of the Indian economy and submitted lists of drainage of Indian resources to the British Parliament. But despite all these condemning reports, the British morale did not change.

Governor-Generals worked without any specific guidelines on the uplift of India's masses. Hyndman in his pamphlet (in a reply to an article of Lord Morley) wrote, "There is no longer any dispute as to the terrible poverty of the agricultural population… so huge a scale is to be found nowhere else on the planet."[3] He wrote that the drawbacks were not discussed in the House of Commons, as Indian policy was made by the government and the ruling party.

William Bolts, a Dutch born British merchant, was a factor in Bengal from 1759–1766 and acquired fortune after joining the company. He was dismissed for disobeying company orders in 1768. Back in England he wrote his memoirs, stating that the Company and its agents regularly flogged and imprisoned weavers forcing them to sell only to the English, and continually harassed peasants to collect revenue.[4] The Company had monopolized everything from commerce to land revenue and justice, and ruined Bengal.

Later among others, Lapierre and Collins wrote that British withdrawal in 1947 left 83% of the Indian populace illiterate.[5] India had become one of the poorest nations on earth with a per capita income 5 cents a day, a quarter of her people being homeless, most of her machines were imported, per capita electricity consumption was a tiny fraction of that in developed nations. Yet it had many acres of lands barren waiting to be irrigated, and a 3800-mile coast line without a proper fishing industry.

Shashi Tharoor enumerated that India's share of world GDP was 23% during the Mughal period, and when the British left it was only 3%.[6] He states that 30 million died because of famines, epidemics, communal riots, wholesale slaughter after the mutiny, the Amritsar massacre, of violence and superior rule. British shareholders made absurd amounts of money by investing in railways which guaranteed extravagantly high rates of return; and Indian railway construction cost per mile in India was twice more than that in Australia or Canada. India was the export market of 10 % of the locomotives produced in Britain. The cost of imports was paid by Indians with interest.

The cultivation and sale of opium replacing production of food grains is a typical example of drain. The sale of opium in India was a strict monopoly, apart from production and sale of salt. For opium cultivation advances were made to the farmers, and if a ryot refused the advance he was forced to accept it especially in Patna district and Banaras. Will Durant, an American historian maintained that 7000 opium shops in India were owned by the British government and that their existence defied protests by the nationalists. The government in 1921 vetoed a bill prohibiting opium cultivation, as one-ninth of annual revenues came from this lucrative drug.

Apart from trade related despatches, Indian money flowed to Britain as salaries of overseas staff, their pensions, interest drawn in England by Indian investments, and other profits. In the Railways even the ticket collector was British until the early 1920s. In the 19th century, India was required to pay taxes to an amount exceeding US $400,000. Hard earned money of millions of Indians living just above the poverty line. Indian investments mainly focused on providing luxury to the Europeans, to military needs and the Railways. Indians were not allowed to travel by train until John Clark Marshman, a missionary son from Serampore working for the railway communications, convinced the authorities to allow the pilgrims to board from Calcutta.[7] White supremacy was rampant, beginning from the time of Cornwallis.

In 1861 Charles Wood, the Secretary of State, said, "you cannot possibly assemble at any one place an Indian person who shall be a real representative of various classes of native population of that empire." Even as late as in 1928, William Hicks, a conservative home minister, in the Stanley Baldwin government said, "We conquered India as an outlet for the goods of Britain... by sword we shall hold it..."[8] Indian academics like Jagadish Chandra Bose were barred from teaching in Presidency College, and Meghnad Shah was refused government service. There were many organizations to do survey work but no Indian was recruited to responsible positions.

Tagore was a critic of English education in India which spread with appreciation during the Bengal Renaissance. Miss Rathbone (a British MP, supporter of imperialism) in her "Open letter to Indians," reprimanding Indians for being "ungrateful" in refusing to support the British war effort, hurt Jawaharlal Nehru writing that the British attempt to enlighten Indians had been misunderstood by Indian intellectuals. Tagore, in last phase of his life, replied it was presumptuous for "so-called English friends" to think that if they "had not 'taught' us, we would still have remained in Dark Ages... education in India ... flowed to our children in schools not the best of English thought but its refuse ... even after a couple of centuries of British Administration only about one per cent of the population was found to be literate in English... And what have the British, who have held tight the purse-strings of our nation... and exploited its resources, done for poor people?"[9]

Taking advantage of people's ignorance and disorganized social structures the British rule continued unabated until the Sepoy Mutiny. The EIC's regime was favorable for the British to get access to resources in the entire subcontinent. During the same period, in Bengal a cultural and intellectual renaissance permeated society. To restrict repetitions of Indian outrage (after the Mutiny of 1857), the British Parliament introduced typical imperial rule taking direct control of Indian administration. From the early phase of this colonial rule, educated Indians prepared themselves to form a national platform for Indians to protect people from unjust government policies which destroyed natives' economy and their freedom.

Such efforts of a section of people were receiving support from growing journalism during the renaissance period. Some British trained lawyers and administrators who returned from England with ideas of liberalism and democratic processes enriched the Indian endeavour. In this climate, the Indian National Congress was formed at the initiative of Allan O. Hume, a retired British civil servant. It was the time when the British Raj was instructed from London to expand military activities to protect the Indian interests in ever expanding territories. First there was the scare of the Russian-Afghan approach from the northwestern border, then wars abroad, and finally there was the Japanese threat from the East. Since then war expenditure of the Raj rose manifold until War II, thereby destabilizing the Indian economy.

The aim of Congress was to look after the welfare of Indians, but the leaders of this nascent party with a limited number of educated people were captives of bookish knowledge on European history. There was a reluctance to implement any political agenda to pressure the administration to be more proactive and ensure justice for Indians. It caused frustration among the young nationalists who started violent activities, but failed being limited in number, even though they were patriots who were prepared to sacrifice their lives. In view of these crucial developments, the British administration became repressive and reverted to a divide and rule policy. Bengal's partition was promulgated in 1905.

A moderate group in Congress with radical elements began direct anti-imperialist movements infusing nationalism among common non-political people. It forged a pan Indian understanding to gain natives' right to protest instead of begging for justice from British rulers. This process put enough pressure on the Government which started relaxing the constitution to restrain the unrest which hindered British exports to India. But this movement lost its edge over the next two decades because its sphere could not be extended beyond the middle class. Politics was given priority over the people of India. Ranaday, Surendranath and Gokhale came forward to rescue Congress from the ill effects of provincialism.

Swami Vivekananda, before the dawn of the century, asked the politicians to shoulder responsibility of the common people first. After World War I, Gandhi entered Indian politics with a protest lodged against oppressive government policies. His novel approach led Congress to grass root level targeting complete freedom, cutting all ties with the British Raj. Gandhiji reached millions of poor people with an attire no better than a poor man, honored the 'Horizons' (*Harijans*), talked with them in their language and attracted the masses to volunteer as Congressmen. Gandhi's love for his countrymen opened a new direction. The masses were trained to fight for self-rule through being nonviolent.

The Raj was bewildered with the approach of such unusual political action where entire India participated against the British. Gandhi himself was a unique blend of character; both a political activist and a practical philosopher (without holding a political office), by practicing truth and non-violence. He learnt by trial and error, and gave up his public activities for a certain period accepting his mistakes. His law training in England helped him to develop a unique strategy to subvert British rule by applying psychological pressure. He was also a wily operator, who used hunger strikes to make his countrymen listen to him.

Gandhi's first major experiment with the salt march of 1930 was a total success as all of India sided with Congress. Nehru and Subhash, who joined Gandhi among many others, rose to the peak of Indian politics as leaders at a national level. They were scholars as well as forceful politicians; they differed from Gandhi ideologically, but never went against him. Both leaders being influenced by Fabian principles, they were inclined to the political left. Their presence in the national arena boosted Indian morale and almost the entire nation accepted them.

The 1930s were a crucial decade in Indian history when the growing political pressure accompanied by a Great Depression persuaded the Raj to yield to Indian hands by passing the 1935 Act. The result of the 1937 election gave Congress the mandate to rule India, albeit with limited power. But then the apparent unity of Congress and Muslim League totally broke down, polarizing the nation into separate camps. During this volatile period World War II broke out, to which Indians refused to cooperate with Britain, even though they were purged by the administration.

Subhas drifted away from the mainstream of Congress when his attempt to push the organization towards a more radical leftist viewpoint. This failed and his proposal to strike Britain aggressively while the nation was preoccupied with War, was opposed by older Congress leaders. Though never a fascist, he unilaterally joined the Germany-Italy-Japan axis with the onset of the War, because it was at enmity with Britain. He received direct Japanese support to strike the British force from the northeastern border of India, when Gandhi's Quit India movement was in full swing. This coincidence was a major challenge for the Raj. Announcing the movement early on during the War, Gandhi called the countrymen to behave as free citizens of India from 9 August 1942. *Quit India* was a unilateral declaration to form a government and (later) a wish to become "an ally of the United Nations."

The following day, 10 August, Leo Amery expressed his apprehension that the Indian administration might be shut down by Gandhi's call. In reality, thousands were killed and one million Indians were arrested; the administration was paralyzed. The Quit India movements affected industry and commerce, administration and law courts, schools and colleges, and even interrupted traffic and public utility services. Not only ordinary civil life and administration was paralyzed, but also the whole war effort was affected. Gandhi was immediately arrested, and released in May 1944 from his final imprisonment. The movement continued over the next three years. Lorraine Boissoneault in her article quoted Gandhi's speech of 8 August 1942 and concluded, "the speech helped advance the Indian struggle to secure her freedom."[10]

The Indian Muslims who had prospered during Mughal rule, felt unhappy under the British. The British were also prejudiced against Indian clerics for their Afghan links. But Muslims were brought closer to the Raj to break Indian unity by giving the Muslim League a separate political identity. The conservative Viceroys pampered the League to weaken the nationalist movements. Jinnah also knew that Pakistan would only be possible with the help of the British. In the 1940s Congress was kept under pressure by synergistic bonding of the League and the administration. The British adopted a divide and rule policy similarly as they had done in Ireland and the Middle East.

Stafford Cripps' 1942 announcement was a reflection of the British desire to create a Central Eastern sphere by separating Pakistan from India. The British contemplated protecting the Straits and the Suez Canal from Russian influence, and establishing British influence over oil rich Iran, Iraq, and Arabia. At that point Congress withdrew ministries in 8 provinces. This was a strategic mistake of Congress; it helped Muslims to consolidate and indirectly supported British policy. Congress also missed the chance of changing the center, especially after Japan joined the War. While it realized that HMG would not take the risk of evicting Congress at that time even if the center was changed, Congress withdrew anyway. Gandhi – who opposed the two nation theory – later conceded to the proposal of a "Muslim majority area" but insisted on a central authority to administer subjects of both the states to keep India united. Jinnah rejected his proposal.

The Emergency Powers (Defence) Act 1939 turned Britain into a totalitarian state for six years with unlimited authority over the Islanders. Britishers were fortunate to keep the Atlantic route open to sustain their food supply. The war dragged on until 1945, but Indian cooperation in the war effort was refused because self-rule for Indians was defied. The Raj, however, was forced to provide 2.3 million soldiers with food and subsistence. When the war in Europe ended by May 1945, Britain emerged weakened in need of recovery of her own. President Roosevelt offered unlimited credits. In India the lesson of the great Calcutta Killings confirmed that there must be Pakistan or else civil war. Lord Wavell was undone when the possibility of keeping India united evaporated.

After Churchill's shock election defeat, the new liberal government "decided" (not recommended) to withdraw, keeping India united by forming a common constitution making body along the proposal of the Cripps' Mission. But the Cripps' scheme provided the Muslim League an opportunity to secure a province-wise Pakistan. The premier of Punjab, Khizar Hyat Khan tried to resist the partition of Punjab but did not get administrative support. With his resignation, the Unionist party dissolved, and the last chance to resist partition was lost.

For twenty years Britain managed the colonies from Ireland to the Middle East to the Indian subcontinent with inefficient manpower. Some British civilians had regretted this, saying, "never in history did ill-breeding contribute so much towards the desolation of the Empire." And, "Eton, Harrow, Winchester … should be razed to the ground."[11] After the War 60–70,000 employees, including many senior officials, lost their jobs. An understaffed government was unlikely to continue beyond 1949 when conflicts between Congress and Muslim League intensified. The residual officers in Indian administration were disarranged and not equipped intellectually to grope with a battery of British-trained Indian lawyers. Gandhi questioned the British morale. Britain was obliged to pay back the credit offered by America as Lend-Lease, and Britain lost supremacy in global politics. The Raj became Britain's liability with its source of finance becoming uncertain.

When Indian parties failed to forge a single successor to British India, Wavell was withdrawn. Attlee requested Mountbatten to replace Wavell.[12] Mountbatten had no reason to disagree with Wavell's administration until June 1946,[13] but he accepted Attlee's offer to take this new responsibility. He shouldered total responsibility for the Indian administration when the interim government fell apart. He used the provisions in the 1935 Act to complete his task of handover by 3 June 1947. Mountbatten said that he did not know of any country in the world which was so fortunate to have a constitution (Act 1935) that could be amended by stroke of a pen. In the end, Mountbatten had no alternative but to agree to the Partition, otherwise he would have to quit leaving India in chaos and uncertainty.

Jinnah had suggested the Partition Act. Lord Mountbatten was supposed to be the Governor-General of both India and Pakistan. But Jinnah requested to be made Governor-General of Pakistan leading to an unforeseen complication, as this decision violated the 3 June agreement. It was solved by withdrawing Muslim League from the interim government formally. Mountbatten accepted the Governor-Generalship of India as he knew that Nehru's government would advise him even from behind bars.[14] But Jinnah would rather be Governor-General than Premier, to provide him with legislative powers to resist any future attempts for reunification.

Mountbatten also acted as the Crown representative of Princely states as the Viceroyalty. He reminded the Chamber of the Princes about their obligation to join any of the new domains, and helped some States like Orissa, Gujarat and Punjab to form princely blocks. Mountbatten's success to convince most of the States to accede by 14 August was a bloodless revolution which recent histories often gloss over. His effort helped India to secure an unfragmented territory. He even took a personal initiative for the accession of Jammu-Kashmir in India but not going beyond his legitimate authority. At present, a part of Kashmir remains under Pakistan occupation as contested, even though the entire territory of Kashmir enjoyed the paramountcy and was accessed to India legally. Pakistan did not agree with the UN's plebiscite proposal to end the Kashmir problem. In a recent court statement made in June 2024, the Pakistan authority admitted that "occupied Kashmir" is foreign land.[15]

The volume of Mountbatten's work was huge. He had to solve many problems that were pending since 1918. So many issues were considered and so many opinions emerged during negotiations that 1,613 files of documents were created to be preserved as records.[16] Mountbatten received full cooperation from Nehru. When Nehru became introspective,

Mountbatten supplied him with dimensions to adjust and prevented him from taking emotional decisions (in Simla). When the transfer of power materialized before the scheduled time frame, Mountbatten said that "history seems sometimes to move with infinite slower speed of a glacier and sometimes to rush forward on a torrent."

Abiding by the principle of partition, the Boundary Commission divided the subcontinent into two territories, but the tragic holocaust of migration could neither be prevented or controlled. About 14 million humans migrated to distant places when troop numbers were completely inadequate. Alan Campbell-Johnson wrote of his experience of flying over the migrants on 1 September 1947,

> Today, however, there is this difference: the number on the move are comparatively greater than ever before, and this time there will be no return.... We flew, in fact, for over fifty miles against this stream of refugees without reaching the source. Every now and then the density of bullock-carts and families on foot keeping to the thin-life line of the road would tail away, only to fill out again in close columns without end... At one point during our flight Sikh and Moslem refugees were moving almost side by side in opposite directions. There was no sign of a clash. As though impelled by some deeper instinct, they pushed forward obsessed only with the objective beyond boundary.[17]

The Partition resulted in a massacre of about 6,000,000 persons who died in Punjab itself. 55,000 soldiers could not keep check on the riots. This news of frenetic cruelty was widely reported in the media. The flow of migrants continued until November. According to Menon, planning for such a huge population exchange was not done ahead of the transfer.[18] Radcliffe was so shocked that he left India immediately after handing over the award; he waived the £2,000 he received as fees.[19] Even Sir Evan Jenkins in Punjab and Sir Olaf Caroe of NWFP, with their experience in India, did not foresee that such a carnage might happen.[20] It was unprecedented.

Wealthy Sikhs were replaced by impoverished Muslims in Northwest Pakistan. Khan Abdul Ghaffar Khan and associates, out of indignation, blamed the Congress as people of their state were forced to stay in Pakistan. A little over a million people lived in Delhi. But being close to Punjab it became overwhelmed by an additional half million refugees. About 400,000 migrants reached the unprepared capital in a short time. Lady Mountbatten with her experience in the Red Cross and St. John's Ambulance built up morale, and looked after the refugee camps not only in Delhi, but also in Lahore where she rescued Hindu migrants sheltered in places more like concentration camps.

On the eastern side of Bengal millions of Hindus migrated to India, crossing a boundary of about 2600 miles long. Gandhi's presence kept Calcutta peaceful. Europeans of the Police force participated in his four day fast (September 1–4). People pledged to maintain peace in their own localities. Gandhi persuaded Suhrawardy to join him after he was refused by Jinnah; he was vanquished by Gandhi's personality (Fig. 29). Gandhi was acclaimed as Mahatma even by the West as in Bengal his power of the soul proved to be more potent than thousands of soldiers posted in Punjab. Mountbatten said, "Our force consists of one man, and there is no rioting."[21] As a serving officer, he paid tribute to the one-man boundary force saying what his moral persuasion did, four divisions failed to achieve by force.[22]

Ranganathananda, a monk of the Ramakrishna Mission wrote, "He (Gandhi) had no army behind him, yet he was tremendously strong. He could move the entire nation by the power of his character… It is same-sightedness coming from atman-awareness."[23]

On the 15th August, Mountbatten read King George VI's message, "On the historic day when India takes her place as a free and independent Dominion in the British Commonwealth of Nations, I send you all my greetings and heart full wishes … with this transfer of power by consent comes the fulfilment of a great democratic ideal to which the British and Indian people alike are firmly dedicated."[24] Mountbatten worked faithfully and complied with the order of his nation. Still a fog of propaganda spread against him.

Mountbatten kept his return to the Navy open until June 1948. Still he was accused of being in a hurry to retain his naval career. Churchill said that Muslims were Britain's friends, and it was terrible that an English man and cousin of the King supported Britain's enemy, and took the initiative to send British trained soldiers and British equipment to crush Muslims in Kashmir. He wanted Mountbatten not to involve the King and his country in further backing traitors.[25] The Communists said that allowing both Partition and dominion status enabled the British to keep control over India.[26]

Mountbatten replied once only saying, "When I went to India, I told myself: I am going to take my decision looking ten years ahead. All my decisions are going to be governed by what it will read like when history is written… I don't care what people say now. I am working for the history of my grandchildren and my great-grandchildren will read. This makes one impervious to short-term criticism."[27]

Lord Mountbatten was applauded too. *The Washington Post* wrote, "Certainly this performance is not the work of a decadent person. This on the contrary is the work of political genius requiring the ripest wisdom and the freshest vigor, and is done with an elegance and a style that will compel and will receive an instinctive respect throughout the civilized world… statesmen can do it not with force and money but with lucidity, resolution and sincerity." Ian Stephen, the then editor of *The Statesman*, wrote later, "… for sheer intellectual range and vigor, for assured grasp of minutes, yet brilliant marshalling of main lines of a long, difficult argument, it was an extraordinary performance."[28]

Raja Rammohan Roy led Indians to come out from the dark age; Vivian Derozio and David Hare came unexpectedly when Indians were in their greatest need. They helped prepare the foundation of the Indian renaissance that awakened Indian nationalism. Swami Vivekananda, a product of this renaissance, realized that in the hundred years after Rammohan, India became the poorest of the poor. His call was to youths to "arise and awake," and work for Indians as selfless soldiers of the freedom struggle.

Indian independence was achieved following an unprecedented path, and there are people who are still confused about how this independence came about. Was it due to the struggle of the nationalists only? Lapierre and Collins wrote, Indian independence was "a war which both sides won, a war without losers."[29] There is no doubt that nationalists put continuous pressure on the British to hasten their withdrawal. But Independence was a result of the tenacity, morale and the strong urge of Congress leaders on one side, and Clement Attlee and Mountbatten's determination to withdraw on the other. British withdrawal was a coincidence of time and situations.

There is also gossip and rumors on the partition issue. Who was responsible and who benefitted? Mountbatten came prepared to complete the transfer process keeping India united. He told Gandhi, "I shall be completely honest. I came here with the firm determination that India would never be split into two separate states." With the advancement of partition, Gandhi asked whether he had changed his mind. Mountbatten replied, "I am not sure what I am saying. However, I admit that I am beginning to see an alternative, if Mr. Jinnah and the Muslim League go on refusing to cooperate."[30] From the beginning, Congress strove for a united India and opposed separate electorates. The conservatives in Cabinet propagated a divide and rule policy for some forty years to keep India under control by weakening the national unity while pampering the League. The Muslim League, at the same time, used British support to get Pakistan.

On Partition, Tagore* stated, "It was a heinous act of separating the spirit of Indians."[31] He also wrote that we would be made responsible for the Hindu-Muslim divide, but it was a conspiracy made secretly by those in high position in administration, and backed by a group within us; otherwise such a disgraceful and uncivilized act would not have occurred in Indian history. The British planted the Muslim League which finally blackmailed Britain when she needed a united India. It is felt that British conservatives

---

* Note: Translated from "Sabhyatar Sankat," or Crisis of Civilization was the topic Rabindranath Tagore's lectured on during the occasion of his 80th year and was published in 1941, the year he died.

were responsible for the Partition; not Congress or Gandhi or Mountbatten. Jinnah worked as a remote control with no connection with the masses. The bloodbath was the result of such a single minded approach. Jinnah had no regret for it. He was an achiever, but with a limited dimension of his character. Muslim League was the only gainer of the Partition.

Congress leaders were exasperated as their struggle for self-rule for more than twenty years got hung up with uncertainty; they lost patience and surrendered to an unforeseen situation that came all of a sudden. Accepting the Partition was perhaps a pragmatic decision of Congress. The alternative was that India would have to live with hardline elements who would have robbed national peace by its agitations similarly as the Muslim League did when it was in the interim government.

All the people of India, including students, their parents, and the victims of partition, encouraged a prolonged struggle until the consummation of independence. They sacrificed with full understanding of the strengths and weaknesses of the leadership. The long process of this struggle gave rise to a cultural shift that helped develop intellectual discourses to compose poems, songs, novels, and journalistic works disseminating the spirit of nationalism.

The British withdrawal was the culmination of a long wedded relationship between the two nations. This separation was mutual and was an indicator of Imperial collapse. British departure practically declared the end of an era of 450 years of European-Indian connection which began with the arrival of Vasco de Gama, the first European to land on this subcontinent. However, the French and Portuguese powers survived only a few more years, before their territories were absorbed into India.

References:

1. H. M. Hyndman, *The Emancipation of India: A reply to the article by the Right Hon. Viscount Morley, O.M., on "British democracy and Indian government" in the "Nineteenth century and after" for February, 1911* (London: The Twentieth Century Press, [1911]), 4.
2. William Samuel Lily, *India and Its Problems* (London: Sands & Co., 1902).

3. Hyndman, Ibid, 5.
4. William Bolts, *Considerations of Indian Affairs: Particularly Respecting the Present State of Bengal and Its Dependencies. With a Map of Those Countries, Chiefly from Actual Surveys* (London: J. Almon, P. Elmsley, Richardson and Urquhart, 1772).
5. Dominique Lapierre and Larry Collins, *Freedom at Midnight* (New Delhi: Vikas Publishing House, 2003), 315.
6. Shashi Tharoor, *An Era of Darkness: The British Empire in India* (New Delhi: Aleph Books, 2016).
7. Barid Baran Mukherjee, *Serampore: Late Medieval and Colonial Era* (Kolkata: Ghosh Publishing Concern, 2021), 239.
8. Shashi Tharoor, *Inglorious Empire: What the British did to India* (Melbourne, London: Scribe Publications, 2017), 173.
9. "Tagore's Last Article." Reprinted from The Tribune in *The Militant*, Volume V, no. 40, (4 October, 1941), 6.
10. Lorraine Boissonneault, "The Speech that Brought India to the Brink of Independence." *Smithsonian Magazine* (August 8, 2017) https://www.smithsonianmag.com/history/speech-brought-india-brink-independence-180964366/.
11. Piers Brendon, *The Decline and Fall of British Empire 1781–1997* (London: Vintage Books, 2008), 342.
12. Alan Campbell-Johnson, *Mission with Mountbatten* (New Delhi, Calcutta: AICO Publishing House, 1951), 17.
13. Ibid, 18.
14. Philips Ziegler, *Mountbatten* (New York: Alfred A. Knopf, 1985), 402.
15. *India Today*, June 1, 2024. https://www.indiatoday.in/world/story/pakistan-occupied-kashmir-pok-foreign-territory-admits-pakistan-government-in-islamabad-high-court-india-relations-2546601-2024-06-01.
16. The Mountbatten files are published as volumes VII–X, entitled, *Transfer of Power 1942–47. The Mountbatten;* and part of the *Constitutional Relations between Britain and India* in *Volumes I–XII*. Nicholas Mansergh Contributor (London: H.M. Stationery Office, 1970).

17. Campbell-Johnson, Ibid, 200–201.
18. V. P. Menon, *The Transfer of Power in India* (Princeton, NJ: Princeton University Press, 1957), 386, 417–18.
19. Lapierre and Collins, Ibid, 356.
20. Lapierre and Collins, Ibid, XVI.
21. Ziegler, Ibid, 461.
22. Campbell-Johnson, Ibid, 181.
23. Swami Ranganathananda, *The Message of Vivekachudamani* (Kolkata: Advaita Ashrama Publication, 2009), 602.
24. Menon, Ibid, 414.
25. J. R. Wood (ed.), "Dividing The Jewel: Mountbatten and Transfer of Power to India and Pakistan," *Review Article: Pacific Affairs*, Vol. 58 (4) University of British Columbia (1985), 653.
26. Menon, Ibid, 383.
27. Lapierre and Collins, Ibid, 24.
28. Menon, Ibid, 382–383.
29. Lapierre and Collins, Ibid, 352.
30. Butler, Ibid, 74.
31. Rabindranath Tagore, in *Sabbatar Sankat* (Crisis of Civilization), Rabindra Rachanabali (Works of Rabindranath), Part 13 (Calcutta: Government of West Bengal, 1990).

Glossary

An Act is a specific law expressed in writing by authorized Government representatives.

Allied Forces are an Alliance formed between Great Britain and France (1940–44) to fight against Germany. The Soviet Union joined the Alliance from June, 1941 and the United States of America from December 1941.

Anarchism. A word used to describe an extreme form of belief in freedom, or use of violence to overthrow the establishment as an indispensable condition without considering anybody's interest and advantage, with belief in democracy, human rights, and rule of law, when Revolutionaries consider advantages and disadvantages of situations for their own interest.

Atlantic Charter. A statement issued on 14 August, 1941 and signed jointly by the American President Roosevelt and British Prime Minister Churchill in the British Naval Base, Newfoundland. This Charter denotes the British and American goal during the end of the Second World War dismantling the British Empire and forming NATO and GATT. The Charter was ultimately accepted by the inter-Allied Council, United Nations.

Axis Power. A group collaborated by Germany, Italy and Japan in the second World War.

Bill is a landmark of an Act in constitutional law that sets out certain basic civil rights.

Black Hole tragedy is an incident that occurred in Calcutta when Siraj-Ud-Daulah captured the Old Fort with British soldiers who were not prepared. 60–70 of prisoners of war (including women and children) were kept in an underground cell measuring 14' × 18' overnight on 29 June 1756. The next morning only 20–30 persons were alive. This tragedy inspired scientists to coin this term to refer to the gravitational collapse of very heavy stars. The incidence of the Calcutta Black Hole tragedy became controversial because some authors described it as a simple hoax.

The **Commonwealth** is a political association of member states of nearly all former territories of the British Empire. It was originally created as the British Commonwealth of nations through the Balfour Declaration in 1926. It became an Imperial Conference with focus on non-governmental relations between member states without legal obligations to one another, but connected through their use of English language and historical ties. Each member state values democracy, human rights, and rule of law to enrich the Commonwealth Charter.

Communist Party of India is an Indian party that follows Communist political ideology. When Russia was in a friendly relationship with Hitler's Germany they supported Russia. After Hitler attacked Russia, the Communist Party of India changed its stand and supported the Allies in the war, designating the war as a People's War. In 1942, Communists worked against the Quit India movement and built up their Indian organization in a vacuum.

Congress Working Committee (CWC) is the executive of the Indian National Congress. It consists of 15 members elected by the members of the All India Congress Committee.

Cossim Bazar is an important commercial center in Murshidabad district from the seventeenth century. It became a silk town in the eighteenth century. The British, in their early days, took interest in occupying the place. Other European nations like the Dutch and French also used Cossim Bazar as commercial centers because of its association with the silk industry.

Durbar Hall is one of the two halls present in the Rashtrapati Bhavan, New Delhi. The hall was featured for holding the British rituals after the Mughals.

His Majesty is a title of respect when referring to the king of England.

Jaigirdary is a form of land tenancy which developed from the 13th century during the Muslim rule.

Lend-Lease means a debt to be dealt at a later date.

Genocide is systematic mass killing by a group to eliminate opponents.

Harijan Patrika (or *Harijan*) was first published in 1933 after the *Poona Pact* by the *Servants of Untouchables Society* in Poona. The first issue of this weekly bulletin contained seven articles written by Gandhi himself, and a translation of a poem of Satyendranath Dutta by Rabindranath Tagore, "Why do they shun your touch … whom cleanliness follows at every step … you help us, like a mother her child, into freshness and uphold…" It was a period of political turmoil and Gandhi said, "I hope that Congressmen will make it a point to read "Harijan'." It was not a political bulletin but acted as an instrument shaping the struggle for freedom apart from reforming a society striving under caste system and untouchability. *Harijans* were debarred from entering the temples, and even using water from a well. Tagore was so much influenced by the movement against untouchability that he wrote 9 articles in the Horizon in 1933, wrote Chandilaka in 1938, and a few poems in 1939 - all concerning untouchability. He was a great patron of the *Harijan*.

Indian National Army (INA) organized by Subhas Chandra Bose.

Indo and Hindu. These two terms are synonyms derived from followers of culture developed from a civilization that grew around the river "Sindhu" (the Indus valley) and the words are the same. Persian traders pronounced Sindhu as Hindu, and Greek scholars simplified it as Indu. After Muslim invasion the rulers used Hindus to distinguish local inhabitants from Turaka. Also, Britishers initially used Hindu or Hindustan (the land where Hindu followers lived) to differentiate from Muslims. Later 'Hindustan' was westernized as 'India' for convenience.

The **Indigo Revolt** took place in Bengal in 1859 when oppressed peasants protested the exploitation of government supported European planters. The peasants received sympathy from middle class Bengalis. A famous play entitled, 'Neel Darpan' (Neel = Indigo) written by Dinabandhu Mitra was performed in different places.

Kanailal Dutta was a freedom fighter from Chandanagar (though a police report states he was from Serampore).

Kohima is a town in Nagaland at the Eastern Indian frontier where INA had a base camp. It was recently reported, in an interview with a 90 year old retired school teacher, Mr. Vezo Swuro, who stated that a place identified as Chesezu, about 55 kilometers from Kohima, was the base camp of the Japanese army and the INA.*

Krishna Menon was educated in Madras Presidency College, India, and then at the London School of Economics. He also earned a degree in law from Glasgow. He was influenced by the theory of Harold Laski. While in London, he worked for the cause of Indian independence and became a member of the Labour Party. In the 1930's Menon met Nehru for the first time, and since then they became close friends with intellectual interests. He became the first ambassador of India in London, and led Indian delegations to the United Nations. Menon also worked as counselor in more than conflicting international interests. Above all he was a great orator, with specialization in foreign affairs.

The **McMahon Line** was named after the chief of the British negotiator, Henry McMahon who signed the agreement of establishing the border line demarcating Tibet and Assam in British India in March 1914. This agreement was signed at the Simla conference (1913–14) in presence of the plenipotentiaries of Tibet, China, and British India, but the Chinese representative refused to sign. China was ruled by the Qing Dynasty (1644–1911), which was dissolved through internal rebellions after 1911. During this time China was in a chaotic state without a defined central authority, and during World War I the French and British expanded their influence in China until the People's Republic was formed (1949). Tibet was also occupied by the Qing dynasty. The Manchus, the people of North

---

* Note: His statement was substantiated by other contemporary persons of the same village who claimed themselves eyewitnesses, said that they remember from their boyhood a soldier with a badge, a kind gentleman, handsome and always smiling. He used to come on horseback, and discussed the development of their village. From Netaji's picture they identified that the handsome soldier was Subhas Chandra Bose.

East Asian origin whose history, language, and identity was distinct from Chinese, founded the Qing dynasty. The McMahon line presently exists as a "Line of Control" between India and China which has been disputed since 1962.

The **Maginot Line** was built in 1930 along the French-German border with large and small fortresses, bunkers, rail lines etc. to prevent invasion of German troops in France. But German troops entered France via Belgium in 1940.

Marattas are residents of the (present) state of Maharashtra.

Mohan Singh was posted in Malaya as a battalion captain in the British army. Due to Japanese occupation of the area he became a prisoner of war (POW) and was approached by a Japanese major, posted there, to form an Indian army with all POWs in S. E. Asia. This army was formed and acted as an ally of the Japanese forces to liberate India from the British. From Kuala Lumpur and Bangkok about 35,000 army personnel were recruited with the help and support of the Japanese, and the local Indian population. Due to differences of opinion and misunderstandings with the Japanese, Mohan Singh was arrested by the Japanese police. After Japan was defeated in 1947, Mohan Singh was repatriated to India and had to face trial. After independence he became a member of the upper house of the Indian Parliament.

Nana Saheb was an adopted son of an educated Indian Brahmin from Deccan, Peshwa Balaji Rao, who was in exile in Bithoor after his defeat in Maratha War III against the East India Company. Nana travelled with his father in exile, and was heir presumptive of Maratha's throne. He was entitled to receive a pension amounting £80,000 per year after the death of Balaji, but the Company refused to pay pension because he was not the biological son of Balaji. Nana, however, managed to secure a job as collector at Kanpur. During the Sepoy Mutiny, the Company wanted to use Nana's help to manage the troops. Nana instead supported the mutineers in 1857.

Noakhali was once a small town situated in the southeastern corner of East Bengal (now Bangladesh).

Pearl Harbor housing the US Naval fleet was surprisingly attacked by the Japanese Airforce on December 7, 1939. The Japanese attack was intended to keep the US Naval Fleet away from interfering against the Japanese military intervention in S. E. Asia. The Japanese force was ultimately defeated.

Plenipotentiary is a term used as an adjective, meaning having full power to make independent decisions.

Princely States and Paramountcy. Each Princely State, a delineated territory, was ruled by a king with due sanction of the British Government. The state enjoyed internal sovereignty with certain restrictions when the British Crown had supreme authority with responsibility to provide protection from external intervention. Paramountcy was a British policy which was introduced by the East India Company by which the Company claimed supreme authority with greater power than the Princely States but with responsibility for providing security.

Quit India Movement. This movement was launched from Bombay by the All India Congress Committee on 8 August 1942. In an open Gowalia Tank Maidan, Gandhi announced an orderly British withdrawal from India. With support of the Muslim League, Hindu Mahasabha and some Princely States, police arrested all Congress leaders soon after the movement was announced.

RAF and RIN are the Royal Air Force and Royal Navy (British).

Rash Behari Bose. Once working closely with the anarchists and posted in Dehradun, Rash Behari Bose escaped to Japan in 1915 after Lord Hardinge survived a botched murder attempt in Delhi. Bose married in Japan and stayed there with his family. After learning of his whereabouts, the British government approached the Japanese government to hand him over. But Japan refused extradition; and Rashbehari took refuge there, never losing interest in Indian politics. After his wife died, Rash Behari started writing on different topics. He respected Gandhi as a person, but once wrote "Gandhi is a person of yesterday." He took a keen interest in the INA soon after it was formed, and attended the INA conference held in Bangkok. He agreed to accept the post of chairmanship. Later Subhas Chandra Bose took over the charge of INA from Rash Behari. Rashbehari died in Japan in 1945 when he was fifty years old.

Revolution means to collectively activate a radical change in a territory by an act of rebellion against the authorities, but with certain interests.

Round Table Conferences are a series of three conferences held in London with participation of the British authority and Indian politicians to discuss Indian constitutional reforms.

Sannyasin. According to Swami Vivekananda, it is a person who sacrifices everything for the good of others. He said, I was sannyasin, who had renounced caste, family, prestige, and everything.

Satyendra, an anarchist, accompanied Kanailal Dutta to assassinate Narendra Nath Goswami in the Alipur jail.

Santals are one of the largest homogenous tribal communities of India.

Sepoys are Indian soldiers (Muslim or Hindu) serving under British and other European orders.

Secretary of State. A position responsible for His (or Her) Majesty's administration and political head of different countries of the British empire and also a British cabinet minister.

Serampore is a historic former Danish town in Bengal. The Danes hosted the British missionaries to settle under the leadership of William Carey.

Simla is a town situated at 2276 m altitude in the Western Himalayas. The Kalka-Simla railway was dedicated by Lord Curzon in November 1903. Functioned as the summer residence of the Viceroy.

Suzerainty is the right of Britain (in present situation) to control foreign policy and relations of the Princely States but allowing their internal autonomy.

V. D. Savarkar was an Indian born political philosopher who was educated in England. He looked after the Indian organization based at India House in London, along with Indian students' organization. He was arrested in connection with anarchist activities from India House and imprisoned for several years in the Andamans. While in jail, he turned to be the proponent of Hindutva (Hinduness) as he believed that every descendant from the Hindu culture is Hindu irrespective of caste, creed and religion. He opposed the Quit India movement in 1942, and the partition of India as the main organizer of Hindumahasava. He refused to take food and water when he became old and physically inactive. Before his death he wrote, "when one's life mission is over and the ability to serve the society is left no more, it is better to end life at will rather than waiting for death." He lived for more than 83 years.

Victoria Memorial Hall is situated in Calcutta. It was built with Indian contributions from 1906–1931 and dedicated to Queen Victoria. The foundation was laid by the Prince of Wales in 1906, and was designed after the Taj Mahal with domes and white marble. The memorial has a museum with 25 galleries with exhibits ranging from sculptures to paintings and armory. Lord Curzon wished that Europeans and natives would visit there to learn history. A lofty garden surrounds the Hall.

V. P. Menon was an ICS officer in the Government of British India with responsibility in the office of constitutional developments in India from 1917 to 1947. From 1942 he worked as Constitutional Advisor to the Governor-General until power was transferred to India. He, as a witness of many episodes, was knowledgeable about the Indian constitutional progress. He wrote books by dint of his direct experience as an administrator.

Viscount Wavell was the penultimate viceroy of India (1943–47) who chronicled his experiences recording an account of declining imperial power and rising nationalistic aspirations during World War II, along with notes on Bengal Famines.

White Calcutta was a half square kilometer residential area for European residents of Calcutta. Europeans who came initially established their residences around Esplanade Row at the east of Fort William and Maidan. Gradually when the European population increased, new settlers moved to Park Street and adjoining areas further south, ultimately reaching Elgin Road. North of white Calcutta was the unplanned densely populated area called **Black Calcutta,** where native Indians lived.

White Officers were British administrative and military officers.

APPENDIX 1

The Bengal Renaissance

The Renaissance,* the period of acquiring and spreading new knowledge to end superstitions and orthodoxy prevalent in Indian society began in Calcutta when the East India Company was rising to power in the early 19th century. This cultural renaissance continued until the first quarter of the 20th century, extending throughout India. It was initiated in Bengal through the inspiration of three leading exponents who all were influenced by western thought. They were Rammohan Roy, David Hare, and Louis Vivian Derozio, whose mission impacted the first batch of Hindu College students. The thrust of this movement was transmitted like ripples to the pupils of the every following generation, bringing a long lasting impact on Indian society.†

---

* Note: Sir Jadunath defines Bengal Renaissance as, "... reforms of language, social reconstruction, political aspirations, religious movements, and even changes in human manners, that originated in Bengal, passed like a ripple from a central eddy, across provincial barriers, to the farthest corners of India."[4]

† Note: Romesh Chunder Dutt wrote, "...vigor and freedom of English literature and English thought, the great efforts of the French intellect of the 18th century, the results of German labor in the field of Philosophy, the Ancient History, positivism, utilitarianism, Darwinism - all these have influenced and shaped the intellect of modern Bengal."[5]

The following is the story of several key persons who imbibed new knowledge and transmitted it to a wider public in phases. It resulted in a cleansing of a slate with the debris of ignorance accumulated for centuries. The story depicts how a new generation came up, how Bengali language and literature developed. Through the growth of journalism, aided by printing, liberal thoughts reached the common people and new directions in art, culture, and science opened up. This important portion of modern Indian history deserves to be retold.

The revival of Indian society was not instigated by Governor-Generals as is often claimed. All reforms – social, political and literary – occurred after the tenure of Warren Hastings through active persuasion of the natives. They urged for initiating English teaching, convinced the government to abolish Sati and to allow legal remarriage of widows, with active support of some European residents in Calcutta.

The major source of information for the following narrative is based on the work of Sivanath Sastri,[1] Romesh Chunder Dutt (1877),[2] and (1893),[3] who witnessed this renaissance.

The renaissance began with western style of education, but was enriched with ancient Indian concepts reintroduced by Rammohan Roy (refer chapter 2.3). He saw that Indian ideals were paralyzed due to lack of education. Unlike their European counterparts, the Indian masses were completely illiterate. The Bengal Renaissance was a fervent period of spreading education through building up groups of recipients, before it showed similar results as the European Renaissance, which had caused the rebirth of European culture after the middle ages. An enlightened section of people improved the vernaculars, revitalized ancient wisdom, and spread new ideas. Rammohan Roy translated the Vedas and Upanishads into Bengali for instruction among common people to help them rise above their unreason as prevailing in a dark age.

Swami Vivekananda said that cultural recovery in India took place more than once. Krishna and Buddha – the two greatest men of ancient India were reformists. Buddhism failed to survive because society had become disjointed from Vedic literature. Sanskrit learning had become iconoclastic, and being overpowered by negative forces, society became engulfed in a miasmatic pool of ceremonials and superstitions, and Buddhism died in the land of its birth. India had to wait for centuries until Sankara and Ramajunam brought a revival of Vedanta. Their work was so impressive that householders began to study the Aranyakas.*

Rammohan Roy set out ideas for revival. The students of Derozio at Hindu College, the Derozians, started the Young Bengal movement by taking over the baton from Rammohan. They developed themselves into a noble class of young intellectuals which challenged the counter-reform forces. Their influence changed religious concepts, social customs, and even tests and manners, and ultimately sowed the seed of nationalism. Groups of successive students advanced the process in stages.

From the 1820s, every following generation gained greater understanding. Bengali prose writing gradually improved, innovation took place in poetry, drama and art, creating new styles. A large number of newspapers, magazines, and books in Bengali and English were published. The national awakening among intellectuals was fuelled by advanced western liberal ideas on nationalism, political and economic thought, and the new scientific processes. After direct exposure to the west, a new generation adjusted to the European system of administration and legal affairs to serve their own people. The era climaxed with a refined talented generation who competed in literature, art, spiritualism, and science at an international level.

The process began from the old Calcutta, the Indian British capital. Some privileged Calcutta Bengalis came into limelight through the mercantile system and European association, and their fortunes helped sponsor the start of this renaissance.

Calcutta at the beginning: The area around the old fort of Calcutta was the home of European settlers who were responsible for tax collection and trade. Many of them were wealthy. Calcutta grew economically and became an attractive city for Europeans. Their presence in turn triggered a migration of natives, which caused a gradual growth of the city (Fig. 35).

---

* Note: Aranyakas are the part of ancient Vedic literature representing the later sections of vedas. The contents explain the theme of Hindu spirituality; interpretations of different ceremonies which could be realized by meditation in the wilderness. There are seven Aranyakas.

322 The Bengal Renaissance

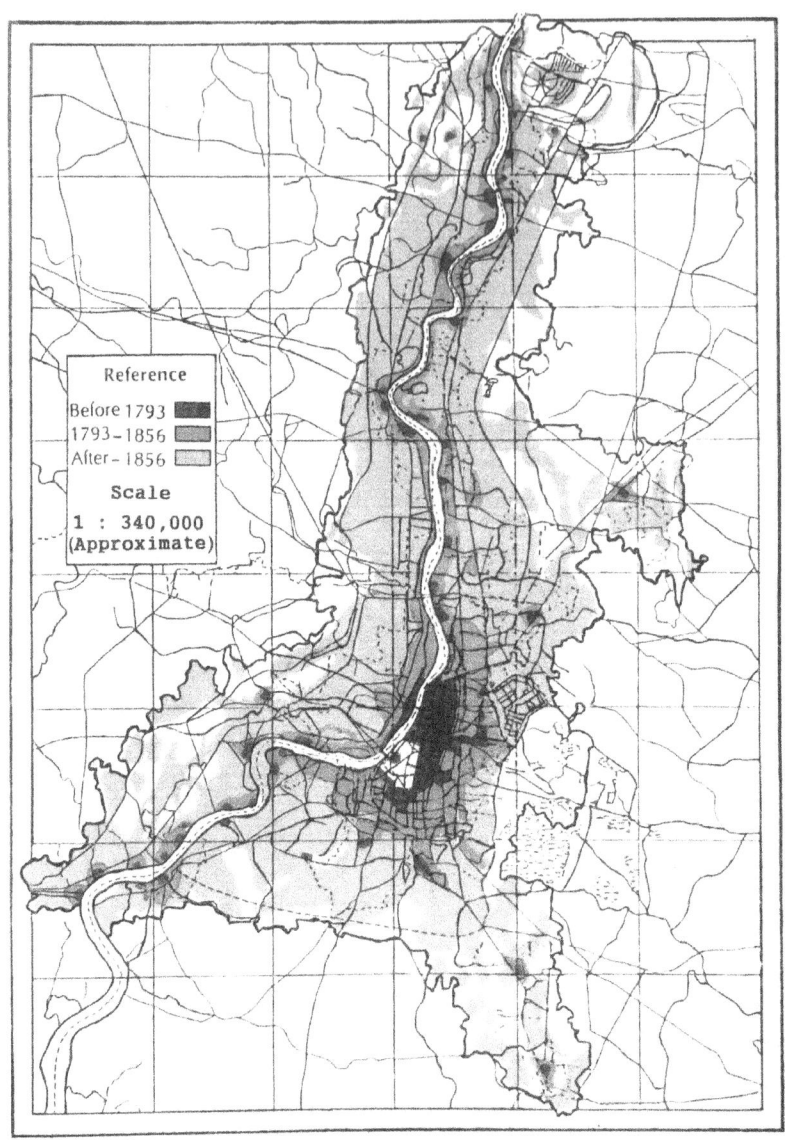

Fig. 35 Growth of Calcutta with its suburbs (NATMO, Salt lake, Calcutta).

The number of wealthy natives (mainly the zamindars) grew from 209 in 1752 to 500 by 1800, and the town area expanded from 216 to 3,115 acres between 1752 and 1794.[6] According to Robert Clive, Bengal was, "...one of the most wicked places in the universe. Corruption, licentiousness and want of principles seem to have possessed the minds of civil servants, by frequent bad examples they have grown callus, rapacious and luxurious beyond conception."[7] Clive saw the dishonesty of his Nayeb, Gobindram, and that of Ganga Gobinda, Dewan of Hastings. Cornwallis dismissed dishonest employees in his government.

Calcutta continuously increased in size and population. Without any regulations, the construction projects in native Calcutta, flourished without regard to the beauty and regularity of the town. This unorganized building boom was to meet the growing demands for housing in large parts of Black Calcutta.[8,9]

British people living in the 18th century Calcutta enjoyed a full social life. There were numerous dinner parties throughout the week, formal balls on Friday, boating, and gambling. Calcutta was a bustling, exotic place, and the goal of every British citizen was to gain riches and leave Calcutta for good. But the Calcutta lifestyle could not be maintained in London unless one returned to India. In Hastings' case, the second time he became successful and returned to London fabulously wealthy in 1786. Europeans generally lived in White Calcutta, where European quarters were well-planned and often magnificent.

Black Calcutta of the natives did not have any infrastructure. It had no reliable drinking water supply and no drainage. Hygienic conditions were poor, and the area was filthy with rodents and insects abounding. People were lazy and immoral. Some of them were wealthy and used to lead luxurious lifestyles. The common people were fond of light entertainment, sometimes vulgar and with bad tastes. Live actions were arranged as Kabi Gan; a fight between two groups by composing songs on social or allegorical topics (more like debates) by two lead singers, some of those were in slang too.

Native' culture was limited to festivals – mainly religious. But they were devoid of deep religious thinking. Brahmins used to worship different gods and goddesses reciting slokas, without understanding their inner meaning. The entire society was sunk in superstition, insinuation, and even immorality.[10]

A few native elites received enlightenment due to their European association, and accumulated wealth through trade and commerce. This small elite native society was contemporary to Rammohan Roy. They supported natives' education and learnt English informally. Some, like Radhakanta Deb, Motilal Seal, Ramkamal Sen, were conservative Hindus and rallied against social reformation. Others, like Dwarakanath Tagore, Kalinath Roy, Mathuranath Mallik, and Prasanna Kumar Tagore, supported Rammohan (Chapter 2).

When Rammohan came to Calcutta, the elites he engaged with were influential natives. **Dwarakanath Tagore** (1794–1846) born at Calcutta, learnt English in a private Anglo-Indian school. He trained in legal affairs through the aid of a Barrister, served as an administrative agent, and became owner of a large business house in Calcutta. He earned a fortune, and spent much on charity. He supported Rammohan's reformation.

Dwarakanath paid scholarships to aspiring Bengali doctors for higher studies in England, set up a district charitable society, a public library, and also paid for the construction of the Calcutta Medical College. His charity reached out to anyone who needed help. He was the grandfather of Rabindranath Tagore.

Radhakanta Deb (1784–1867), born in the Shovabazar Raj family (North Calcutta), was a conservative Hindu. He was proficient in English, Arab, Persian and Sanskrit, a social worker and writer. He became a founding member of Calcutta School Book Society (1817) and School Society (1818). He encouraged young men in their studies, composed *Shabda Kalpa Drum* (a dictionary of Sanskrit words), and wrote a book on women's education. Opposed Rammohan's reformation.

Ramkamal Sen (1783–1844) was born in Naihati, 24 Parganas, but was brought up in Calcutta. He first worked at the Hindustan Press, then as a clerk at the Asiatic Society. Through his proficiency of English, he was promoted to become Indian secretary of this Society. He served as Dewan of the Mint, and became the treasurer of the Bengal Bank. He was the principal of the Sanskrit College at its beginning, and was inducted in the committee of the Hindu College in 1817. He worked as a member of the Medical Commission set up by Lord Bentinck. Ramkamal Sen authored an English-Bengali dictionary composed of 58,000 words in two volumes. His *Hitopodesha* –a collection of fables in Bengali prose– was published at the Serampore Mission in 1820. Like Deb, he was an orthodox Hindu, a pro-sati activist who opposed Rammohan. However, Keshab Chandra Sen, his grandson, supported Brahmos and opposed Hindu conservatism.

Motilal Seal (1792–1854) was born in Coolutola, Calcutta. He did not get formal education because of the early death of his father. But he learnt English and after his marriage he built up his career. He was an ordinary employee of Fort William, but later became a successful business entrepreneur. He also worked as an interpreter in Calcutta Port and helped the crews of foreign ships. He became a wealthy man who engaged in philanthropy. He established a Free School and College in 1842 and was active in social work.

Dwarakanath Tagore established Zamindari Association in 1838 (later name changed to Landowners' Association) along with Radhakanta Deb, Ramkamal Sen, Prasanna Kumar Tagore, and Bhabani Charan Mitra. Their association aimed to protect landlords' interest and demanded rent-free tenures. They urged for extension of Permanent Settlement all over India. This association convinced the government to grant lease of waste lands to their occupants and lobbied for reforms of the judiciary, police and revenue departments for natives' interest. Their society secured 10 bigha rent free land for the service of idols and temples. Though organized for zamindars only, it was the first Indian native organization with a political agenda.

Fig. 36 Henry Louis Vivian Derozio (Public Domain).

Fig. 37 Statue of David Hare, Calcutta (Wikipedia).

Derozio and the Derozians (Pioneer reformists): Henry Louis Vivian Derozio (1809–1831) (Fig. 36), a teacher at Hindu College, imbibed new ideas to his students, while receiving moral and material support from David Hare (Fig. 37). His students became popularly known as Derozians. Being influenced by their teacher, these students studied the literature, science and political concepts that were advancing in Europe, and embraced free thought of the west. Some of them even gave up ancient Indian cultural traditions or rebelled against it. But most of them learnt Sanskrit and read ancient scriptures side by side with English literature.

Derozio was born in Calcutta as the son of a Portuguese father and an Indian mother. He read with David Dromed in his school at Dharmatala, who greatly shaped Derozio's personality. Dromed was a pandit of English literature and Philosophy, who was a supporter of the French Revolution and cherished the concept of free thinking. From him Derozio learnt to accept logic, reason, and empirical observation to arrive at a belief, avoiding any conformity with religion, creed or a messiah. Derozio's talent was expressed when he was fourteen or fifteen years old. He finished reading classical works in literature and philosophy, and developed the power to evaluate critical works when he was still young. He started writing poems in the *Indian Gazette* and was familiar among thinkers and educationists in Calcutta.

Derozio was appointed in Hindu College in March 1828 to teach literature and History to the students of fourth class.[11] He taught his students to build up their belief, principle, character, and self-reliance in the same way as he learnt. But his magnetic personality attracted students from all different classes, and within one year an integrated group of students were raised at his close supervision, and his personal touch extended from classrooms to outside. He influenced his students to read books and poems written in the post-revolutionary period of Europe.

Some of his students became so infatuated that they condemned everything Indian as ancient, and accepted everything in the west as modern and good. They landed in conflict with the older generation in family and society. They were criticized for too much inclination to the West. But they learnt free thinking and obeyed at their hearts' behest. In the twenty years between 1825 to 1845, many of Derozio's students became pillars of the Bengal Renaissance.

Mr. Edward, Derozio's biographer, wrote,

> … the students of first, second, and third classes had the advantage of attending a conversation established in the school by Mr. Derozio, where readings in poetry, literature, and moral philosophy were carried on. The meetings were held almost daily after or before school hours. Though they were without the knowledge or sanction of the authorities yet Mr. Derozio's disinterested zeal and devotion in bringing up the students in these subjects was unbounded and characterized by a love and philanthropy which, up to this day, has not been equalled by any teacher either in or out of service.
>
> The students in their turn loved him most tenderly; and were ever ready to be guided by his counsels and imitate him in all their actions in life. In fact, Mr. Derozio acquired such an

ascendancy over the minds of his pupils that they would not move even in their private concerns without his counsel and advice. On the other hand, he fostered tests in literature; taught the evil effects of idolatry and superstitions; and so far formed their moral conceptions and feelings, as to place them above the antiquated ideas and aspirations of the age. Such was the force of his instructions, that the conduct of the students out of the college was most exemplary and gained them applause from the outside world, not only in the literary or scientific point of view, but what was of still greater importance, they were all considered men of truth. ... those that remember the time, must acknowledge, such a boy is incapable of falsehood because he is a college boy.[12]

Derozians were involved in self-development through extra-curricular activities. They organized debates, published magazines, and formed an *Academic Association* in Maniktala – a meeting place for students to carry on open discussions on various topics relevant to social and moral affairs. Ramgopal Ghosh, Rasik Krishna Mallik, and Krishna Mohan Bandyopadhyay were the main speakers in such meetings. Radha Nath Sikdar, Dakshina Ranjan Mukhopadhyay, Ramtanu Lahiri, Peary Chand Mitra, Shiv Chandra Dev were enthusiastic listeners. Derozio acted as the chairman. Often the subjects of discussions were engaging and used to attract David Hare, private secretary of Lord Bentink, high ranking military officers, and even the principal of Bishop's College, joining them as attendees.

Haramohan Chattopadhyay, a clerk of Hindu College, attended meetings like a student. He wrote, "Principles and practices of the Hindu religion were openly ridiculed and condemned, and angry disputes were held on moral subjects; ... degraded state of Hindus formed the topic of many debates; their ignorance and superstition were declared to be cause of such state, and it was the resolved that nothing but a liberal education could enfranchise the minds of people... the question at a very large meeting was carried unanimously that Hindu women should be taught."[13]

When some students of Hindu College engaged in public protests against Hindu customs, their relationship with family members became embittered. Those students from Brahmin families refused their regular evening worship and discontinued to wear sacred threads. They, instead, began to recite from Homer's *Iliad*. Their behavior enraged social conservatives who rumored that Derozio was using the students to do away with Hinduism. The College authorities called for Derozio's explanation. David Hare, however, emphasized that Derozio was always an excellent teacher. The committee decided to close teachers' discussions on religious issues. This incident in Hindu College coincided with the passing of the Sati Regulation Act by Lord William Bentinck (4 December 1829) and the Brahmo Samaj inaugurating their new building in February of 1830. Orthodox Hindus were so annoyed that they not only spoke against Derozio, but also demanded Rammohan and Brahmo Samaj members to be socially outcast.

In a special committee meeting of Hindu College called in April 1831, Ramkamal Sen, an influential member, wanted to know whether Derozio would be allowed to continue as a teacher, or whether allowing Derozio to continue would be harmful for the College. David Hare and Dr. Wilson strongly pleaded for Derozio to continue for the benefit of the students. But Derozio immediately resigned stating that what he did was for the good of the students. Derozio died on December 24th, 1831 of Cholera. Calcutta mourned the death of a prime teacher who brought a new era in Bengal. However, the ripple Derozio created did not subside in his absence.

The Charter 1833 was passed allowing Indians to hold higher posts like Dy. Collector and Dy. Magistrate in government services. In the same year Mahesh Chandra Ghosh and Krishnamohan Bandyopadhyay, two Derozians, converted to Christianity in protest of being ill-treated by their own families and society, because they opposed the Hindu orthodoxy. Krishnamohan was also influenced by Alexander Duff.

Derozians like Ramgopal Ghose, Rasik Krishna Mallick, Kashi Prasad Ghosh, Shiv Chandra Dev, Hara Chand Ghosh, Peary Chandra Mitra, Radha Nath Sikdar, Kashi Prasad Ghosh, Ramtanu Lahiri, Tarachand

Chakraborty, Daskhina Ranjan Mukhopadhyay, etc. were noteworthy of their time. They were contemporary in Hindu College but of different age groups, and admitted strictly on merit basis. At that time, Hindu College had no power to confer degrees.

Debendranath Tagore usually kept himself aloof from the Derozians as he was of a different mind. Most Derozians came from Calcutta except a few like Ramtanu Lahiri. Not all students were from affluent families. David Hare arranged their admission in Hindu College from Hare School. He also arranged their scholarships from the School Society of which he was a founder member.

These students learnt to assimilate knowledge through debates, literary and journalistic works. They founded *Societies* for *Acquisition of General Knowledge* and the *Epistolary Association*. Tarachand maintained a circulating library when the Academic Council became defunct (1834). They edited a number of magazines like *Jnanannesan, Inquirer, Hindoo Patriot*, etc., sometimes in individual capacity; and regularly contributed articles in *Bengal Spectator, Bengal Hurkaru, Englishman, Calcutta Review*, etc. Prose writing in Bengali was initiated by Kashi Prasad Ghosh who edited the *Hindu Intelligencer*, and encouraged budding journalists to contribute to it.

Tarachand Chakraborty edited and published *The Quill*. He wrote critical articles usually suggesting reorientation of government policies for natives. Kashi Prasad Ghosh criticized James Mill's *History of British India* (1817) which denounced Hindu culture by establishing that Hindu rulers of the golden age were always secular, and ruled with cultural cooperation. Many Derozians learnt Sanskrit to acquire knowledge of ancient Indian culture.

Ramgopal Ghosh started political activities farming an association which for the first time organized opposition to the Black Acts. He was influenced by George Thomson, an anti-slave trade activist of England and US. Thompson came to visit Calcutta with Dwarakanath Tagore to create a political atmosphere in India. Ramgopal learnt from him how to deliver political speeches in public places. Thompson also helped establish the *Bengal British India Society*, (which in 1851 was merged with the *Landholders' Society*) forming the *British Indian Association* that sought administrative justice for natives. In the 1860s, Debendranath Tagore as the secretary of this association, submitted a petition to the government asking to take administrative steps to improve the conditions of natives.

Rasik Krishna was also a good orator and an efficient editor. He actively worked to foster Rammohan's mission. Radhanath Sikdar, while in service in Geographical Survey, used his own mathematical design in establishing that Mount Everest was the highest peak in the Himalayas. Peary Chand Mitra became the librarian of the Public Library when it was transferred to Metcalf Hall.

During this period, when many Derozians were vocal against the Hindu customs, Debendra Nath Tagore adhered to reforming Hinduism through the Brahmo Samaj. He established *Tattvabodhini Sabha* with a pathshala, and published *Tattavabodhini Patrika* to promote nationalism and spread knowledge on ancient scriptures among common people.

Many Derozians supported the Brahma Samaj which followed the essence of Hinduism, and worked to free the society from religious dogma, superstition, and casteism. They also urged the spread of western science and to revise the teaching program from 1834. In response to Derozians' campaign, press restrictions were lifted from September of 1835. Their journalistic work influenced the government to replace Persian with English in district courts. Derozians started the monthly *Bengal Spectator* in Bengali and English versions from 1842. David Hare died in 1842 ending a glorious era. The residents of Calcutta farewelled him with wet eyes.

Several students of the first group of Derozians gained opportunities to hold important positions in the government services and teaching. A few of them became self-employed and earned fortunes. They lived with mutual understanding and remained faithful to each other and contributed to building a healthy society. They never forgot what they had learnt from Derozio, and how they received help from David Hare. Ramgopal Ghose collected funds for establishing statues of David Hare near Hindu School (present name), and in the Medical College campus.

David Hare (1775–1842), a Scottish watchmaker, was a pioneer who initiated English education in Calcutta. He collaborated with Rammohan Roy and others to found *Hindu College*, the *School Society* and the *School Book Society* (Fig. 37). The *Calcutta School Society* founded in 1818 was responsible for opening new English and Bengali schools in different places, while the *School Book Society* took responsibility of printing English and Bengali books for the students and teachers when there was no suitable printed matter. They availed the printing facility from the Serampore Mission Press.

David Hare owned a watch shop at Lalbazar area in Calcutta. He was not a family man and sold his shop to become a free man to work for the natives' education. Each day he would fix up schedules for inspection of his schools and look after the needs of poor students. He routinely left his Grey street house every morning using a hand carried palanquin to visit the schools before arriving at the Hindu College at the end of the day.

David Hare treated the school students with tender care and supplied them with food and medicine whenever they needed. He even collected 'balls' for the entertainment of children. His charity in cash and kind helped many students of Hindu College to continue their studies. He stood by Derozio and supported the Young Bengal movement. David Hare did not have any university degree but devoted his life to uplift education of Bengali natives until his death in 1842.

Post Derozians: From around the 1835, post Derozian students became significant in all India contexts. Iswar Chandra Bandopadhyay (Vidyasagar), Akshay Kumar Dutta, Peary Chand Mitra, Madhusudhan Dutta etc. experimented with Bengali prose and poetry writing. They advanced Bengali literature and developed new styles in poetry and drama, improved journalism, enriched the Brahmo Samaj, and brought social changes. Their contribution was massive.

Vidyasagar published *Betal Panchabinsati* in 1847 as an improved version of Bengali prose-writing initiated by a Derozian. Inspired by its success, he published several books one after another. Ram Ram Bose along with

William Carey and Ganga Prasad had introduced Bengali prose writing from the early 1800s. Next, Rammohan Roy took up the translation of ancient scriptures in Bengali.

Ishwar Chandra Vidyasagar (1820–1891) born in a remote village, was a student of Sanskrit College in 1835. He also acquired knowledge in Law, and got a service as the judge-pandit in the Maharaja of Tripura's estate. His next assignment was the head pandit in Fort William College, where he learnt English from his European associates. Mr. Bethune, the then secretary of the Education Council, appointed him as principal in Sanskrit College. Vidyasagar was a reformer. He changed Sanskrit teaching methods by writing *Vyakaran Kaumudi*, reprinted some ancient Sanskrit Punthis, and opened up admission to Sanskrit College for everyone, irrespective of caste and creed. He also introduced English teaching there. His strong personality became evident when he refused the military to set up camps in the College during the Mutiny.

Vidyasagar served as the school inspector of Burdwan, Midnapur, Hooghly and Nadia districts. He resigned when his proposal for opening girls' schools, in addition to boys' schools in the districts he was in charge of, was opposed by the Director of Education. From the early 1850s Vidyasagar lobbied for legalizing widow remarriage by writing extensively in its favor and contradicting all counter arguments raised by the orthodox Hindus. He influenced the government to frame the Hindu Remarriage Act 1856. Sirish Chandra Vidyaratna married a widow in 1856. For nearly two of his final decades he worked for the advancement of social and economic conditions of tribal people (Santals) in and around Karmater presently in Jharkhand.

Akshay Kumar Dutta and Iswar Chandra Gupta also worked harmoniously for improvement of Bengali writing. Akshay Dutta taught in Tattvabodhini Pathshala from 1840. From 1843 he edited the *Tattvabodhini Patrika* which disseminated general knowledge among common people, which under his pen became one of the best Bengali journals. Akshay Dutta introduced changes in the fundamental concept of Brahmo Samaj which influenced Debendranath Tagore to compile the essence of Brahmo

Dharma in his book, *Spiritualism and Unitarian Concepts*. Akshay Dutta also compiled a book entitled, *Indian Community of Spiritual Seekers* from his sick bed.

Iswar Chandra Gupta was born with a poetic skill. Jogendra Mohan Tagore encouraged him to write in his weekly magazine *Sambad Prabhakar* which he started in 1830. Iswar Gupta, as the editor, raised the standard of Prabhakar and encouraged young writers like Bankim Chandra Chattopadhyay and Dinabandhu Mitra to publish poetry in his paper.

Madhusudhan Dutta (1824–1873) (Fig. 38), one of the most talented writers in Bengali literature, was not interested in Mathematics, but he possessed an exceptional memory. He was a student of Hindu College between 1837 and 1841. Madhusudan was influenced by Captain Richardson to write poems during his college life. He was no ordinary person. He learnt Greek, Hebrew, and Latin during 1843–1847 at Bishop's College. Afterwards, while staying in Madras, he started writing in English papers, and published *Captive Lady* in 1849. He gained a reputation as a poet in the English language. After his return, Bethune advised him to express his talents in Bengali literature and develop the language. He started writing dramas.

European residents of Calcutta began a play house in Lal Bazar from 1756. They established another play house at the northern side of Clive's Street near Writers Building where *Merchant of Venice*, *Hamlet*, *Romeo and Juliet* were staged. Female actors were not conventionally used until 1813. Wealthy natives loved watching English performances. They took initiative to get similar theatrical facilities in Bengali. But no good Bengali drama script was available.

A turning point came in Madhusudhan's career when he watched a Bengali drama, *Ratnabali*, translated from Sanskrit in the Belgachia theater. He translated *Ratnabali* into an English drama, opening a new chapter in his career. He researched critical aspects of Sanskrit dramas, and then started writing Bengali dramas, beginning with *Sarmista* in 1858. It was staged in the Belgachia Hall with great success. His next drama *Padmavati* was also successfully played. This encouraged him to focus on Bengali writing when prose was still in its nascent stage.

Jyotirindra Nath Tagore created infrastructures and arranged for staging *Sakuntala* and *Benisanghar* written by Madhusudhan, which were successfully performed. Madhusudhan then added a new chapter to Bengali literature by introducing Sonnets with new rhythms. He published *Tilottama Sambhaba* in 1860.

Bengali literature was further diversified by Lal Behari Dey, when he introduced folk literature in Bengali. He read in Duff's General Assembly Institution (Scottish Church College) from 1834 to 1844. After writing *The Falsity of Hindu Religion* in 1842, he accepted Christianity in 1843. He edited *Arunodaya*, a fortnightly journal dedicated to the cause for educating people in Bengali medium, and influenced the Education Commission to initiate education in Bengali for the commoners. He was a great writer, an efficient editor and a reformer.

Dinabandhu Mitra wrote a drama named *Nil Darpan* (mirror of indigo farmers) with a plot based on the peasantry of Jessore district, which was published in 1860. This drama, full of pathos depicting cruelty in European Indigo factories, was unusually popular. It was translated into English by Madhusudhan Dutta keeping the writer's name undisclosed. The success of this play inspired Dinabandhu to write more dramas.

Harish Chandra Mukhopadhyay started journalism by coming in touch with Kasiprasad Ghosh, the editor of *Hindu Intelligencer*. He received much appreciation when one of his articles protested Lord Dalhousie's Oudh Campaign. The *Hindoo Patriot* became very popular when it regularly published articles on the Sepoy Mutiny in 1857. During the Mutiny he took the role of a peacemaker, which pleased Lord Canning. Haris Chandra was influenced by Dinabandhu's *Nil Darpan* and staged protests against the European Indigo farmers. His articles influenced the formation of the Indigo Commission. As a witness before the Commission, he disclosed every detail on how the peasants were victimized by the factory owners. As a consequence, the *Hindoo Patriot* was sued in the Supreme Court. Henceforth he broke his health through all his xertions, did not recover and died when he was only 37 years old.

Fig. 38 Madhusudhan Dutta. By Atul Bose (Victoria Memorial Collection).

Fig. 39 Bankim Chandra Chattopadhyay (Public Domain).

Fig. 40 Sivanath Sastri (Public Domain).

Bankim Chandra Chattopadhyay (1838–1894) was one of the earliest students in Presidency College (Hindu College) (Fig. 39) who obtained the bachelor degree from Calcutta University. He began his career by writing poems in *Prabhakar* in a period when the Bengali mind was fully occupied with Madhusudhan's *Megnath Bodh Kavya*. Bankim decided to write novels after publishing a few short stories in Bengali prose.

His first novel, *Durgesh Nandini* published in 1864, was an unprecedented creation that changed the direction of Bengali literature. Thereafter he did not stop. He introduced a new style in his novels that analyzed characters in different ways and published several novels one after another. His writings attempted to avoid Sanskrit words in Bengali prose and improved it further.

Bankim Chandra's grasp of English and Sanskrit literature was manifested in his writings. He expressed his deep feelings for the motherland in *Vande Mataram*. This song was incorporated in his *Anandamath* (1882) written with the background of the Sanyasi Revolution of the late

18th century in mind. The song became a major source of inspiration among the freedom fighters after Rabindranath Tagore introduced rhythms to it.

Bankim wrote on various topics, from serious to seriocomic, to satirical, and most of those were published in his *Bangadarsan* (1872) which began a new era in published Bengali magazines. His writings on ancient literature projected the nobility of Hindu ideals. But his *Krishnacharit* portrayed Lord Krishna as a legendary pragmatic person behind centuries of myth. Rabindranath Tagore's literary work was much influenced by Bankim's writings.

Bankim was influenced by Rooso, and at the same time he accepted both J. Bentham and J. S. Mill. According to R. C. Dutt, "no [other] living writer has done so much to enrich the Bengali language."[14] Aurobinda Ghosh regarded him as an inspiration and saw in him as "…a new spirit leading the nation towards resurgence and independence." Bankim sharpened the intellect of future generations. He was one of the pillars of the Bengali Renaissance.

Biharilal Chakraborty was a great poet of his time. Rabindranath Tagore was influenced by him and complimented him as "Morning Bird." Biharilal was also a journalist, and editor of several literary magazines.

Keshab Chandra Sen (1838–1884), was one of the sons of Peary Mohan Sen and a grandson of Ramkamal Sen. Keshab met Debendranath in 1858 after he joined the Brahmo Samaj, and they started working together. The period between 1856 and 1861 was significant in Bengal history, as it witnessed the widow marriage movement, Sepoy Mutiny, and Indigo Movements. Those events influenced writers to develop journalism which propagated nationalism among Indians.

In this period when Bengal was progressing intellectually, Keshab Chandra's oration attracted many talented youths to join the Brahmo Samaj, and in the 1860s they drove the social movement forward. Keshab Chandra and Debendranath established a *Brahmo Vidyalay* to train up youths. Keshab introduced a core group of intellectuals as the *Sangat Sabha* where the youth members were trained in self-development by realizing truth and learning how to sacrifice. Keshab himself gave up his material ambition, and stood as a strong societal pillar with support of his co-workers. The Brahmo Samaj developed into a hub of intellectuals.

The Bengal youth vowed to propagate Brahmo-ism throughout India, and the Brahmo Samaj was established in Punjab, Sindh Pradesh, Bombay, and Madras. They indirectly carried the message from Bengal when Indian people needed intellectual progress in all spheres. In 1865 Keshab Chandra visited different eastern districts of Bengal along with Bijoy Krishna Goswami and Aghore Nath Gupta and worked hard to take the Samaj to village level. From 1866 Brahmo Samaj promoted social revolutions by publishing magazines and worked for a total development of the womenfolk through women empowerment.

A group of Brahmos came forward to promote progressive ideas against Hindu customs and Brahmo Samaj grew in numbers by working on societal reformation, female education, abolishing drinking, etc. The Samaj urged the government to pass the Civil Marriage Act, which was passed in 1872 restricting eligibility of only those who would declare that they were not believers of a conventional religion.

Keshab Chandra was influenced by Christ "who was an Oriental," and did not hesitate to adopt Christ. He comprehended that Christ and humanity were one, but not in the way that Christ and God were one. Keshab Chandra and some of his close associates were attracted by Sri Ramakrishna who believed in secular spiritualism. They deviated from the Unitarianism of the Brahmo Samaj being influenced by Ramakrishna's logical discrimination, even while knowing fully well that Ramakrishna practiced idolatry. Romain Rolland wrote, "Keshab's disciples pressed around the two sages at the porthole of the cabin, like a swarm of flies. And as the honey of his words began to flow from Ramakrishna's lips, the flies were drowned in its sweetness."[15] Keshab Chandra brought him in the limelight when he was not known by many. Ramakrishna was a man of profound knowledge and high intelligence, and a person who never made a mistake in decision making. His personality overpowered Keshab Chandra and his talented associates. Swami Vivekananda, also a talented person, tested Ramakrishna several times before accepting him as his guru, and preached the spiritual concept of Ramakrishna in the Parliament of World's Religions in Chicago (1883).

In reality, Brahmo Samaj is inseparable from the Hindus. When some extremists of Brahmo Samaj declared that they were not Hindus, Debendranath lamented that Brahmo Samaj was established by Rammohan Roy to propagate the essence of Hinduism in Hindu society and not to create new sects.

The Poet **Nabagopal Mitra** (1840–1894) to make Indians self-sufficient, organized the National Fair (Jatiya Mela) in 1867–1868 along with Gogenengra Tagore. The Mela was the venue for exhibiting India made products including nationalist literature on indigenous thinking, culture and songs. The purpose of this fair was to return to Indian customs and practices. It became a campaign for independent thought and the promotion of love for the country, through national songs and poetry. Satyendra Nath Tagore wrote, "Gao Bharoter joy..." (Recite and rejoice in the victory of India) at the Belgachia mela. This led to the founding of a Jatiya Sabha where only Bengali was spoken. Later early twentieth century Swadeshi movements were built on the agendas of Jatiya Sabha.

Nabagopal and other Hindu organizers intended to propagate the specialties of Hinduism, accepting the Brahmos as Hindus. Rajnarayan Basu was invited by the organizers as the main speaker and Debendranath Tagore presided over the meetings arranged by a Hindu group, though both of them belonged to Brahmo Samaj. It was a period in Bengal when the ultra progressive members of Brahmo Samaj opposed every Hindu societal practice.

Rajnarayan Basu began translating the *Upanihsads* into English. From 1849 he was a teacher in Sanskrit College where Iswar Chandra Vidyasagar, Dwarakanath Vidyabhusan, Madanmohan Tarkalankar, and Ramgati Nayaratna used to read English with him. Rajnarayan published the pamphlet, *A Society for The Promotion of National Feeling Among the Educated Natives of Bengal* for propagation of nationalism among Indians. As a monotheist, he did not equate Brahmos with Hindus, and he was loved by all.

Ramkinkor Sen, Akshay Kumar Dutta, Kali Pressana Ghosh, Braja Sundar Mitra, Rasbehari Mukhopadhyay, etc. were active workers in the Dacca Brahmo Samaj. In 1875 Eden *Female School* was founded in Dacca. Braja Sundar Mitra established a girls' school in his village in 1864. Keshab Chandra played an amazing role in bringing the youth community of Dacca, Coomila, and Maimansingha into Brahmo Samaj. They worked for social reformation at village level. Govinda Prasad Roy published the weekly *Dacca Prakash*. The Hindu community separately formed *Hindu Rakshini Sabha* and published *Hindu Hitoisini patrika*.

Dwarakanath Gangopadhyay was publishing a weekly, *Abalabandhab* (Friends of Females) from East Bengal. Once he joined the Calcutta Samaj, *Abalabandhab* became popular among young Brahmo women. Durga Mohan Das, a renowned lawyer in the High Court of his time, joined him. Durga Mohan helped in speeding up female education by establishing *Hindu Vidyalaya* (school) in 1873. An educated British lady, Miss. Ekroed came to Calcutta with a mission to educate native women. She became the administrator of this school. Dwarakanath arranged education facilities for girls of poor families. After Anandamohan Basu, a fresh Barrister, returned to Calcutta and joined with the mission of Dwarakanath and Durgamohan, the name of this school was changed to *Bango Mahila Vidyalaya*. This school was amalgamated with Bethune School, which was upgraded to Bethune College in 1879. Kadambani Devi, wife of Dwarakanath, was the first lady doctor in western medicine in South East Asia.

In the 1870s, Peary Charan Sarkar took a leading role to promote alcohol prohibition with direct support of Vidyasagar and Keshab Sen. In 1874, Peary Charan, in agreement made with Mr. Lethbridge, a professor of Krishnagar College, edited the *First Book for Native Children*. Later it was named a*s First Book of Reading* and it gained popularity in Bengal, Behar and Orissa. He also established the *School Book Press* for printing books. Peary Charan also worked for female education by establishing a girls' school in Barasat in 1847, before Bethune School opened.

Sambhu Chandra Mookherjee was a student of the *Oriental Seminary*, established in North Calcutta by Gour Mohan Addy in 1829 as a private school for teaching English to natives with Hindu parents. At that time, the popularity of Sanskrit was declining. Sambhu Chandra had studied in *Hindu Metropolitan College* under D. L. Richardson, formerly the English teacher in Hindu College. He developed a propensity in English, but he equally loved Bengali.

Sambhu Chandra started journalism with great interest along with Krishna Das Pal, his college mate and editor of *Hindoo Patriot*. Though he believed in liberal thought and was a proponent of political modernization, Sambhu Chandra was supposed to be pro-British. But he opposed the income tax policy imposed on Indians around the 1860s. He described Lord Canning as an inconsiderate Viceroy. His greatest contribution was compiling *Mutinies and People*,* a collection of clippings on the 1857 Mutiny from the *Times, The Edinburgh Review, Englishman,* some *Quarterly Reviews*. Sambhu Chandra was one of the founders of *India League* along with Anandamohan Basu, Sisir Kumar Ghosh and Durga Mohan Das.

Kaliprassana Singha (1841–1870) was born in a zamindar family in north Calcutta. He discontinued his studies from Hindu College in 1857, and founded *Vidyotsahini Sabha*, a cultural organization promoting Hindu theatre, when he was only 14 years old. He was supported by Peary Chand Mitra, Radhanath Sikdar, and Krishnadas Pal. Vidyasagar was amazed to see a boy of his age could attract so many eminent people. He wrote *Hootum Pyanchar Naksha*, a satirical book on middle class babu-culture of Bengal. He edited *Paridarsak*, a Bengali daily, *Sarvatattwa Prakashani,* and *Bibidharta Sanghara*. Kalipressana even arranged translation of the *Mahabharata* into Bengali prose order under supervision of Vidyasagar. Kaliprasanna distributed this Bengali version of Mahabharat free, spending lakhs of Rupees. He also translated the *Gita* into Bengali.

Kaliprassana contributed to *Tattvabodhini Patrika, Somprakash, Hindoo Patriot,* and *Mookerjee's Magazine*. He helped Haris Chandra Mukherjee's family in need, and rescued James Long from conviction by paying his large fine when he was tried for printing the unnamed English version of *Nil*

---

* Note: This book was published in London when printing in India was restricted because of the Press Act of Lord Canning. Mr. Malcolm Lewin, a former judge of Madras, helped him publish this book in 1857, and it was reprinted in 1905, and then in 2007 by the Asiatic Society, Calcutta.

Darpan. He also supported widow remarriage. Kaliprassana was appointed as Honorary Magistrate and Justice of Peace in 1863, and then as Chief Presidency Magistrate. Unfortunately, he died of liver failure when he was only twenty-nine years old.

Because special education and professional training were not available locally, Indian students were encouraged to go to Britain for higher education. Between 1853 and 1922 Indians were required to sit for Indian Civil Service (ICS) examination in Britain. To advocate in Indian courts with the right to defend or prosecute criminals, they required a call to the Bar in Britain. A few men born in the 1840s in Bengal availed this opportunity. After retirement many officers and lawyers worked for the Indian National Congress.

Satyendranath Tagore (1842–1923), the second son of Debendranath, was the first Indian to qualify for ICS in 1863. Monomohun Ghosh, a contemporary of Satyendranath at Presidency College, accompanied him to London and became a Barrister. Satyendranath, though taking on an administrative position, was also a poet and contributed to the development of Bengali literature. The nationalist song, *"Mile Sobe Bharat Santan..."* was his composition. Monomohun became a famous lawyer. He helped poor people by rendering free legal services when they were harassed by the administration. He was a social worker and associated with Congress as well.

Surendra Nath Banerjee (1848–1925) of Calcutta, after his graduation from Calcutta University, went to London in 1868 to qualify for the Civil Service Examination along with Rameshchandra Dutta and Beharilal Gupta. Surendra Nath appeared in the ICS examination of 1869 but was barred because he was too young. He qualified in 1871 and was posted as Dy. Magistrate in Sylhet. In 1875 he left government service and took a teaching job in the Metropolitan Institution, and engaged in social work. He campaigned for public awareness on nationalism and liberal politics, and along with Anandamohan Bose, founded the *Indian National Association* in July of 1876 to promote national unity. Manomohun Ghose courteously helped the association by providing an office and legal services.

Surendranath founded Ripon College (now Surendranath College, Calcutta) in 1882. He was engaged in journalism and edited *Bengalee*, which he purchased in 1879 from Girish Ghose. In 1883 he was arrested for contempt for writing an article in *Bengali*. He again went to London the following year to study law at the Middle Temple, but returned as he felt discriminated against.

Surendranath was influenced by the liberal thoughts of Edmund Burke. He was a good orator with a colourful political career. It is said that his strong analytical mind prevented his invitation to the inaugural session of Congress in 1885, but his Indian National Association was merged with Congress in the Calcutta session of 1886. By 1903, he was elected president of Indian National Congress twice.

The political activities of Surendranath have been discussed in chapter 3. At the end of his political career he left Congress to form a new party. He lost to Dr. Bidhan Chandra Roy, a Swaraj Party candidate, in the election of the Constituent Assembly, Bengal. He was offered the Knighthood and a ministerial berth in the Bengal government. As minister he improved the democratic processes in the administration of the Calcutta Municipal Corporation.

Anandamohan Bose (1847–1906) was born in Mymensingh district in an orthodox family and was extremely talented. He stood first in all his examinations and his favorite subject was mathematics. He got a Masters degree from Calcutta University and obtained the Rai Chand-Premchand fellowship. He served the Bengal Engineering College as a teacher. Anandamohan joined Brahmo Samaj in 1869. In 1870 he accompanied Keshab Sen to England and read in Cambridge. He was a Cambridge Wrangler with first class honors. Anandamohan's interest in politics brought him in touch with Britons who supported Indians. Mr. H. Fawcett, an expert in political economy and Cambridge alumni, who served as a member of the Indian finance committee in the 1870s, actively supported Bose.

Back to India in 1874 as a barrister, Anandamohan shouldered many responsibilities. He supported overall development of the student community, and worked for women's empowerment, jointly with Dwarakanath Ganguly and Durgamohan Das. He was the co-founder of the Indian National Association with Surendranath Banerjee. Anandamohan acted as the secretary of the Sadharan Brahmo Samaj, after amalgamating different factions. From 1877 Anandamohan was a member in the Senate and then the Syndicate of Calcutta University. He along with Sivanath Sastri and Surendranath Benergee established City School (later City College) as a trust of Brahmo Samaj. His involvement in social work overtook his law professional engagements.

At the merger of the Indian Association and the Indian National Congress Anandamohan got involved in politics. He toured England to organize meetings, and campaigned for natives' welfare. Back in India he served as president of Indian National Congress for two terms. He proposed founding the Federation Hall for the unity of Indians after the partition of Bengal in 1905. Due to his illness, Rabindranath Tagore read his address when the Federation Hall was inaugurated. He died the year after.

Sivanath Sastri (1847–1919) (Fig. 40) did his Masters in 1872 at Sanskrit College. He was greatly impacted by Keshab Chandra Sen and joined the Brahmo Samaj against his father's wishes. He actively worked for social reformation. Sivanath, while teaching in Bhawanipur South Suburban School, started promoting women's education. He worked against child-marriage, and promoted widow re-marriage along with the Indian *Reform Association*. He accompanied Keshab Sen and urged the government to legalize the minimum marital age of girls at 14 years, promoted a secret society in 1877 to restrain the caste system, and lobbied for educated youths to receive government jobs.

He was one of the early Congress pioneers who were in politics for getting complete freedom from colonial rule. Sibnath was a good writer and improved Bengali prose. He wrote his book *Ramtanu Lahiri and Tatkalin Banga Samaj* about Bengal society as he knew it. A major portion of this chapter has been sourced from Sastri's book.

Nabin Chandra Sen was a famous Bengali poet who lived after Madhusudhan Dutta and before Rabindranath Tagore. He contributed to the *Education Gazette* edited by Peary Chand Sarkar. He wrote *Palashir Juddha*, an epic poem based on nationalism. His autobiography depicts how Bengali literature helped shape Indian politics.

Beharilal Gupta was a student of Hare School and Presidency College. As stated above, Beharilal accompanied his friends to England and passed the Indian Civil Service examination in 1869 as a student of University College of London. Beharilal was also called to the Middleton Bar. Back in Calcutta in 1871, he joined the Civil Services and was posted in the districts. In Calcutta, he, as an Indian, obtained the post of Presidency Magistrate and Coroner from 1881 to 1886. This office became a source of controversy among some British officers who opposed him being recruited for such a coveted post, but he was allowed to continue after the Ilbert bill was passed.* He became a member of Bengal legislative Council, and became Remembrancer of Legal Affairs.

Romesh Chunder Dutt was a son of a Dy. Controller. Before completing his Bachelors, Romesh Chandra left for England to sit the Indian Civil Service examination with his friends in 1868. He cleared the ICS exam, and was called to the Bar at the Middle Temple in 1871. He entered the Indian Civil Service in 1871 and worked in various places in Bengal, facing difficult situations like the famines in 1874–76 and a cyclone in 1877. He was promoted to Divisional Commissioner and became the first Indian holding this position.

After retirement in 1898 he taught Indian History at the University College of London and completed his thesis on *De-industrialisation of India Under British Rule*. His interest in economic nationalism brought him in contact with Dadabhai Naoroji. Romesh Chandra was President of Indian National Congress in the 1899 session. He presided over the literary society Bangyo Sahitya Parisad.†

---

* Note: Lord Ripon's Ilbert Bill of 1883 allowed Indians to become members of the Covenanted Civil Service to try Europeans from which they were debarred by criminal procedure code of 1872. When the Ilbert bill was passed, the Indian Legislative Council was divided. Sir Ashley Eden, Lieutenant Governor of Bengal, forwarded the bill for adoption to the Government of India. The Bill was then passed in a different form to settle the dispute, with the amended bill having wider scope.

† Note: Bangyo Sahitya Parisad was founded in 1893 in Maniktala, north Calcutta. Romesh Chunder Dutt (or Ramesh Chandra Dutta) was the first President. Vice presidents were Rabindranath Tagore and Nabinchandra Sen.

With personal experience in the civil service Romesh Chandra wrote, "... modern Bengal society with all its vices and follies and hypocrisy, is an improvement on the past. There is more honesty, truthfulness, real earnestness, and genuine love of country in the modern days than in the past... English education and contact with the west have already borne their rich fruit. Young Bengal has already outlived the description of his character in which Anglo-Indians delighted fifty years ago. There is a reason for pride and joy."[16] He authored several books like *The Literature of Bengal Peasantry of Bengal, Rajput Jiban Sandhya, Hindu Sastra, History of Civilization in Ancient India, England and India, Mahabharata, Ramayana, Shivaji, The morning of Maratha Life, Indian Famines, De-industrialization in India Under British rule*, and a Bengali version of the *Rig Veda*.

At the terminal phase of the Bengal Renaissance a special generation which excelled in literature, art, spiritualism and science came into being. Rabindranath Tagore, Swami Vivekananda, Aurobinda Ghosh, Jagadish Chandra Bose, Prafulla Chandra Roy, Abanindranath Tagore and others, forming a galaxy of eminent persons who earned international reputation. Except Aurobindo Ghosh, none worked directly in politics, but all worked for the welfare of Indians. Activities of Aurobindo Ghosh were discussed in chapter 3.

Jagadish Chandra Bose (1858–1937) and Prafulla Chandra Roy (1861–1944) initiated western science in India and helped develop self-reliance for the future generations of India.

Nazrul Islam and Sarat Chandra Chattopadhyay wrote on social and political issues of contemporary Bengal. The work of Abanindra Nath Tagore is discussed in the text. Chittaranjan Das, a great nationalist and politician, was also one among this pre-independence generation. His reputation in the legal field is well known. He bailed out Aurobinda Ghosh from the Alipore bomb case. How he advanced nationalistic movements is already discussed. His nobility and charity knew no bounds.

Rabindranath Tagore (1861–1941) and Swami Vivakananda (1863–1902) are well known for their contribution in their own field. Tagore was writer–cum–philosopher and Swamiji was a spiritual leader and philosopher. Both of them were concerned about Indian people and the political situation during British rule. Tagore expressed his opinion on contemporary political situations and analyzed advancing social issues during his lifetime. Vivekananda inspired youths to work for upliftment of poor Indians. Some of their opinions and advice relevant for this work have been discussed briefly in the Conclusion.

Percolation of Renaissance: The Bengal Renaissance gradually percolated to other regions of India. In the West and South, Dadabhai Naoroji, Bal Gangadhar Tilak, Gopal Krishna Gokhale, Govind Ranade, and others were enlightened through western education and became nationalists responding to the calls vibrating from the East. Gokhale organized the *Servants of India Society* and looked after the spread of girl's education. Lala Lajpat Rai turned out to be a hard core Punjab leader with legal expertise. With the spread of journalism by 1870, aspiring educated Indians came closer to each other.

During the termination of the renaissance, several persons with leadership qualities from different parts of India established contact with each other and exchanged ideas with aims to integrate cultural and political activities on all India level. However, in Maharashtra and Madras the domination of Brahmins could not be eliminated. But prosperous middle class Maharastrians protested issues like caste domination. The Brahmins of Madras were educated and financially well off. The majority Dravidian community of Madras influenced by the renaissance began expressing themselves.

Many people of nobility and political acumen maintained respectful contact with one another and discussed national issues. Gandhi accepted Gokhale as his mentor. Gokhale was a fan of Bengali intellectuals who in turn recognized him as an efficient parliamentarian. Sarala Devi, a niece of Tagore, who in her 30s was an active participant in swadeshi movements, was allured by Gokhale's wisdom. Gokhale's speech in the 1902 budget session convinced even some British politicians.*

---

* Note: Gokhale's political acumen also impressed Lord Curzon. He wrote, "He was, if I may so describe him, the leader of the opposition in the Imperial Legislative Council over which I presided… I have never met a man of any nationality more gifted with what one could describe in this country as parliamentary capacities than was Mr. Gokhale." Quoted from *Debates on Indian Affairs, House of Lords Session 1914–16*. Vol. 18–20 (London: Hansard, 1916), 119.

Brahmabandhab Upadhyay was a close associate of Tagore in establishing Brahmacharya Ashram called Tagore *Gurudev*. Later he left Santiniketan and became involved with the anarchists. Tagore assigned Gandhi as *Mahatma*. Gandhi maintained a long association with Santiniketan from the time when he returned to India with students of Phoenix Ashram in South Africa. Those students were accommodated at Santiniketan through the mediation of Mr. Andrews. At the time of Gandhi's departure from Santiniketan on 19 February 1940, Tagore requested him to declare Santiniketan as a national property. Gandhi in reply wrote Tagore that he had accepted Santiniketan as his second home and would take it closest to him. Several letters of Tagore were published in the *Harijan Patrika*. Gandhi used to consult Tagore for every major political decision he took, though they sometimes differed in opinion. Jagadish Chandra Bose, Sister Nivedita, and Tagore maintained intellectual relations with each other. Aurobinda Ghosh, after his return from England, sought Tilak's help to ascertain the right direction in his political activities.

The influence of scientific research initiated in Bengal was thereafter transmitted to Madras. Srinivasa Ramajuan (1887–1920), without having formal training made such contributions in mathematics during the short span of his life, that many of his works remain unexplored till date. According to *Britannica*, Ramanujan left behind so many unpublished documents (the so-called "lost notebook") that mathematicians still continue to study them. After more than hundred years of his death, his discoveries are still being understood and some are still a mystery. Also, Madras born C. V. Raman (1888–1970) obtained a Nobel Prize in physics working from Calcutta.

Even the *Arya Samaj* which gained popularity in northern India was influenced by the Bengal Renaissance. It was built upon the principles of the Vedas and Upanishads, leaving aside all superstitions. Arya Samaj even supported widow marriage which Vidysagar endeavored to bring under the legal code.

References:

1. Sivanath Sastri, *Ramtanu Lahiri O Tatkalin Bango Samaj* (trans. Ramtanu Lahiri and Contemporary Bengal), first published in December, 1903, and 2nd edition was published in March 1909 by the author himself.

(This is the 3rd reprint, 2019 of the first edition retaining each single word of original text to depict how the Bengali prose was written at the end of the 19th century), published by Shyamalendu Das, Rubi Publishers, Kolkata.

2. Romesh Chunder Dutt, *The Literature of Bengal* (Calcutta: I.C. Bose, 1877).
3. Romesh Chunder Dutt, *The Economic History of India Under Early British Rule: From the Rise of the British Power in 1757 to the Accession of Queen Victoria in 1837*. Trübner's Oriental Series (London, New York: Routledge, 2000) (Originally published in 1893).
4. Nitish Sengupta, *Land of Two Rivers: A History of Bengal from the Mahabharatha to Mujib* (New Delhi: Penguin Books, 2011), 210.
5. Dutt, Ibid, 169.
6. Rama Deb Roy, "Glimpses on the History of Calcutta: 1600–1800," *Annales des Démographie Historique* (Paris: E.H.E.S.S., 1989), 243–257.
7. Geri Walton, "18th Century Calcutta: Life for the British." January 13, 2020 (blog) https://www.geriwalton.com/18th-century-calcutta-life-for-the-british.
8. Evan C. Cotton, *Calcutta Old and New: A Historical and Descriptive Handbook of the City of Calcutta* (London: W. Newman, 1907), 87.
9. Caroline Franklin (ed.), *Womens' Travel Writing 1750–1850: Letters from Mrs. Kindersley* (London: Taylor and Francis, 2006).
10. Sastri, Ibid, 42–44.
11. Ibid, 69.
12. Ibid, 82–83.
13. Ibid, 83–84.
14. Dutt, *The Literature of Bengal*, 195.
15. Romain Rolland, *The Life of Ramakrishna* (Kolkata: Advaita Ashram, 2022), 123. (originally published at Yavati Almora: Advaita Ashram, 1932).
16. Dutt, Ibid, 206.

APPENDIX 2

Princely States

The Princely States in India covered about two fifths of the subcontinent (Fig. 35 Map), housing about 180 million people against 123 million in British India. The 565 recorded states varied in size from territories as large as European nations to smaller landlords controlling a few thousand acres. Some of the princes were hereditary rulers from the middle ages, some were more recent and had acted as vassals for the Mughal empire, and some states like Bhopal, Cochin and Jhansi, were ruled by females. Most of the states were autocratic. During the tenure of Lord Dalhousie almost all states came under British command. From 1858, the Princes were kept in power at the wish of the British. The Crown permitted some states to choose their own heirs, adopted, or otherwise.

These States – outside British India proper – enjoyed paramount power through treaties. The Viceroy had dual status to function as Governor-General of British India, and as the Crown's representative of Indian States. Large states like Hyderabad and Mysore were provided with railways and telegraph lines. They also developed roads, sanitation and schools, etc.

Some of the Princes were provided with permanent residences and pursued their studies in England. They had to accept a colonial presence of soldiers and revenue collectors. These States had no liberty in external affairs but stayed under British protection. But the bond between the Raj and the States was regularly weakened through mutual suspicions. Rani

Lakshmibai of Jhansi rebelled against the British when she got involved in the Sepoy Mutiny. In 1857 many states turned against Europeans. The States lacked mutual understanding and never attempted to be united until the twentieth century. In 1921 a Chamber of Princes was formed, presided over by the Viceroy. During World War II some states aided the British with troops and funding.

Princely States and Politics: Most of the Princes ignored the nationalists, though some of them became interested in Indian politics when the parties received electoral rights. Others cherished having more liberty and political affiliation, especially after Lord Minto in 1909 declared the possibility of a partnership with the States in Udaipur.

After the 1917 declaration on self-governing institutions, some States tried to improve collaboration among themselves. States like Baroda allowed the Lok Parishad to look after her subjects. Within the next ten years the *All India States' Peoples' Conference* was formed with headquarters in Bombay. The Nagpur Congress in 1920 opened up membership for residents of the States, and advised the Princes to act as responsible governments. In the same year tribals living in Gujarati and Rajasthani States opposed the Jagirdars' land taxation system through the inspiration of Gandhi, but States generally preferred to solve local problems by themselves.

In 1929, Nehru, in his presidential speech, said that residents of Indian States cannot live separate from other Indians. He asked Princes to allow their subjects to decide their own fate. He demanded all States to become associated with the All India States Peoples' Movement. Subhas Chandra Bose, as president of the Haripura Congress, proposed to render moral support to these peoples' movements.

Many Princes opposed Congress' involvement in their affairs and wished to retain their independence. Some liberal southern States were open to constitutional reforms, but did not pursue any federation. However, after the 1935 Act was passed, many States recognized that British influence was waning and opted for more liberty. During the 1937 election, visionary Congress leaders invited the States to be represented in the federal assembly.

Accession of the States in the Indian territory: On 25 July 1947, Mountbatten, as the Crown's representative, began the process of starting talks with the States in the Chamber of Princes. He proposed that accession of a State was based on personal discretion of the ruler provided that 1) geographical continuity of the state in the successor Dominion was maintained, 2) the communal composition of the State was not compromised, and 3) if needed, a plebiscite (referendum) would be held to ascertain the will of the people. How accession of the States materialized has been discussed in chapter 9.

Kashmir, Junagadh, Hyderabad, Tripura and Manipur refused to accede before 15 August 1947. The first three had in common that the ruler of each state used to rule subjects of a different community who were the majority. Hari Singh was a Hindu Maharaja of Muslim dominated Kashmir, Nizam was Muslim ruler of Hindu dominated Hyderabad, and in Junagadh a Muslim king ruled the Hindu dominated State. The formation of Kashmir and its accession has been alluded to in chapters 2 and 9. Tripura and Manipur had always maintained their independence.

British paramountcy as the protecting authority was due to expire from 15 August 1947. Accessions of some States had been accepted after 15 August as the interim government was awaiting the outcome of local referendums to determine the will of the people. How these last independent States were acceded is discussed below.

Accession of Kashmir: In 1846, the British acquired Jammu and Kashmir and sold it to Gulab Singh under the Treaty of Amritsar. After his uncle's death in 1923, Hari Singh, the only remaining descendant of Gulab Singh, became the Maharaja. As stated before, the Hindu Hari Singh refused accession and opted to remain independent.[1] In opposition was Sheik Mohammed Abdulla, a political leader who worked for the majority Muslim people of Jammu and Kashmir representing the Kashmir Muslim Conference (in 1939 changed to *Secular National Conference*). When in 1946 Abdulla agitated for democracy and self-rule in Kashmir, Hari Singh put him in custody. Unpopular as he was, Hari Singh keeping his options open in a Muslim majority state, refused accession to either India or Pakistan three days before the time limit of the Standstill Agreement terminated.[2] The power vacuum caused by the Maharaja's indecision gave rise to a Pakistan backed Pashtun invasion in October, when the Indian government was preoccupied with problems in Punjab and Junagadh. But Jinnah would overplay his hand if he thought he could frighten Hari Singh into joining Pakistan.

On 24 October 1947, at a dinner party Nehru first spoke of tribesmen on military transport up the Rawalpindi road.[3] The next day, the Defence Council meeting received a telegram stating that five thousand tribesmen had attacked and captured Muzaffarabad and Domel, and a considerable tribal enforcement could be expected soon. Jinnah had sent Pathan tribes to invade Kashmir on a cold moonless night of October. Reports further indicated that they proceeded less than thirty miles from Srinagar.[4] The Kashmir forces were completely taken by surprise. Jinnah was careful not to involve the Pakistani army (a tribal force was sent instead) to fool British officials who had stayed as observers after 15 August.

At Srinagar, trucks loaded with Pathan tribals lined the side of the Jhelum river. They were kept waiting until the Muslim troops of Hari Singh, instigated to revolt beforehand, had overpowered the Hindu officers inside. At the opportune moment the Pathan troop would cross the river into the town, disconnecting Srinagar from the outside world by cutting the telephone lines.[5] Mr. Mehar Chand Mahajan who was first Prime Minister (1947–48) after accession of Kashmir to India wrote the same story in his autobiography republished in 1963.

The British officers posted in Pakistan, who were initially unaware of the move, soon got wind of what was going to happen in Kashmir and sent the telegram to General Sir Robert Lockhart in Delhi which was read in the Defence Council meeting of 25 October. Details on the size, armament, and location of the Pathan forces were also sent.[6]

Lord Mountbatten was worried. V. P. Menon, who had been inducted into the Government of India by Patel just after independence, also received the news of the Pathan invasion of Kashmir. Nehru, who originated from Kashmir, took the issue very serious. He planned with Patel to send Indian forces to Kashmir immediately. But Mountbatten, being the chief of the Indian administration, opposed violating international laws. He asked Nehru to wait till Hari Sing signed for accession.

V. P. Menon was immediately sent to Srinagar along with two military officers to convince Hari Singh for accession to India. Menon saw the Maharaja completely unnerved without army support. The urgency of the situation compelled him to agree to sign after consultation with Mehar Chand Mahajan, his administrative chief. Menon came back to Delhi in the evening of 26 October, and the formality of acceptance of Kashmir by the Indian government was disposed of.[7] Thus, Kashmir was lawfully acceded to India leaving no scope for a referendum on its future state any further.

Many British citizens residing in and around Srinagar, targeted by the pillaging Pathans, were rescued by British officers. As the accession was formally made on 26 October 1947, Mountbatten urged the Indian army to proceed to Kashmir to resist the Pathan invasion before they broke through to Srinagar.

Mountbatten himself improvised the air lifting operation, which quickened the troops' fly-in. Troops reached Srinagar airport on the morning of 27 October.* Jinnah had not calculated on that. Ziegler quotes one of Mountbatten's staff saying, "The mantle of the Governor-General fell from him and he assumed the garb of the supreme commander."[8] The Pathan advancement was halted some 25 miles ahead of Srinagar, but was not defeated. Indian intelligence from Pakistan reported that a few more Pakistani-led troops in disguise of tribesmen were deployed to help Pathans to keep their foothold in Kashmir.

---

* Note: Mountbatten extracted a pledge from Nehru and Patel to accept the decision by Hari Singh to join Pakistan (if he opted) before he flew to Srinagar (before 14 August 1947) and tried to convince Hari Singh to accede Jammu Kashmir to Pakistan. Hari Singh refused and told Mountbatten that he would become head of an independent State.

When the Pakistani attack was averted, Jinnah wanted to talk to Mountbatten. Jinnah would not accept the accession of Kashmir to India. He said it was based on fraud.[9] Baramulla was recaptured. The military situation in Kashmir apparently stabilized after the capture of Uri.

On 1 November, Mountbatten along with Ismay, met Jinnah in Lahore for negotiations on behalf of the Indian Government. It was a bilateral talk. Jinnah wanted India to withdraw its troops. Mountbatten said that there was no question of India withdrawing its troops from Kashmir. He told him, "Mr. Jinnah, as a servant of the Indian Government I must tell you that their action was perfectly legal. Hari Singh signed for accession, and troops were in Kashmir to drive off the large raiding party of Pathans, whose sole interest was loot… Fourteen European nuns were raped and killed at Baramulla convent. I would register a formal protest to your government in due course." This was a clear case of formal accession of Kashmir to India.[10] Mountbatten proposed a plebiscite conditional to Pakistan withdrawing military support to Azad Kashmir. He also stipulated that the Indian army would stay to defend Kashmir. Mountbatten's role in Kashmir accession to India remains beyond controversy.[11]

Jinnah retained his claim for Kashmir, but admitted responsibility for his involvement in sending troops, and said that he would pull out the Pathans if Indian troops were removed. He did not advocate a complete solution. The prospect of serious conflict between the two nations was temporarily averted. On 27 October 1947, Sheikh Abdullah was released and made the Head of the Provincial Administration.

To find a permanent solution, the Kashmir invasion was taken up by the UN Security Council. The Government of India requested to set up a commission. Resolution 47 was adopted by the Security Council on the basis of a 1948 report made by the *United Nations Commission for India and Pakistan* (UNCIP). The Commission's judgment reads, "Measure imposed immediate cease fire and called on the Pakistan government to secure withdrawal from the state of Jammu and Kashmir of tribesmen and Pakistan nationals not normally resident therein who have entered the state for the purpose of fighting. It also asked the government of India to reduce its force to minimum strength before a plebiscite could be put into effect on the question of accession of the state to India or Pakistan."[12] It called for a free and impartial referendum to be held.

Jinnah thought that a plebiscite in presence of Indian troops with Sheik Abdullah in power meant that the average Muslim would be intimidated to vote for India instead of Pakistan, and rejected the proposal of UNCIP. Jinnah demanded for parity, to which India objected.[13] The referendum was never conducted and the Kashmir problem has continued to rear its head since then.

Sheikh Abdullah was appointed as Chief Minister of Kashmir in 1948. Since then, India's strategy (until recently) has been that Kashmir would be treated as a normal state with special provisions for a measure of self-rule.

Accession of Hyderabad: The Nizam of Hyderabad initially ignored all appeals to join a domain, as he was afraid for bloodshed between the communities and wished to retain his status. Three months after independence, he sent a delegation led by Nawab Moin Nawaz Jung, a member of the Nizam's government, to meet the Viceroy in Delhi to negotiate a form of association with self-rule. Also present were premier Chhatari, and Sultan Ahmed, president of the Executive Council of the Nizam, who had advised him to secretly loan part of his wealth to Pakistan. Mountbatten was empowered to negotiate a Stand Still Agreement beyond 14 August, ensuring that administrative arrangements of the British Crown between remaining Princely States would continue unaltered. Upon Mountbatten's and Monakton's persistence that defence and external affairs would remain with the central government, the delegation agreed that V. P. Menon would be sent to Hyderabad to carry on negotiations. But the day before Menon was due to leave Delhi, his visit was cancelled on the grounds that counter demonstrations were organized for his arrival. On 10 October, W. Monckton, legal advisor of the Nizam advised for accession to India with a symbolic status for the Nizam as head. Then on 22 October a Stand Still Agreement was drafted with various revisions acceptable to Nizam's next delegation.

When the draft was shown to Nizam's Executive Council, although three members disagreed, Nizam was still advised to sign the agreement. The Nizam for the time committed not to accede to Pakistan. Ultimately he did not sign the agreement. In the early morning following, thousands of local residents swarmed around the residences of Monckton, Chhatari and Sir Sultan Ahmed and prevented the delegates from leaving. Kasim Razvi, the Razakar leader of Hyderabad's Muslim national party Ittehad, convinced the Nizam that an agreement meant the death of Hyderabad. A new delegation included the three members who disagreed with the draft. But at 8 a.m. the Nizam sent a message to the delegates not to leave for a few days, and a telegram to Mountbatten informing that sending the next delegation would be delayed.

Both Monckton and Chhatari warned that the postponement would be disastrous, and they resigned. The Kashmir accession was completed by 26 October. The new delegation led by Moin Nawaz Jung reached Delhi, and on 27 October they expressed that the Nizam wanted Hyderabad to remain independent with close association to both India and Pakistan, and foreign policy in general in conformity with India's. Mountbatten spoke sternly and said that he never experienced such naive procedure as Hyderabad was trying to adopt, and made the delegation aware that the Stand Still Agreement, as proposed by them, was not terminated. If the Nizam continued to repudiate his own decision, the responsibility would be his own.

The Nizam who had completely withdrawn from all central affairs from 1926, he retired after a clash with Lord Reading, was out of touch with the new ground realities. The delegation finally advised him to accept the agreement, but Hyderabad wanted to buy more time by postponing the procedure until 15 November. When Mountbatten agreed to wait, the Nizam put conditions that his Council, a) would have control over Hyderabad's overseas export trade; b) would station troops for emergency; and c) would rule in absence of any arbitration clause.

On 29 November 1947, India refused to accept any of Hyderabad's conditions. But the Standstill Agreement allowed a breathing space of one year. By that time Ittehad's efforts to introduce democratic policies uniting the Muslim population to support the Nizam were successful. Still there was no indication that the Nizam was willing to sign an agreement to join India and break his relations with Pakistan. Ultimately, on 13 September 1948, the Government of India started Operation Polo and took over Hyderabad at the cost of thousands of casualties.[14]

Accession of Junagadh: The State of Junagadh was 5000 sq. miles with three sides surrounded by Indian territory and one side to the Arabian Sea. This Muslim dynasty with 80% Hindu population chose to accede to Pakistan on 15 August 1947. It argued that though it did not have geographical continuity, it was linked to Pakistan by sea route. After the dynasty's accession, Pakistan posted its troops for the ruling families' protection. Nehru, concerned for growing communal tensions, requested Liaquat Alikhan for their withdrawal. For three weeks, Liaquat did not reply and rejected the demand for a plebiscite in the Defense Council meeting of 16 October 1947.

This accession to Pakistan caused the Junagadhis to agitate. From 1 November 1947 Indian forces entered the two subject states of Mangrol and Babariawad. On 7 November, Junagadh's court, facing a collapse, invited India to take it over. That day the Dewan formally invited the Government of India to take over the State and save it from complete breakdown. The Nawab complied with consent of the public and the State Council. The India government immediately informed the Regional Commissioner in Rajkot to implement the accession which was finalized on 20 February 1948, after a plebiscite was held in early February. More than 95% of the population favored accession to India.

The states of **Tripura and Manipur** were made to accede to Indian territory in October 1949.

References:

1. Philip Ziegler, *Mountbatten* (New York: Alfred A. Knopf, 1985), 447.
2. Alan Campbell-Johnson, *Mission with Mountbatten* (New York: Atheneum, 1985), 223–24.
3. Ibid, 224.
4. Ibid.

5. Ziegler, Ibid, 249.
6. David Butler, *Mountbatten: The Last Viceroy* (New York: Pocket Books, 1985), 223.
7. Ibid.
8. Ziegler, Ibid, 249.
9. Butler, Ibid, 242.
10. Ibid, 447.
11. Dominique Lapierre and Larry Collins, *Freedom at Midnight* (New Delhi: Vikas Publishing, 1983), XIV.
12. For UN Resolution 47 refer: http://unscr.com/en/resolutions/47
13. Campbell-Johnson, Ibid, 225.
14. Syed Akbar, "Hyderabad had tried 'NRC' 71 years ago and failed," in *The Times of India*, September 15, 2019. https://timesofindia.indiatimes.com/city/hyderabad/hyderabad-had-tried-nrc-71-years-ago-and-failed/articleshow/71132138.cms.

APPENDIX 3

Scholastic Europeans in India

During the tenure of the East India Company several administrators and educators like Sir William Jones, Charles Grant, J. Groundwater Bethune, and missionaries like William Carey and his associates at Serampore worked selflessly for the cause of Indians. Some made India their home and died here. Contributions of several Europeans were discussed in the text. Many of them, known and unknown, started working on preserving Indian treasures.

As the first, Governor-General Warren Hastings supported Charles Wilkins to translate the *Bhagavad Gita* (Dialogue of Krishna and Arjun). Wilkins, who had learned Sanskrit in Benares, translated a portion of the Mahabharata from Sanskrit. He also worked on Brahmin scripts. His major contribution was creating Devanagari and Bengali fonts. After his return to London, Wilkins worked as the first director of the India House library (now British Council). Warren Hastings also supported Nathaniel Brassey Halhed to write the first Bengali grammar which was printed in 1787 on his Hooghly Press. Wilkins commissioned the casting of the first Bengali fonts. His technique of font making led to the development of a type foundry at Serampore Mission Press. Halhed also translated the *Gentoo Code* from Persian to English. This was an important legal code relating Hindu social system originally written in Sanskrit.

When London bureaucracy became anti-Indian, two contemporary Governors, Thomas Munro (1820–27 in Madras) and Mountstuart Elphinstone (1819–27 in Bombay), worked to enlighten Indian subjects to make them capable of governing themselves. Thomas Munro died in India.

According to David Gilmour, the majority of the British Indian officers favored the British conservatives and were not interested in working routinely following ICS manuals and avoided club culture. But there were some officers who spent time on intellectual activities and Indian affairs. Gilmour maintained names of several such officers who preferred to be posted in places away from the city. Philips Mason was happier in Garhwal. Mildred Archer and her husband Bill, both scholars, served in Bihar in 1934. They were sceptical of keeping a connection with Raj. Mildred was an art historian who wrote a book on paintings in Patna. John Merriman, a commissioner in Ranchi and author of a book on British Social Life in India, wrote that scholarly people were forced to suppress their knowledge and had difficulty publishing their findings.

In the 1860s an officer in the Hyderabad Residency translated Homer from Greek. Some important areas of Indian research were initiated by Europeans. William W. Hunter, a statistician, studied Indian historical culture and science as a hobby. Douglas Dewar wrote a book on Indian birds. Bill Archer, a magistrate, wrote on songs and poetry of the Uraons–an aboriginal tribe of central India, and was interested in primitive Indian sculptures. John Muir, a district Judge, worked on Sanskrit texts. A. C. Burnell, a judge, prepared a catalogue of Sanskrit manuscripts in the palace of Tanjore. John Beams completed a comparative grammar of modern Aryan languages. George A. Grierson wrote on *Bihar Peasant Life* and compiled a grammar of 18 dialects and subdialects of Bihari languages in 8 volumes. Robert Caldwell, Hermann Sunder, and Ferdinand Kittel worked on Tamil, Malayalam, and Kannada languages respectively. Most of such labours were done during the 18–19th centuries.

There were anthropologist ICS officers like John Hunter who spent his career in the Naga Hills (1909–35) and wrote on Naga tribes. James Mill also wrote three books on Nagas.

Reference:

David Gilmour, *The British in India: A Social History of The Raj* (New York: Farrar, Straus and Giroux, 2018), 414–419.

APPENDIX 4

List of Governor-Generals and Viceroys

I. Governor-Generals   1772–1858

Warren Hastings	1773 – 1785
Cornwallis	1786 – 1793
John Shore	1793 – 1798
Wellesley	1798 – 1805
Cornwallis	1805
George Barlow	1805 – 1807 (acting)
Minto	1807 – 1813
Hastings (Moira)	1813 – 1823
Amherst	1823 – 1828
Bentinck	1828 – 1835
Metcalfe	1835 – 1836 (acting)
Auckland	1836 – 1842
Ellenborough	1842 – 1844
Hardinge	1844 – 1848
Dalhousie	1848 – 1856
Canning	1856 – 1858

II. Viceroys from 1858–1947

Canning	1858 – 1862
Elgin	1862 – 1863
Lawrence	1864 – 1869
Mayo	1869 – 1872
Northbrook	1872 – 1876
Lytton	1876 – 1880
Ripon	1880 – 1884
Dufferin	1884 – 1888
Lansdowne	1888 – 1894
Elgin II	1894 – 1899
Curzon	1899 – 1905
Minto II	1905 – 1910
Hardinge II	1910 – 1916
Chelmsford	1916 – 1921
Reading	1921 – 1926
Irwin	1926 – 1931
Willingdon	1931 – 1936
Linlithgow	1936 – 1944
Wavell	1944 – 1947
Mountbatten	1947 – 1948

Note: All titles have been omitted.
Governor-Generals and Viceroys who were acting for less than one year have been omitted.

Bibliography

Akbar, Syed. "Hyderabad had tried 'NRC' 71 years ago and failed." *The Times of India*, September 15, 2019. https://timesofindia.indiatimes.com/city/hyderabad/hyderabad-had-tried-nrc-71-years-ago-and-failed/articleshow/71132138.cms.

Bairoch, Paul. *Economics and World History, Myths and Paradoxes*. Chicago: University of Chicago Press, 1995.

Bandyopadhyay, Sekhar. *Constraints in Bengal Politics, A History of Modern India*. Hyderabad: Orient Longman, 2004.

Bandyopadhyay, Shyamal Chandra. "America's Rise & End of an Empire." *The Statesman (Durga Puja Special)*, Calcutta (2011), 45.

Banerjee-Dube, Ishita. *A History of Modern India*. Cambridge: Cambridge University Press, 2015.

Banerjee, Brojendra Nath. "Rammohan Roy an Educational Pioneer." *Journal of Bihar and Orissa Research Society*, Vol. 16 (June 1930), 154–175.

Basu, Prasenjit K. "How The British Raj Ultimately Fell to INA Trial." Dailyo.in dated 16.06.2017. https://www.dailyo.in/arts/subhas-chandra-bose-ina-trials-british-raj-empire-azad-hind-fauj-19004.

Bengal Government, Confidential report No. 1876-C, dated 31st August 1908, preserved as *Assassination of Narendra Nath Goswami* in the Bengal Government file on *Assassination* in *Documents in the Life of Sri Aurobindo*. https://incarnateword.in/documents/assassination-of-naren-goswami.

Bhalla, Parveen. *The Life and Times of Subhas Chandra Bose*. Kolkata: Prabhat Prakashan, 2020.

Boissonneault, Lorraine. "The Speech that Brought India to the Brink of Independence." *Smithsonian Magazine* (August 8, 2017) https://www.smithsonianmag.com/history/speech-brought-india-brink-independence-180964366/.

Bonnerjee, W. C., *Indian Politics. With an introduction by W. C. Bonnerjee*. Madras: G. A. Natesan & Co., 1898.

Bose, Krishna. *Netaji Subhas Chandra Bose's Life, Politics and Struggle*. New Delhi: Picador India, 2022.

Bose, Sankari Prasad. *Vivekananda O Samakalin Bharatbarsha*. Kolkata, 1955.

Bose, Subhas Chandra. *The Indian Struggle 1920–1942*. New Delhi: Oxford University Press, 1964, 1997.

Bolts, William. *Considerations of Indian Affairs: Particularly Respecting the Present State of Bengal and Its Dependencies. With a Map of Those Countries, Chiefly from Actual Surveys*. London: J. Almon, P. Elmsley, Richardson and Urquhart, 1772.

Bowen, H. V. "Sinews of Trade and Empire: The Supply of Commodity Exports to East India Company during the Late Eighteenth Century." *The Economic History Review*, 55 (3) (March 2003), 466–486.

Brendon, Piers. *The Decline and Fall of British Empire 1781–1997*. London: Vintage Books, 2008.

Bridge, Carl. *Holding India to the Empire: The British Conservative Party and the 1935 Constitution*. Burlington, VT: Vantage Press, 1986.

Butler, David. *Lord Mountbatten: The Last Viceroy*. New York: Pocket Books, 1985.

"Calcutta Riot 1946: Mass Violence and Resistance." *Research NetWork* (Science pst), 8 November, 2007.

Campbell-Johnson, Alan. *Mission with Mountbatten*. New Delhi, Calcutta: AICO Publishing House, 1951 and New York: Atheneum, 1985.

Carson, Penelope. *East India Company and Religion 1698–1858*. Volume 7 of Worlds of the East India Company. Woodbridge, UK: Boydell Press, 2012.

Chamberlain, Neville and Robert C. Self, ed., *The Neville Chamberlain Diary Letters: The Heir Apparent*, Vol. 3. Farnham, UK: Ashgate, 2000.

Chandra, Bipin, M. Mukherjee, A. Mukherjee, S. Mahajan, K. N. Panikar, *Indian Struggle for Independence 1857–1947*, 2nd Ed. Kolkata: K. P. Bagchi, 1994.

Childs, David. *Britain Since 1945: A Political History*. London, New York: Routledge, 1979.

Chattopadhyaya, Haraprasad. *The Sepoy Mutiny, 1857: A Social Study and Analysis*. Calcutta: The Author, 1957.

Colville, Jock. *The Fringes of Power*. Guilford, CT: John Lyon Press, 2002.

Cotton, Evan C. *Calcutta Old and New: A Historical and Descriptive Handbook of the City of Calcutta.* London: W. Newman, 1907.

Crawford, Dirom Gray. *A Brief History of the Hughly District.* Calcutta: Bengal Secretariat Press, 1903.

Curzon, George Nathaniel. *Speeches of Lord Curzon of Kedleston*, Part 1. Calcutta: Government Print, 1900.

Dalrymple, William. "The East India Company: The Original Corporate Raiders." *The Guardian*, 4 March 2015, 16.

Digby, William. *Prosperous' British India: A Revelation from Official Records.* London: T. Fisher Unwin, 1901.

Dutt, Romesh Chunder. *Literature of Bengal: Attempts to Trace the Progress of National Mind and Various Aspects of Literature.* Calcutta: I.C. Bose & Co., Stanhope Press, Bow Bazar St., 1877.

Dutt, Romesh Chunder. *The Economic History of India Under Early British Rule: From the Rise of the British Power in 1757 to the Accession of Queen Victoria in 1837.* Trübner's Oriental Series. London, New York: Routledge, 2000. (Originally published in 1893).

Edwardes, Michael. *British India 1772–1947.* New Delhi: Rupa, 2019.

Esteban, Javier Cuenca. "The British Balance of Payments 1772–1820: India Transfers and War France." *The Economic History Review*, Vol. 54, No. 1. (February 2001), 58–86.

Franklin, Caroline (ed.), *Womens' Travel Writing 1750–1850: Letters from Mrs. Kindersley.* London: Taylor and Francis, 2006.

Gandhi, M. K. "Mahatma Gandhi's Statement." *The Indian Annual Register*, Vol. 1 (April 1941), 327.

Gandhi, M. K. *The Collected Works of Mahatma Gandhi*, Vol. 69. New Delhi: Government of India, Publication Department, 1999.

Gilmour, David. *The British in India: A Social History of the Raj*. New York: Farrar, Straus and Giroux, 2018.

Glendevon, John. *The Viceroy at Bay: Lord Linlithgow 1936–43*. London: Harper Collins, 1971.

Gokhale, G. K. and G. A. Natesan, eds. *Speeches of Gopal Krishna Gokhale*. Madras: G. A. Natesan, 1916.

"Gopinath Saha" in *Marxist Indiana: An Encyclopaedia of Freedom Fighters in India in Alphabetic Order*. Blog Post No. 188 (November 23, 2013).

Goswami, Devaprasad. *Twelve Great Men of Hindustan*. Kolkata, 2020.

Grover, B. L. *A Documentary Study of British Policy Towards Indian Nationalism 1885–1909*. Delhi: National Publications, 1967.

Gupta, Amit Kumar. "Defying Death: Nationalist Revolution in India, 1897–1938." *Social Scientist*, 25 no. 9–10 (Sept-Oct 1979), 3–27.

Hicks, Pamela. *Daughter of Empire: My life as Mountbatten*. New York: Simon & Schuster, 2012.

Hindu, A. *The Mutinies, the Government and the People*. Calcutta: D' Rozario and Co., 1858.

Hodges, William. *Travels in India during 1780–83*. New Delhi: Munshiram Memorial, 1794, 1999.

Hopkirk, Peter. *On Secret Service East of Constantinople*. Oxford: Oxford University Press, 2001.

Hoover, Karl. "The Hindu Conspiracy in California, 1913–1918." *German Studies Review*, 8 no. 2 (1985), 245–261.

Hutchins, F. G. *Spontaneous Revolution: Quit India Movement*. New Delhi: Manohar, 1871.

Hyndman, H. M. *The Emancipation of India: A reply to the article by the Right Hon. Viscount Morley, O.M., on "British democracy and Indian government" in the "Nineteenth century and after" for February, 1911*. London: The Twentieth Century Press, [1911].

Jayanta, Sanyal. "Goyenda Report O Ramakrishna Mission, Kichu Aprakasita Tatta." *Udbodhan*. No. 8, (2021–22), Swami Krishnananda Ed., 635–643.

Kelly, Nigel. *History and Culture of Pakistan*. Delhi: Peak Publishing/Danesh Publications, 2009.

Kora, Aloke. "Rakkahas Khalir Tamralipi– Bhumi Dan Sankranta Dalil." *Udbodhan* 126 (February 2024), 58.

Lapierre, Dominique and Larry Collins, *Freedom at Midnight*. New Delhi: Vikas Publishing House, 1997.

Lawrence, James. *The Making and Unmaking of British India*. New York: St. Martin's Press, 1998.

Lily, William Samuel. *India and Its Problems*. London: Sands & Co., 1902.

Macaulay, Thomas Babington. "Minute Upon Indian Education (1835)." H. Sharp, ed. *Selections from Educational Records Part I, 1781–1839*. Calcutta: Government Printing, 1920.

Maddison, Angus. *Contours of World Economic History: Essays of Macro Economic History*. Oxford: Oxford University Press, 2007.

Majumdar, Ramesh Chandra. *History of the Freedom Movement in India*. Calcutta: Firma K. L. Mukhopadhyay, 1971.

Mallick, Samar Kumar. *Adhunik Bharoter Derso Bochor (1707 to 1857)*. Kolkata: West Bengal Publishers, 2003.

Marshall, P. J. *East Indian Fortunes: The British in Bengal in the Eighteenth Century*. Oxford: Oxford University Press, 1976.

Marshall, P. J. "The White Town of Calcutta under the Rule of the East India Company." *Modern Asian Studies* Vol. 34, No. 2 (May 2000), 307–331.

Mehrotra, R. S. *The Emergence of the Indian National Congress*. Delhi: Vikas Publications, 1971.

Menon, V. P. *The Transfer of Power in India*. Princeton, NJ: Princeton University Press, 1957.

Metcalf, Barbara D. and Thomas R. Metcalf, *A Concise History of India*. Cambridge: Cambridge University Press, 2005.

"Military Report, 24 August, 1946" (E. C. & Personal, No. 5705/3/CSI b) National Archives, 12 A.P.C. Road, Kolkata. Report No. 216/66.

Mookherjee, Sambhu Chandra (A Hindu), *The Mutinies and the People, Or, Statements of Native Fidelity: Exhibited During the Outbreak of 1857–58*. London: Smith Elder, 1858.

Moor, Pendon (ed.), *Wavell: The Viceroy's Journal*. Oxford: Oxford University Press, 1973.

Moore, R. J. "Mountbatten, India and the Commonwealth." *Journal of Commonwealth and Comparative Politics*, Vol. 19 (1) (1981), 1–4. (Publ. online in 2008).

Mountbatten, Louis F.A.V.N. *Transfer of Power 1942–47*. The Mountbatten [Files] in *Constitutional Relations between Britain and India* in *Volumes I–XII*. Nicholas Mansergh Contributor. London: H.M. Stationery Office, 1970.

Mukherjee, Barid Baran. *Serampore: Late Medieval and Colonial Era*. Kolkata: Ghosh Publishing, 2021.

Nehru, J. L. *Jawaharlal Nehru: An Autobiography*. London, New Delhi: Oxford University Press, 1936, 1982.

Nehru, J. L. and S. Gopal, ed. *Selected Works of Jawaharlal Nehru*, Vol. 7. Oxford: Oxford University Press, 2015.

Purani, A. B. *The Life of Sri Aurobindo*. Pondicherry: Sri Aurobindo Ashram, 1958.

Puri, Harish Kumar. "Revolutionary Organization: A Study of the Ghadar Movement." *Social Scientist* 9, no. 2/3 (1980): 53–66.

Raj, J. L. *Making and Unmaking of British India*, Abacus Publication Office, London War Office, 208/761A, 1997.

Ranganathananda, Swami. *The Message of Vivekachudamani*. Kolkata: Advaita Ashrama Publication, 2009.

Read, Antony and David Fisher, *The Proudest Day: India's Long Road to Independence*. New York: W. W. Norton and Co., 1999.

Rehman, Mohsinur. "The National Riots: Forgotten Noakhali Hindu Massacre." *Category History*, Noakhali, 14 August, 2014.

Robert, Andrew. *Eminent Churchillians*. London: Weidenfeld & Nicolson, 1994.

Rolland, Romain. *The Life of Ramakrishna*. Kolkata: Advaita Ashram, 2022. (originally publ. 1931).

Roy, Rama Deb. "Glimpses on the History of Calcutta: 1600–1800." *Annales des Démographie Historique* (Paris: E.H.E.S.S., 1989), 243–257.

Sengupta, Nitish. *Land of Two Rivers: A History of Bengal from the Mahabharata to Mujib*. New Delhi: Penguin Books, 2011.

Sevareid, Eric. *Not So Wild a Dream*. New York: Simon and Schuster, 1946.

Sastri, Sivanath. *Ramtanu Lahiri O Tatkalin Banga Samaj*. 3rd ed. Kolkata: Rubi Publishers, 1903, 2019.

Sialkoti, Zulfiquar Ali. "An Analytical Study of the Punjab Boundary Line Issue." *Pakistan Journal of History and Culture*, XXXV, Vol. 2 (2014), 71–111.

Springate, Susan. "Lady Pamela Hicks on the Real Story Behind Viceroy's House." *The Telegraph*, 25 February, 2017.

Stein, Burton. *A History of India*, 2nd. ed. David Arnold. Sussex, UK: Wiley-Blackwell, 2010.

Tagore, Rabindranath. "Tagore's Last Article." Reprinted from "The Tribune" in *The Militant*, Volume V, no. 40 (4 October, 1941), 6.

Tagore, Rabindranath. *Sabbatar Sankat*, in Rabindra Rachanabali (Works of Rabindranath), Part 13. Calcutta: Government of West Bengal, 1990.

Tagore, Saumyendranath. *Rammohan Roy: His role in Indian Renaissance*. Calcutta: Asiatic Society, 1975.

Tharoor, Shashi. *Nehru: The Invention of India*. New Delhi: Penguin, 2007.

Tharoor, Shashi. *An Era of Darkness: The British Empire in India*. New Delhi: Aleph Book Company, 2016.

Tharoor, Shashi. *Inglorious Empire: What the British did to India*. Melbourne, London: Scribe Publications, 2017.

"The 20th Eventful Century: Forging The Modern Age 1900." II Series *Readers Digest*. Pleasantville, NY: The Reader's Digest Association, 2000.

Tomlinson, B. R. "India and British Empire 1880–1935." *The Indian Economic & Social History Review*, 12 no 4 (1975), 337–380.

Tomlinson, B. R. "The Political Economy of the Raj: decline of Colonialism." *Journal of Economic History*, Vol. 42, no. 1 (March 1982), 133–137.

Tomlinson, B. R. "India and British Empire, 1880–1935." *Sage Journal*, Vol. 2, Issue 4 (1975), University of Cambridge, Published online 26 July 2016.

Waley, S. D. *Edwin Montagu: A Memoir and an Account of his Visits to India*. Bombay: Asia Publishing House, 1964.

Walton, Geri. "18th Century Calcutta: Life for the British." January 13, 2020 (Internet blog). https://www.geriwalton.com/18th-century-calcutta-life-for-the-british.

Wood, J. R. (ed.), "Dividing The Jewel: Mountbatten and Transfer of Power to India and Pakistan." *Review Article: Pacific Affairs*, Vol. 58 (4) University of British Columbia (1985), 653–662.

Ziegler, Philip. *Mountbatten*. New York: Alfred A. Knopf, 1985.

Index

Academic Association, 328
Acharya, Rajagopal, 157, 174, 187, 189, 190, 217
Afghan war, 59, 104, 105
Afghan, 28, 31, 104, 105, 107, 114, 140, 181, 221, 298, 301
Agra, 26, 27, 60, 92, 189
Agriculture, 51, 60, 86, 87, 107, 141, 146, 149, 170, 188, 295
Alam, Shah, 36
Alam, Shah, II, 2, 31, 33, 34, 37, 53
Alan-Campbel, 8, 9, 197, 262, 264, 290, 309, 359
Ali, Asaf, 218, 229
Ali, Hyder, 17, 28, 32, 33, 48
Aligarh, 77, 135
Alipore Bomb Case, 127, 129, 134, 157, 162, 347
All India Radio, 273
Allahabad Congress, 127, 147
Allahabad, 2, 31, 53, 60, 77, 84, 112, 127, 147, 158, 163

Allied Force, 220, 222, 311
Ambedkar, 179
Amboina, 14
American, 85, 90, 110, 141, 209, 212, 216, 226, 233, 234, 255, 276, 297, 311
Amery, Leo, 208, 227, 300
Amery, Lord, 220
Amherst, 58, 67, 74, 79
Amrita Bazar Patrika, 114, 251
Amritsar massacre, 146, 150, 156, 164, 296
Andaman, 104, 131, 133, 147, 187, 221, 230, 317
Anglo-American War, 90, 141, 295
Annie Besant, 118, 138, 146, 148, 149, 164
Anti Compromise Conference, 204
Anusilon Samity, 128
Arabia, 301
Arah, 37

Arundal, George, 138
Arya Samaj, 349
Asoka Hall, 58
Assam, 87, 120, 158, 208, 219, 238–240, 252, 265, 272, 281, 314
Atlantic Charter, 201, 209, 219, 311
Attlee, Clement, 167, 179, 191, 211, 229, 244, 252, 256, 259–261, 265, 273, 274, 275, 276, 289, 302, 307
Auchinleck, Claude, 219
Aurangzeb, 12–15, 18, 20, 22–27, 32
Aurobinda, 6, 123, 124, 127, 338, 347, 349
Austria, 190
Awadh, 33, 36, 41, 60, 82–84, 115, 156, 189
Axis Force, 209
Azad Brigade, 222, 226
Azad Hind Government, 221
Azad Hind Radio, 220
Azad, Abul Kalam, 152, 157, 207, 228
Azad, Chandrasekhar, 162, 163

Babur, 11
Badal, 161, 162
Bahadur Shah, 82, 84
Bahadur, Tej, 220, 229
Bal, Loknath, 172
Balasore, 17, 134, 160

Baldwin, 169, 176, 297
Balkan Plan, 264–266, 270
Ballav, Gobinda, 192
Balochistan, 238, 239
Banaras, 49, 65, 71, 73, 147, 154, 163, 217, 296
Bandel, 15, 18
Bankar, 138, 149
Bankim, 48, 78, 113, 334, 336–338
Bara bazar, 245
Bardoli, 160
Baroda, 91, 122, 123, 154, 218, 352
Batavia, 134
Belgium, 205, 315
Benerjee, Surendranath, 105, 121
Bengal Chemical, 125
Bengal Engineering College, 77, 344
Bengal Ladies Society, 79
Bengal National College, 123
Bengal Partition, 119, 120–122, 124, 126, 136, 137, 147, 280, 281
Bengal riots, 244
Bengal Volunteer Organization, 159
Bengali, 9, 49, 64–67, 71, 72, 75, 78–80, 89, 90, 92, 96, 97, 102, 107, 105, 115, 120, 123, 250, 255, 295, 320, 321, 324, 330–335, 337, 338, 340–345, 347, 348, 350, 361
Benoy, 161, 162, 173

Bentinck, 59, 66, 69, 74, 77, 87, 90, 324, 329
Bentink, Lord, 328
Berlin Committee, 131–133
Bethune, 79, 80, 109, 172, 333, 334, 341, 361
Betor, 20
Bharatpur, 26, 58, 88
Bhulabhai, 229, 230
Bihar, 7, 25, 28, 34–37, 42, 45, 83, 97, 109, 147, 149, 153, 154, 184, 189, 218, 243, 244, 250, 252, 362
Birla, 173, 190
Bishops College, 75, 77
Black Act, 102, 109, 110
Black Hole, 29, 312
Board of Council, 36
Boer War, 119
Bombay Presidency Association, 114
Bombay, 11, 14, 15, 17, 18, 22, 28, 43, 45, 55, 58, 75, 81, 83, 90, 91, 101, 102, 106, 111, 112, 114, 115, 117, 122, 124, 135, 138, 142, 144, 146–148, 150, 152, 153, 155, 156, 165, 168, 178, 184, 187, 190, 198, 207, 217, 218, 231, 266, 316, 339, 352, 362
Bonnerjee, W. C., 115, 143
Bose, Anandamohan, 111, 114, 121, 343–345
Bose, Krishna, 161, 223, 224, 225, 234
Bose, Rash Behari, 122, 131, 134, 221, 316
Bose, Sisir Kumar, 208, 224
Bose, Subhas Chandra, 6, 9, 154, 159, 161, 163, 166–168, 170, 173, 186, 190–194, 196, 197, 201, 202, 207, 208, 212, 216, 220–224, 230, 231, 234, 235, 313, 314, 317, 352
Boundary Commission, 272, 275, 278, 279, 304
Brahmabandhab, 121, 349
Brahmo Samaj, 67, 68, 80, 329, 331–333, 338, 339–341, 344, 345
Brain, 252
British Empire, 9, 21, 97, 106, 144, 152, 166, 197, 199, 207, 210, 212, 311, 312
British India, 5, 7, 39, 60, 71, 85, 98, 99, 101, 142, 143, 146, 165, 167–292, 302, 314, 330, 331, 351
Brochman, 262
Buddhism, 62, 320, 321
Burma, 1, 53, 58, 60, 82, 84, 105–107, 120, 133, 139, 161, 171, 181, 184, 222, 226, 290
Butler, 262, 284, 291, 292, 310, 360
Buxar, 2, 36, 37, 41, 83

Cabinet Mission Plan, 237, 238, 240, 243, 264–266, 269, 271
Cabinet Mission, 214, 233, 237, 238, 240, 241, 243, 253, 256, 264–266, 269, 271
Calcutta Corporation, 93, 120, 123, 159, 161
Calcutta famine, 226, 254
Calcutta Gazette, 49
Calcutta Museum, 318
Calcutta, 283–285, 293, 297, 302, 305, 309, 310, 312, 318–327, 329–332, 334, 337, 341–346, 349, 350
Cambridge, 9, 39, 76, 97, 122, 143, 154, 166, 198, 199, 234, 344
Carnatic war, 16
Census, 89, 94, 104, 139, 184, 245, 272, 279, 280
Central Provinces, 120, 147, 158, 159
Chamber of Princes, 352, 353
Champaran, 149, 154
Chandannagar, 30, 122, 129, 130
Charles, Grant, 361
Charnock, Job, 18, 19, 38
Chattopadhyay, Virendranath, 131
Chauri Chaura, 156
Chelmsford, 122, 139, 145, 178
Chittagong Armory, 173
Chittaranjan, 123, 152, 157, 347
Chowdhury, Raja, 123
Church Missionary Society, 79

Clive, 3, 18, 19, 28–31, 34, 35, 38, 41, 42, 47–49, 94, 294, 322
Coastal China, 210
Cochin, 15, 17, 351
Colebridge, T. N., 73
Colville, 199, 235
Commonwealth, 106, 138, 210, 214, 227, 239, 263, 265–268, 273–275, 277, 285, 291, 305, 312
Congress constitution, 164
Constituent Assembly, 176, 183, 187, 203, 206, 211–214, 216, 232–234, 238–244, 253, 256, 260, 268–271, 273
Cornwallis, 3, 33, 49–51, 53, 87, 108, 297, 323
Coromandel Coast, 11, 90
Cossimbazar, 17–19, 29, 35, 36
Cotton, 86, 88–90, 93, 96, 104, 120, 121, 126, 141, 142, 158, 162, 165, 180, 182, 294, 295, 350
Cotton, Henry, 120
Cowasji, 131
Cripps Mission, 213, 216, 302
Cuddalore, 17
Curzon, 54, 79, 107, 119–122, 126, 131, 135, 139–141, 143, 317, 318, 348

Dalhousie, 3, 60, 81, 91, 335, 351
Dandi, 171–173
Danish, 18, 25, 72, 73, 317

Das, Bina, 173, 252
Das, Chittaranjan, 123, 152, 157, 347
Daula, Siraj-Ud, 23, 29, 36–38, 41
Deb, Radhakanta 67, 68, 323–325
Deccan, 13, 24, 26–28, 32, 115, 148, 315
Defence Committee, 140
Defence Council, 201, 202, 210, 211, 232, 354
Denmark, 205
Depressed Class, 146, 179, 241
Derozians, 108, 109, 321, 326, 328–332
Derozio, 306, 319, 321, 325–329, 331, 332
Desai, Bhulabhai, 229, 230
Desai, Mahadev, 149
Deshmukh, 27
Dev, Naren, 202
Devi, Sarala, 125, 128
Dhan Gopal, 132, 133
Dhingra, Madanlal, 122
Dig Darshan, 72
Dinabandhu, 313, 334, 335
Dinesh, 161, 162
Direct Action, 242–244, 254, 256, 282, 284
Diwani, 37, 43
Do or Die, 217
Dominion status, 158, 159, 164, 167–170, 185, 203–205, 267, 269, 271, 274–276, 306

Dufferin, 106, 116, 117, 120, 135
Dunkirk, 205
Dupleix, 30, 37
Durani, 28
Durbar Hall, 58, 282, 312
Dutch, 14, 15, 17–19, 25, 42, 58, 85, 210, 212, 293, 296, 312
Dutta, Ramesh Chandra, 346
Dyarchy, 145, 157, 184
Dyer, 151

East Africa, 140
East India Company, 1, 9, 11–100, 102, 109, 315, 316, 319, 361
Edinburgh Review, 342
Edward VII, 126
Edwina, 261
Egypt, 53, 140, 181, 237
Election-1945, 229
European indigo planters, 148
Executive Council, 45, 102, 111, 136, 146, 182, 203, 204, 206–208, 210, 211, 214, 239, 241, 242, 270, 357, 358

Famine, 42, 47, 48, 87, 104, 105, 114, 118, 119, 121, 139, 142, 226, 227, 233, 245, 254, 255, 295
Federalcourt, 184, 185, 244, 252
Federation Hall, 121, 345
Female Juvenile Society, 79
First World War, 132, 148

Fort St. David, 17–19
Fort St. George, 15, 18–20
Fort William, 22, 47, 49, 54, 71, 72, 73, 75, 83, 91, 132, 133, 318, 325, 333
Fort William College, 49, 54, 71–73, 75, 91, 333
French East India Company, 30
French, 15–19, 22, 23, 25, 28–31, 33, 36, 38, 39, 48, 53, 55, 105, 137, 186, 293, 308, 312, 314, 315, 319, 326
Friend of India, 69, 70, 72, 91

Gandhi Brigade, 223
Gandhi, M.K., 5, 6, 117, 124, 131, 132, 135, 138, 145, 148–157, 160, 163, 164, 166, 167, 169, 170–174, 176–179, 182, 187–189, 191, 192, 196, 198, 201, 203–208, 211, 215, 217–220, 222, 223, 226–228, 252, 253, 262, 264, 269, 273, 276, 281–286, 290, 299–302, 305, 307, 308, 313, 316, 348, 349, 352
Gandhi-Irwin Pact, 177
Ganpati Festival, 124
Gaya Congress, 157, 163
Geneva, 186
Geological Survey, 95
George VI, 287
German, 131, 133, 144, 186, 205, 209, 220, 221, 315, 319
Ghadar, 131–133, 138, 144, 150
Ghosh, Ganesh, 172
Ghosh, Ramgopal, 109, 110, 328, 330
Gladstone, 105, 112
Gokhale, 117, 124, 127, 138, 143, 299, 348
Golconda, 24
Government house, 46, 54, 217
Government of India Act 1858, 102
Government of India Act 1919, 139, 145–147, 164
Government of India Act 1935, 5, 183–185, 195, 263, 270, 276
Govindpur, 22
Great Calcutta Killings, 244, 302
Great depression, 174, 181, 300
Gujarat, 14, 26, 27, 54, 90, 106, 149, 154, 155, 160, 171, 288, 303
Gulf Countries, 140
Gupta, Kamala Das, 252
Gurkah Brigade, 223

Halhed, Nathaniel, 71
Hardinge, 59, 75, 122, 126, 316
Hare, David, 66, 67, 74, 75, 306, 319, 326, 328, 329, 330–332
Harijan Weekly, 215
Harris, Bret, 227
Hastings, Lord, 54, 69
Hastings, Warren, 3, 35, 36, 39, 45–50, 53, 60, 71, 94, 295, 320, 361

Havell, Ernest Binfield, 78
Hind Swaraj, 131, 132, 148
Hindu College, 68, 74–76, 78, 80, 95, 321, 324, 326–330, 332, 334, 337, 342
Hindu Mahasabha, 147, 157, 168, 217, 233, 240, 245, 316
Hindustan Republican Association, 157, 160
Hitler, 216, 220, 221, 227, 312
HMG statement, 272, 273, 275, 301
Holkars, 27, 54
Holland, 205
Home Rule, 138, 149, 150
Hooghly, 17–20, 73, 75, 76, 92, 106, 160, 162, 250, 333, 361
Horizon, 299, 313
Howrah Bridge, 92, 93
Howrah Station, 91
Hume, 106, 114, 115, 152, 298
Huq, Fazlul, 188, 219
Hyderabad, 3, 24, 27, 31, 32, 53, 84, 95, 198, 266, 287, 288, 351, 353, 357–359, 360

Ilbert Bill, 105, 111, 346
Imperial Library, 79
Imphal, 222
INA, 213, 221–223, 226, 229–233, 235, 313, 314, 316, 317
INA trial, 229–231, 233, 235
Independence of India League, 168

Indian Council Act 1892, 117
Indian High Courts Act 1861, 45
Indian Independence Act, 8, 286
Indian Independence Committee, 131
Indian National Congress, 3, 4, 101, 106, 107, 111, 114–116, 120, 143, 148, 298, 312, 343–346
Indian National Pact, 158
Indigo Commission, 335
Indigo, 44, 81, 85, 87–89, 96, 102, 108, 109, 113, 148, 149, 313, 335, 338
Indonesia, 210
Instrument of accession, 287
Interim Government, 227, 232, 238–244, 252–254, 256, 263, 264, 267, 269, 277, 303, 308, 353
Iran, 24
Iraq, 301
Irwin, 160, 164, 167, 169–171, 176–178, 180–182, 194, 195, 254, 260
Irwin, Lord, 160, 164, 167, 169, 178, 180, 181, 254, 260
Ismay, 264–266, 356

Jackson, Stanley, 173
Jadavpur, 77, 123
Jagadish, 297, 347, 349
Jagirdars, 352
Jahangir, 14

Japan surrender, 229
Japan, 15, 122, 126, 134, 137, 210, 212, 215, 216, 221, 223, 229, 230, 233, 256, 300, 301, 311, 315–317
Jats, 3, 13, 26
Jinnah, 135, 137, 152, 153, 168, 171, 188, 189, 196, 201, 204–207, 210, 216, 220, 227, 228, 232, 233, 238, 240, 242–244, 252, 256, 264, 268–270, 272–275, 277, 289, 290, 301, 303, 305, 307, 308, 354–357
Jitendra, 132–134
Johnson, Louis, 216
Joshi, 193
Judiciary Act 1781, 45
June 3 Plan, 277

Kanailal, 129, 130, 314, 317
Karachi, 92, 155, 176, 177, 231, 272, 282
Karmayogin, 123
Karnataka, 28, 32, 218
Khadi, 149, 153–155, 158, 165, 170, 173, 191, 290
Khalifat, 156
Khan, Abdul Goffor, 174, 178, 275, 277, 305
Khan, Alivardi, 23
Khan, Khizar Hyat, 302
Khan, Liaquat Ali, 264, 280
Khan, Murshid Quli, 23, 25
Khan, Shah Nawaz, 229
Khan, Syed Ahmed, 80, 116, 135
Khudiram, 122, 128, 129
Kishore, Brojendra, 123
Kohima, 222, 314
Koh-I-Noor, 25
Kolkata, 9, 20, 22, 54, 57, 97, 99, 143, 144, 166, 198, 256, 309, 310, 350
Kripalani, J.B., 149
Krishnagar, 341
Kumar, Aswani, 121

Labour Party, 5, 229, 234, 314
Lahore Congress, 169, 170
Lahore Resolution, 211, 220
Lalbazar, 20, 332
Laldighi, 20
Lansdowne, 116, 117
Lawrence, Pethick, 237, 240
Liakat, 121
Libya, 293
Linlithgow, 185, 188, 198, 201–204, 206, 219, 238, 269
Lockhart, 354
Lord, Birkenhead, 159, 171
Lucknow Congress, 137, 187
Lucknow Pact, 147, 157, 196
Lytton, 104, 105, 112, 114, 139

MacDonald, Ramsay, 169, 178
Madhusudhan, 108, 332, 334–336, 345

Madras, 11, 15, 16, 19, 20, 22, 23, 28, 32, 33, 37, 43, 45, 47–49, 55, 58, 59, 70, 75–77, 80, 81, 83, 90, 91, 94, 101, 102, 112, 114, 115, 118, 121, 124, 127, 133, 135, 138, 139, 143, 146, 152, 153, 155, 168, 174, 188–190, 202, 231, 295, 314, 334, 339, 342, 348, 349, 362
Mahajan Sabha, 114
Maharaja, 31, 48, 73, 121, 288, 333, 353, 355
Malaysia, 210, 261
Malda, 17, 120, 281
Malvia, Madan Mohan, 127, 179
Manipur, 106, 107, 222, 223, 230, 353, 359
Maratha, 18, 27, 28, 32, 54, 90, 124, 315, 347
Marwar, 32
Marwari, 255
Masulipatnam, 15, 16, 17
Mayor's Court, 43, 44, 122, 129
Menon, Krishna, 267, 268, 314
Metcalfe Hall, 79, 331
Middle East, 137, 202, 301, 302
Midnapur, 34, 37, 130, 154, 333
Miéville, Eric, 262, 272
Military report, 246, 256
Minority quota, 196
Minto Morley Act, 127, 136–137

Minto, 54, 73, 122, 126, 127, 135, 136
Mitra, Peary Chand, 79, 110, 328, 329, 331, 332, 342
Mohammedan Anglo Oriental Association, 135
Montagu, 122, 139, 144–146, 165
Morley, 126, 127, 135, 136, 295, 308
Moscow, 211
Mountbatten – Nehru Deal, 271
Mr. Scott, 162
Mughals, 3, 12, 13, 18, 23–29, 31–33, 35, 38, 53, 80, 312
Mukherjee, Ajoy Kumar, 218
Mukherjee, Jadu Gopal, 157
Mukherjee, Shyamaprasad, 274
Municipal, 103, 120, 159, 344
Munro, 37, 76, 362
Muraripukur, 122, 129
Murshidabad, 19, 34–36, 41, 47, 281, 312
Muslim League, 3–5, 101, 113, 134, 135, 137, 147, 153, 158–160, 177, 185, 188, 189, 196, 201–203, 205, 208, 211, 213–215, 217, 219, 227–230, 232, 238, 240–245, 251, 252, 254, 256, 261, 263–265, 268, 271, 273, 275, 277, 283, 290, 300–303, 307, 308, 316
Mysore, 3, 17, 28, 32, 33, 52, 53, 94, 266, 351

Nabagopal, 125, 340
Nagaland, 222, 314
Nagas, 363
Nagpur Congress, 352
Nairs, 146
Naoroji, 111, 116, 117, 127, 295, 346, 348
Napoleon, 53, 68
Narayan, Joyprakash, 202, 217, 218
Naren, 129, 144, 202
Natal, 148
National Council of Education, 123
Nazi, 226
Nehru Brigade, 222
Nehru Mountbatten Plan, 273
Nehru, Motilal, 6, 151–154, 157–159, 163–165, 168–170, 177, 178, 185–187, 190–193, 196, 198, 202, 203, 207, 210, 212, 215, 217, 221, 222, 225, 226, 229, 230, 232, 235, 242–244, 253, 261, 263–275, 280, 282, 284, 287, 297, 300, 303, 314, 352, 355, 359
New India, 138, 270, 285
New York Times, 172
Nil Darpan, 108, 335
1937 election, 195, 196, 203, 232, 300, 352
Nivedita, 128, 349
Nizam, 16, 27, 28, 32, 33, 53, 288, 353, 357–359

Noakhali riot, 244, 250
Non-violence, 132, 148, 153, 158, 163, 174, 192, 217, 232, 286, 299
North Western Frontier Provinces, 188
North Western Frontier, 107, 119, 174, 178, 184, 188, 204

Old Fort William, 22
Oldham, 120
Operation freedom, 162
Opium Tea, 87–88, 96
Oriya, 120
Oudh, 25, 31, 33, 335

Pal, Behari, 123, 125, 152
Pal, Bipin, 124
Pamela, 261, 291
Pan Indian Mutiny, 133
Paris Indian Society, 131
Paris, 131, 350
Parliamentary Delegation-1946, 232
Parliamentary system, 146, 168
Patel, S. Vallabhbhai, 149, 154, 155, 157, 160, 186, 203, 230, 231, 253, 269–272, 275, 280, 287, 354, 355
Patel, Vithubhai, 186
Pathan, 354, 355
Patna, 17–19, 34–36, 64, 76, 154, 179, 217, 296, 362

Patrick Spens, 246
Patriot, 108, 330, 335, 342
Pearl Harbor, 210, 316
Permanent Settlement, 51, 52, 60, 68, 81, 86, 89, 95, 108, 229, 325
Persia, 15
Persian, 12, 47, 64–67, 69, 72–74, 80, 313, 324, 361
Peshwa, 27, 28, 54, 76, 315
Philippines, 210
Pitt's Act, 49
Plassey, 29–31, 33, 34, 37, 43, 48
Police report, 115, 130, 314
Poona Pact, 179, 313
Poona, 26, 27, 53, 54, 76, 115, 117, 148, 179, 206, 219, 313
Portuguese, 14, 15, 17, 48, 308, 326
POW, 315
Prafulla, 111, 128, 129, 347
Prasad, Rajendra, 157, 203, 285
Presidency College, 77, 154, 297, 314, 337, 343, 346
Princely States, 1, 8, 45, 60, 84, 102, 104, 136, 154, 168, 169, 171, 179, 183–185, 195, 196, 201, 213, 214, 218, 237–240, 259, 266, 270, 276, 286, 288, 303, 316, 317, 351–360
Provincial, 11, 24, 32, 49, 102, 104, 105, 116, 136–138, 141, 142, 145, 153, 157, 158, 161, 168, 170, 179, 181, 183–185, 187, 195, 202, 203, 214, 226, 227, 230, 233, 238–240, 242, 245, 263, 265, 267, 269, 271, 272, 279, 299, 319, 356
Public Library, 79, 324, 331
Pulin, 128
Punjab, 7, 26, 28, 31, 32, 53, 55, 59, 60, 65, 107, 115, 122, 124, 138, 145, 147, 150, 153, 155, 158, 162, 173, 188, 204, 207, 208, 232, 238, 239, 244, 250, 263, 265, 266, 268–270, 272–274, 277, 279, 281, 290, 302–305, 339, 348, 354
Pusa, 141

Qasim, Mir, 34–37, 43, 86
Quit India, 5, 176, 213, 216–219, 221, 233, 234, 256, 300, 312, 316, 318

Radcliff, 280, 281
RAF, 316
Rahaman, Sheikh Mujibur, 250
Rai, Lajpat, 119, 121, 124, 125, 147, 152, 157, 162, 168, 190, 348
Railway, 91–93, 125, 156, 158, 295–297, 317
Raimangal, 134
Rajguru, Shivaram, 162, 163
Rajkot, 148

Rajnarayan, 73, 125, 340
Rajput, 13, 26, 27, 32, 48, 63, 347
Rajputana, 53, 266
Rajshahi, 120
Ranaday, 299
Ranade, 111, 348
Ranchi, 76, 362
Rangpur, 65
Rani of Jhansi Regiment, 222
Rao, Baji, 27, 82
Rashbehari, 121, 123, 134, 316, 317
Regulatory Act Bengal 1773, 43
Rehman, Mohsinur, 251, 256
Renaissance, 2, 3, 8, 55, 69, 96, 97, 107, 119, 157, 297, 298, 306, 319–349
Richardson, D.L., 76, 342
Rickshaw pullers, 245, 247
RIN, 231, 316
Ripon, 105–107, 111, 181, 344, 346
Rishikesh, 130, 131
Rolland, Romain, 339, 350
Roosevelt, 209, 210, 216, 302, 311
Roy, Bidhan Chandra 252, 344
Roy, P. C., 125
Roy, Rammohan, 3, 5, 6, 61, 62, 64–70, 74, 97, 107, 108, 111, 295, 306, 319–321, 323, 324, 329, 331–333, 340
RSS, 148

RTC, 168, 170, 171, 177, 182, 183
Russia, 119, 126, 137, 194, 209, 221, 312

Sabarmati Ashram, 124, 148, 171
Sahajan, 17
Saheb, Nana, 82, 315
Sahgal, Prem, 229
Salt Act, 171
Salt March, 175, 194
Sambalpur, 120
San Diego, Java, 133
San Francisco, 131
Sanyal, Sailendranath, 157
Saptagram, 18, 20
Sastri, 8, 9, 48, 64, 84, 97, 98, 108, 143, 320, 337, 345, 349, 350
Sati, 59, 62, 64, 66, 320, 324, 329
Satish, 123, 128
Savarkar, 132, 147, 317
Seal, Motilal, 73, 78, 323, 325
Second Christmas Day Plot, 131
Second World War, 201, 222, 229, 311
Sen, Keshab, 338
Sen, Ramkamal, 67, 77, 323–325, 329, 338
Sen, Surya, 172
Sepoy, 1, 4, 38, 41, 45, 48, 53, 60, 81–85, 95, 98, 122, 181, 298, 315, 317, 335, 338, 352

Serampore, 18, 65, 66, 69, 72, 73, 75, 79, 91, 97, 129, 130, 132, 160, 245, 250, 297, 309, 314, 317, 324, 332, 361
Servants of India, 348
Seth, Jagat, 36
Shah, Meghnad, 297
Shah, Nader, 24
Shantiniketan, 125
Shivaji, 18, 20, 26–28, 118, 347
Shylet, 239
Sikh war, 59
Silver Rupee, 142
Simla Conference 1945, 218, 227, 228, 233, 314
Simon Commission, 167, 168, 177, 261
Simon, 167, 168, 170, 171, 177, 198, 261, 291
Sindh, 53, 59, 183, 184, 188, 204, 219, 232, 233, 238, 239, 339
Sindhia, 54
Singapore, 216, 221
Singh, Bhagat, 162, 163, 166, 173
Singh, Gulab, 59, 353
Singh, Gurbaksh, 229
Singh, Hari, 288, 353–356
Singh, Ranjit, 31, 55, 59
Sinha, 136
Smrities, 47
Sonnet, 335
Srinagar, 354, 355

Sriniketan, 125
St. Xavier's College, 76
Stafford Cripps, 211, 216, 233, 237, 240, 301
Straits, 301
Suez Canal, 91, 301
Sultan, Tipu, 33, 53, 94
Sultanate, 15, 26
Supreme Court, 43, 45, 50, 58, 64, 66, 71, 102, 246, 335
Surendranath, 105, 111, 114, 115, 117, 118, 121, 122, 124, 153, 299, 344, 345
Survey, 43, 68, 73, 85, 94, 95, 113, 119, 149, 297, 309, 331
Suryakanta Acharya, 123
Sutanuti, 22
Swadeshi movement, 92, 118, 124, 140, 152, 340, 348
Swadeshi, 78, 92, 118, 124–127, 140, 142, 152, 165, 180, 185, 340, 348
Swaraj party, 157–160, 344
Swaraj, 118, 121, 125, 127, 131, 132, 138, 148, 152, 153, 155–160, 168, 344
Sylhet, 120, 265, 272, 273, 277, 281, 343

Tagore, Abanindranath, 78, 79, 125, 347
Tagore, Debendranath, 67, 80, 110, 112, 330, 331, 340

Tagore, Dwarakanath, 69, 80, 324, 325, 330, 340, 341, 344
Tagore, Prassana Kumar, 110
Tagore, Rabindranath, 78, 113, 121, 123, 125, 151, 179, 307, 310, 313, 324, 338, 345–347
Taj Mahal, 58, 318
Tamil, 81, 152, 362
Tarachand, 329, 330
Taraknath, 130
Tata, J. N. 142
Tattvabodhini Patrika, 333, 342
Tegart, Charles, 160
Telegraph, 60, 91, 92, 112, 291, 351
Telugu, 81, 124, 152
The Times, 63, 98, 360
Tibet, 65, 119, 126, 127, 314
Tilak Memorial Fund, 155
Tilak Swaraj fund, 153
Tilak, 117, 118, 121, 123–127, 137, 138, 153, 155, 157, 348, 349
Tipperah, 120
Tribune Kesari, 114
Trigonometric Survey, 94, 95
Tripura, 55, 353, 359
Turkish empire, 152
Tyabji, Badaruddin 135

Ullaskar, 129
Unionist Party, 302
University Act, 120, 123
Upanishads, 65, 66, 320, 349
Urdu, 12, 205, 245

Vellore, 53
Veto power, 227, 228, 239, 240, 241
Vidyasagar, 332, 333, 340–342
Vivekananda, 70, 117, 122, 128, 130, 144, 154, 247, 299, 306, 317, 320, 339, 347, 348

Wadia, B. P., 136
Wardha, 215, 217
Wavell, Viscount, 218, 219, 227, 228, 233, 235, 237, 238, 252, 253, 256, 259–261, 269, 280, 289, 302, 318
Wellesley, 3, 28, 33, 46, 52–55, 71, 72, 88, 102, 110
Widow marriage, 338, 349
William Ward, 120
Willingdon, 178, 182, 188
Wyllie, Curzon, 122, 131

Zafar, Mir, 24, 29, 34
Ziegler, Philip, 262, 291, 309, 355, 359

Front cover: East India House at Leadenhall Street, London, in 1817, the HQ of the East India Company until 1857. National Maritime Museum, Greenwich, London.